WOMEN'S SOURCE LIBRARY

WOMEN'S SOURCE LIBRARY

VOLUME I
The Education Papers
Edited by Dale Spender

VOLUME II
The Radical Women's Press of the 1850s
Edited by Ann Russo and Cheris Kramarae

VOLUME III
Barbara Leigh Smith Bodichon and the Langham Place Group
Edited by Candida Ann Lacey

VOLUME IV
The Revolution in Words
Edited by Lana F. Rakow and Cheris Kramarae

VOLUME V
Before the Vote was Won
Edited by Jane Lewis

VOLUME VI
The Sexuality Debates
Edited by Sheila Jeffreys

VOLUME VII
Women's Fabian Tracts
Edited by Sally Alexander

VOLUME VIII
Suffrage and the Pankhursts
Edited by Jane Marcus

VOLUME IX
The Non-Violent Militant
Edited by Carol McPhee and Ann Fitzgerald

Women's Source Library

VOLUME VII

Women's Fabian Tracts

Edited by
Sally Alexander

ROUTLEDGE
ROUTLEDGE
Taylor & Francis Group

London and New York

First published 1988
by Routledge
2 Park Square, Milton Park, Abingdon, Oxon, OX14 4RN

Simultaneously published in the USA and Canada
by Routledge
270 Madison Ave, New York NY 10016

This edition first published 2001

First issued in paperback 2010

Routledge is an imprint of the Taylor & Francis Group

Typeset in Times by Keystroke, Jacaranda Lodge, Wolverhampton

British Library Cataloguing in Publication Data
A catalogue record for this book is available from the British Library

Library of Congress Cataloging in Publication Data
A catalog record for this book has been requested

ISBN 978-0-415-25669-8 (Set)
ISBN 978-0-415-25692-6 (hbk) (Volume VII)
ISBN 978-0-415-60643-1 (pbk) (Volume VII)

Publisher's note
The publisher has gone to great lengths to ensure the quality of this reprint
but points out that some imperfections in the original book may be apparent.

Contents

Contents

Acknowledgement

The Fabian pamphlets have been reprinted with the kind permission of the Fabian Society.

Introduction

Fabian socialism

The Fabian Society was formed in London in 1884. One of several socialist sects founded in the 1880s, the Fabians were a breakaway from the Fellowship of the New Life, a small group of women and men who were inspired by the ideas of Thomas Davidson, a wandering scholar, philosopher, and advocate of the 'new life'. Davidson taught that the regeneration of mankind would come through regeneration of the self and a repudiation of the waste and excess of capitalism. The cultivation of love, wisdom, and unselfishness would lead to the 'new life' which would be based on mutual though voluntary co-operation.[1] 'Everyman', Davidson believed, 'must be his own philosopher', a tenet which, according to Beatrice Webb (leading Fabian, and autobiographer), was one of the two 'most characteristic assumptions' of the 1870s and 1880s (the other being that 'physical science could solve all problems').[2]

Hampstead, Bloomsbury, and Chelsea in the 1880s were filled with frustrated young idealists searching amid the debris of Christian belief and the fading ethos of liberal individualism for a moral creed powerful enough to vitalize the 'new life'. Those who broke away from the Fellowship were those sceptics who modestly feared, in George Bernard Shaw's words, that the ideal society would have 'to wait an unreasonably long time if postponed until they personally attained perfection'.[3] The Fabians wanted the 'new life' too, but they were – as Havelock Ellis, the sexologist and anarchist member of the Fellowship put it – 'more political'.[4] Shaw was more explicit: 'socialist militants' was his uncompromising retrospective epithet. The inner life – though in need of refurbishment – pressed less urgently on Fabian consciousness than the poverty and squalor in which the mass of the population lived and

1

the conditions of which could be seen every day in the streets of London.

In 1884 Fabian socialism was rudimentary. It meant a belief in collectivism and the priority of the social question: that is, poverty. The huge gap in living standards between rich and poor was *the* social evil in the late nineteenth century. Not only did such gross inequality cast a blight on the prosperity of the imperial and commercial capital of the world, but the predicament of the poor also preyed on the consciences of the well-to-do. Both Shaw in his novels and plays, and Beatrice Webb in her autobiography have evoked the awakening 'consciousness of sin' among the privileged and propertied classes, anxious to hold on to political and economic power and fearful of the newly enfranchized working classes.[5] In the 1880s Britain was in the throes of severe economic depression with the characteristics – now again familiar – of lavish wealth for the few, a relatively high level of income among the employed, while the unemployed (a term which entered the English language in those years) lived in chronic want.

There were bitter divisions among all sectors of public opinion about the solutions for industrial dislocation and its effects. 'Social questions are the vital questions of today', Beatrice wrote in her diary in 1884, several years before she herself became a socialist: 'they take the place of religion'.[6] And indeed, socialism in the 1880s and 1890s had something of the enthusiasm of a religious revival. People of all classes spoke of their 'conversion' and spent much time and energy spreading the word. Hubert Bland, journalist and husband of Fabian novelist Edith Nesbitt, referred in his Fabian essay of 1889 to 'the deep discontent, a spiritual unrest' which he experienced at the 'constant presence of a vast mass of human misery'.[7] For the Fabians, it was the spectacle of poverty in the midst of plenty rather than their own or the poor's spiritual imperfections which provoked a vigorous critique of bourgeois economics, industrial inefficiency, and party political inertia. And although a vein of spiritual regeneration ran through the society, the Fabians prided themselves on a 'practical socialism', a determined pragmatism, a refusal – in Shaw's phrase again – of 'sentimental cant'.[8] Their very first tract was simply called 'Why are the many poor?' and Amber Reeves, a member of the Fabian nursery before the First World War, told me that the socialism of her mother and friends had been about 'being fair to the poor'.[9]

Fabian socialism was always intellectual. It took shape in critical dialogue with others. It never had, and only once or twice had any ambition to have, a popular base. The first Fabians were writers, teachers, journalists, civil servants, and one or two stockbrokers and clerks. Mostly young, in their early twenties, several of them impoverished, they were of heterodox religious and philosophical opinions: unitarians, lapsed Anglicans, secularists, anarchists, Hegelians, Marxists, and feminists. They met in each others' rooms to talk: of Marxist economics or revolutionary anarchism; the causes of poverty or the progress of municipal socialism. And then they went out into the streets or public platforms to influence hearts and minds through exhaustive propaganda. 'For years past', wrote Shaw in the 1890s, 'every Sunday evening of mine has been spent on some more or less squalid platform, lecturing, lecturing, lecturing, and lecturing.'[10] Since the Fabians included at this time Annie Besant, the secularist and birth controller; Charlotte Wilson, feminist and anarchist; Ramsay Macdonald, future leader of the Labour Party, and other authors and propagandists including Shaw, their street oratory was as prolific and distinguished as their written propaganda.

All this talk took place against a background of riots of the unemployed in the mid-1880s and the strikes of the matchgirls, dockers, and other unskilled workers in London in 1889 and 1890. Fabian socialism was shaped then and during the equally turbulent years of Irish nationalism, women's suffrage, and syndicalist militancy before the First World War (1906–14), years when, as Virginia Woolf remarked, the mental life of the nation changed. Some Fabians had participated in these struggles working alongside trade unionists and socialist militants. But this experience of working-class militancy filled them with unease. Fabians had studied Marx and rejected his theory of class struggle as well as the labour theory of value.[11] The collectivist spirit and growth of the state were the motors of history, according to the Fabians, not class struggle. Socialism they conceded might be inevitable, but it would not emanate from the working class. The poor lacked the education and leisure to think and to organize – for this reason, as Ruth Cavendish Bentinck argues below (pp. 129–44) in a tract which reveals the élitism latent in some Fabian thought, 'no Socialist has nor ever will come from the slums'.[12]

In this respect Fabian socialism owed more to John Stuart Mill's cautious collectivism than to the revolutionary creeds of either Marx or Kropotkin. Indeed, their name was taken from the Roman General whose motto was: 'deliberate before striking hard'. And Mill's reservations about the benefits of mass democracy, the fear that the desires of civilized minorities would be swamped by the uncultivated majority was more to the forefront of much Fabian thought than that openhearted goodwill of, for instance, the Independent Labour Party or even the humanist imperatives of Auguste

3

Comte. Socialism was as necessary as political democracy was unavoidable, but it must be a socialism based on the study of facts not the encouragement of feelings (except collectivist ones). As Sidney Webb, husband of Beatrice, admonished the enthusiastic socialist missionary Katherine St John Conway (who like Ramsay Macdonald and others was a member of both the Fabians and the Independent Labour Party) in 1892, 'study the facts of modern industry' not 'the aspirations of socialists'.[13] Socialist aspirations were unsettling, they were for the unconverted. The characteristics of Fabian socialism identified by Beatrice Webb would certainly have dampened chiliastic ardour:

> They translated economics and collectivism into the language of prosaic vestrymen and town councillors. They dealt largely in statistics; they talked about amending factory acts, and municipalising gas and water supplies. Above all they were prolific of facts, ideas and practical projects of reform. They were, indeed, far more extreme in their opinions and projects than their phrases conveyed to the ordinary citizen. Their summary of Socialism, which was found in the ensuing decade to have a strong appeal, was put in the following terms. It comprised, they said, essentially collective owner-ship wherever practicable; collective regulation everywhere else; collective provision according to need for all the impo-tent and sufferers; and collective taxation in proportion to wealth, especially surplus wealth.[14]

There was no mention of the women's movement, the suffrage, or women, which was odd because women formed between one-third to a half of the membership, sat on the Executive, and contributed fully to the political life of the Society. But then, Fabian socialism through Beatrice's lens (and she was one of its architects) was dry and passionless; the product of reason. The Woman Question, on the other hand, aroused passions not always amenable to reason because it opened up (and still does) those vexed questions of marriage, the family, and the 'sex-relation'. The first Fabians refused to think politically about sexual differ-ence, except in very limited ways, which is why some women found it necessary in 1908 to form the Fabian Women's Group. But the Society's commitment to democracy and egalitarianism, their opposition to virile displays of revolutionism, their – on the whole – decorous socialism, created a tolerant atmosphere in which feminists could pursue their aims. So who were the Fabian women, and what were their aims?

4

Socialism and the 'sex-relation'

The Fabian Women's Group (FWG) first met in the drawing-room of Maud Pember Reeves, wife of a New Zealand diplomat, in early 1908 after a winter of suffrage agitation of increasing violence. Women had not made themselves or their cause felt powerfully enough in the Society, they believed; nor, although Fabian women belonged to about a dozen different suffrage organizations, had they participated effectively in the movement as a group. At the first meeting they resolved first to further the principle of equal citizenship within and without the Society, and second to 'study women's economic independence in relation to socialism'. To this end they threw themselves into activity: standing for local elections as Poor Law Guardians; joining the Women's Labour League, the women's circles of the Independent Labour Party, and trade unions; working for reform of divorce (they wanted divorce by consent), prisons, and the feeding of London schoolchildren; and running well-attended lecture series and conferences on women's employment and training, motherhood, and domestic workers as well as speaking on socialism and aspects of the Woman Question wherever they were invited. They wanted to forge links between the two most vital movements of their time: socialism and women's emancipation.

In so far as they conceived of the Woman Question as a problem of 'economic liberty' then Fabian women went a long way towards thinking through the connections past and present between this problem and socialism. Their historical writings and empirical research on the economic condition of women still form a vital element in feminist thought. Beatrice Webb's explanations (culled from trade unionists) of women's low pay, her arguments for factory legislation and the 'rate for the job'; Maud Pember Reeves's description of domestic life on a pound a week; Barbara Hutchins's uncovering of the different economic needs of women at different phases in their lives; Barbara Drake's study of women and trade unions; Alice Clark's account of the effects of capitalist production on women's economic position remain unsurpassed.[15]

But it was the 'sex-relation' that was more difficult to reconcile with socialism in thought or practice. In spite of some remarkable women among its membership, the Fabian Society was silent on the Woman Question in its first years. It had something of the character of a men's debating society, and informal reminiscence conveys Fabian men's hesitancy to speak publicly on marriage, divorce, and the 'sex-relation'. However, in the first years of the twentieth century the Women's Movement gathered in momentum and militancy. Women joined trade unions in large numbers, their independent voice as industrial workers being heard through the National Federation of Women Workers (1906–21); while the Women's Co-operative Guild (1883–) spoke with authority for the working-class housewife and mother. Fabian women belonged to these and other organizations and were often among their leadership: Mary MacArthur, the leader of the NFWW, for instance, or Margaret Bondfield, shopworker and first woman cabinet minister; Marion Phillips, who organized the Women's Labour League or Susan Lawrence, who became a Labour MP in the 1920s. Like Fabian men, the women were writers, journalists, lecturers, teachers – occupations which had always been open to women of ability and audacity. But they were also drawn from the new – to women – and militant professions: doctors, nurses, local government officers, sanitary inspectors, and trade union officers.[16] Some list no occupation and were perhaps single women of means, or wives and mothers with leisure, property, and servants enough to combine the study of social conditions with plans for their alleviation: Charlotte Shaw, for instance, wife of the playwright and with a private income of her own; Maud Pember Reeves; or Charlotte Wilson, the anarchist wife of a stockbroker in whose Hampstead cottage the first Fabians had met to study Marx's *Capital* in the 1880s. She had then left the Society, rejoining in 1908 to become the first secretary of the FWG.

These women came – in Beatrice Webb's own self-definition – from that class of persons who 'habitually gave orders',[17] which is probably why they could imagine a state, Parliament, and even industrial forces responsive to their collective and egalitarian will. (The other reason, of course, was their optimism. They believed, before the First World War disabused such illusions, both that human nature was perfectable and industrial forces tractable.) More anguished were their attitudes towards domestic servants, most of whom were women and some of whom seemed absolutely necessary. Some Fabian women refused to employ any but the most essential; others ate with them; most characteristic were the several schemes for their better training and industrial organization. Domestic servants themselves, manual workers, and wives of working men were not visibly or vocally represented in the Group (which numbered 211 out of a total membership of a few thousand at its peak in 1910), though clearly not all the typists, office workers, or the one weaver I discovered, came from the wealthy reaches of the middle class.

Fabian women, then, recognized class difference among women and made it central to their analysis of women's economic

6

condition. The industrial revolution, they argued, had reduced wealthy women to economic 'parasitism' within the family, and confined working-class women to sweated industry and starvation wages. But while they were alert to the fact that class division meant that women's immediate demands might differ, their ultimate interests were the same. First, the parasitic status of women of property obliged them to expose and reform the poverty in which the majority of women lived and died. And second, what united women (apart from their lack of the franchise) was their economic dependence and their 'sex-function'. In the minds of employers, Members of Parliament, male trade unionists, or factory inspectors, economic dependence and sex were linked. Fabian women wanted to separate them. A woman's economic liberty depended upon her either receiving the rate for the job in industry – irrespective of her sex – or a state pension if she were a mother. That the biological function of motherhood had no ill-effects on a woman's capacity and so her economic value was, Fabian women realized, an assertion that had to be proved. Unlike the *Freewoman*, an anarchist journal celebrated by Rebecca West because it 'mentioned sex loudly and clearly and repeatedly and in the worst possible taste', Fabian women determined to pin down the differences between the sexes scientifically.[18] But Edith Nesbitt, opening the first series of lectures on the subject, cast all caution to the wind by claiming that: 'women . . . are predominantly creatures of sex, whose paramount need is a mate and children: and also they are heavily weighted throughout life by physical and mental disabilities unknown to men.'[19] Not surprisingly this statement aroused 'much opposition' and produced an avalanche of argument to prove that women's 'disabilities' of strength and skill were the result not of natural difference, but – in the age-old plea of feminism – of the artificial exaggeration of sex differences. Fabian analysis went on to argue that this exaggeration was historical, patriarchal, and that its effects radiated adversely through domestic and industrial production.

'We women are the slaves of slaves'[20]

Women's economic dependence was twofold: within the family they were subordinate to father, husband, son; while in waged work they were fixed as unskilled and cheap labour. Both positions stemmed from the past and had a single cause: the custom of marriage by capture or purchase (of wives by husbands), and the exclusive focus on a woman's sex which a man's wish for legitimate heirs imposed on his wife. Men had defined women through their sex rather than their common humanity. Motherhood united women, but motherhood was, in Emma Brooke's words, a 'stigma' when it should have been recognized as a 'valuable act of citizenship' and rewarded with state pensions and co-operative households. If a woman's biological function was the explanation of her impoverishment in the home (and Maud Pember Reeves's research into household budgets in Lambeth showed how poor this was) then her sex also lowered her value in the labour market.

Wherever Fabian women looked, the sexual division of labour seemed in evidence. Women were domestic servants, unskilled and sweated workers. Industrial production was not to blame. The factory system 'provides the great market for women's labour', if only women would raise themselves up and organize and refuse to accept wages below subsistence level.[21] Hitherto, women had made 'poor trade unionists', a failing which had perpetuated their cumulation in 'backward' sectors of the economy, the sweaters' dens, and backstreet workshops beyond the reach of factory legislation and trade boards. The unskilled woman worker was her own worst enemy Beatrice Webb had argued in the 1897 tract on *Women and the Factory Acts*, because of her partial subsistence from within the family, her lack of training and skill, her low standard of living, and, as Sidney Webb had noted earlier in an influential survey of women's wages published in the *Economic Journal* in 1891, because she had something to sell other than her labour.[22]

Women then, were caught on a treadmill. Their economic dependence, their poverty, forced them not only into sweaters' dens and a 'narrow range of occupations' in which the unskilled and low-paid woman worker became the 'enemy' of her own sex, but worse, it led them into compulsory sexual relations with men – whether prostitution or marriage, the latter being merely a legalized form of the first. 'To be compelled to marry to escape destitution' exclaimed Emma Brooke, 'is clearly sexual slavery.'[23] What form free and proper sexual relations should take, Fabian women were not prepared publicly to opine, except to stipulate first, that women should enter them freely and not out of economic need, and second, that women might have both work and sexual fulfilment.

Fabian women's analysis of women's economic dependence was as thorough in its details as it was circumspect in its demands. When they looked into themselves to define women's wants then their voice became bolder. The modern feminist, declared M.A. (Mabel Atkinson) in her 1914 tract on *The Economic Foundations of the Women's Movement*,[24] wants not *either* love or work but both:

8

She wants work, she wants the control of her own financial position, and she wants education and the right to take part in the human activities of the State, but at the same time she is no longer willing to be shut out from marriage and motherhood.

This want (which in the twentieth century has tormented educated and ambitious feminists as much as it has exasperated their socialist male comrades) has ebbed and flowed with the changing conditions of women's lives. Articulated as a dream in the eighteenth and nineteenth centuries, in the early twentieth century industrial development, birth control, and women's suffrage seemed to promise the possibility of a new epoch in the 'sex-relation'. But, at a more mundane level, the demand was also formulated in defiance of the limits, as Fabian women understood them, of the feminisms of earlier generations.

'Serious-minded ladies'

Nineteenth-century feminism, M.A. argues (inaccurately incidentally), was a movement of elderly spinsters, and she quoted Lydia Becker (secretary of the Manchester Suffrage Society in the 1860s) to the effect that 'a good husband is much better worth having than a vote'.[25] Twenty years later Beatrice Webb (Potter as she then was) forcing herself into intellectual work as an antidote to sexual desire, echoed these thoughts: 'I have not despised the simple happiness of a woman's life; it has despised *me* and I have been humbled as far down as woman can be humbled.'[26] Even when Beatrice wasn't dwelling in the slough of unrequited love, she firmly believed from her observation of the hardworking philanthropic and socialist women around her, that a woman could be a mother ('the highest calling') or have a career, but she could not have both. Younger Fabian women had less respect for custom and public opinion; they were less stoical.

The first generation of Fabian women had the grit of pioneers. They were the 'serious-minded ladies' as Amber Reeves described her mother's friends, whose intellectual path to socialism was strewn with the thorns of theology, political economy, secularism, idealist philosophy, and Marxist economics. They exhorted each other to learn, to educate, spurring each other on with reminders of women's 'undeveloped civic sense', lack of mental discipline, or the habits of trade unionism. Education was the path to collective as well as individual self-improvement as it was for so many working men. The minutes of the FWG reverberate with intentions to pursue and spread rational thought and education in citizenship, and this austerity and single-mindedness is reflected in their personal lives. Beatrice Webb remarked wryly at the end of her life on the bourgeois respectability of the first Fabians (forgetting perhaps Shaw's philanderings, or Hubert Bland's several sexual liaisons). 'My mother was chaste to the last degree', Amber Reeves told me, 'not a hint of scandal about her', whereas she herself rocked both her family and the Fabian Society in 1909 by having an affair and a baby with H.G. Wells, marrying a loyal suitor (also a Fabian), and then keeping everyone on anxious tenterhooks while she wavered between them.[27] Margaret Cole, a young Edinburgh graduate before the First World War – pipe-smoking and mop-haired – said in her autobiography that feminism to her was about free love as well as economic independence.[28] This was a sentiment that Beatrice's generation of Fabian women was unlikely to have voiced. Beatrice's diary is dotted with interesting asides on the love affairs of younger socialist women, and her accounts of the pre-war Fabian summer schools portray them as evidently glorious opportunities for the young to at least talk about sexual liberation in the 'sex-relation' even if the chaperonage was too vigilant to permit much practice.

But if sexual desire and its implications could be felt, and sometimes lived, more fully by some younger Fabians before the First World War, it still remained the most volatile element in the delicate relationship between the movements for women's emancipation and socialism. The time was not yet ripe for their harmonious resolution. Fabian men greeted the 'new' woman more unequivocally than the women; in some sense they invented at least her literary existence. Unwilling or unable to explore the political implications of women's emancipation within the Society, the issue spilled over into men's novel- and play-writing. 'We are discovering women', H.G. Wells wrote with excitement in the autobiographical *New Machiavelli* (1910), which meant that he and other male writers were exploring the literary possibilities of the 'sex-relation' without the marriage tie.[29] Fabian women on the other hand argued, as we have seen, that the Woman Question was essentially an economic question. A woman could achieve economic liberty so long as the laws of the market were tempered in waged work by judicious legislation and responsible trade unionism and in the home by state pensions and co-operative households. What women should not have to do was to rely on men's property or wages for their subsistence. As far as it went, theirs was a powerful and rational analysis.

But the 'sex-relation' could not be compressed into an economic

10

relation. By urging the woman wage-earner to become more like a man, and the state to take responsibility for the maintenance of the child, Fabian women were in fact evading the difficulty of what sort of relation should exist between the sexes. Fabian women sought self-fulfilment. Women were bound to men not just economically, they argued, but by their very identity: 'women [are] bred to please men'. Femininity was merely a veneer. To discover themselves, women had to throw off the chains of economic slavery and mental subservience. Many agreed with Shaw, who wrote in a clever essay on Ibsen that self-sacrifice, the least attractive human quality, was the essential attribute of the 'womanly woman' in late Victorian Britain.[30] The search for an identity independent of men (and children?) and self-fulfilment was hard to reconcile with the collective socialist will – a dilemma feminists and socialists have yet to resolve.

After the First World War Fabian feminism faded, individuals moving into women's or labour organizations, and in the 1930s into the Communist and Peace movements too. Many wrote books. The Fabian Society's socialism influenced the Labour Party whose constitution it had helped to draft. Some Fabian principles of piecemeal reform and a responsible state, may be discovered in the policies of the Attlee government of 1945. But the socialism of the Labour Party has never been able to contemplate women as other than wives and mothers, fastened to the home, or else in carefully demarcated sectors of the labour market. Feminists inside and out of the Labour Movement during the 1920s and 1930s strove to force a way to make it consider women as independent persons, but independence does not stick to the category 'wives and mothers'.

I am left only with a question. Does it reveal the limits of the English socialist vision that women remain fixed in its thought as wives and mothers, and as sources of cheap labour? Or is wanting something more the impossibility of feminist desire? There's no doubt though, that without the work of the Fabian women, thinking through the history of women's lives and the relationship between them and the movements for economic and political equality would be much more difficult. The following tracts, for their richly researched empirical detail and the generosity of their imagination, deserve to be better known.

Sally Alexander
September 1987

Notes

1 For the birth of the Fabian Society, see A. M. MacBriar, *Fabian Socialism and English Politics, 1884–1918*, Cambridge: Cambridge University Press, 1962, chapter 1; see also Havelock Ellis, *My Life*, Boston: Houghton Mifflin, 1939, pp. 199–203.
2 Beatrice Webb, *My Apprenticeship*, London: Longman, 1926, p. 57.
3 G. Bernard Shaw, 'The Fabian Society: its early history', London: Fabian Society, 1892, tract 41, p. 30.
4 Havelock Ellis, *My Life*, op. cit., p. 203.
5 Beatrice Webb, *My Apprenticeship*, op. cit., pp. 177–8.
6 Norman and Jeanne Mackenzie (eds), *The Diary of Beatrice Webb*, vol. 1: *Glitter Around and Darkness Within*, London: Virago, 1982, p. 115.
7 Norman and Jeanne Mackenzie, *The First Fabians*, London: Quartet Books, 1979, p. 115.
8 G. Bernard Shaw, Fabian tract 41 *passim*; The Venturists in Mrs. Humphry Ward's *Marcella* (1894), London: Virago, 1984, are based on the Fabians.
9 Interview with Amber Blanco White, (née Reeves), summer 1978.
10 Peter Clarke, *Liberals and Social Democrats*, Cambridge: Cambridge University Press, 1978, p. 34.
11 The Fabians extended David Ricardo's theory of rent to explain the genesis of both surplus value and political and cultural inequality. Differential rents on land, capital, and brains were the cause of social injustice.
12 Ruth Cavendish Bentinck, 'The point of honour', London: Fabian Society, 1910, tract 151, see below p. 129.
13 Norman and Jeanne Mackenzie, *The First Fabians*, op. cit., p. 185. The Mackenzies describe Kate Conway: 'The daughter of a Congregational minister and a graduate in classics from Newnham College, [she] was the kind of New Woman who was becoming familiar in socialist circles, fusing religion, social justice, and female emancipation into an emotional euphoria of the kind that Webb distrusted.'
14 Beatrice Webb, *Our Partnership*, London: Longman, 1948, p. 107.
15 The tracts by Beatrice Webb (no. 67) and Maud Pember Reeves (no.162) are reprinted below. Barbara Drake, 'Women in trade unions' (1920) and Alice Clark, 'Working women in the seventeenth century' (1919) are both reprinted by Virago. See also Beatrice Webb's minority *Report* from The War Cabinet committee on women in industry, 1919, vol. 31 and B. L. Hutchins, *Women in Modern Industry* (1915), West Yorkshire: E. P. Publishing Ltd, 1978.
16 See also E. J. Hobsbawm, 'The Fabians reconsidered', in *Labouring Men*, London: Weidenfeld, 1964, and S. Alexander, 'Introduction', Maud Pember Reeves: *Round About A Pound A Week* (1913), London: Virago, 1979.
17 Beatrice Webb, *My Apprenticeship*, op. cit., p. 43.
18 Jane Marcus (ed.), *The Young Rebecca: Writings of Rebecca West, 1911–1917*, London: Virago, 1983, p. 5.

19 Fabian Women's Group, 'Three years' work, 1908–1911', London: Fabian Society, see below p. 154. See also the Minutes of the FWG at the Nuffield Library, Oxford.

20 Ibid., see below p. 153.

21 Beatrice Webb, 'Women and the Factory Acts', London: Fabian Society, 1896, tract 67; see below p. 29.

22 Sidney Webb, 'Women's wages', in Sidney and Beatrice Webb, *Problems of Modern Industry*, London: Longman, 1902, pp. 78–9.

23 Emma Brooke and others, 'A summary of six papers and discussions upon the disabilities of women as workers', London: Fabian Society, 1909, see below p. 108.

24 M.A., 'The economic foundations of the women's movement', London: Fabian Society, 1914, tract 175, see below pp. 273–4.

25 Ibid., see below p. 280.

26 Norman and Jeanne Mackenzie, *The Diary of Beatrice Webb*, vol. 1, op. cit., p. 160.

27 *The Diary of Beatrice Webb*, vol. 3: *The Power to Alter Things*, through 1908 and 1909. H. G. Wells's *Ann Veronica* (1909) was based on his vision of Amber and the love affair; *The New Machiavelli*, London: Odham's Press, 1910, included an account of his quarrel with the Fabians and a very convincing satire of the Webbs.

28 Margaret Cole, *Growing Up into Revolution*, London: Longman, 1949, pp. 43–5.

29 H. G. Wells, *The New Machiavelli*, op. cit., p. 16.

30 G. Bernard Shaw, *The Quintessence of Socialism*, London: Walter Scott, 1891, pp. 31–44.

The tracts

FABIAN TRACT No. 67
(February 1896)

WOMEN AND THE FACTORY ACTS[1]

Beatrice Webb

The discussions on the Factory Act of 1895[2] raised once more all
the old arguments about Factory legislation, but with a significant
new cleavage. This time legal regulation was demanded, not only
by all the organizations of working women whose labor was
affected,[3] but also by, practically, all those actively engaged in
Factory Act administration. The four women Factory Inspectors
unanimously confirmed the opinion of their male colleagues. Of
all the classes[4] having any practical experience of Factory legislation, only one – that of the employers – was ranged against the
Bill, and that not unanimously. But the employers had the
powerful aid of most of the able and devoted ladies who have
usually led the cause of women's enfranchisement, and whose
strong theoretic objection to Factory legislation caused many of
the most important clauses in the Bill to be rejected.

The ladies who resist further legal regulation of women's labor
usually declare that their objection is to special legislation applying
only to women. They regard it as unfair, they say, that women's
power to compete in the labor market should be 'hampered' by
any regulation from which men are free. Any such restriction,
they assert, results in the lowering of women's wages, and in
diminishing the aggregate demand for women's work. I shall, later
on, have something to say about this assumed competition between
men and women. But it is curious that we seldom find these
objectors to unequal laws coming forward to support even those
regulations which apply equally to men and to women. Nearly
all the clauses of the 1895 Bill, for instance, and nearly all the
amendments proposed to it, applied to men and women alike. The
sanitary provisions; the regulations about fire-escapes; the pre-
eminently important clause making the giver-out of work responsible for the places where his work is done; the power to regulate

17

unhealthy trades or processes; all these made no distinction between the sexes. Yet the ladies who declared that they objected only to inequality of legislation, gave no effective aid to the impartial sections of the Bill. If we believe that legal regulation of the hours and conditions of labor is found, in practice, to promote the economic independence and positively to add to the industrial efficiency of the workers concerned, why should we not help women workers in unregulated trades to gain this superior economic position, even if Parliament persists in denying it to the men? It is clear that there lurks behind the objection of inequality an inveterate scepticism as to the positive advantages of Factory legislation. Indeed, the most energetic and prominent opponents of women's Factory Acts openly avow as much. Mrs. Henry Fawcett and Miss Ada Heather-Bigg, for instance, usually speak of legal regulation as something which, whether for men or for women, decreases personal freedom, diminishes productive capacity, and handicaps the worker in the struggle for existence. I need not recall how firmly and conscientiously this view was held by men like Nassau Senior and John Bright in the generation gone by. To-day there are evidently many ladies of education and position superstitiously clinging to the same belief. Therefore before discussing whether any particular Factory Act is good for women or not, we had better make up our minds on the general question. Does State regulation of the hours and conditions of labor increase or decrease the economic independence and industrial efficiency of the workers concerned?

Now those who object to further Factory legislation are right in asserting that the issue cannot be decided by harrowing accounts of factory tyranny, or particular cases of cruelty or hardship. I shall not trouble you with the long list of calamities in the unregulated trades, on which the official report of the Chief Inspector of Factories lays so much stress – the constitutions ruined by long hours in dressmakers' workrooms or insanitary laundries, the undermining of family life by the degradation of the home into a workshop, the diseases and deaths caused by white lead and lucifer matches. And, I hope, no one in the discussion will think it any argument against Factory Acts that some poor widow might find it more difficult to get bread for her starving children if she were forbidden to work at the white lead factory; that some sick man's daughter would not be allowed to earn the doctor's fee by taking extra work home after her factory day; or that some struggling laundress might find it impossible to make a living if she could not employ her girls for unlimited hours. Either way there must be hard cases, and individual grievances. The question is whether, taking the whole population and all considerations into account, the evils will be greater under regulation or under free competition.

Let us concede to the opponents of Factory legislation that we must do nothing to impair or limit the growing sense of personal responsibility in women; that we must seek, in every way, to increase their economic independence, and their efficiency as workers and citizens, not less than as wives and mothers; and that the best and only real means of attaining these ends is the safeguarding and promoting of women's freedom. The only question at issue is how best to obtain this freedom. When we are concerned with the propertied classes – when, for instance, it is sought to open up to women higher education or the learned professions – it is easy to see that freedom is secured by abolishing restrictions. But when we come to the relations between capital and labor an entirely new set of considerations come into play. In the life of the wage-earning class, absence of regulation does not mean personal freedom. Fifty years' experience shows that Factory legislation, far from diminishing individual liberty, greatly increases the personal freedom of the workers who are subject to it. Everyone knows that the Lancashire woman weaver, whose hours of labor and conditions of work are rigidly fixed by law, enjoys, for this very reason, more personal liberty than the unregulated laundry-woman in Notting Hill. She is not only a more efficient producer, and more capable of associating with her fellows in Trade Unions, Friendly Societies, and Co-operative Stores, but an enormously more independent and self-reliant citizen. It is the law, in fact, which is the mother of freedom.[5]

To understand the position fully we must realize how our long series of Factory Acts, Truck Acts, Mines Regulation Acts, and Shop Hours Acts, have come into existence.[6] All these are based upon a fundamental economic fact which has slowly forced itself into the minds of economists and social reformers – the essential and permanent inequality between the individual wage-earner and the capitalist employer. When the conditions of the workman's life are settled, without any collective regulation, by absolutely free contract between man and man, the workman's freedom is entirely delusive. Where he bargains, he bargains at a hopeless disadvantage; and on many of the points most vital to his health, efficiency, and personal comfort, he is unable to bargain at all.

Let us see how this comes about. I will not, to prove my point, take a time of bad trade, when five workmen are competing for one situation: I will assume that the whole labor market is in a state of perfect equilibrium; that there is only one workman wanting work, and only one situation vacant. Now, watch the process of bargaining between the employer and the workman. If the capitalist refuses to accept the workman's terms, he will, no doubt, suffer some inconvenience as an employer. To fulfil his orders he will have to 'speed up' some of his machinery, or insist on his workpeople working longer hours. Failing these expedients he may have to delay the delivery of his goods, and may even find his profits, at the end of the year, fractionally less than before. But, meanwhile, he goes on eating and drinking, his wife and family go on living, just as before. His physical comfort is not affected: he can afford to wait until the laborer comes back in a humbler frame of mind. And that is just what the laborer must presently do. For he, meanwhile, has lost his day. His very subsistence depends on his promptly coming to an agreement. If he stands out, he has no money to meet his weekly rent, or to buy food for his family. If he is obstinate, consumption of his little hoard, or the pawning of his furniture, may put off the catastrophe; but sooner or later slow starvation forces him to come to terms. This is no real freedom of contract. The alternative on one side is inconvenience; on the other it is starvation. I need not remind you that the fallacy of free and equal contract between capital and labor has been long since given up by the economists. If you read, for instance, our foremost economist, Professor Marshall, he will tell you that the employer is a combination in himself, with whom the individual wage-earner is seriously at a disadvantage.[7] No competent authority would now deny that unfettered individual bargaining between capitalist and workman inevitably tends to result, not in the highest wage that the industry can afford, but in the lowest on which the workman and his family can subsist.

Here, then, we have the first justification for something more than unfettered bargaining between man and man. But this is not all. We often forget that the contract between employer and workman is to the employer simply a question of the number of shillings to be paid at the end of the week. To the workman it is much more than that. The wage-earner does not, like the shop-keeper, merely sell a piece of goods which is carried away. It is his whole life which, for the stated term, he places at the disposal of his employer. What hours he shall work, when and where he shall get his meals, the sanitary conditions of his employment, the safety of the machinery, the atmosphere and temperature to which he is subjected, the fatigue or strains which he endures, the risks of accident or disease which he has to incur: all these are involved in the workman's contract and not in his employer's. Yet about the majority of these vital conditions he cannot bargain at all. Imagine a weaver, before accepting employment in a Lancashire cotton mill, examining the quantity of steam in the shed, the strength of the shuttle-guards, and the soundness of the belts of the shafting; an engineer prying into the security of the hoists and cranes, or the safety of the lathes and steam hammers among which he must move; a dressmaker's assistant computing the cubic space which will be her share of the workroom, criticising the ventilation, warmth and lighting, or examining the decency of the sanitary accommodation; think of the woman who wants a job at the white lead works, testing the poisonous influence in the particular process employed, and reckoning, in terms of shillings and pence, the exact degree of injury to her health which she is consenting to incur. No sensible person can really assert that the individual operative seeking a job has either the knowledge or the opportunity to ascertain what the conditions are, or to determine what they should be, even if he could bargain about them at all. On these matters, at any rate, there can be no question of free contract. We may, indeed, leave them to be determined by the employer himself: that is to say, by the competition between employers as to who can most reduce the expenses of production. What this means, we know from the ghastly experience of the early factory system; when whole generations of our factory hands were stunted and maimed, diseased and demoralized, hurried into early graves by the progressive degeneration of conditions imposed on even the best employers by the reckless competition of the worst.[8] The only alternative to this disastrous reliance on a delusive freedom is the settlement, by expert advice, of standard conditions of health, safety, and convenience, to which all employers, good and bad alike, are compelled by law to conform.

We see, therefore, that many of the most vital conditions of employment cannot be made subjects of bargain at all, whilst, even about wages, unfettered freedom of individual bargaining places the operative at a serious disadvantage. But there is one important matter which stands midway between the two. In manual work it is seldom that an individual can bargain as to when he shall begin or leave off work. In the most typical processes of modern industry, individual choice as to the length of the working day is absolutely impossible. The most philanthropic or easy-going builder or manufacturer could not possibly make separate arrangements with each of his workpeople as to the times at which they should come and go, the particular intervals for meals, or what days they should take as holidays. Directly we get machinery and division of labor – directly we have more than one person working at the production of an article, all the persons concerned are compelled, by the very nature of their occupation, to work in concert. This means that there must be one uniform rule for the whole establishment. Every workman must come when the bell rings, and stay as long as the works are open; individual choice there can be none. The hours at which the bell shall ring must either be left to the autocratic decision of the employer, or else settled by collective regulation to which ever workman is compelled to conform.

We can now understand why it is that the representative wage earner declares, to the astonishment of the professional man or the journalist, that a rule fixing his hours of labor, or defining conditions of sanitation or safety, is not a restriction in his personal liberty. The workman knows by experience that there is no question of his ever settling these matters for himself. There are only two alternatives to their decision by the employer. One is their settlement by a conference between the representatives of the employers and the representatives of the organized workmen; both sides, of course, acting through their expert salaried officials. This is the method of collective bargaining – in short, Trade Unionism. The other method is the settlement by the whole community of questions which affect the health and industrial efficiency of the race. Then we get expert investigation as to the proper conditions, which are enforced by laws binding on all. This is the method of Factory legislation.

No greater mistake can be made in comparing these two methods than to assume that Trade Unionism sacrifices the imaginary personal liberty of the individual workman to make his own bargain any less than Factory legislation. Take, for instance, the Oldham weaver. Here we see both methods at work. The rate of wages is determined entirely by Trade Unionism; the hours of labor and sanitary conditions are fixed by law. But there is no more individual choice in the one than in the other. I do not hesitate to say, indeed, that an employer or a weaver would find it easier and less costly to defy the Factory Inspector and work overtime, than to defy the Trade Union official and evade the Piecework List of Prices. Or, take the Northumberland coal-miner. He, for particular reasons, objects to have his hours fixed by law. But we need be under no delusion as to his views on 'personal liberty'. If any inhabitant of a Northumberland village offered to hew coal below the rate fixed by the Trade Union for the whole county, or if he proposed to work two shifts instead of one, the whole village would rise against him, and he would find it absolutely impossible to descend the mine, or to get work anywhere in the county. It is not my business to-day either to defend or to criticise Trade Union action. But we cannot understand this question without fully realizing that Trade Unionism, in substituting for the despotism of the employer or the individual choice of the workman a general rule binding on all concerned, is just as much founded on the subordination of the individual whim to the deliberate decision of the majority as any law can be. If I had the time I could show you, by elaborate technical arguments, how the one method of over-riding the individual will is best for certain matters, and the other method more expedient in regard to other matters. Rates of wages, for instance, are best settled by collective bargaining; and sanitation, safety, and the prevention of overwork by fixed hours of labor are best secured by legal enactment.

But this question of the relative advantages of legislative regulation and Trade Unionism has unhappily no bearing on the women employed in the sweated industries. Before we can have Trade Union regulation we must build up strong Trade Unions; and the unfortunate women workers whose overtime it was proposed to curtail, and whose health and vigor it was proposed to improve, by Mr. Asquith's Bill of 1895, are without any effective organization. The Lancashire women weavers and card-room hands were in the same predicament before the Factory Acts. It was only when they were saved from the unhealthy conditions and excessive hours of the cotton mills of that time that they began to combine in Trade Unions, to join Friendly Societies, and to form Co-operative Stores. This, too, is the constant experience of men's trades. Where effective Trade Unions have grown up, legal protection of one kind or another has led the way.[9] And it is easy to see why this is so. Before wage-earners can exercise the intelligence, the deliberation, and the self-denial that are necessary for Trade Unionism, they must enjoy a certain standard of physical health, a certain surplus of energy, and a reasonable amount of leisure. It is cruel mockery to preach Trade Unionism, and Trade Unionism alone, to the sempstress sewing day and night in her garret for a bare subsistence; to the laundrywoman standing at the tub eighteen hours at a stretch; or to the woman whose health is undermined with 'Wrist-drop,' 'Potter's-rot,' or 'Phossy-jaw.' If we are really in earnest in wanting Trade Unions for women, the way is unmistakable. If we wish to see the capacity for organization, the self-reliance, and the personal independence of the Lancashire cotton weaver spread to other trades, we must give the women workers in these trades the same legal fixing of hours, the same effective prohibition of overtime, the same legal security against accident and disease, the same legal standard of sanitation and health as is now enjoyed by the women in the Lancashire cotton mills.

So much for the general theory of Factory legislation. We have still to deal with the special arguments directed against those clauses of the 1895 Bill which sought to restrict the overtime worked by women in the sweated trades. If, however, we have fully realized the advantages, both direct and indirect, which the workers obtain from the legal regulation of their labor, we shall regard with a good deal of suspicion any special arguments alleged in opposition to any particular Factory Acts. The student of past Factory agitations sees the same old bogeys come up again and again. Among these bogeys the commonest and most obstructive has always been that of foreign competition, that is to say, the risk that the regulated workers will be supplanted by 'free labor' – whether of other countries or of other classes at home. At every step forward in legal regulation the miner and the textile worker have been solemnly warned that the result of any raising of their standard of sanitation, safety, education or leisure would be the transference of British capital to China or Peru. And to my mind it is only another form of the same fallacy when capitalists' wives and daughters seek to alarm working women by prophesying, as the result of further Factory legislation, the dismissal of women and girls from employment, and their replacement by men. The opposition to Factory legislation never comes from workers who have any practical experience of it. Every existing organization of working women in the kingdom has declared itself in favor of Factory legislation. Unfortunately, working women have less power to obtain legislation than middle-class women have to obstruct it. Unfortunately, too, not a few middle-class women have allowed their democratic sympathies and Collectivist principles to be overborne by this fear of handicapping women in their struggle for employment. Let us, therefore, consider, as seriously as we can, this terror lest the capitalist employing women and girls at from five to twelve shillings a week, should, on the passage of a new Factory Act, replace them by men at twenty or thirty shillings.

First let us realize the exact amount of the inequality between the sexes in our Factory Acts. All the regulations with respect to safety, sanitation, employers' liability, and age apply to men and women alike. The only restriction of any importance in our Labor Code which bears unequally on men and women is that relating to the hours of labor.[10] Up to now there has been sufficient influence among the employers, and sufficient prejudice and misunderstanding among legislators, to prevent them expressly legislating, in so many words, about the hours of labor of adult men. That better counsels are now prevailing is shown by the fact that Parliament in 1892 gave power to the Board of Trade to prevent excessive hours of work among railway servants, and that the Home Secretary has now a similar power in respect of any kind of manual labor which is injurious to health or dangerous to life and limb. I need hardly say that I am heartily in favor of regulating, by law, the hours of adult men, wherever and whenever possible.[11] But although the prejudice is breaking down, it is not likely that the men in the great staple industries will be able to secure for themselves the same legal limitation of hours and prohibition of overtime that the women in the textile manufactures have enjoyed for nearly forty years. And thus it comes about that some of the most practical proposals for raising the condition of the women in the sweated trades must take the form of regulations applying to women only.

It is frequently asserted as self-evident that any special limitation of women's labor must militate against their employment. If employers are not allowed to make their women work overtime, or during the night, they will, it is said, inevitably prefer to have men. Thus, it is urged, any extension of Factory legislation to trades at present unregulated must diminish the demand for women's labor. But this conclusion, which seems so obvious, really rests on a series of assumptions which are not borne out by facts.

The first assumption is, that in British industry to-day, men and women are actively competing for the same employment. I doubt whether any one here has any conception of the infinitesimal extent to which this is true. We are so accustomed, in the middle-class, to see men and women engaged in identical work, as teachers, journalists, authors, painters, sculptors, comedians, singers, musicians, medical practitioners, clerks, or what not, that we almost inevitably assume the same state of things to exist in manual labor and manufacturing industry. But this is very far from being the case. To begin with, in over nine-tenths of the industrial field there is no such thing as competition between men and women: the men do one thing, and the women do another. There is no more chance of our having our houses built by women than of our getting our floors scrubbed by men. And even in those industries which employ both men and women, we find them sharply divided in different departments, working at different processes, and performing different operations. In the tailoring trade, for instance, it is often assumed that men and women are competitors. But in a detailed investigation of that trade I discovered that men were working at entirely separate branches to those pursued by the women. And when my husband, as an economist, lately tried

25

to demonstrate the oft-repeated statement that women are paid at a lower rate than men, he found it very difficult to discover any trade whatever in which men and women did the same work.[12] As a matter of fact, the employment of men or women in any particular industry is almost always determined by the character of the process. In many cases the physical strength or endurance required, or the exposure involved, puts the work absolutely out of the power of the average woman. No law has hindered employers from engaging women as blacksmiths, steelsmelters, masons, or omnibus-drivers. The great mass of extractive, constructive, and transport industries must always fall to men. On the other hand, the women of the wage-earning class have hitherto been distinguished by certain qualities not possessed by the average working man. For good or for evil they eat little, despise tobacco, and seldom get drunk; they rarely strike or disobey orders; and they are in many other ways easier for an employer to deal with. Hence, where women can really perform a given task with anything like the efficiency of a man, they have, owing to their lower standard of expenditure, a far better chance than the man of getting work. The men, in short, enjoy what may be called a 'rent' of superior strength and endurance; the women, on their side, in this preference for certain employments, what may be called a 'rent' of abstemiousness.

I do not wish to imply that there are absolutely no cases in British industry in which men and women are really competing with each other. It is, I believe, easy to pick out an instance here and there in which it might be prophesied that the removal of an existing legal restriction might, in the first instance, lead to some women being taken on in place of men. In the book and printing trade of London, for instance, it has been said that if women were allowed by law to work all through the night, a certain number of exceptionally strong women might oust some men in book-folding and even in compositors' work.[13] We must not overlook these cases; but we must learn to view them in their proper proportion to the whole field of industry. It would clearly be a calamity to the cause of women's advancement if we were to sacrifice the personal liberty and economic independence of three or four millions of wage-earning women in order to enable a few hundreds or a few thousands to supplant men in certain minor spheres of industry.[14]

The second assumption is, that in the few cases in which men and women may be supposed really to compete with each other for employment, the effect of any regulation of women's hours is pure loss to them, and wholly in favor of their assumed competitors who are unrestricted. This, I believe, is simply a delusion. Any investigator of women's work knows full well that what most handicaps women is their general deficiency in industrial capacity and technical skill. Where the average woman fails is in being too much of an amateur at her work, and too little of a professional. Doubtless it may be said that the men are to blame here: it is they who induce women to marry, and thus divert their attention from professional life. But though we cannot cut at the root of this, by insisting, as I once heard it gravely suggested, on 'three generations of unmarried women,' we can do a great deal to encourage the growth of professional spirit and professional capacity among women workers, if we take care to develop our industrial organization along the proper lines. The first necessity is the exclusion of illegitimate competitors. The real enemies of the working woman are not the men, who always insist on higher wages, but the 'amateurs' of her own sex. So long as there are women, married or unmarried, eager and able to take work home, and do it in the intervals of another profession, domestic service, we shall never disentangle ourselves from that vicious circle in which low wages lead to bad work, and bad work compels low wages. The one practical remedy for this disastrous competition is the extension of Factory legislation, with its strict limitation of women's hours, to all manufacturing work wherever carried on.[15] It is no mere coincidence that the only great industry in which women get the same wages as men – Lancashire cotton weaving – is the one in which precise legal regulation of women's hours has involved the absolute exclusion of the casual amateur. No woman will be taken on at a cotton mill unless she is prepared to work the full factory hours, to come regularly every day, and put her whole energy into her task. In a Lancashire village a woman must decide whether she will earn her maintenance by working in the mill or by tending the home: there is no 'betwixt and between.' The result is a class of women wage-earners who are capable of working side by side with men at identical tasks; who can earn as high wages as their male competitors; who display the same economic independence and professional spirit as the men; and who are, in fact, in technical skill and industrial capacity, far in advance of any other class of women workers in the kingdom.[16] If we want to bring the women wage-earners all over England up to the level of the Lancashire cotton weavers, we must subject them to the same conditions of exclusively professional work.

There is another way in which the extension of the Factory Acts to the unregulated trades is certain to advance women's industrial position. We have said that the choice of men or women as workers is really determined by the nature of the industrial process. Now these processes are constantly changing; new inventions bring in new methods of work, and often new kinds of machinery. This usually means an entire revolution in the character of the labor required. What to-day needs the physical strength or the life-long apprenticeship of the skilled handicraftsman may, to-morrow, by a new machine, or the use of motive power, be suddenly brought within the capacity of the nimble fingers of a girl from the Board School. It is in this substitution of one process for another that we discover the real competition between different classes or different sexes in industry. The tailoring trade, for instance, once carried on exclusively by skilled handicraftsmen, is now rapidly slipping out of their hands. But it is not the woman free to work all the night in her garret who is ousting the male operative. What is happening is that the individual tailor, man or woman, is being superseded by the great clothing factories established at Leeds,[17] or elsewhere, where highly-paid skilled designers prepare work for the costly 'cutting-out' guillotines, and hundreds of women guide the pieces through self-acting sewing and button-holing machines, to be finally pressed by steam power into the 'smart new suit' of the City clerk.

Now this evolution of industry leads inevitably to an increased demand for women's labor. Immediately we substitute the factory, with its use of steam power, and production on a large scale, for the sweater's den or the domestic workshop, we get that division of labor and application of machinery which is directly favorable to the employment of women. It is to 'the factory system, and the consequent growth of the ready-made trade,' declares Miss Collet, that must 'be traced the great increase in the number of girls employed in the tailoring trade.'[18] The same change is going on in other occupations. Miss Collet notices that the employment of female labor has specially increased in the great industry of boot and shoe making.[19] But, as in the analogous case of the tailoring trade, the increase has not been in the number of the unregulated women workers in the sweaters' dens. Formerly we had a man working in his own room, and employing his wife and daughter to help him at all hours. Some people might have argued that anything which struck at the root of this system would deprive women of employment. As a matter of fact, the result has been, by division of labor in the rapidly growing great boot factories, to substitute for these few hundreds of unpaid assistants, many thousands of independent and regularly employed women operatives. For we must remember that when these changes take place, they take place on a large scale. Whilst the Society for Promoting the Employment of Women is proud to secure new openings for a few scores or a few hundreds, the industrial evolution which I have described has been silently absorbing, in one trade or another, hundreds of thousands of women of all classes. It is therefore infinitely more important for the friends of women's employment to enquire how an extension of the Factory Acts would influence our progress towards the factory system, than how it would affect, say, the few hundred women who might be engaged in night-work book-folding.

If there is one result more clearly proved by experience than another, it is that the legal fixing of definite hours of labor, the requirement of a high standard of sanitation, and the prohibition of overtime, all favor production on a large scale. It has been the employers' constant complaint against the Factory Acts that they inevitably tend to squeeze out the 'little master.' The evidence taken by the House of Lords' Committee on Sweating conclusively proved that any effective application of factory regulations to the workplaces of East London and the Black Country would quickly lead to the substitution of large factories. Factory legislation is, therefore, strenuously resisted by the 'little masters,' who carry on their workshops in the back slums; by the Jewish and other subcontractors who make a living by organizing helpless labor; and by all who cherish a sentimental yearning for domestic industries. But this sentiment must not blind us to the arithmetical fact that it is the factory system which provides the great market for women's labor. Those well-meaning ladies who, by resisting the extension of Factory legislation, are keeping alive the domestic workshop and the sweaters' den, are thus positively curtailing the sphere of women's employment. The 'freedom' of the poor widow to work, in her own bedroom, 'all the hours that God made'; and the wife's privilege to supplement a drunken husband's wages by doing work at her own fireside, are, in sober truth, being purchased at the price of the exclusion from regular factory employment of thousands of 'independent women.'

We can now sum up the whole argument. The case for Factory legislation does not rest on harrowing tales of exceptional tyranny, though plenty of these can be furnished in support of it. It is based on the broad facts of the capitalist system, and the inevitable results of the Industrial Revolution.[20] A whole century of experience proves that where the conditions of the wage-earner's life are left to be settled by 'free competition' and individual bargaining between master and man, the worker's 'freedom' is delusive. Where he bargains, he bargains at a serious disadvantage, and on many of the points most vital to himself and to the community he cannot bargain at all. The common middle-class objection to Factory legislation – that it interferes with the individual liberty of the operative – springs from ignorance of the economic position of the wage-earner. Far from diminishing personal freedom, Factory legislation positively increases the individual liberty and economic independence of the workers subject to it. No one who knows what life is among the people in Lancashire textile villages on the one hand, and among the East End or Black Country unregulated trades on the other, can ever doubt this.

All these general considerations apply more forcibly to women wage-earners than to men. Women are far more helpless in the labor market, and much less able to enforce their own common rule by Trade Unionism. The only chance of getting Trade Unions among women workers lies through the Factory Acts. We have before us nearly forty years' actual experience of the precise limitation of hours and the absolute prohibition of overtime for women workers in the cotton manufacture; and they teach us nothing that justifies us in refusing to extend the like protection to the women slaving for irregular and excessive hours in laundries, dressmakers' workrooms, and all the thousand and one trades in which women's hours of work are practically unlimited.

Finally, we have seen that the fear of women's exclusion from industrial employment is wholly unfounded. The uniform effect of Factory legislation in the past has been, by encouraging machinery, division of labor, and production on a large scale, to increase the employment of women, and largely to raise their status in the labor market. At this very moment the neglect to apply the Factory Acts effectively to the domestic workshop is positively restricting the demand for women workers in the clothing trades. And what is even more important, we see that it is only by strict regulation of the conditions of women's employment that we can hope for any general rise in the level of their industrial efficiency. The real enemy of the woman worker is not the skilled male operative, but the unskilled and half-hearted female 'amateur' who simultaneously blacklegs both the workshop and the home. The legal regulation of women's labor is required to protect the independent professional woman worker against these enemies of her own sex. Without this regulation it is futile to talk to her of the equality of men and women. With this regulation, experience teaches us that women can work their way in certain occupations to a man's skill, a man's wages, and a man's sense of personal dignity and independence.

Notes

1 Reproduced, with some additions, from papers read at the Nottingham Conference of the National Union of Women Workers (October, 1895), and the Fabian Society (January, 1896).
2 Factory and Workshop Act, 1895 (58 and 59 Vict. ch. 37).
3 Petitions were sent in, and meetings held in support of the Bill by, I believe, all the Trade Unions of Women, as well as by the Women's Co-operative Guild, which is mainly composed of women textile workers, whose hours of labor have, for nearly forty years, been rigidly fixed by law.
4 See the *Report of the Chief Inspector of Factories* for 1894, C. 7745, price 5s. 3d.; also the *Opinions on Overtime*, published by the Women's Trade Union League (Club Union·Buildings, Clerkenwell Road, London). The evidence before the Royal Commission on Labor was decidedly in favor of an extension of, and the more rigid enforcement of Factory legislation: see, in particular, the Minority Report (published separately, price 2d., by the Manchester Labor Press, Tib Street, Manchester).
5 This was pointed out by the Duke of Argyll, in the final chapter of his *Reign of Law*, which deals with Factory legislation.
6 See W. C. Taylor, *The Modern Factory System*; Von Plener's *English Factory Legislation*; and Miss Victorine Jeans' *Factory Act Legislation*.
7 See, for instance, the *Elements of the Economics of Industry* [1892], p. 382.
8 Some account of this development is given in the first chapter of my *Co-operative Movement in Great Britain*. See also Engels' *Condition of the English Working Classes in 1844*, or Arnold Toynbee's *The Industrial Revolution*.
9 For proof of this see *The History of Trade Unionism*, by Sidney and Beatrice Webb, particularly the first chapter.
10 *The Law relating to Factories and Workshops*, by May Abraham and A. Llewelyn Davies (Eyre and Spottiswoode, 1896, 5/-), contains a convenient summary of all the Acts. With regard to hours, the main provisions are as follows: Textile factories employing women or children, may work only between 6 a.m. and 6 p.m. (or 7 a.m. and 7 p.m.), only 56½ hours net per week, and overtime is absolutely prohibited. In non-textile factories and in ordinary workshops, women may be worked 60 hours per week, overtime is (usually) permitted under certain conditions, and the day's work may (except on Saturdays) range over a period from 6 a.m. to 8 p.m., or, if no children or young persons are employed, even from 6 a.m. to 10 p.m. This absence of a precisely determined legal working-day makes it practically impossible to enforce the law. In 'domestic workshops' there is no restriction on women's hours, and in laundries the only limit is a general one of sixty hours per week (or fourteen in any one day), without regulation of the hours of beginning or ending, or of mealtimes. This is quite illusory.
11 See Fabian Tract, No. 48, *Eight Hours by Law: a Practicable Solution*.
12 'The Alleged Difference between the Wages of Men and Women,'

Economic Journal, December, 1891; see, on the general question, *Economic Studies*, by Professor W. Smart, and the valuable report by Miss Clara Collet, on the *Statistics of Employment of Women and Girls*, published by the Labor Department of the Board of Trade (C-7564), price 8d.

13 With regard to the employment of women as compositors, an article by Amy Linnett, in the *Economic Review* for January, 1892, should be referred to.

14 Looked at from the point of view of the whole community, and not merely from that of one sex, it would, of course, be a matter for further consideration whether, and in what directions, it is socially desirable that men should be replaced by women as industrial operatives. Throughout this paper I have abstained from discussing this consideration.

15 See Fabian Tract, No. 50, *Sweating: its Cause and Remedy*.

16 See the introduction, by Mr. A. J. Mundella, to Von Plener's *English Factory Legislation*.

17 See 'Women's Work in Leeds,' by Miss Clara Collet (*Economic Journal*, September, 1891, pp. 467–72).

18 *Statistics of Employment of Women and Girls*, C-7564, p. 11.

19 Ibid., p. 73.

20 See Fabian Tract, No. 23, *The Case for an Eight Hours Bill*.

FABIAN TRACT No. 130
(January 1907)

HOME WORK AND SWEATING:
The Causes and the Remedies

Miss B. L. Hutchins

Between 1886 and 1889 the public became very much excited over
the horrors of the 'Sweating System.' The revelations of hideous
suffering, overwork and want brought home for a brief space to
the minds of the middle and upper classes 'how the poor live.'
Gradually the excitement died away: new topics absorbed the
interest of the public; and of Sweating and the Sweating System
we heard little. In 1906, however, the *Daily News,* following the
example of a philanthropic society at Berlin, arranged an exhibition
of sweated industries. Workers were shewn, in a London hall,
actually manufacturing match-boxes, blouses, etc., or carding
hooks and eyes, and so forth; and though for obvious reasons
neither the long hours of work nor the insanitary conditions which
too generally characterize similar employments, could be permitted
or represented in an exhibition, full explanatory details of rates of
pay, cost of materials, etc., were given to visitors, and each day
there was a lecture by some person qualified to describe and illustrate not only the seen but the unseen side of sweating. The show
attracted a vast deal of attention. Pity and sympathy were freely
expressed; but along with the pity was mingled a note of sheer
bewilderment, and almost daily, when question-time followed the
lecture, came the cry, 'What can be done? what can we ourselves
to, to stop it?' The present Tract is an attempt, not to revive the
useless public excitement, but to set plainly before the workers
themselves – and especially before the organized Trade Unionists,
who can do most to bring about a reform – the actual facts as to
Sweating, and the way in which it can be abolished.

What is meant by the Sweating System

The phrase, the Sweating *System* is misleading. All experts agree that there is no one industrial system co-extensive with, or invariably present in, the Sweated Trades. Mr. Booth expresses this by saying that it is not with one but many sweating systems we have to deal: Mr. Schloss says that no sweating *system* whatever is discoverable; and the House of Lords Committee, whilst reporting that the evils complained of could 'scarcely be exaggerated,' said that they had been unable to find any precise meaning attached to the phrase. An enquiry into sweating resolves itself, therefore, into an enquiry into the conditions under which the 'sweated industries' are worked. Here at least a painful and striking uniformity is met with, and accepting it as a starting point, the Lords Committee defined Sweating as:–

> 1.–Unduly low rates of wages.
> 2.–Excessive hours of labor.
> 3.–Insanitary state of the workplaces.

Mr. Schloss has added the important point, taxing of working-power to an unreasonable extent, or getting sixpenny-worth of work out of fourpenny-worth of pay ('driving'). The broadest definition we can find for the term sweating, is, 'grinding the faces of the poor.' Professor Ashley[1] has given us a new and vivid phrase, 'cheap and docile labor,' which helps to explain the special characteristic of sweated industry. Sweated workers are sweated because either by reason of sex, age, infirmity or want of organization and support, they have to let their work go cheap. They are compelled by need to sell their labor to the first purchaser who will take it, and cannot make conditions. They must work at the rates of pay the employer thinks good enough for them, and the smallness of the pay automatically extends the hours of work.

Sweating is no new thing. It occurs usually as a symptom of one of two kinds of industrial change: either as the decay of a handicraft or as an extension or offshoot of the factory system. Handloom weaving is an instance of the former kind that will occur to us at once. Long before machinery was introduced we find the scattered weavers suffering from their lack of organization, subject to continual oppression by the factors who disposed of the stuff. Elizabeth's ministers were so impressed with the gravity of the evil that they drafted a bill to 'avoid deceits done by Spinners of Woollen yarn and Weavers of Woollen cloth, and *to increase their wages.*' (S. P. Dom. Eliz. Vol. 244.) In more recent times the handloom weavers vainly petitioned Parliament to revive the assessment of wages in their trade. In 1815 it was argued before

Peel's Committee on the Employment of Children in Cotton Mills that it was unjust to limit the hours of children working in the mills while the handloom weavers, being grievously underpaid, often had to keep their children working far into the night to make up a living. In Germany and Austria and elsewhere the decaying handicraft, or Hausindustrie, is well known and widely spread. It is not only the competition of hand work with machinery that cuts down the rates of pay. The chain making at Cradley Heath shews that a handicraft can be grossly underpaid and sweated, although as yet no machine has been invented to do the work. But in England the sweated industry now more often takes the form of an auxiliary to the factory. Tailoring, clothing, shirts, blouses, ties, shoes, slippers and various trifles such as toys, crackers, match-boxes, instead of being made in the factory, are given out to be made or partly made in the workers' homes. This at first sight seems mysterious, for the economy and efficiency of factory industry (production on a large scale) has been demonstrated over and over again, in theory and in practice. How is it that blouses or match-boxes continue to be made in homes if they could be better and more cheaply made in a factory?

The Reason why Sweating Pays the Sweater

Although, broadly speaking, the factory is the more economical method, yet the employment of home-workers offers an advantage, in that very little capital is needed for starting or extending a business, and also because the sweating employer or contractor is able to shift some of the cost on to other people's shoulders. The manufacturer has to pay rent and rates for his factory; the sweater leaves the workers to pay rent for themselves. The manufacturer has to observe Factory Act requirements as to the cleaning, ventilation and sanitation of his factory; the sweater does not trouble about the condition of the workrooms to which he gives out work, as long as he gets the work done. The manufacturer may only employ women, children and young persons, for a certain period and within certain hours; the sweater's hands may work all night if they and he see fit. But there is another circumstance which gives the sweater an advantage, or apparent advantage, and that is in the complete lack of organization among these out-workers. It is true, no doubt, that factory women also are generally unorganized, but the mere fact of working and being paid together helps to maintain some sort of a standard, though often low enough. Out-workers are mostly very poor people, scattered about in their little homes, knowing nothing of one another; sometimes very shy and shrinking; they are often women

35

who sorely need a few shillings to supplement the more or less irregular earnings of the head of the house, but are not entirely dependent on their own industry. If they ask for better pay or attempt to protest against a reduction of rates, there is one answer for them; others will be thankful to get the work. Some of these women get a little charity; many have poor relief; some have husbands who earn 16s. or 17s. a week when they are lucky enough to be in work at all. Some depend entirely on their wretched trade, and their case must be little better than prolonged starvation. All of them constitute however a force of 'cheap and docile labor' which can be made profitable after a fashion, though it can obviously be applied to some industries only. Work that depends on delicate or costly machinery, or on skilled supervision and organization, is safe from any competition from the home. But the needlework trades and certain small objects that can be made with little skill, boxes, toys, crackers, etc., offer a field to the enterprise of the sweating employer, because the work can so easily be transferred from the factory or shop to the home. And the peculiarly unfortunate feature of this competition between the two industrial modes is that every improvement in the Factory Law or in its administration tends to drive work out of the factory into the home. If a local authority resolves to adopt a higher standard of requirements in regard to 'suitable and sufficient' sanitary accommodation, the occupier of a workshop may decide to send away women and give them work to do at home; on the other hand, stricter inspection of out-workers will help to disgust their employer, who will think he would rather take on more indoor hands than be worried over the infectious diseases of people he knows very little about. The exact effect of the law in force in deciding the choice between outdoor and indoor employment is a point on which fuller information is much needed. But one thing is plain; the legal regulation of home work must be amended and extended in order to do away with the unfair advantage obtained by the employer; otherwise the benefit of the Factory Act to the worker will in certain industries involve the giving more work out to homes.

Wages

The unfair advantage enjoyed by the sweater is of two kinds: first, the evasion of factory legislation, already mentioned; second, the extreme lowness of the wages paid. Of the low wages so much has been heard lately that it is hardly necessary to labor the point further. We may take a few instances at random from the *Daily News* Exhibition Handbook.

36

A. Trouser maker, widow with 4 children, works 10 or 12 hours a day, her best earnings (exceptional) are 10s. 6d. a week; more often 3s. or 4s.: receives parochial relief.
B. Match-box maker, works 12 hours a day, earns on an average less than 5s. a week. Highest earnings 8s. 2d. for a full week including Sunday.
C. Button carder. Two old people work together, earn 3s. 6d. per week.

Such instances could be multiplied *ad nauseam*. The Cradley Heath chain makers, after deducting cost of fuel, earn only 5s. to 6s. weekly for hard work, of a kind really skilled in its way, and not yet replaceable by machinery. The present writer has personally visited home workers in London, Birmingham and Cradley Heath, and has met with one, a skilled waistcoat maker, who was paid a living wage. The next most favourable instance was that of a remarkably quick, capable girl, making girls' frocks, lined throughout and trimmed, at 8d. each, deducting cost of cotton. She said she could make five or even six a day on occasion; but 'you have to move yourself to do it'; and one could well believe it. This was an exceptionally quick worker; what would have been the earnings of an average or slow worker? In match-box making and similar wretched trades, about 1d. per hour seems to be what the piece rates yield. The lowest depths of all perhaps are reached by workers who sew hooks and eyes, buttons, etc., on cards. Carding hooks and eyes I have found paid at 14d. per gross cards in Birmingham. The employer was threatening to reduce the price to 10½d. for there were middlewomen who could farm the work out to 'very poor people,' and thus cut the recognized price of 14d. per gross. The average earnings of women in this work are only about 3s. 3d. weekly, even when they work long hours.[2] In all these small home industries the wages appear to tend steadily downwards, although in factory work women's wages have been rising for a considerable period.[3] The explanation is not far to seek; whereas the factory industry, aided not only by machinery which can be seen, but by improvements in organization and supervision which are not seen (or not so easily), becomes more efficient and produces at a less cost, in home work there is no scope for these improvements, and employment is given to 'cheap and docile labor' only. In so far as these women consent to take lower and lower rates, they can get work.

Sweating is not 'cheap' to the community

The sweater, as we have seen, may squeeze a profit out of such 'cheap and docile labor,' in so far as he can shift the cost of subsistence on to other people, or compel his employees to do with wages insufficient to keep them in health. How far is such labor really 'cheap'? The cost to the community in physical deterioration and poor relief is impossible to estimate in £. *s. d.*, but obviously it must be considerable. In many cases the children are pressed into the service, and set to sew buttons or hooks on cards as soon as they come in from school. A home worker will tell you she can make so-and-so per week 'with the children helping.' If the children are too young to work, the result of the mother's home work is that they are neglected. A young married woman, perhaps with a recent baby and two or three little ones beside, tries to supplement her husband's irregular or scanty earnings by taking some work; finishing babies' boots, for instance. The boots thus made are usually hard, stiff, wretched little things, of a kind no baby should ever wear; meantime the worker, tired, dejected, underpaid and underfed, uses all her small strength to make a few pence over this wretched employment, and has little energy left to clean her room or care for her own children, who stray about unwashed, half-clothed, and neglected. It is impossible to imagine a more deplorable misdirection of energy. Let illness come, and the possible results are such as no one can contemplate without a shudder. A 'notifiable' infectious disease may perhaps be discovered in good time, if the inspector is watchful, and stops the work before it is too late; but we are coming more and more to realize that most diseases are infectious, and that tuberculous disease is especially so. The germs of disease or vermin may and doubtless often are, carried from one poor little child to another in the shoes, clothing or toys made under these conditions. The deterioration of physique that must result in children brought up in these miserable surroundings and on insufficient food is so evident that it needs no emphasis.

What Has Been Done

Successive enquiries and reports have brought these conditions before the public. The Commission on Children's Employment, 1863–7, advised the extension of the Factory Act to homes in which certain industries were carried on. But no government has had the courage to take such a step, each in turn having been daunted, partly no doubt by a vague dread of infringing 'the sanctity of the home,' but still more, probably, by the practical difficulties of administering such an Act. The law in regard to home work consists of a few very mild provisions. Lists of out-workers' names and addresses must be kept by employers or contractors in certain specified trades, and must be forwarded to the district or town council (in London the Metropolitan Borough Council) and the names and addresses of out-workers residing outside the borough or district must be forwarded on by the authority to the authority of the district or borough in which the out-worker resides. Giving out work to be done in unwholesome premises, or to a house in which any person is suffering from an infectious disease, is punishable by fine, unless the contractor can plead ignorance, which of course in many cases he can. These regulations are not strong enough to fix the responsibility for the conditions under which the work is done on the shoulders of the employer, and there is good reason to suppose that even as they stand, the regulations are not well observed.[4]

In domestic workshops, viz., those workshops in which only the members of a family are employed, the hours of work are unregulated as regards women, and are regulated for children and young persons on an elastic system, by which the number of hours the child or young person may work is restricted, but the period of employment and meal-times need not be stated, save only that work must cease at night, viz., between 9 p.m. and 6 a.m. Now all experience tends to show that a regulation of hours which does not include a statement of the period of employment is very illusory. In these cases the inspector cannot do much more than check the employment of children and young persons at night. No regulation as to hours applies to out-workers, unless the out-worker is himself an employer of a child, young person, or woman, as sometimes happens, in which case the work place is a 'workshop' and as such is under the Factory Act. But the solitary home-worker, and the worker whose employment is 'irregular and does not furnish the whole or principal means of living of the family,' may work any hours that seem to them good.

The hours of work of out-workers are, however, closely bound up with the question of wages. The employer does not directly compel them to work long hours, but he exercises compulsion indirectly through the miserable rates of pay. Out-workers would not work so many hours if they could get a decent remuneration without so doing. It is often urged by religious and benevolent persons who are shocked when these facts come to light, that the purchasers of wares so unjustly made are guilty, and ought to satisfy themselves that goods are not made by sweated labor. Can pressure be brought to bear by customers to ensure better wages?

Consumers' Leagues and Trade Union Labels

Private consumers cannot exercise much influence. It is doubtful whether consumers' leagues, by issuing 'white lists,' can do much to favor the good employer, for the reason that trade is so complicated that it is practically impossible to trace the production of any article through its stages. We may please ourselves with the notion that Messrs. Barkley or Whiterod, or whoever it is we prefer, is 'all right,' and provides seats or afternoon tea for his young people, which no doubt is all to the good as far as it goes. But who can trace the clothing, the jam, or the toys sold by Barkley and Whiterod, back to the dealer, and thence to the actual makers of the goods, who may be scattered all over England, or, indeed, the world? Consumers' leagues might however exercise a very good educational influence by agitation, by disseminating instruction among their members and the public, and even by raising the standard of public opinion on the two points of (*a*) paying bills regularly, (*b*) treating tradespeople with more consideration in the matter of giving orders for clothing,, etc., with a reasonable time allowed for carrying them out. In both these ways the well-to-do classes, sometimes from hard callousness, but much more often from sheer ignorant thoughtlessness, help to tighten the pressure of competition on the tradesman, and through him on the workers, and here there is a real field for the educating influence of the consumers' league. Again, the committees of philanthropic societies and religious bodies should before all others see that their own hands are clean. It is not a pleasant thought that bibles are frequently stitched and folded at starvation rates of pay; and illegal overtime on church embroidery before festivals has been so frequent as to be specially mentioned by the Chief Lady Inspector. The committees also of working-men's clubs, co-operative societies, friendly societies and trade unions might scrupulously pass the 'rat-shop' printer by, however cheaply he may offer to do the work. Some good, perhaps, might be done by the requirement of a label on goods for sale, stating that the goods were tenement made, in unhealthy conditions, or the reverse. This plan has been tried in Massachusetts and Pennsylvania, it is said, with some success; but the extreme ease with which a label can be forged or destroyed makes the provision of doubtful value. It is better to face the fact that the customer is for the most part powerless to ascertain where or how his purchases have been produced; and though the 'education of demand' may do a little to check sweating, much cannot be hoped from it. Much sweating, moreover, is carried on not for the supply of public authorities or even for the English customer, but for export. It becomes evident, then, that only the collective authority of the community acting through its organized representatives can take effective action.

Protection of Home Industries

Protection of home industries is sometimes urged as a possible remedy for sweating. The evidence collected for the Berlin exhibition of sweated industries shewed however that sweating is quite as rampant in protected Germany as in free-trade England; and there are colonies of home-workers in Chicago and New York where even the very high tariff maintained in America does not make wages or conditions any better than in the worst parts of London. Regulation of sweating would do far more for trade than any import duty on manufactured goods, as it would deprive the sweater of the unfair advantage he now gets by employing 'cheap and docile labor' in unregulated workrooms, and more custom and a larger share of the export trade would then go to the traders who are carrying on business honestly under fair conditions.

Alien Immigration

Restraint of immigration is often urged as a remedy for sweating, but the Aliens Act of 1905 achieved little or nothing, and it is unlikely that even a much more drastic Act would really check the evil. It must be remembered that the alien population is comparatively small, though, no doubt, in one or two districts it forms a high percentage. Sweating is quite equally rampant where the alien is a negligible quantity. There are practically no foreigners in the cutlery or nail and chain-making industries, yet there the sweater flourishes. Even in the tailoring trades, the competition of destitute foreigners is as nothing compared with the great mass of unskilled and unorganized female labor which crowds the market. The removal of all Jews from the sweated trades would be but a partial and temporary relief. The evil effect of the Jew's competition lies in the characteristics which render him a fit subject for the pestilential conditions of home work: he overcrowds whole districts; his standard of comfort is low; and his ingenuity has created or organized new industries to suit the circumstances. In the factory, English skilled labor has the preference: abolish the conditions that now specially favor the demoralizing competition of the Jew, and the difficulty will be got over without an impracticable policy of exclusion. The latest factory inspector's report from New Zealand (June, 1906) says that though there has been a considerable influx of labor into the colony of late years, no displacement or unemployment of their own people has ensued. Why? Because *the system*

41

of employment in the colony permits no undercutting in wages, and 'thus gives to those possessing knowledge of local conditions and requirements advantage over the visitor, unless the latter shows decidedly superior attainments.'

How Wages have been Raised

If we want to decide how to raise the wages of sweated workers we are fortunately not compelled to rely on theory alone, for in the colonies of Australasia two distinct methods of regulating wages have been in operation for ten or eleven years, and the results can be studied on the spot, or in reports issued on the subject. The two methods were initiated respectively by New Zealand in 1894 and by Victoria, Australia, in 1896. In New Zealand the machinery designed for the prevention and settlement of labor disputes is made use of to abolish sweating. 'The colony was divided into districts, in each of which a local board of conciliation might, if petitioned for, be set up, composed of equal numbers of masters and men, with an impartial chairman. At the request of any party to an industrial dispute, the district board was to call the other parties before it, and hear, examine and award. As soon as a dispute stood referred to a board, anything in the nature of striking or locking-out was forbidden. . . . A board's award, however, was not to be enforceable by law, but was only to be a friendly recommendation to the disputants. In case these, or any of them, refused to accept it, any party might appeal to the court of arbitration, or the conciliators themselves, if hopeless of effecting a settlement, might themselves send a case thither.'[5] The court is presided over by a Judge of the Supreme Court, and it rests with the court to say whether the award is to have the force of law or to be merely in the nature of good advice. If it is to have legal force, it must be filed in the Supreme Court and then it has the weight of an ordinary submission to an award, and any party to it can, by leave of the judge, get an order exacting a penalty for breach of it. Decisions of the court are binding not only on the parties to the dispute, but on all employers and trade unions registered in the trade, and since 1900 decisions are equally binding on anyone entering the industry regulated by them.

For present purposes we are concerned with this New Zealand measure, not as a means of settling disputes, but for the regulation of sweating. The basis of the institution is trade unionism, and it might therefore seem as if it could effect little for unorganized workers, especially women. But in practice it has done much. If sweated workers want to have a revision of the conditions of their work, they have but to file a statement of claim in the office of the nearest conciliation board, and they are at once in the position of a union. Working women have invoked the aid of the law to good purpose. For instance, in Auckland, as lately as 1892, it had been found impossible to establish a tailoresses' union or a fair factory log, but under the Arbitration Act they gained an increase of wages estimated at fifteen per cent. The latest factory inspector's reports from New Zealand state that the Arbitration Act is working most satisfactorily. The wages of workers have been increased, and employment has become more regular.

Inspectors of awards have been recently appointed, and these inspectors are often able to settle disputes without having recourse to the courts at all, and in cases where employees have been sweated or unfairly paid, the payment of arrears can be claimed. The report for 1904–5 says that 295 informations of breach of contract were laid, of which 232 were won by the workpeople. Three hundred and twelve cases were settled without having recourse to the courts, and £1,463 of back wages secured for the workers, besides what was obtained at arbitration. In 1905–6, £788 of arrears were obtained for the workers by the inspector, plus £1,153 obtained under award of the court.

It will be seen that a great deal is done by agreement and adjustment. A noteworthy feature of the arbitration law is a provision for filing in the Supreme Courts contracts embodying working conditions agreed upon by employers and unions. These documents, called industrial agreements, are, when filed, binding for the period mentioned in them, which must not exceed three years. Numbers of these agreements are voluntarily entered into, and the arbitration court sometimes orders the parties to a dispute to execute an industrial agreement.

In Victoria wages have been regulated by the plan of having special boards for each trade, consisting of equal numbers of members elected as representatives of employers and employed, with a chairman elected by the board. A board may be appointed to fix wages and piece rates for persons employed either inside or outside factories. It must also fix the hours for which the rate of wage is fixed, and the rate of pay for overtime; and in fixing wages must take into consideration the nature, kind and class of work, the age and sex of the workers, and any matter which may be prescribed by regulation.

This Act was passed in 1896 in order to stamp out the sweating which had been shewn to exist in Melbourne and elsewhere in Victoria. It has met on the whole with great success, and the inspector's reports state that sweating has been practically stamped out. South Australia followed Victoria, and passed a Wages Board

Act in 1900. The main difference between the two methods is that in the case of New Zealand, the unit of administration is the district; in the case of Victoria it is the trade. In the former case the authority is *judicial*; in the second it is *elective*.

Suggestions

I. – SANITARY REGULATION

Short of regulating wages, we do not believe that any real or adequate control of the sweater can be maintained. But undoubtedly efficient sanitary inspection of homes used as workrooms may do some good indirectly, in that it protects the consumer from the very real danger of dirt and infection, and also in that it checks the giving out of work in some degree, and is likely to ensure more work being done in factories and workshops, 'to which the employer has the right of access and control.' Two competing suggestions are now before the public; these are known respectively as the Tennant Bill and the Women's Industrial Council's Bill, the latter usually introduced jointly by some friends or members of the Women's Industrial Council and of the Scottish Council for Women's Trades. Mr. Tennant's Bill aims at placing the responsibility for the conditions under which work is done in home workrooms on the giver-out of work; and would place the administration in the hands of the local sanitary authority, who already receives the out-workers' lists. The Women's Industrial Council Bill involves more of an innovation; it would place inspection of out-workers under the factory inspectors, and all out-workers would have to produce a certificate shewing that their workrooms had been inspected and found suitable for the work to be carried on, having regard to the health of the persons to be employed therein. This measure would involve a considerable increase in the inspecting staff, but as that is for other reasons highly necessary and desirable, it does not in itself constitute an objection. In New Zealand and some other colonies any workroom where two or more persons are employed, the employer counting as one, constitutes a factory within the meaning of the Act. The employment of children by their parents does not constitute an exception. Those who have studied the history of factory legislation can see that this is by far the best method, and the only one that can check sweating in home work and prevent unfair competition with well-conducted industry. It would however be very difficult to pass such a measure all at once, in an old country like ours. The Women's Industrial Council's Bill or Mr. Tennant's Bill would form an intermediate

44

stage, and help the transition to the more logical and comprehensive measure adopted in New Zealand.

II. – TRUCK AND PARTICULARS

A recent legal decision has held out-workers to be outside the operation of the Truck Acts, and thus, Miss Squire says,[6] placed thousands of workpeople outside the protection they had hitherto successfully claimed. This anomaly will it is to be hoped be righted before long by legislation. A provision recommended by the International Conference for Labor Regulation, Geneva, 1906, was that 'particulars' of work and wages (now required under our law to be given to the worker) should also be exposed in the employer's pay office. This might be very useful and perhaps would help towards the difficult work of organizing the trades in question.

III. – WAGE REGULATION

While measures for better inspection of home work and for improved sanitary conditions should have all the support that can be given them, and the restricted hours of work in domestic workshops should be enforced as far as possible, and made binding on home workers wherever children are employed, yet these measures by themselves will almost certainly prove inadequate. The utmost cleanliness and the strictest enforcement of an Eight Hours Day will not provide food for the sweated worker's child or make six shillings a week into a decent wage for a woman.

The Wages Boards are supported by the high authority of Sir Charles Dilke, who has several times introduced a Bill on the lines of the Victorian measure. The advantage of the New Zealand plan however is that instead of confiding the regulation of wages to the representatives of sectional interests, an impartial and unbiassed authority of high legal knowledge and position is set up, who after hearing and weighing the evidence of those immediately concerned, can fix minimum rates binding on an industry within a given district, and the same authority also has power to decide disputes as to hours and conditions of employment (so far as these are not already regulated by the Factories Act), while the wages board is really an *ad hoc* body dealing with wages and nothing else. Without attempting to discuss every detail of the machinery that would have to be set in motion in England, we suggest that the Conciliation Act, 1896, might be amended and extended so as to deal with sweated trades.[7] The Board of Trade might be empowered to appoint a commissioner to enquire into the conditions of home work in some special district, and if much sweating were discovered, the commissioner should form a board, consisting of

45

himself and two persons thoroughly conversant with the trade, as representatives of employers and employed. Home-workers might then register as unions under the board, every care being taken to make the process as simple as possible. The board would then proceed to take evidence as to the rates of pay, in order to discover what piece rates yield a living wage per hour. Having drawn up a scale, which should be published in the district and made known as far as possible, every effort should be used to induce the employers to adopt the scale voluntarily as a minimum. The factory inspector might be charged with the duty of discovering how far the minimum rate was adopted, and of calling the attention of employers to the decision. If difficulties were made, and the standard rate was not adopted, recourse should be had to a Court of Arbitration, whose decisions should have the force of law, and be binding for the trade within the district concerned. The experience of New Zealand shews that the inspector can do a great deal to bring about amicable arrangements and fair agreements as to wages, without recourse to the Court, when it is known that he has that measure in reverse. A very difficult question would be the decision of the amount of the standard minimum wage, for which the assistance and advice of experts would have to be called in. It would have to be remembered that many sweated workers are working as supplementary earners only; therefore the most effectual method would be, not to require a living *weekly* wage, which would certainly be evaded wholesale, but a scale of piece rates which would yield a fair remuneration *per hour*. Supposing it was decided that 15s. should be the standard minimum weekly wage for women, the piece rates should be calculated so as to yield about 3½d. per hour, which would mean a very substantial increase to most home workers. Inspectors of awards, as in New Zealand, should be appointed to enforce the law. It would probably be wise not to attempt to fix a really living wage at once, but to try and effect a moderate rise first, and revise the rates after two or three years. If a system of this kind was tried first in one or two districts notorious for sweating, it might then gradually be extended and develop into a national minimum.

We believe that the New Zealand Arbitration Court offers great advantages in the superior judgment and detachment of mind that could be brought to bear by a skilled expert, who would have the opportunity of hearing evidence from different trades, as compared with the method of leaving the solution to the decision of those themselves concerned in any particular industry, and we also believe that the encouragement given to women's organizations by making it cheap and easy for any little group of workers to register as a union, might have most valuable results. Experience shews that efficiency in the administration of the Factory Act regulations approaches perfection most nearly where the workers are best organized, and themselves take an intelligent interest in the measures enacted for their good. Women have hitherto proved apathetic and weak-kneed as trade unionists, but they are improving year by year. It is noticeable that a commission appointed in Victoria to enquire into the working of the various labor laws of the Australasian colonies strongly commended the New Zealand regulations. It reported as follows:– 'The New Zealand Conciliation and Arbitration Acts remain to-day the fairest, most complete, and most useful labor law on the statute books of the Australian States . . . protecting on the one hand the fair-minded employer from the dishonest competition of the sweater, who keeps down cost of production by paying miserably low wages, and on the other, the toiling thousands to whom a rise in wages of a few shillings a week when an industry can fairly bear it, often means the difference between griping poverty and comparative comfort. Its main provisions have stood the test of time; and while employers and workers alike keenly criticize each other's actions in connection with its operations in certain industrial centres, *in no part of the colony* which we visited *did we hear any general desire expressed for its repeal.*'

Special consideration would also have to be given to those industries which are decaying handicrafts rather than auxiliaries to the factory. These, as already said, are relatively inconsiderable in England, but nevertheless occupy quite a large proportion of the population in certain districts. In some Highland villages the poor people have two or three sheep of their own, shear the wool, spin it into yarn, and knit it into stockings, for which they receive about 1s. a pair from the dealer. No wage regulation could touch this form of sweating, and it is likely enough that in the chain-making, the specially sweated industry at Cradley, the employers would soon be sharp enough to arrange to sell the iron and buy the chain, instead of paying wages, so that they would avoid the minimum wage altogether. In cases like these it would be desirable for the Government to take measures to instruct the people as to co-operative association for buying their own material, and to organize them for self-help and mutual protection, by lending capital, and so forth. Measures of this kind have been adopted in Austria for the assistance of the ancient crafts and rural industries, with very good effect. It would of course be better still to take over the whole industry and carry it on in Government shops with fair wages and good conditions.

IV. – Direct Employment

To those who follow the argument here supported,[8] that sweating, though apparently an inexpensive method of production, is ruinous to the community through the physical and moral deterioration induced in the sweated and their workers, it will be at once evident that the abolition of sweating is an important incidental advantage of direct public employment. The establishment of the Army Clothing Factory has saved thousands of workers from sweating dens without any increase in the cost of production.[9] The enlargement of that factory so as to produce in it not only some but all the clothing required for the army, militia and volunteers, would rescue thousands more from their present fate. The workshops at Woolwich could be expanded so as to render unnecessary that contracting for saddlery work, chains and hardware, which now promotes sweating. A navy clothing factory might supersede all sweating of the garments of sailors, coastguards, and marines. The Government factories should produce also all the uniforms of the customs, police, prisons, post office, and other official staffs, as well as all the boots, shoes, saddlery, and accoutrements required.

And if local authorities followed suit – if the London County Council were given power to set up its own clothing factory, and to supply other local governing bodies – if it became the practice to manufacture all asylum, hospital, police, and fire brigade uniforms required by any Town or County Council or other public body, either in its own factory or in that of some other public body – if a similar course were pursued with regard to boots and shoes, saddlery, and general leather work, chains, furniture, and other commonly sweated wares, part, at least, of the evil would disappear. For it would be easy to ensure that the factories of the Government or the Town Council would be well-built, well-ventilated and well-equipped; that the hours of work would be regular and short; that the employment would be steady, and the wages at any rate as high as those paid in the best shops elsewhere.

V. – Anti-Sweating Clauses in all Public Contracts

But however rapidly we press on the establishment of public factories for the supply of public wants, many public bodies will, for a long time to come, have to buy goods which are at present usually the product of sweating. The Government contracts all contain some clause which is intended to secure a fair wage for the workers, and to restrain the practice of sub-contracting. For instance, the form of tender for clothing to be delivered by the contractor to the War Office includes among the required conditions that no portion of the contract be transferred without the written permission of the Secretary of State; that all garments shall be cut out and made up in the contractor's own factory, and no work shall be done in the homes of the workpeople; that the wages paid shall be those current in each trade for competent workmen in the district in which the work is carried out, and that the wages shall be paid to the workers direct, and not through any foreman or intermediary. So far back as 1891 the House of Commons passed a resolution that the Government's duty was to make every effort to secure the payment of fair or current wages for work done by workmen under Government contracts. But these provisions where out-workers are concerned are at present often neglected.

Though sub-letting and home work are expressly prohibited, there are hundreds of home-workers openly employed in Government work, and except in work where the workers are organized in trade unions there is no provision for ensuring a standard of wages. In 1906, the Minister for War, Mr. Haldane, had his attention drawn to the matter by some representatives of the Women's Industrial Council, and assured them that he would introduce some system of effective inspection. He also kindly assisted the committee of the Sweated Home Industries Exhibition by lending materials on which to employ the Government workers, who shewed the low prices at which they had to work for Government contractors. Municipal and other public authorities have the same difficulty, and probably will continue to have it if they employ middlemen. A case has been discovered where a contractor gave a worker a job to do for a municipal contract, and paid her the fair price insisted on by the municipality, but on condition that she should do other work for him at a rate lower than usual, so that her average wage is not protected by the fair wage clause. 'The only satisfactory solution to prevent such evasions is the extension of direct employment without the medium of a private contractor by the Government and other public authorities.'[10] The extension of employment under fair conditions will benefit the sweated workers not only directly, in so far as they themselves obtain employment under those conditions, but indirectly, as the payment of fair wages to the men employed would lessen the competition for work by married women. Nothing comes home more forcibly to the investigator of home work than this fact, that many of the women would not take work out at all if their husbands could obtain a decent remuneration. A great deal of sweated work by women is simply an indirect result of the under-payment or irregular employment of men.[11]

Conclusion

There are those who will say that the measures of reform here sketched out will have the effect of throwing out of work those poor people who are not worth employing at the wages and under the conditions that would be required under an amended Factory Act, with a minimum wage and strictly sanitary conditions required for out-workers as well as indoor hands. M. Aftalion, in a recent interesting study,[12] declares that to regulate home work is to destroy it, and cites the example of Victoria, where the establishment of a minimum wage has driven almost all the work into factories. We believe, judging from the analogous case of factory regulation, that the unemployment which would result from a well thought out scheme of home work regulation would be much less than these critics expect. Some workers would go to the factory; some, as already pointed out, would no longer need to take work out, if the head of the family were assured a living wage. Some workers, now underpaid, underfed, underwarmed, and badly clothed, would quickly respond to improved conditions and pay, and would in a short time become really more efficient. Moreover, we must remember that the payment of larger wages to a class of workers previously underpaid would in itself be a beneficial stimulus to trade, and lead to an increased demand for employment in the production of the food and clothing required. But let us admit that most probably there would be some workers unable to earn the minimum wage, and consequently thrown out of employment. These, we must remember, would be the workers either so unhealthy, so old, or so exhausted with a life of underpaid toil, that they would not be worth employing under the changed conditions and improved standard set. Here, surely, if ever, is the case for liberal poor relief. It would be far cheaper to the community in the end to pension off these victims of unregulated competition than to allow them to compete in the labor market, lower the rate of wages, and through their cheapness thrust the more capable out of work. For it must be remembered we are not here discussing those who are 'unemployable' because of drink, extravagance or excess. The pathetic part of the sweated industries is that it is often the very virtues of these people that are their ruin. Miss Clementina Black, in her introduction to the cases investigated and tabulated by the Women's Industrial Council,[13] says 'many of them are of the highest respectability and maintain a standard of conduct and cleanliness quite heroic. . . . The majority of these 44 women are industrious, even painfully industrious; most are thoroughly respectable; scarcely one is paid a living wage.' They will sit up all night, and work for what is given them, and submit. Theirs is indeed 'cheap and docile labor.' They represent an out-of-date tradition and a superseded method, and only the wise and careful intervention of the State can save them and their children from a slow process of deterioration through want. 'There is no person in this kingdom – or in any of the states that are called civilized – who does not partake of the proceeds of underpaid labor; and the conditions of such labor are not growing better; they are, if anything, growing worse, and underpayment is rather spreading than decreasing.'[14]

NOTE. – A few sentences of Fabian Tract No. 50 are incorporated above, by permission.

POSTSCRIPT. – The Wages Board Bill (see p. 13) was re-introduced by Mr. Henderson, and read a second time in the House of Commons, February 21st, 1908.

Notes

1 *Th Tariff Pro am*, 1903, p. 110.
2 *Daily News Handbook*, p. 39.
3 See G. H. Wood, F.S.S., in the *Journal of the Statistical Society*, June, 1902.
4 The statistics contained in the Return presented to Parliament, No. 211 of 1906, shew that in a considerable number of districts little use has been made by the local authorities of their powers under the home work provisions of the Factory Act. In October, 1906, the Home Office issued a Memorandum to the Clerks of Town and Borough Councils urging the importance of thorough administration.
5 Reeves, *State Experiments in Australia and New Zealand*, Vol. ii., p. 102.
6 Factory Inspector's Report for 1905, p. 323.
7 It may be noticed that the measures for regulating wages here suggested are not entirely identical with those advocated in Fabian Tract No. 128. The discrepancy is one of detail merely. The writer of the present Tract is entirely in sympathy with the principles laid down in 'The Case for a Legal Minimum Wage,' but doubts the advisability of employing the local authorities in the manner there suggested.
8 It is developed with much more fulness in *Industrial Democracy*, by S. and B. Webb (Longmans, 1902, 12s.).
9 Even if there were some increase in cost of production, it would still be good policy for the country to pay a living wage. The private sweater can send his worn-out workers to the workhouse when he has done with them: the country has to maintain its bye-products of pauperism, (See *Common Sense of Municipal Trading*, by Bernard Shaw, Constable, 1904, 2s. 6d.) It is a fact less well-known than it should be, that municipal contractors have been found giving out workhouse clothing to be made up by women who were compelled to ask for

51

out-relief from their own union to supplement their wretched earnings. One way or another – *the country pays.*

10 Interim Report on Home Work, by Mrs. J. R. MacDonald; Women's Industrial Council, 1906; p. 35.

11 An ex-out-worker told the present writer she had given up taking work – her 'old man said it wasn't worth it.' Many 'old men' would say the same if they could earn their own wages. See on this point Cadbury's *Women's Work and Wages*, which shews that men's wages for the less skilled kinds of work in Birmingham are often not more than 17s. or 18s.

12 *Le Développement de la Fabrique, et le Travail à Domicile*, Paris: Larose; 1906.

13 Interim Report on Home Industries of Women, p. 44.

14 Ibid., p. 45.

FABIAN TRACT No. 140
(December 1908)

CHILD LABOR UNDER CAPITALISM

Mrs. Hylton Dale

The Industrial Revolution and Child Labor

At the end of the eighteenth century England ceased to be predominantly agricultural and became the most important manufacturing country in the world.[1] Child Labor being regarded by the manufacturers as absolutely essential to the speedy piling up of fortunes, the morality of which no one questioned, it was universally employed in the cotton mills and factories which suddenly sprang up in the land. Manchester, specially the seat of the cotton trade from its earliest days, was the greatest employer of Child Labor, and became wealthy and populous. In ten years – from 1780–1790 – the population almost doubled, owing to the inrush from the country of people, who were tempted by high family earnings to barter their infinitely healthier existence on the land for life in crowded slum cities. A positive majority of the workers in the cotton mills were young children.

Until the middle of the eighteenth century spinning and weaving had been done in cottage homes with the simple hand looms which had altered but little from primitive times. But with the introduction of elaborate and costly machinery into factories the work changed its character. New methods, new buildings, new modes of life superseded those of the rural life of the English peasantry. The latter at first refused to allow their children to work in the factories and mills which had been built by their streams and rivers from which was derived the water-power which worked the machinery. The parents at first considered it derogatory and degrading work for young people. But to procure the cheapest form of labor was considered not only justifiable but almost a mandate from heaven. The wealth that poured into the country, notably into the pockets of the manufacturers, was regarded as a reward from God for industry and self-help. Unfortunately in the workhouses of London and other large towns manufacturers easily found the cheap material they required. Shoals of unwanted children of all ages, even as young as five and six, were transported from workhouses and sent as parish apprentices to remote districts wherever their labor was wanted. The parish authorities, whose callousness was equalled by the manufacturers, were only too anxious to be rid of the burden of rate-supported children, and they actually stipulated – so little did humanity and pity rule their hearts – that a due proportion of feeble-minded children must be taken as part of the contract. As far as is known no further interest by the overseers was shown in the fate of these hordes of victims of ungoverned industrialism. No one can tell how many thousands died unknown and untended over a long series of years. No records were kept. It was no one's business to see after such children. Employers for the most part regarded their apprentices as of less value than their machines, which at any rate were kept clean and carefully preserved. The masters themselves were frequently men of low type, with little or no education, who had often come from the ranks of manual labor themselves, and who were intoxicated with their own sudden wealth. They had little sympathy for the class from which they had sprung. Children worked side by side with adults and for the same length of time. They worked all day and sometimes all night; they were cruelly beaten if fatigue overcame them at their work; they worked in bad air without ventilation or sanitation, and with no regard to cleanliness or decency (the two sexes being herded together at night in huts); they received no personal care morally or physically, no education, no love. Many were living skeletons, some almost gibbering idiots. They died off like flies from various diseases, especially pneumonia, fostered by the sudden changes of temperature from damp heat in the mills to cold outside. Malignant fevers decimated them from time to time, and of those who survived many were in poor health, ignorant of the commonest things, and destitute of all education, secular, religious or moral.[2]

The work in the mills was, perhaps, not in itself hard. It consisted of piecing together the broken threads of cotton, of removing obstructions from the machinery, and of cleaning its parts. But accidents were not infrequent. And the children of all ages stood at their work the whole day through (often from twelve to fifteen hours at a stretch, with one and a half hours' interval for meal times), under pitiless taskmasters.

The conscience of society gradually became aroused to the evils of the system when the sins committed upon the hapless children reacted upon itself. When infectious fevers, originating in the dens where the little apprentices festered, were caught by children and adults outside, it was brought home to people that some foul wrong existed somewhere.

In 1784 the Manchester magistrates requested a committee of medical men, led by Drs. Percival and Ferriar, to investigate an outbreak of fever in the Radcliffe cotton factories. Dr. Percival, F.R.S., President of the Manchester Literary and Philosophical Society, had had his attention specially called as a medical man to the evils and ravages of disease among the Poor Law apprentices in the town.

The first report, from which all subsequent factory legislation sprang, was that presented in 1796 to the Manchester Board of Health by Dr. Percival on the abuses and cruel conditions of life under which all the operatives, and especially the children, lived and died. It was resolved by the Board to invoke the aid of Parliament to establish laws 'for the wise, humane, and equal government of all such works.'

Robert Owen

On the Board sat Robert Owen, cotton spinner, embryo philanthropist, and pioneer of factory legislation. He and his two partners subsequently purchased the cotton mills of New Lanark belonging to David Dale (whose daughter Owen married), and who was one of the few instances of a humane and enlightened master of that period. Owen carried on the work at New Lanark in the same humane spirit as his predecessor, and instituted a series of reforms in Child Labor. He raised the minimum age of the workers to ten, and refused to take any more Poor Law apprentices, preferring to gather in as employés children who lived at home with their parents. He established infant schools where children from one year old were kept in a very superior crêche and kindergarten combined. In his schools for older children he established co-education, and had dancing, military drill, natural science, botany, arithmetic, geography, history, singing and music taught. He allowed no punishments of any kind. The whole atmosphere of his schools was one of love. He, more than any educationist before or since, recognized that children are like plants, in that they want more than care and attention; they want love.

The First Factory Act

In 1802, Sir Robert Peel the elder, himself an owner of cotton factories, inspired by what he knew of his own mills at Radcliffe and the report of the Manchester Board of Health, introduced and got passed the first Factory Act known as 'The Health and Morals of Apprentices Act.' By this Act the hours of labor were limited to twelve a day, and the children were forbidden to work at night. They were to go to church once a month, and were to be taught reading, writing and arithmetic. Girls and boys were not to sleep in the same apartment. The factories were to be ventilated and periodically whitewashed. All this seems little enough to the modern sense, but it called the attention of right-minded people to the subject, and raised a standard of humanity which has never been lowered, and from it came, slowly it must be confessed and after fierce struggle, all subsequent factory legislation.

Employment of 'Home' Children

One result of this Act, which dealt solely with Poor Law apprentices, was the substitution for them of children who lived at home, on whose behalf the law had not interfered. The evils of excessive work were now transferred to the 'home' children, and continued to be borne by them for many long and weary years. Steam power, after 1802, having replaced water power, factories were built in towns, and, as the children lived with their parents, many of the ghastly and horrible outrages on health and decency disappeared. But the hours of work were just as terrible. Seven was the age at which children began to work in the mill, but cases of even six and five were not uncommon, and they worked twelve hours a day – thirteen hours at a stretch with an interval for dinner only, breakfast and tea being snatched while at work. No seats were provided, and the children stood the whole day through. Many had to clean the machinery on Sundays.

The Cotton Mills Act of 1819

In 1819, through Robert Owen's influence and ceaseless endeavor, Sir Robert Peel the elder got passed the Act known as the 'Cotton Mills Act' of 1819. Although shorn of all the chief provisions dear to Owen's heart, for which Sir Robert Peel himself had striven, 'The Act of 1819,' as Mr. Podmore says in his life of Robert Owen, 'marks the first and the most important step in the long procession of Factory Acts. Under it for the first time the State assumed the rights of parent and guardian to the children of the free, and took upon itself to prescribe the hours of work and the general condition of their labor.'[3] This Act referred solely to cotton mills. The minimum age of employment was fixed at nine. The hours of labor were to be twelve per day. No provision was made for education, although this had been most strenuously urged by Owen.

The Acts of 1833–44

It was not until 1833 that provision was made by the Act of that year for the appointment of paid Government inspectors. The hours of children's work were restricted to nine per day. But this Act failed to work satisfactorily, and the Act of 1844 was passed, enacting (1) that children from eight to sixteen must not work without a medical certificate; (2) that factories were to be inspected and registered; (3) that children under thirteen might only work half time. Extensions and amendments of this Act were made in 1867, 1874, 1878, 1883, 1891 and 1895.

The Coal Mines Regulation Act

In 1887 the 'Coal Mines Regulation Act,' amending the statute of 1872 (which had replaced that of 1842), forbade girls and women and boys under twelve to work in any mine below ground and forbade it for boys from twelve to sixteen for more than ten hours a day or fifty-four hours a week.

The Factory and Workshops Act of 1901

But the twentieth century has seen the most vital changes of all, the most important respecting Child Labor since Robert Owen pleaded nearly a century ago, viz., the consolidation and amendment of all the previous Acts into 'The Factory and Workshops Act of 1901.'

Child Labor To-day

It comes as a surprise to the majority of present day people to learn that Child Labor still exists all over Great Britain, and for the most part to a highly injurious extent. This is more flagrantly the case in Yorkshire and Lancashire, where the 'half time system' is in full play. According to the Report of the Board of Education for the year 1906–7 there were no fewer than 82,328 of these half timers or 'partial exemption scholars' – to give them their official name. In 1904–5 the number was 80,368, and in 1903–4 it was 78,876. So the numbers are increasing.[4]

The three areas in which the largest number of 'partial exemption scholars' are found are the Administrative County of Lancashire, with over 11,900, and the West Riding of Yorkshire and the County Borough of Bradford, each with over 8,000. All three areas show an increase in the number of these scholars in 1905–6 as compared with 1904–5. The County Boroughs of Oldham,

Sheffield and Burnley also show noticeable additions to the number of 'partial exemption scholars.'

These half timers are children over twelve years of age who have obtained a labor certificate, and who are then allowed by law to be sent to work half a day in mills or factories, provided that they are sent to school the other half of the day. Employment in the mill has to be either in morning or afternoon shifts, or on the alternate day system. One set of children begin work at 6 a.m. or 6.30 a.m. and go to school in the afternoon; the afternoon set go to work in the mill at 1 p.m. and end at 5 p.m. or 6 p.m., and attend school in the morning. A child may not be employed in the same shift either morning or afternoon for two consecutive weeks. No child may be employed on two successive Saturdays, nor on any Saturday if he has worked for five and a half hours on any day in the previous week. The maximum time for work for half timers is twenty-seven and a half hours a week.

Many of the children on the first shift rise at 5 a.m. (Mr. J. C. Clynes, M.P., states that he rose about 4.30 a.m. as a half timer); and sometimes they have to walk a mile to the mill in all weathers and be there by six o'clock. They have half an hour for such breakfast as they can afford. At mid-day they walk home to their dinners. At 2 p.m. they are in school.

Is it any wonder these children are worn out and that they fall asleep over their desks; or that the merciful teacher lets them sleep? The education that they receive is of very little use, whilst the injury done to their health by their double work is often irreparable.

Miss Clementina Black, President of the Women's Industrial Council, states: 'I shall never forget the impression made on my mind by the peculiar mixture of pallor and eagerness on the faces of the little half timers the first time that I ever went over a weaving mill. The place was light and airy and the work was not hard, and the management considerate; but as to the children, any London doctor or any woman accustomed to the care of children, would have thought their appearance unhealthy and their expression of face abnormal.'[5] Miss Black adds: 'Labor in childhood inevitably means, in nine cases out of ten, decadence in early manhood or womanhood; and the prevalence of it among ourselves is perhaps the most serious of national dangers. It is an example of that most cruel form of improvidence described by the French proverb as "eating our wheat as grass." '

Bradford, a pioneer town as regards its admirable arrangements for the scientific feeding of the necessitous children at school, is one of the principal offenders of the sin of the half time system.

Miss Adler, a member of the Education Committee of the L.C.C. and Hon. Sec. of the Committee on Wage-earning Children, recently made personal enquiries at two manufacturing centres in the north of England, one having over 5,000 half timers, the other 800. She said the appearance of the children was sickly and pallid owing to the fact that the processes of cotton and wool spinning have to be carried on in a humid and warm temperature. All authorities whom Miss Adler interviewed stated that the children lost 50 per cent. of their education; and she added that 'teachers consider their whole moral tone is lowered, and that there is a visible deterioration which is most heart-breaking.'[6]

Is there any plea that can be urged for the continuation of such a system? Yes, there is. This is what the Right Hon. H. O. Arnold-Foster (late Secretary of State for War), writes by way of opposing Socialist reform: 'The great cotton industry of Lancashire, the wool and worsted industry of Yorkshire, and many other industries in a less degree, *are at the present time dependent on Child Labor*'; and he gives, as a plea for its justification and absolute necessity – exactly as Nassau Senior did three-quarters of a century ago: 'The minute margins of profit and loss' owing to competition; adding: 'The fierce competition of the world, especially in those countries in which Child Labor and long hours are prevalent, has to be met.'[7] No statement could be more condemnatory of our present social system based on competiton.

Inspectors, managers, teachers, members of education committees are agreed as to the evils resulting from children working during the years that they attend school. Nor do the parents' necessities compel such child-slavery. All who have studied this question testify that, as a rule, it is the children of men earning good wages who are sent to the mills as early as the law allows, in order to gain a mere pittance of 2s. 6d. for twenty-six or twenty-seven hours work a week. One penny an hour is the usual rate of wages for a half time child working at the textile trade in Yorkshire. It is not the very poorest parents who are the greatest exploiters of their children. It is to be noted that all these children and their work come under the jurisdiction of the Factory and Workshops Act; and that, accordingly, their lives for the most part are deliberately regulated and controlled by the State.

Children not under the Factory and Workshops Act

As regards children whose work does not come under the jurisdiction of the Factory and Workshops Act, and therefore escapes Government inspection, they may be classed as those employed (1) in shops, or by shopkeepers as errand boys and girls, and

59

carriers; (2) in domestic work; (3) in street trading; (4) in agriculture; and (5) in various miscellaneous industrial employments at home or abroad.

The Parliamentary Committee of 1903 came to the conclusion that there were in England alone (apart from the half timers) 200,000 children thus employed as wage earners. It can easily be seen how such uninspected Child Labor may be exploited, and how extremely difficult, and, in many cases, how impossible it is to supervize and prevent its abuse.[8]

In London the half time system has been abolished, but there is very little else upon which the Metropolis can be congratulated as regards Child Labor.

Child Labor in Domestic Work

The abuse of Child Labor in ordinary domestic work is the most difficult of all to control. Miss Bannatyne, a school manager and Acting Warden of the Women's Settlement at Southwark, stated before the Inter-Departmental Committee of 1903 that children are often absent from school one or two days a week on account of domestic employment. The casual labor is bad for the boys' character, and the long hours unfit them for school work. The girls suffer from drudgery in their own homes, which she saw no way of preventing. But if the half days could be prevented and the attendance at school more regularly enforced, she believed that whilst much Child Labor would be prevented it would not affect the family income to any appreciable extent. Thus, a stricter attendance must be enforced at school.

'Ay! There's the rub.' If regular attendance at school were really enforced, the parents, knowing the law could not be evaded, would accept the situation. It would be an enormous gain all round; first, to the children, who are now overworked, and whose education is spoilt by irregular attendance; secondly, to the managers and teachers, many of whom are unceasingly worried over this question; and thirdly, it would be a great saving of expense, as a large staff of attendance officers has to be kept under our present system to compel the parents to send their children regularly to school.

Even in the special schools for mentally defective children in Bermondsey, the writer has found cases of girl children who are such pitiful little drudges at home that the officer of the N.S.P.C.C. has had to be sent to 'warn' the parents, with the result that the children are worked less hard, but only, it is feared, when closely supervized by the officer. Another little girl in a special school gets 1d. a week and her tea for going after school to help a neighbor in domestic work and nurse the baby. (This

60

penny she deposits regularly every week with the teacher for her own boot fund).

Of play, so absolutely essential to the proper physical and mental development of childhood, many of these children have next to none. They are old before their time and incapable of joy, and are weighed down by the responsibility of life.

Child Wage-Earners in London and the Provinces

Miss Adler gave evidence before the Inter-Departmental Committee on Employment of School Children in March, 1901.[9] In the summary of evidence it is stated that: 'For the purposes of the present enquiry Miss Adler had caused about 4,000 London cases and 3,000 cases in the provinces to be investigated. Those employed are about 10 per cent. of the total number of children. Miss Adler put in very voluminous tables, from which it appeared that out of 107 London schools containing 42,097 children, 3,897 were employed – 633 in domestic work, 136 as barbers, 723 errand boys or girls, 1,227 in shops, 341 milk carriers, 386 street hawkers, 451 in other miscellaneous employments. Out of 3,527 cases in which the hours were clearly specified, 2,652 worked less than thirty hours a week, fifty-three worked over fifty hours in addition to school. The figures show that it is not the most needy parents who employ the children excessively. Some cases are very extreme; as, for instance, a girl employed sixty hours a week at trouser-making. Saturday work is often excessive. In the provinces returns were collected from some schools in twelve towns, showing out of 67,865 children that 3,049 were employed. The nature of employment and hours worked were much the same as in London, and many cases of excessive hours were to be found. In London the street traders were about one-tenth of those employed. In the provincial towns they amounted to nearly one-fourth of the total employed. Of the employments, domestic work, that is, going in to clean knives and boots, is the least harmful. Street selling is always bad.'

Wage-Earning Children in Hoxton and Bermondsey

In March (1908) the writer accompanied Miss Adler in her inspection of wage-earning children at a boys' school in Hoxton and at a girls' school in Bermondsey. They found 15 per cent. of the boys in the Hoxton school were wage earners. They were employed as errand boys to take out bottles, parcels and papers; at a tea shop, at a coal shop, at an upholsterer's, at a barber's. As street sellers they sold laces, salt, pot-herbs, vegetables, blacking. One 'picked over green stuff' for a greengrocer; one ran errands for a maker of doll's arms; one looked after a crippled boy; one helped at a whelk and mussel stall; one made capsules, one cardboard boxes, one sticks; whilst one covered steels.

At the girls' school in Bermondsey some ran errands, some minded neighbors' babies, some sold vegetables in the streets, or helped at coster stalls, some played with neighbors' children, some sold alone in the streets, which is illegal. The boys' occupations are the most varied and interesting. Those of the girls are often very heavy, tiring and dreary. 'Bright girls,' Miss Clementina Black truly says, 'are put to work far too soon, and they become apathetic, listless women at thirty-five who might be fifty.'

Mrs. Hogg's Report

Nine years have passed since the evils of Child Labor were brought officially to the notice of our rulers, and that by a woman. Mrs. F. G. Hogg (Secretary of the Education Committee of the Women's Industrial Council), made a special study of the subject and organized a deputation to Sir John Gorst, then Vice-President of Committee on Education, respecting it. A Parliamentary enquiry was instituted, and the facts brought to light were so terrible and unexpected that Sir John Gorst in the House of Commons called it 'a perfectly sickening document which threw a lurid light upon the social conditions of a large part of the population.' One manager stated: 'Without exaggeration I can truthfully assert that there are to-day in our National and Board schools thousands of little white slaves.'

This Parliamentary report stated that 144,000 boys and 34,000 girls worked regularly for money out of school hours, but nothing was said of casual or seasonal work. Of the children regularly at work, 131 were under six years of age, 1,120 between six and seven, 4,211 between seven and eight, 11,027 between eight and nine, and 22,131 between nine and ten. One little boy peeled onions twenty hours a week for 8d. a week. A milk boy received 2s. a week for twenty-eight hours labor a week – less than 1d. an hour. One boy received 6d. for twenty hours work a week. A little boy engaged in pea-picking received 3d. a week. A little girl under six carried milk for thirty-five hours a week for her parents, and earned no wages. Another under six was a nurse girl who worked for twenty-nine hours a week for 2d. and her food. A boy of ten worked seventy-two hours a week for a farmer for 3s. A newspaper boy worked 100 hours a week, including Sundays (over fourteen hours a day), and received 3s. 6d. a week and his meals. One girl of twelve was employed before, between and after school for six and a half hours a day for 3d. a week. Another girl of twelve got 9d. a week and her food for carrying out parcels for six and a half hours daily during the intervals when she was not at school. A greengrocer's boy of twelve started for the London market every day at 2.30 a.m. He returned at 9.30 a.m. and then went to school!

One would have thought that after such revelations as these were officially made known to Parliament it would have bestirred itself to remedy the evil. But the usual delays occurred.

The Inter-Departmental Committee on the Employment of School Children, formed in 1901, represented three of the great Departments of State – the Home Office, the Board of Education, and the Board of Trade. As a result of this, in 1902, a Bill to deal with Child Employment was introduced, but, as Sir John Gorst says,[10] 'was not proceeded with, the time of Parliaments being occupied with subjects more interesting to the governing classes. It was introduced again in 1903, and, by great good luck, became law on January 1st, 1904; but in 1906, in most places, in spite of the Act of January 1st, 1904, the deliverance of over-worked children is still a long way off. The local authorities belong, to a very great extent, to the governing class, and are not much under the influence of working-class opinion.'

The Need for a Socialist Party

Sir John Gorst winds up his chapter on 'Overworked Children' thus: 'The story of this attempt at reform illustrates the impotence which threatens our social system, and the incapacity of the governing classes to carry out the simplest measure of social reform, even one which does not affect their interests, and on the necessity for which they themselves are agreed. It seems to justify the people in revolting against the parties into which the governing classes have divided themselves, in forming independent labor parties and in endeavouring to take the regulation of Society into their own hands. The present holders of power, according to the view of the rising party of the people, have had their opportunity; they have failed to avail themselves of it, and the carrying out of necessary reforms must now pass into other hands.' Moreover, as Sir John Gorst adds: 'Had the counsels of women been more sought after and attended to, many of the lamentable blunders that men have made in the treatment of children would have been avoided.'

Bye-Laws to be Framed by Local Bodies under Act of 1903

After all these delays, the Employment of Children Act of 1903 conferred powers on the London County Council and the councils of other counties and boroughs to frame bye-laws to regulate Child Labor. Mrs. Alden, M.D., states:[11] 'The Act contains regulations which, if they were enforced, would have great value. The failure to enforce the regulations is due largely to the laxity of local authorities, who have neglected to frame bye-laws, and who have failed in some cases to put into operation even the statutory provision of the Act.'

Bye-laws were framed by the London County Council in 1905, but only now, in 1908, are they at length to be enforced. The employment of children under eleven is forbidden. If attending school, children are only to be employed in industrial work at home between 5 p.m. and 8 p.m., or on other days between 9 a.m. and 12 noon, and between 5 p.m. and 8 p.m., or on Sundays. Three and a half hours are to be the maximum of work if attending school, and eight hours a day when the school is not open. If attending school they are not to be employed outside the home between 8 a.m. and 5 p.m., or before 6 a.m. or after 8.30 p.m. Street trading is regulated for all children under sixteen. Girls under that age are to trade only when accompanied by a parent or guardian. Boys under sixteen are to wear on the right arm a badge provided by the Council. On Sundays children are not to be employed for more than three hours and between the hours of 7 a.m. and 1 p.m.

But the enforcement needs more officers than are at present employed. A school attendance officer recently told the writer that in addition to his ordinary visiting (he has 3,200 children to look after), owing to these bye-laws, he has to be out in the streets until midnight on Saturdays in order to prevent children being employed beyond the legal hour – 8 p.m. in the winter and 9 p.m. in the summer months.

In a return to the House of Commons dated June 25th, 1907, it is stated only sixty-six local authorities in England and Wales (out of more than 300), twenty-six in Scotland and five in Ireland had framed bye-laws.

The Prevention of Cruelty Acts

The Act of 1894, among other useful provisions for the protection of children, made their employment in theatres or other places of entertainment conditional on the obtaining of a magistrate's licence, to be granted only when the magistrate is satisfied that the child is physically fit for the work and that proper provision has been made for its health and kind treatment. This Act has been amended and extended in the Act of 1904 and the Children's Act, 1908. The dangerous training of acrobats is subject to regulation.

Child labor under capitalism

The Education (Provision of Meals) Act, 1906–7

This Act authorizes the levying of a halfpenny rate, if necessary, for the feeding of necessitous children, by any county, borough, or urban district council in England and Wales which is an education authority under the Education Acts of 1902–3. The Act, being permissive, has, in London, lamentably missed fire so far. Although members of the London County Council were moved to tears in the autumn of 1907 by Mr. Crooks' eloquent speech on behalf of the feeding of poor children, a majority of them voted against the levying of the halfpenny rate to buy food, for fear of placing additional burdens on the ratepayers. The London County Council, so far as concerns the feeding of necessitous children, contents itself with co-operating with private agencies and charitable societies, which are, in many cases, far from satisfactory. In Bermondsey the children have often to be given a penny by the head teacher and sent to the cook shops, as no provision can be made for them at the schools. The food provided by the caterers is often most unsuitable for children, especially for those who have delicate stomachs. Even if parents are able to provide food for their children in the slum districts, it is often of the most unwholesome kind, such as fried fish (bought cold), eels, meat pies, coarse parts of meat (especially pork), bloaters, cheap jam and bread, vinegar and pickles, whilst tea is a universal drink. (The tea being more of the nature of a 'stew' can hardly be called tea at all.) Milk porridge, bread and milk, and milk puddings are almost unheard of, whilst maccaroni is unknown. The children's taste is vitiated by the strong flavored viands which they are given; and at first it is often difficult to get them to eat food suitable for their age and delicacy. Children fed at home are not infrequently sick over their desks in school. It is, of course, far easier for many parents to buy cooked food than to cook in their own poor rooms, with an impossible firegrate, no oven, no water supply, no sink, and no dustbin for vegetable refuse. To cater properly for the children, a system such as that prevailing in Bradford must be organized. In the matter of feeding the children England expects every city to do its duty at least as well as Bradford.

In the Report of the Inter-Departmental Committeee on Physical Deterioration in 1904, Dr. Eichholz, one of H.M. Inspectors of Schools, estimated the number of underfed children in London at 122,000, or 16 per cent. of the whole.

Up and down the United Kingdom there are at least as many children at school hungry as in London. Dr. W. L. Mackenzie, Medical Member of the Local Government Board for Scotland,

65

said that in the slums of Edinburgh a large proportion of children were half starved. Dr. Kelly, Roman Catholic Bishop of Ross, stated in 1904 that in the South of Ireland it was commonly the case that children came to school underfed.

Medical Inspection under Section 13 of Act of 1906–7

This Act provides for the medical inspection of all school children. But though medical inspection is of the utmost importance, it is of little use without medical treatment and proper feeding. It is believed that half the children in the mentally defective schools are thus defective, or backward, owing to improper feeding or semi-starvation. Their brains are anaemic, their eyes are often sore, their ears deaf, their teeth ache, their heads and bodies are verminous. Such children, when grown up, swell the ranks of the unemployed and unfit, and will continue to do so until the scientific feeding of school children is undertaken.

There is no more instructive reading respecting the physique of children than the *Report by Dr. W. Leslie Mackenzie and Captain A. Foster on a Collection of Statistics as to Physical Condition of Children attending the Public Schools of the School Board of Glasgow*, which was issued by the Scotch Education Department.

This Report gives the results of the most extensive investigation ever undertaken in Great Britain as regards the physique of the children. The heights and weights of children in seventy-three schools in Glasgow were dealt with. Returns were obtained for 72,857 children in seventy-three schools, which were divided into four social groups, representing, among other things, the distribution of one, two and three or more roomed homes.

At each age from five to eighteen the weight of the children was found to be uniformly below the standard of the average of the population as ascertained by the Anthropometrical Committee of the British Association. Up to the age of fourteen the children were distinctly below the standard.

Boys and girls in Group A, the poorest districts, fell very much below the anthropometric standard. At the age of ten the boys' average weight was 10.8 pounds below the standard, and the average height 2.9 inches below. At thirteen the average weight was 11.1 pounds below the standard, the average height 3.1 inches below. The facts were practically parallel with regard to the girls.

As surely as boys or girls came from Group A, the one-roomed group, the children were always on an average distinctly smaller and lighter than the children from the two-roomed group; and those from the two-roomed group were smaller and lighter than children from the three-roomed group; and those from the three-roomed group than the children from the four-roomed group. The Report says: 'The numbers examined are so large, and the results are so uniform, that only one conclusion is possible, viz., that the poorest child suffers most in nutrition and growth. It cannot be an accident that boys from two-roomed houses should be 11.7 pounds lighter on an average than boys from four-roomed houses and 4.7 inches smaller. Neither is it an accident that girls from one-roomed houses are, on an average, 14 pounds lighter and 5.3 inches shorter than the girls from four-roomed houses.'

Now, many of these undersized children are employed as wage-earning children. It is fair to assume that if as comprehensive a report were made of children in London as in Glasgow, the results would be equally startling.

Pernicious Effects of Street Trading

As regards street trading, all the witnesses before the Inter-Departmental Committee and all inspectors, managers, members of education committees, and clergymen, are agreed that its influence on children is entirely pernicious. Mr. Chilton Thomas, who was for ten years Hon. Manager of Father Berry's Roman Catholic Homes at Liverpool, stated: 'The more we have to do with street trading, the more baneful we find it. Would that it could be abolished. I do think the street trader is such a social leper that he ought to be kept quite apart from the errand boy who has some sort of trade for his after life.' In 1892, Mr. Chilton Thomas said they had a home for these street trading boys. He had 3,000 of them pass through his hands; but they had to shut up the home, as they found it did not do the boys a bit of good without regulations by the City Council (now in force in a measure), and without the care of parents or guardians. He also said the hours of labor on Saturday were terrible.

As regards street trading for girls, Miss Florence Melly, formerly a member of the Liverpool School Board, stated: 'Our day industrial evidence would go to this, that no girl remains good after fourteen years of age who has had street trading. "Chip girls" and "step girls" should be included, as they go from house to house and come in contact with anyone who opens the door.'

Mr. Alderman Watts, Chairman of the Sub-Committee of the Watch Committee of Liverpool, said: 'To have a pleasant looking child in the streets is flying in the face of the greatest possible danger. I have a strong opinion that if girls are kept out of the way of temptation during the earlier period of their lives, they will grow up respectable women; but if the temptation is thrown in their way, as it must be in the street, the danger is very great indeed. Liverpool a few years ago was, perhaps, one of the worst cities in this respect – as bad as London, in fact – but you will not find it here now. The death rate,' Alderman Watts continued, 'amongst children is abnormal and awful. Children cannot be exposed in the streets or elsewhere without very serious danger to their lives. Nine out of ten of little girls are of delicate frame.'

Mr. Alderman Rawson, Chairman of the Watch Committee of Manchester City Council, said: 'We are quite certain that the trading by girls in the streets leads to loose life. We have illustrations to that effect of a very painful character. The selling of newspapers and matches by girls in the streets is often a mere cloak for solicitation. There are girls that come from homes so bad, from parents so dissolute, that we believe the selling is simply a pretence, and that parents send them out knowing it is a pretence.'

So much for the efficacy of parental control, guidance, and care under certain conditions of life. All the Councils of Liverpool, Nottingham, Birmingham, and Manchester were in favor of the total prohibition of street trading for girls.

But why only for girls? Sir Lambert Ormsby, President of the Royal College of Surgeons in Dublin, bore witness before the Inter Departmental Committee on Physical Deterioration in 1904 to the miserable physique of the little street traders in Dublin and the frequent cases of pneumonia among them in the children's hospital, the death rate being quite abnormal.[12] And there is a concensus of opinion that it is from street trading boys that spring most of the unemployed, the casuals, the loafers, the gamblers, and many others who form the most difficult problems of modern society.

As a matter of fact, it is found that child labor and unskilled labor go hand in hand. For, in the first place, child labor is itself unskilled labor, and unskilled labor of a kind very attractive to certain employers. It is cheap; fresh supplies are always ready to hand; and, most important of all, it is intelligent unskilled labor, at any rate until the training of the school has lost its effect. Secondly, it leads to a supply of unintelligent unskilled labor. The child who is working cannot be learning, and the child whose mental development is checked is the child who becomes in later years the laborer too stupid to employ except at the lowest wages. Finally, even if he could escape from this dreary fate, he has no desire to do so. The bent has been given to his tastes; he has been taught to regard earnings, and not prospects, as his sole goal in life, and to sacrifice the last for the sake of the first.[13]

As regards the general employment of children, the Head Master of the Anglesea Place Board School of Bristol declared that the evils of employment have shown themselves over and over again in the following ways:–

1. The boys are often late for school, some habitually so.
2. They come to school utterly worn out.
3. There is a grave moral deterioration.
4. Their mental power is diminished. It is very rarely a wage-earning boy does his school work well. The injury done to children is very great.[14]

In the Michael Faraday School in Walworth, Mr. Marshall Jackman said that, out of 227 wage-earning boys in his school, only 61 were in really good health. Dr. Thomas, the Medical Officer of the L.C.C., examined 2,000 children in schools, and he found that, out of 384 wage-earning boys, 233 showed signs of fatigue, 140 were anaemic, 131 had nerve signs, 63 per cent. showed nerve strain, 64 were suffering from deformities from the carrying of heavy weights, 51 had severe heart signs, 27 had severe heart affection, and 72 per cent. of barbers' boys were anaemic.[15]

Mrs. Pankhurst, at one time a member of the Manchester School Board and member of the Board of Guardians, stated that wage-earning by children was 'demoralizing,' and that 'it would be distinctly an advantage to the parents in the long run that the children should be withdrawn from these employments. The more intelligent artizan does not believe in sending out his children to work for wages. . . . It competes with adult labor.'

Child Labor in Agriculture

In the agricultural districts the attendance at school is constantly evaded. It frequently happens that the local magistrates and county councillors are landlords or farmers, who must have cheap labor, even at the expense of the children's well-being. The children are employed in milking and tending cattle, in picking up stones off the land, in weeding, in picking strawberries (often at 3 a.m. in the season in all weathers), in hop picking, and in minding and leading horses. The work is extremely fatiguing. There is still in this twentieth century a wearing struggle between the educationist and the child exploiters, although it is not as bad as it used to be. In certain country districts 75 per cent. of attendances – instead of 95 per cent. – is still considered high.

The Children's Act of 1908

But there are signs everywhere now of the awakening of the public conscience to the infamy of Child Labor. Although this Act does not deal directly with the labor question, there are, under it, to be established Juvenile Courts, in which all charges concerning the welfare of children will be heard, including applications for committal to industrial schools and reformatories.

The Immediate Reforms to Work for

The evils disclosed are grave. Leaving aside for the moment all schemes of social reconstruction, what immediately practicable reforms will bring prompt, if only partial, remedies? There is a vast amount to be done by mere administration of the existing law. It may safely be said that no local authority yet makes anything like full use of its powers under the Education Acts, the Shop Hours Acts, the Children's Act, etc. An enormous amount of good would result if members of education committees and of town or county councils could be induced merely to put the existing laws fully in operation. But amendments of the law are urgently required. In agreement with practically all those who have studied the question, we recommend:–

1. That for children under five for whom adequate home care is not available, there should be a sufficient provision of small day nurseries, under the administration of the local health authority, where these infants can remain all day, either gratuitously or at fees representing only the cost of the food supplied.

2. That attendance at school of all children between five and fourteen be rigorously enforced (the poorest parents being adequately assisted to enable them to let their children attend), an adequate supply of suitable efficient schools being everywhere provided under due public control, including special schools for sub-normal children of various kinds, 'open-air' schools and vacation schools.

3. That children in attendance at school be not permitted to be employed for hire under any pretence whatever.

4. That in order to ensure the welfare of the coming generation of citizens the responsibility for the care and maintenance of children of school age, being destitute, be transferred from the Poor Law to the local education authorities.

5. That it be made obligatory upon the local education authorities to organize throughout the whole year a system of providing, at the expense of the rates and under direct public control, suitable meals of a simple kind for all children found at school in an underfed condition; such meals to be provided under skilled and salaried supervision with the amenities of civilization.

6. That it should be made obligatory for every public elementary school to have attached to it a 'Children's Care Committee' of members whose duty it should be to take cognizance of every child attending school in a neglected or necessitous condition; to visit its home and discover what is amiss; to afford such friendly help as may be required; and to bring to light any cases of ill-treatment which call for criminal prosecution.

7. That in all cases in which a child is provided for by what is now Poor Law relief, reports should be obtained upon its adequacy and the character of the home; and that where it is not considered expedient to grant to the parent enough for the full maintenance of the child, or where the child is found, in fact, to be suffering from lack of nourishment or lack of care, the child be sent to a day industrial school, where it will receive meals and care during the whole day.

8. That where it is found that the parents are of such vicious life and character as to be wholly unfit to have the care of children, the guilty parents should be criminally prosecuted for their neglect, and the children sent to residential schools, so as to secure their proper upbringing.

9. That the minimum age at which children may leave school to be employed in industry at all be raised at once to fourteen, and as soon as possible to fifteen (as in Switzerland).

10. That in view of the need of securing effective technical and domestic training for all boys and girls, the 'half time' provisions of the Factory and Workshops Acts be extended for all industries up to the age of eighteen, no boy or girl under eighteen being allowed to be employed in industry for more than thirty hours per week.

11. That provision be made for the compulsory attendance of boys and girls between fourteen and eighteen at technical institutes for a combined course of physical training, technical education and continuation classes, absorbing the thirty hours per week which they will no longer give to their employers.

Notes

1 *The Industrial Revolution*, by Arnold Toynbee; *Growth of English Industry and Commerce*, by W. Cunningham; *Capital*, by Karl Marx.
2 *Life of Robert Owen*, by F. Podmore; *History of Factory Legislation*, by B. L. Hutchins and A. Harrison.
3 *Life of Robert Owen*, by F. Podmore, p. 208.
4 See also the *Report on the Employment of Children in the United Kingdom*, by Constance Smith (British Association for Labor Legislation).
5 *Sweated Industry*, by Miss Clementina Black, p. 122.
6 *Child Workers and Wage Earners*, by Miss Adler.
7 *English Socialism of To-day*, by the Right Hon. H. O. Arnold-Foster, pp. 99, 100.
8 The Government has appointed an Inter-Departmental Committee to enquire into the working and result of the half time system. The Trades Union Congress at Nottingham in September, 1908, passed a resolution urging its abolition.
9 Minutes of Evidence taken before the Inter-Departmental Committee on Employment of School Children in 1901, pp. viii. and 70–73.
10 *The Children of the Nation*, by Sir John Gorst.
11 *Child Life and Labor*, by Mrs. Alden, M.D., p. 110.
12 *Juvenile Wage Earners and their Work*, by Miss Adler, p. 4.
13 See *The Town Child*, by Reginald Bray, L.C.C.
14 Report of Inter-Departmental Committee, Appendix No. 32.
15 Barbers' shops in London are now, by bye-law, barred to boy workers.

FABIAN TRACT No. 142
(March 1909)

RENT AND VALUE

Adapted by Mrs. Bernard Shaw from 'The Economic Basis of Socialism' in 'Fabian Essays'

'There is nothing *specific* in Socialism except its economics. . . . There is absolutely nothing peculiar to it except its economic demonstration that private property produces the phenomenon of privately appropriated economic rent and all the consequences of it.'—G.B.S.

PART I. – RENT

Socialists, protesting against the present state of society, have lately been often met by two somewhat contradictory assertions. We are told that too much stress has been laid upon figures, statistics, and 'dry' things such as political economy: that what is wanted is a 'great wave of emotion,' 'genuine religious feeling,' a 'change of heart'; that these and these only will rectify the cruelties and injustices of the present state of society. And in the same breath it will often be illogically maintained that 'you can't change human nature'; and that as human nature has brought about the present state of things it is no use trying to make any radical alteration.

Now I propose to shew that human nature, whether it can be changed or not, did not bring about the present state of things; but that it was rather the present state of things which brought about human nature; that the existing conditions of society are the result of economic laws which work inexorably, indifferent to the weal or woe of the human race, and unconscious of its existence. I also propose to shew that should the human race become conscious of the existence of such economic forces, and capable of directing them, these laws can be made to subserve man's welfare as powerfully as, left to themselves, they have been working for his destruction. A change of heart, if it be in the right direction, seems incidentally desirable; but by itself, and unaccompanied by the requisite knowledge of economic laws, it will be as useless as would be a wireless telegraphy station sending messages into space were there not somewhere a receiver to collect those messages.

The Origin of Rent

Picture then to yourself a vast green plain of country, virgin to the spade, awaiting the advent of man. Imagine the arrival of the first colonist, the original Adam. He drives his spade into, and sets up his stockade around, the most fertile and favorably situated patch he can find. Metaphorically Adam's little patch is a pool that will yet rise and submerge the whole land. Other Adams come all sure to pre-empt patches as near as may be to the first Adam's, partly because he has chosen the best situation, partly for the pleasure of his society and conversation, and partly because where two men are assembled together there is a two man power that is far more than double one man power. And so the pool rises, and the margin spreads more and more remote from the centre, until the pool becomes a lake, and the lake an inland sea.

But in the course of this inundation that specially fertile region upon which Adam pitched is sooner or later all pre-empted and there is nothing for the newcomer to pre-empt save soil of the second quality. Also, division of labor sets in among Adam's neighbors; and with it, of course, comes the establishment of a market for the exchange of the products of their divided labor. Now it is not well to be far afield from that market because distance from it involves extra cost for roads, beasts of burden, and time consumed in travelling thither and back again. All this will be saved to Adam at the centre of cultivation, and incurred by the newcomer at the margin of cultivation.

The Establishment of Rent

Let us estimate the annual value of Adam's produce at £1,000 and the annual produce of the newcomer's land on the margin of cultivation at £500, assuming that Adam and the newcomer are equally industrious. Here is a clear advantage of £500 a year to Adam. This £500 is economic rent. For why should not Adam let his patch to the newcomer at a rent of £500 a year? Since the produce will be £1,000, the newcomer will have £500 left for himself; that is, as much as he could obtain by cultivating a patch of his own at the margin; and it is pleasanter to be in the centre of society than on the outskirts of it. The newcomer will himself propose the arrangement, and Adam may retire (not in consequence of any special merit of his own, any extra industry or brain power, but simply because he was fortunate enough to get the best place at the right moment) as an idle landlord with a perpetual pension of £500 of rent. The excess of fertility of Adam's land is thenceforth recognized as rent and paid, as it is to-day, regularly by a worker to a drone.

The Origin of the County Family

So Adam is retiring from productive industry on £500 a year; and his neighbors are hastening to imitate him as fresh tenants present themselves. The first result is the beginning of a tradition that the oldest families in the country enjoy a superior position to the rest, and that the main advantage of their superior position is that they enjoy incomes without working. Nevertheless, since they still depend upon their tenants' labor for their subsistence, they continue to pay Labor, with a capital L, a certain meed of mouth honor; and the resultant association of prosperity with idleness, and praise with industry, practically destroys morality by setting up that incompatibility between conduct and principle which is the secret of the ingrained cynicism of our own time.

According to our hypothesis, the area of cultivation has now spread into the wilderness so far that at its margin the return for a man's labor for a year is only £500. But it will not stop there; it will at last encroach upon every acre of cultivable land, rising to the snow line on the mountains and falling to the coast of the actual salt water sea, but always reaching the barrenest places last of all, because the cultivators will not break bad land when better is to be had. But suppose that now, at last, the uttermost belt of free land is reached, and that upon it the yield to a man's year's labor is only £100. Clearly now the rent of Adam's primeval patch has risen to £900, since that is the excess of its produce over what is by this time all that is to be had rent free.

Dual Ownership

Adam has yielded up his land for £500 a year to a tenant. It is this tenant accordingly who now lets Adam's patch for £900 a year to the newcomer, who of course loses nothing by the bargain, since it leaves him the £100 a year, with which he must be content any way. It has, in fact, come to this, that the private property in Adam's land is divided between three men, the first doing none of the work and getting half the produce; the second doing none of the work and getting two-fifths of the produce; and the third doing all the work and getting only one-tenth of the produce.

Here is private property in full swing, produced (let us emphasize the fact) not in the least by 'human nature,' but by the natural working of economic laws of which the settlers were unconscious. Probably if the first colonists when they were still on their original patches had been asked 'would you tolerate a state of things in which there should be not only loafers, but in which the loafers should be the richest people in the country,' they would have repudiated the idea with profound and genuine indignation.[1]

All this, however, is a mere trifle compared with the sequel. When the total cultivable area has reached its confines; when there is nothing but a strip of sand round the coast between the furrow and the wave; when the very waves themselves are cultivated by fisherfolk; when the pastures and timber forests have touched the snow line; when, in short, the land is all private property, there appears a man in a strange plight: one who wanders from snow line to sea coast in search of land, and finds none that is not the property of someone else. On the roads he is a vagrant: off them he is a trespasser: he is the first proletarian.

Rent of Ability

Now it may be that this second Adam, the first father of the great proletariat, has one of those scarce brains which are not the least of nature's gifts. If the fertile field yields rent, why not the fertile brain? Here is the first Adam's patch still yielding its £1,000 to the labor of the tenant who, as we have seen, has to pay £900 away in rent. How if the proletarian were boldly to bid £1,000 a year to that man for that property and contrive – invent – anticipate a new want – turn the land to some hitherto undreamed of use – wrest £1,500 a year from the soil and site that only yielded £1,000 before? If he can do this, he can pay the full £1,000 rent, and have an income of £500 left for himself. This is his profit – the rent of his ability – the excess of its produce over that which it would yield to ordinary stupidity.

Origin of the Proletariat

But in due replenishment of the earth there follows upon the footsteps of this first proletarian another who is no cleverer than other men, and can do as much, but not more, than they. For him there is no rent of ability. What is to be his fate? It is certain that by this time not only will the new devices of the renter of ability have been copied by people incapable of inventing them, but division of labor, the use of tools and money, and the economies of civilization will have greatly increased man's power of extracting wealth from nature. So that it may well be that the produce of land on the margin of cultivation, which, as we have seen, fixes the produce left to the cultivators throughout the whole area, may rise considerably.

Scarcity Value

This rise has nothing to do with the margin of cultivation. It is not the difference between the best and worst land. It is not, to put it technically, 'economic rent.' It is a payment for the privilege of using land at all – for access to that which is now a close monopoly; and its amount is regulated, not by what the purchaser could do for himself on land of his own at the margin, but simply by the landowner's eagerness to be idle on the one hand, and the proletarian's need of subsistence on the other. In current economic terms the price is regulated by supply and demand. As the demand for land intensifies by the advent of fresh proletarians, the price goes up and the bargains are made more stringent. Sooner or later the price of tenant right will rise so high that the actual cultivator will get no more of the produce than suffices him for subsistence. At that point there is an end of sub-letting tenant rights. The land's absorption of the proletarians as tenants paying more than the economic rent stops.

Advent of the Proletarian

And now what is the next proletarian to do? For all his forerunners we have found a way of escape; for him there seems none, for where is his subsistence to come from, if he cannot get at the land? Food he must have, and clothing; and both promptly. There is food in the market, and clothing also; but not for nothing. Hard money must be paid for them, and money can only be procured by selling commodities. This presents no difficulty to the cultivators of the land, who can raise commodities by their labor; but the proletarian, being landless, has neither commodities nor the means of producing them. Sell something he must: yet he has nothing to sell – *except himself.*

The first 'Hand': 'Labourer': 'Mechanic': 'Servant': 'Wage-Slave'

The idea seems a desperate one; but it proves quite easy to carry out. The tenant cultivators of the land have not strength enough or time enough to exhaust the productive capacity of their holdings. If they could buy men in the market for less than the sum that these men's labor would add to the produce, then their purchase would be sheer gain. Never in the history of buying and selling was there so splendid a bargain for buyers as this. Accordingly the proletarian

77

no sooner offers himself for sale in 'a new country' than he finds a rush of bidders for him, each striving to get the better of the others by offering to give him more and more of the produce of his labor, and to content themselves with less and less of the surplus. But even the highest bidder must have some surplus or he will not buy. The proletarian, in accepting the highest bid, sells himself openly into bondage. He is not the first man who has done so; for it is evident that his forerunners, the purchasers of tenant right, had been enslaved by the proprietors who lived on the rents paid by them. But now all the disguise falls off: the proletarian renounces not only the fruit of his labor, but also the right to think for himself and to direct his industry as he pleases. The economic change is merely formal: the moral change is enormous. We shall see presently what happens in 'an old country' when the rush of buyers of labor becomes a rush of sellers.

PART II. – VALUE

It is evident that in our imaginary colony labor power is now in the market on the same footing as any other ware exposed for sale: it can be purchased as men purchase a horse or a steam engine, a bottle of wine or a pair of boots.

Exchange Value of Human Beings

Since human labor therefore turns out to be a commodity, marketable just as a basket of eggs or a woollen shirt is marketable, if we want to know what is going to happen to our proletarian in a state owned by private individuals, as our colony is owned, we must proceed to find out what fixes the price of commodities in general (since his price will be fixed in the same way); and what causes the series of arrangements between buyers and sellers which have been named 'supply and demand,' for our proletarian is now supplying *himself* in answer to a demand.

Contradictions and difficulties soon show themselves.

It would seem on the surface that the selling value, or exchange value, of anything must depend upon its utility, for no one will buy a useless thing. Yet fresh air and sunlight, which are so useful as to be quite indispensable, have no money value; whilst for a meteoric stone, shot free of charge from the firmament into your back garden, the curator of a museum will give you a considerable sum. A little reflection will show that this depends upon the fact that fresh air is plentiful and meteoric stones scarce.

Scarcity Value

If by any means the supply of fresh air could be steadily diminished, and the supply of meteoric stones, by celestial cannonade
or otherwise, steadily increased, the fresh air would presently
acquire an exchange value which would gradually rise; whilst the
exchange value of meteoric stones would gradually fall, until at
last fresh air would be supplied through a meter and charged for
like gas, and meteoric stones would become as unsaleable as ordinary pebbles. The money (or exchange) value, in fact, decreases
as the supply increases; or, in other words, as the supply pours in
the demand falls off, until finally, if the supply continues to pour
in, the demand ceases altogether and what is left of the supply is
valueless.

How Exchange Value is Fixed

But besides this fact of the exchange value of any commodity
being dependent upon the amount there is of it in any market at
any one time, another equally important fact must be carefully
mastered, viz., that the value of our commodity is fixed not by
the rarest and most useful part of the stock of it, but by the least
costly and least useful. This can be explained quite simply by an
illustration. If the stock of umbrellas in the market were all alike
and sufficiently large to provide two for each umbrella carrier in
the community, then, since a second umbrella is not so necessary
as the first, the instinctive course would be to ticket half the
umbrellas at, say 15s., and the other half at 8s. 6d. But no man
will give 15s. for an article which he can get for 8s. 6d.; and when
people came to buy, they would buy up all the 8s. 6d. umbrellas.
Each person being thus supplied with an umbrella, the remainder
of the stock, though marked 15s., would be in the position of
second umbrellas, only worth 8s. 6d. It may very likely occur to
the reader that if he was the seller of umbrellas, he would charge
15s. all round and put away half his stock until the number of
umbrellas actually and immediately necessary to his fellow
townsmen was sold. But a moment's reflection will remind him
that there will be other tradesmen in the town who sell umbrellas.
In the next street will be a shop where umbrellas can be purchased
for 10s. 6d., and near by another where they can be had for 7s.
6d.; so that, granted all the umbrellas are of the same quality, the
customers will go to the shop where they are to be had for 7s.
6d., and my reader's 15s. ones will remain on his hands unsold.[2]
The only limit to this 'competition' is obviously the actual cost of
the manufacture of the umbrella. One more illustration of a

different kind. You want to get and sell coal. You begin by going to the point where coal is on the surface – where you can shovel it up with ease. But when that supply is exhausted, you must sink a shaft; you must burrow under ground, eviscerate mountains, tunnel beneath the sea, at an enormous cost in machinery and labor. Yet when you have made your greatest effort, another man may still be in possession of a mine near the surface where he gets his coal for half, a quarter, a tithe of the labor you expend upon yours. In spite of this, when you both bring your coal to market and offer your supplies for sale, you cannot say 'I have been at great expense to get mine and I will charge 20s. a ton.' Your rival is offering his for 15s. a ton, and you must sell at the same price or you will get no customers. Let us suppose that it has cost you 18s. per ton to get your coal, and that it has cost him 5s. per ton to get his, the whole difference between the 5s. and the 18s. is economic rent gained by him, not by superior industry or ability (for it is you who have had these), but by the fact of his privately owned coal mine being in a more advantageous situation than yours. In this manner the exchange value of the least useful and least costly part of the supply fixes the exchange value of all the rest.

The Law of Indifference. – Final Utility (Marginal Utility)

Technically this is called the Law of Indifference. And since the least useful unit of the supply is generally that which is last produced, its utility is called the *final utility* of the commodity.

TOTAL UTILITY

The utility of the first and most useful unit is called the *total utility* of the commodity.[3] The main point to be grasped is, that however useful any commodity may be, its exchange value can be run down to nothing by increasing the supply until there is more of it than is wanted. The excess, being useless and valueless, is to be had for nothing; and nobody will pay anything for a commodity so long as plenty of it is to be had for nothing. This is why air and other indispensable things have no exchange value, whilst scarce gewgaws fetch immense prices.

These, then, are the conditions which confront man as a producer and exchanger. If he produces a useless thing, his labor will be wholly in vain: he will get nothing for it. If he produces a useful thing, the price he will get for it will depend on how much of it there is for sale already. This holds good of the whole mass of manufactured commodities. Those which are scarce, and therefore relatively high in value, tempt men to produce them until the increase of the supply reduces their value to a point at which there is no more profit to be made out of them than out of other commodities. And this process, unless deliberately interfered with, goes on until the price of all commodities is brought down to their cost of production.

Cost of Production

But here is a new question. What does the *cost of production* mean?

We have seen that, owing to the differences in fertility and advantage of situation between one piece of land and another, cost of production varies from district to district, being highest at the margin of cultivation. But we have also seen how the landlord skims off as (economic) rent all the advantage gained by the cultivators of superior sites and soils. Consequently, the addition of the landlord's rent to the expenses of production brings those expenses up even on the best land to the level of those incurred on the worst. Cost of production, then, means cost of production at the margin of cultivation, and is equalized to all producers, since what they may save in labor in favorable situations is counterbalanced by the greater amount of rent they have to pay in those situations. So far from commodities exchanging, or tending to exchange (as some economists allege that they do), according to the labor expended in their production, commodities produced in the most favorable situations, well inside the margin of cultivation, with the minimum of labor, will fetch as high a price as commodities produced at the margin with the maximum of labor. *And all the difference between the two goes to the landlord.* So man's control over the value of commodities consists solely in his power of regulating their supply. Individuals are constantly trying to decrease supply for their own advantage. Gigantic conspiracies have been entered into to forestall the world's wheat and cotton harvests, in order to force their value to the highest possible point. Cargoes of East Indian spices have been destroyed by the Dutch as cargoes of fish are now destroyed in the Thames, to maintain prices by limiting supply. All rings, trusts, corners, combinations, monopolies, and trade secrets have the same object.

The Vital Point

Now we have come to the most important part of this paper: the part which will explain why we Socialists are attacking this private monopoly system – this capitalist system – this *laissez faire* system – with all our strength and ingenuity. Go back to our proletarian. We found that he had come to our colony when all the land, from the sea to the snow line was occupied and owned; when the utmost rent of ability had been screwed out of it; and when its scarcity value had been exploited to the last penny. It was therefore imposs- ible for him to produce any of the commodities by the sale (or exchange) of which men live. But we found that he had one commodity the sale of which he could effect with ease – the sale of himself. We found that men ('laborers,' 'hands,' 'mechanics,' 'working men,' 'servants' – how expressive words are!) were in the market, and traffic in them could be carried on precisely on the same terms as traffic in any other commodity.

Now reflect for a moment upon the laws we have been exam- ining which regulate the exchange of commodities. We found that 'if the supply continues to pour in, the demand ceases altogether, and what is left of the supply is valueless.' We also found that, by the Law of Indifference, 'the exchange value of the least useful part of the supply fixes the exchange value of all the rest.' What will be the result of the action of these laws upon the human commodity we have called a proletarian? The commodity he deals in is one over the supply of which he himself has practically no control. True, at first there is only one of him in our colony; but others pour in, population increases by leaps and bounds, soon there are twenty, one hundred, one thousand, five thousand, and men continue so to multiply that their exchange value falls slowly and surely until it disappears altogether. This is the condition of our English laborers to-day: they are no longer even dirt cheap: they are valueless. The proof of this is the existence of the unem- ployed, who can be had for nothing.

You will immediately say 'no labor can be had for nothing': you will very likely add that you 'wish it could,' and instance the high wages given to 'hands' and 'servants.' The answer is deplorably simple. Suppose horses multiplied in England in such quantities that they were to be had for the asking, like kittens condemned to the bucket. You would still have to feed your horse – feed him well if you used him as a smart hunter – feed him and lodge him wretchedly if you used him only as a drudge. But the cost of his keep would not mean that the horse had an exchange value. If you got him for nothing in the first instance, if no one would give you anything for him when you had done with him, he would be worth nothing, in spite of the cost of his keep. That is just the case of every member of the proletariat who could be replaced by one of the unemployed to-day. Their wage is not the price of themselves, for they are worth nothing; it is only their keep. If you have to give your footman a better allowance than your wretched hewer of wood, it is for the same reason that you have to give your hunter oats and a clean stall instead of chopped straw and a sty.

The Capitalist System Guilty

This, then, is the economic analysis which convicts private property of being unjust from the beginning, and utterly impossible as a final solution of the problem of the distribution of wealth. All attempts yet made to construct true societies upon it have failed: the nearest things to societies so achieved have been civilizations which have rotted into centres of vice and luxury, and eventually been swept away by uncivilized races. It is sometimes said that during this grotesquely hideous march of civilization from bad to worse, wealth is increasing side by side with misery. Such a thing is eternally impossible; wealth is steadily decreasing with the spread of poverty. But riches are increasing, which is quite another thing. The total of the exchange values produced in this country is mounting, perhaps, by leaps and bounds. But the accumulation of riches, and consequently of excessive purchasing power in the hands of one class, soon satiates that class with socially useful wealth, and sets it offering a price for luxuries. Luxuries are not social wealth: the machinery for producing them is not social wealth: labor skilled only to manufacture them is not socially useful labor: the men, women, and children who make a living by producing them are no more self-supporting than the idle rich for whose amusement they are kept at work. It is the habit of counting as wealth the exchange values involved in these transactions that makes us fancy that the poor are starving in the midst of plenty. They are starving in the midst of plenty of jewels, velvets, laces, equipages, and racehorses; but not in the midst of plenty of food. In the things that are wanted for the welfare of the people England is abjectly poor. Yet private property, by its nature, must still heap the purchasing power upon the few rich and withhold it from the many poor.

Conclusion

Now Socialism claims to have discovered in this private appropriation of land the source of those unjust privileges which the Socialists seek to abolish. They assert that *public property in land and the means of production is the basic economic condition of Socialism.* How the economic change from private to public ownership can be brought about with the least suffering to individuals does not come within the scope of this paper; but if we have got as far as an intellectual conviction that the source of our social misery is no eternal wellspring of confusion and evil, not the depravity of human nature or the hardness of human hearts, but only an artificial system susceptible of almost infinite modification and readjustment – nay, of practical demolition and rearrangement at the will of man, then a terrible weight will be lifted from the minds of all except those who are clinging to the present state of things from base motives. It is to economic science – once the dismal, now the hopeful – that we are indebted for the discovery that though the evil is enormously worse than we knew, yet it is not eternal – not even very long lived, if we only bestir ourselves to make an end of it.

Notes

1 The reader will observe that, to avoid complications, no mention has been made of capital as such. The monopoly of land produces the monopoly of capital. All capital begins as spare money, no matter what it may finally be turned into: mines, railways, canals, houses. In the first instance the possession of capital always means that some individual has received more rent than he desires or chooses to spend. Colloquially, one property with a farm on it is said to be land yielding rent; whilst another, with a railway on it, is called capital yielding interest. But economically there is no distinction between them when they once become sources of revenue. Shareholder and landlord live alike on the produce extracted from their property by the labor of the proletariat.
2 There is indeed another way. The reader might buy up all the umbrellas in the town and arrange that none should be brought in from anywhere else. This is to 'corner' the market – but that is another story.
3 Some economists, transferring from cultivation to utility our old metaphor of the spreading pool, call final utility 'marginal' utility.

FABIAN TRACT No. 145
(September 1909)

THE CASE FOR SCHOOL NURSERIES

Mrs. Townshend

School Attendance of Children under Five

Till quite recently it has been the practice in England and Wales for children between three and five to attend school if their parents so desired and for school authorities to make regular provision for such children. 'During the fifteen years previous to 1907 at least a third of all such children were on the registers of public elementary schools.'[1] Soon after the passing of the Education Act, 1902, however, the question as to whether school attendance for very young children was desirable began to be much discussed. It was pointed out that the compulsory age limit was lower in England than in any other country, and that the methods employed in most of our infant schools were unsuited to the needs of such very young children. Enquiries were set on foot by some of the new education authorities and by the Board of Education, with the result that in the Code for 1905 the following clause was inserted:–

'Where the Local Education Authority have so determined in the case of any school maintained by them, children who are under five years of age may be refused admission to that school.'

Accordingly no obligation rests at present on local education authorities to provide for children under five. There are in England and Wales three hundred and twenty-seven such authorities, and of these thirty-two wholly exclude children under five from their schools, one hundred and fifty-four retain all children between three and five who are sent to school, while the remaining one hundred and thirty-six take a middle course, retaining some and excluding others.[2]

Reasons for Excluding Children under Five from Elementary Schools

The reasons given for this exclusion are of two kinds; some have reference only to the ordinary infant school as it exists at present in England, others to any kind of public provision whatever. Among the former may be mentioned:–

1. THE VENTILATION DIFFICULTY

It has been urged that under existing conditions of air space proper ventilation is almost impossible, and that the air has been actually found to be more impure in schools than in the dwellings of the poor.[3] It is argued that in the case of older children the risks from bad air are less while the advantages of education are greater, that it is a heavy and needless risk to herd very young children together in bad air. Such objectors take for granted that the present unsatisfactory conditions as to ventilation are to be looked on as inevitable, but, 'it certainly seems anomalous, to say the least, that elementary schools should be allowed to remain as the classical example of bad ventilation, and that children should thus be taught by practical example to tolerate foul air.'[4] It must be remembered, too, that the bad smell and intolerable stuffiness of the ordinary schoolroom, which are the outward and sensible sign of injurious air conditions, are due rather to dirt than to actual deficiency of air. 'Far more could be done by cleanliness than by ventilation. The floors and walls should be capable of being properly cleansed, and the children themselves and their clothes kept clean and tidy.' Now in the nursery school cleanliness would always be specially insisted on, would indeed take the very first place among subjects of instruction, so that it may be hoped that the air would in them be less laden with impurities than in the ordinary elementary school. It must be noticed, too, that the children in such schools ought to spend a large part of their school time out of doors, and that no day nursery or nursery school is complete without ample playgrounds, both roofed and open, with facilities for resting out of doors in good weather.

2. THE DANGER OF INFECTION

'In proportion to the number of children, the spread of infectious diseases caused by school attendance is greater before five than after; but it must be remembered that if more escape *before* five, the greater will be the incidence of the disease *after* five.' It is also noteworthy that 'with the better training of teachers on the hygienic side and the appointment of school medical officers, a state of things will arise, and, in fact, is arising, in which attendance at school will become a means of decreasing the diseases (more especially diphtheria and scarlet fever).'[5]

3. The Danger of Premature Mental Strain

'The question of overpressure has been rather exaggerated. Practically it does not exist in infants' schools, except in the case of children with defects to start with, children highly nervous or badly nourished, for whom the work is too much. At the same time, much of the instruction now given is without doubt unsuitable. . . . Play is the best way of educating young children; let them follow their natural instincts as in the nursery. . . . Above all, avoid any idea of enforcing discipline. Fine muscular movements (as of the eye or fingers in reading, writing, or sewing, etc.) should be postponed until the child has obtained a fuller control over its muscles. . . . Drill is very important, and should consist of "coarse" movements as contrasted with the "fine" movements mentioned above. Organized games can be made into a very severe lesson; their value is much exaggerated.'[6] This danger of overstrain through unsuitable treatment is of the utmost importance; and it is the special claim of the nursery school to avoid it by providing just that atmosphere of freedom and kindly encouragement which a sensible mother gives to her child, avoiding alike over stimulation and needless restraint.

But in addition to these special and more or less avoidable dangers, general objections are raised against making any public provision for little children which would facilitate their removal from home. There is, for instance:–

4. The Danger that Parental Responsibilty may be Weakened

Experience has shown over and over again that the parental burden is too heavy. All observers agree that children attending school are better looked after by their parents, kept cleaner and tidier, than they would be if they stayed at home. A marked difference may be noticed in almost any poor district in the appearance of the children on Saturdays and during the holidays. It would be much nearer the truth to say that any arrangement which involves the child's being periodically submitted to outside inspection would raise the standard of parental responsibility, and that this influence would be greatly increased by teaching and illustrating what the needs of young children really are. The hollowness of this objection is apparent when one considers that the wealthy ladies who think it so dangerous to relieve the hardworked mother of any of her duties to her little ones find it necessary to depute all such duties in their own case to a nurse. This fact furnishes an answer also to another objection which is often urged, viz., that little children require such constant individual and loving attention that they are better looked after by their mothers than by anyone else. Let us look at the facts. How does the rich mother who has free choice in the matter act? Does she keep her three year old child constantly with her when she is reading, writing, talking to her friends, or eating her meals? No; she devotes, perhaps, a few hours in the day to it when she can give it a fair share of attention, and for the rest of the time she places it with a skilled attendant either out of doors or in an airy, sunny apartment, where it can play about freely under due supervision. What does the poor mother do? If she is able to remain at home, she will allow her three year old to crawl about the kitchen floor or play in the street, or, perhaps, if he be a venturesome child, will tie him to the leg of the table, so that he may not tumble into the fire, while she is busy with the dinner, the housework, or the family washing. If, on the other hand, she has to go out to work, she will leave him with a 'minder,' usually some old or feeble person who is not able to do more active work, or, if she can manage to hoodwink the attendance officer, with an elder brother or sister kept at home for the purpose. Can it be seriously alleged that it would be a disadvantage to the child to be removed from the minder, or even from the home kitchen and the tail of his mother's eye, to a nursery resembling that which the rich mother provides for her own child, but shared with a number of little neighbors of its own age? It is just because little children require constant and watchful attention that collectivist nurseries are so much needed. One capable, motherly, experienced woman, with a suitable number of trained assistants, can superintend the tending and training of a large number of infants; while one woman with a house to clean, a family to feed and clothe, and the washing to do, cannot properly care for one.

5. The Danger of Encouraging Bottle Feeding

But though this dread of lightening the responsibilities of motherhood may for the most part be dismissed as sentimental, yet there is one aspect of it, affecting our dealing with infants of only a few months old, the importance of which cannot possibly be exaggerated. The right place for a suckled infant is with its mother, and in a well ordered State no woman would be allowed to undertake work away from home until her child was nine months old; but any legal prohibition of this kind seems, unfortunately, a long way off, since it would necessarily imply State maintenance for nursing mothers. Meanwhile, as long as husbands are liable to be underpaid or unemployed, mothers who should be nursing their babies will accept laundry work or charing; and when this happens the unfortunate baby will fare better in a crèche, where it will receive pure milk, suitably diluted, out of a clean bottle, than with the casual minder. It does not necessarily follow, however, that the crèche baby should be hand fed. After the first few months, when the feeding has become less frequent, it is quite possible for nursing mothers to visit the crèches at suitable intervals. In French and Belgian crèches a room is usually set apart for this purpose.

The Need for Public Provision for Children under School Age

It seems clear, notwithstanding all difficulties and objections, that public provision must be made for some children under school age. Even if we decide with the Consultative Committee that the proper place for such children is at home with their mothers, yet we are bound to admit, as they do, that the home surroundings of large numbers of children are not satisfactory, and that children from these homes should be sent during the daytime to places specially intended for their training.[7] No responsible person in London, for instance, is prepared to recommend that the children under five now at school should be turned into the streets.

Kind of Provision Required

We have already said that of actual teaching, in the ordinary sense of the word, children under five ought to receive very little. Information should be given very sparingly and only in response to awakened curiosity. Restraint, compulsion, and punishment should be almost unknown; but there is one kind of education which must take place in these early years if at all, and on which health and efficiency in after life largely depend, I mean the formation of physical habits.[8] People are apt to forget that breathing, walking, eating, speaking and sleeping have to be learnt, and that there are right and wrong ways of doing each. They are all difficult arts to the baby learner, and he may be much helped in acquiring them by an expert and watchful guardian. As soon as a child is born one may begin to teach him regularity and periodicity in sleeping, eating and the evacuations of the body, and by the time he is a year old he is ready for one or two new lessons. Every year a little more may be done in the way of checking injurious habits and encouraging useful ones; and it must be remembered that these nursery lessons are not less but far more important than the reading, writing, and counting that are taught in the ordinary infant schools. If we consider what are the differences that distinguish a well-bred person from an ill-bred one, we shall find that they depend for the most part on habits acquired in babyhood, modesty, refinement, consideration for others shown in such everyday matters as eating, drinking, and moving about, accurate and distinct utterance, and little points of personal cleanliness. Training of this kind should find a place in the crèche and the nursery school, while it is almost impossible that it should be given by the overworked mother in a workman's home.

Children must be Taught:

How to Wash

Cleanliness is, perhaps, the most important aspect of the question. The wish to be clean is not born with us. It has to be taught and trained. If a child can be induced to feel uncomfortable when he is dirty, a great step has been taken towards civilizing him and towards the establishment of a higher standard in living for the next generation. This is a point that needs emphasizing, for there is no doubt that we rank lower in regard to cleanliness of clothes and person than other European countries. One's nose testifies to this fact if, after travelling in crowded workmen's trains in England, one does the same thing in France or Germany.

In England the crusade for cleanliness in the schools is only just beginning. The first step was taken when nurses were appointed to examine the children's heads. Some teachers insist on clean hands and faces, but investigations have seldom proceeded further. Now that medical inspection is at length instituted, terrible disclosures are being made of verminous bodies and diseases engendered by dirt. Now cleanliness is a lesson that can be taught. Few lessons are easier to teach, provided that necessary appliances are at hand, and none bring to the pupil a more immediate and obvious blessing. None certainly are more important if the first aim of our schools is to extend to the children of the poor the opportunity of leading a decent life. But this important lesson is not one that can wait for the school age. The evil results of dirt affect the health of a young child even more than of an older one. A child of two or three years old preyed on by parasites is an object so deplorable that nothing could be more absurd than to permit children to remain in this condition till they are five years old and then expend large sums on teaching them the three R's, often without any cleansing process at all.

In any public nurseries which may be established in England the bathing apparatus would have to play a very important part, and clothing would have to be rigorously inspected and, when necessary, replaced. A time may come some day when English mothers, like French ones, may be required to provide clean under-linen twice a week for their children and a clean pocket handkerchief every day; but to anyone familiar with our schools in poor districts such a time seems remote.

How to Sleep

The children of the poor suffer almost as much from want of sleep as from want of food.[9] The regular midday rest, which is such an important feature in the régime of the nursery, is a luxury of the rich, and in a two roomed household it is almost impossible to put the little ones to bed early enough at night. Undisturbed sleep at regular intervals is in itself invaluable, especially as the means of forming a periodic physical habit which will last a lifetime. Any schools for children under six should be provided with suitable and sufficient sleeping accommodation. 'The babies must be allowed to sleep when they want to, and should all be trained to sleep during the day.'

How to Eat

Another very important nursery lesson is the right way to eat. Recent experience in organizing school feeding has amply proved the need for it. That we teach children to read and write before they know how to eat is an example of our topsy turvey methods. If we instructed them early in the use of their teeth, and were careful to provide suitable materials for that instruction, we should need to spend less later on in dentistry. The dinner table, too, with its code of manners, founded on consideration for others, provides an admirable field for moral instruction and for laying the foundations of civilized life.

How to Talk

Second only to the importance of learning to wash, to sleep, and to eat, is that of learning to talk. Speech, the widest and most distinctively human of the arts, must begin in the nursery; and much depends on whether it begins there well or ill. Nothing is more noticeable and more distressing to the visitor in our schools than the inarticulateness of the children. One has to delve deep to reach a response. To receive an answer prompt, fearless, and distinct is so rare as to be absolutely startling. There are many reasons for this, but the most obvious is an actual difficulty in utterance. The children have never been taught to speak, and most of them make very clumsy attempts at it. Of course, they soon acquire a code of half articulate sounds, which serve to express their more urgent needs and emotions; but their ears are not trained to recognize nice distinctions of sound, and as they grow older the possibility of such discrimination is lost. The vocal organs, too, having no demands made on them, lose their flexibility and become unmanageable. Bad habits of breathing, too, pass unnoticed, which are difficult to cure and have very bad results.

To impart some familiarity with spoken language, the child should be taught to pronounce very simple words correctly and delicately; and his vocabulary should be extended gradually as his field of observation widens. This should be the chief educational aim of the nursery school. No child can think to much purpose till he can speak, or make any real use of information till he can frame his thoughts into sentences. The power of expression is absurdly neglected throughout our schools. We proceed to teach children to read while they are still, to all intents and purposes, dumb, which is like forcing food on a sick man who can't digest.

But though speech is the most important of the nursery arts, it is not the only one. Much can be done to assist that long, unwearied, ingenious campaign which any healthy child will devise and carry on for himself, and which has for its unconscious aim the control of his own nerves and muscles.

Limit of the Nursery Period

It is impossible to make hard and fast rules as to the dividing points in a child's life. One child will be more developed at four than another at six, and it is difficult to decide at what age the sort of training sketched above should give place to ordinary school methods. There is much to be said, however, for fixing the break at six or seven rather than at five; and in this we may, perhaps be guided by the practice in well-to-do households, where children migrate from nursery to schoolroom at about that age. For it is well to bear in mind that what we are pleading for is, after all, a peculiarly English institution. Those very advantages, unfortunately, on which the English middle class specially pride themselves, they are the least eager to share with their poorer neighbors. We boast of the playing fields of Eton, and of the admirable training in self-control and esprit de corps to be gained in them, and leave our elementary schools with a wretched square of asphalte, where nothing can occur but a disorderly scramble. We are proud of our English cleanliness and our cult of the daily morning bath, and yet we are content to allow our school children to remain the most filthy and ragged in Europe. So though England is the home of the nursery (the word being untranslatable), and the wealthy mother in Russia or Italy makes a point of securing an English nurse for her children, yet a nursery for the children of labor is a notion of foreign growth, and we must turn to France, to Belgium, and to Hungary to see anything like an adequate realization of it.

In all these countries the school age is six, and provision is made for children below it in two separate institutions, the crèche and the école maternelle or école gardienne, as it is called in Belgium.

The following account of these institutions is compiled from reports published by the Board of Education:–

The Crèche in England and France[10]

In Paris the first crèche was opened in 1844 by private enterprise and supported by charity. Mothers paid twopence a day per child, emphasis being laid on the intention of helping those who were obliged to earn their living, rather than merely of feeding and sheltering the children of the indigent. In 1847 the Society of Crèches was inaugurated at the Hotel de Ville, and in 1869 it was recognized as an institution of public utility. In 1904 Paris, with a population of two and three-quarter millions, had sixty-six crèches accommodating two thousand four hundred and ninety-one children under three years old. It is instructive to compare these figures with those for London, where, with a population of four and a half millions in 1904, there were fifty-five crèches, accommodating one thousand six hundred and ninety-three children under three. 'In other words, London had crèche accommodation for one child in every two thousand five hundred, Paris had crèche accommodation for one child in every thousand. The crèches in London are private, with no aid from State or municipality, while those in Paris have received both since 1862. London has no registration or system of State inspection. Paris has both, the crèches being inspected daily by doctors. Lastly, the London crèches are distributed quite irregularly, some of the poorest boroughs having none at all, while Paris crèches are evenly distributed among twenty arrondissements. Even more startling are the differences outside the capitals. France, not including Paris or the Department of the Seine, has three hundred and twenty-two crèches. England, not including London, or greater London, has nineteen.'[11]

English crèches, or day nurseries, are, for the most part, organized by committees of ladies. They are mostly parochial and supported entirely by voluntary contributions. Few of them are in houses built for the purpose: most are in adapted premises.[12] Any private person may open a crèche in England without leave from any public body; crèches are unregistered and under no inspection.

The crèche in France, though not State supported, is generously subsidized. In the year 1904 Paris crèches received from the Minister of the Interior £1,468, from the Ville de Paris £67,045, and from the Conseil General des Départments £1,376.

No crèche may be opened in Paris without leave from the prefect of the department. In order to receive a grant it must be subject to inspection, conform to certain rules, and be administered by a council presided over by the mayor of the locality.

At the head of every crèche is a directress. Under her there is a berceuse to every six children and a gardienne to every twelve children under the age of one and a half years. In a large crèche there are also a cook and a laundry maid.

Each crèche has twenty or thirty 'dames patronesses' or managers under a lady president. They are appointed by the mayor. Each lady has certain days or weeks in the year allotted to her and is definitely responsible for certain duties of management.

Children are admitted at the age of fifteen days and kept till the age of three. The mother is requested to bring the child clean. While she is feeding it herself she must come regularly to the crèche at least twice a day. She must pay her contribution, twopence for one child, threepence for two, every morning, and she must show that she is obliged to go to work or is incapable of attending to the child at home.

Illegitimate children are admitted after due investigation.

The cost per day per child at the Paris crèches averages about one shilling, so that the mother's payment covers only one-sixth of it.

The children are supplied with clothes. These are changed when they arrive and again at night.

There are usually seven or eight doctors attached to a crèche, one of whom visits it every day. In many cases these doctors, who give their services entirely free, form a committee to decide all questions connected with hygiene.

To some crèches is attached a 'School for Mothers,' to which infants not in the crèche are brought for weekly inspection, and tables are kept of the weight and progress of each child.[13]

The forty-five crèches in Paris receiving municipal grants are subject to inspection. In addition to the ordinary inspectors, a lady inspector of crèches has recently been appointed.

All the Paris crèches can be visited by anyone who is interested in them without introduction.

The Crèche in other Countries

The chief characteristic of the Belgian crèche is that it is nearly always run in connection with an école gardienne or nursery school, which admits children up to the age of six.

The crèche system is not by any means so widely developed in Belgium as in France (outside the capital the only town at all adequately provided being Liège, which has six crèches), but in the poorer suburbs of Brussels there are one or two crèches admirably installed and managed which far surpass anything of the kind in England.

Crèches or Krippen exist in most German and Swiss towns,[14] and are usually separate from the kindergartens or nursery schools. The krippe admits children from six weeks to three years, and is intended only for the children of mothers who are out at work. It is open from 5.30 or 6 a.m. till the factories close in the evening, or sometimes till 8 p.m. The charge is usually about twopence a day; sometimes, to nursing mothers only, one penny a day. Illegitimate children are not excluded. Krippen are, as a rule, in the charge of Sisters (Catholic or Protestant), with voluntary helpers, who have nearly always been trained in the management of infants. The krippen are not municipally organized or supervized, but they receive in many towns municipal grants varying a good deal in amount. The cost varies from sixpence to tenpence a head.

Nursery Schools

Between the crèche and the elementary school there is obvious need for a half-way house. This is already supplied, after a fashion, in some parts of the country by the baby class in the infant school, but nowhere in England is it sufficiently recognized that what is needed is not a school at all in the ordinary sense. Children under five (or, as I should prefer to say, under six or seven) should receive little or no definite instruction. They need plenty of freedom for spontaneous activity among wholesome surroundings under the guidance and supervision of attendants who have been trained in matters relating to health, to conduct, and to the growth of intelligence. Large rooms, well lighted, well aired, well warmed, and a pleasant open air playground where, if possible, plants and animals can be watched and tended, not too much interference, but the constant care of kind and watchful nurses; these are the requisites for a nursery school. In England, although a kindergarten here and there comes near to this ideal, no attempt has been made to supply the need for them all over the country. For anything of the kind on a national scale we must turn to France, Belgium, or Hungary.

THE ECOLE MATERNELLE (FRANCE)

Yet it is consoling to our national vanity when we look up the history of the French écoles maternelles, from which we have now so much to learn, to find that in their origin they owe a good deal to an Englishman and a Socialist.

For their first germ, indeed, we must go to Switzerland and to the year 1771, when Pastor Oberlin started his first école à tricoter in the Vosges. Mme. Pastoret transplanted the idea to Paris in 1801 when she opened a salle d'hospitalité, where the children of working mothers could be taken in and cared for; but it was not till 1826 that anything approaching the modern maternal school was opened, and by that time Mme. Pastoret had learned all she could about the infant schools which had been started by the English cotton manufacturer, Robert Owen, in 1812.

It was in the blackest hour of English child slavery that these schools appeared like a dawn of hope, an illusory dawn unfortunately. Robert Owen, roused by the pitiable condition of the poor children collected together from public charities and poor houses in order to work in the cotton mills, put a stop in his own mills to the practice of employing them from the age of six, and persuaded the parents to send them to school at two and keep them there till ten. Of these eight years the earlier were, in his opinion, even more important than the later. His reasons for thinking so are to be gathered from the very interesting evidence which he gave in 1816 before the Select Committee of the House of Commons to Enquire into the Education of the Lower Orders in the Metropolis. In describing the treatment of the infants, he says:–

They were perpetually superintended, to prevent their acquiring bad habits, to give them good ones, and to form their dispositions to mutual kindness and a sincere desire to contribute all in their power to benefit each other. . . . In fine weather the children are much out of doors that they may have the benefit of sufficient exercise in the open air. . . . The children were not to be annoyed with books, but were to be taught the uses and nature or qualities of the common things around them by familiar conversation, when the children's curiosity was excited so as to induce them to ask questions. . . . All rewards and punishments whatever, except such as nature herself has provided . . . are sedulously excluded. . . . A child who acts improperly is considered an object not of blame, but of pity. . . . No unnecessary restraint is imposed on the children. . . . The dress worn by both boys and girls is composed of strong white cotton cloth of the best quality that can be procured. It is formed in the shape of the Roman tunic, and reaches in the boys' dresses to the knees and in the girls' to the ankle. These dresses are changed three times a week that they may be kept perfectly clean and neat. The parents of the older children pay threepence a month. Nothing is paid for the infant classes. . . . The infants, besides being instructed by sensible signs – the things themselves or models or paintings – and by familiar conversation, were from two years and upwards daily taught dancing and singing.[15]

Owen had some difficulty in finding teachers who would adopt his views and could carry them out.

I had therefore [he says] to seek among the population for two persons who had a great love for, and unlimited patience with, infants and who were thoroughly tractable and willing unreservedly to follow my instructions. The best to my mind in these respects that I could find in the population of the village was a poor simple hearted weaver, named James Buchanan, who had been previously trained by his wife to perfect submission to her will, and who could gain but a scanty living by his now oppressed trade of weaving common plain cotton goods by hand. But he *loved* children strongly by nature, and his patience with them was inexhaustible.

This man was afterwards sent to London to superintend the first English infant school, which was opened in Westminster under the patronage of James Mill and other distinguished men. Owen gives an amusing account of his disappointment on the occasion of a surprise visit to this school:–

On entering the school, the first object that I saw was Mrs. Buchanan, whom I had never seen in the New Lanark school, brandishing a whip and terrifying the children with it. Buchanan I saw in another part of the room without authority or influence, and as much subject to his wife as the children.

Owen was full of ideas, and none of them were more original and valuable than those as to the education of infants; but, as one may judge from the above extract, he does not seem to have had the knack of gathering round him the people who could satisfactorily carry out those ideas and render permanent the institutions which sprang from his warm heart and fertile brain. But England was deep in the trough of laissez faire, and one need not wonder that here Owen's preaching fell on deaf ears and produced no permanent results.

France, quickened by a stirring of revolt and intellectual awakening, offered more hopeful soil; and there, as we have seen, the seed germinated when the first salle d'asile (or salle d'essai, as it was at first called) was opened in the Rue du Bac in 1826. Seven years later the salles d'asiles received their first recognition by the State, and in 1837 a commission was appointed to draw up rules for their conduct. These rules were revised from time to time, and a special training school for infant teachers was opened; and at last, in 1881, the old name of salles d'asiles was changed to écoles maternelles, and the rules as to admission and the program were settled and codified.

At the head of every école maternelle is a directress, a certificated teacher, whose salary, paid in part by the State, in part by the commune, begins at one hundred and sixty-eight pounds a year, and rises gradually to a maximum of two hundred and eight pounds, with a right to a pension at the end of twenty-five years. She is helped by a number of assistants (one for every forty children), whose salaries begin at eighty-eight pounds, and rise to one hundred and twenty-eight pounds. There are, in addition, a number of nurses or servants chosen by the directrice and paid by the commune, whose wages vary from forty pounds to fifty pounds.

The directress has various registers to keep, which must be at the disposal of the inspectors.

On the arrival of the children in the morning, she must ascertain by personal inspection that each one is in good health and clean. She also inspects their baskets, and sees that each child has brought a pocket handkerchief. She receives the pence and keeps a list of those who are fed free of charge, and she supervizes the school canteen.

The assistants must be over seventeen and certificated. Each has a separate class, and a great deal depends on the ingenuity and child love of the teacher. They help with the midday meal if required. The school hours being very long, they take it in turns to stay overtime.

The nurses, or femmes de service, are a most important addition to the staff. There is one, at least, in every school; two, if the numbers justify it. Their duties are very various. They sweep out the school every day, and open it at eight in winter and seven in summer for any children whose mothers go early to work, taking charge of the children till the directress and assistants arrive at nine o'clock. The femme de service superintends the children at the water closets every morning and again at one o'clock. This, from a hygienic point of view, is most important and is much neglected in English infant schools. She also washes the children's hands and faces twice a day and, in some schools, gives them a weekly bath and helps to wait on them at the school dinner. As in the case of the crèche, the general superintendence of the school is in the hands of a committee of ladies presided over by the mayor. Members of this committee visit the homes of the children.

The école maternelle is optional and free. Children between the ages of two and six are admitted on producing a note of admission from the mayor of the commune. Mothers are specially asked to bring the children clean and to pack in their school bucket a spoon, a dinner napkin, some bread and wholesome drink.

The schools are entirely paid for out of public funds, the cost being divided between the State, the department, and the commune.

The 'Caisses des Ecoles' is a benevolent society subsidized and controlled by the State. It originated in 1849 and has grown into an organization of great importance. It covers much the same ground as our newly established Care Committees, its object being to provide clothing, boots, and food to necessitous children. It also provides for country holidays and vacation schools.

About a third of the children in the écoles maternelles pay for their food and the rest have it free. The list of the latter is kept by the mayor. The food consists chiefly of milk, vegetable purées and other soups, maccaroni, semolina, and tapioca, with very little or no meat.

Many of the large towns in France are spending great sums in feeding the children in the écoles maternelles. Marseilles has made all the feeding in them free. St. Etienne charges three halfpence, for which wine is given.

The écoles maternelles, like the other French schools, are inspected at least twice a month by the medical inspector; but besides these there is a large staff of special lady inspectors.

With regard to medical inspection of Paris schools, it must be remembered that in every district there is, under the caisse des écoles, a free dispensary for children subsidized by the municipality. Here children from the schools can have baths, hair cut and washed, medical advice with regard to teeth, eyes, ears, etc.; while a free distribution of cod liver oil is made to necessitous children in the winter.

It is difficult to give any idea of the school program in a few words. It includes games, manual work, such as building with bricks or cards and making artificial flowers, the first principles of moral education, knowledge of everyday things, drawing, and lessons on language. Reading is taught to children over five, but not much insisted on. The little talks on familiar subjects are, perhaps, what strike one most. Take this, for instance: 'The house, the kitchen. Let the child describe it. What can we see? Kitchen fire, table, etc. The use of each object. What does mother do? Each child? Cat? Children should help their parents without complaining.' Or this: 'The pocket handkerchief. What is it? What is its use? Blowing your nose, spitting. Each must have a handkerchief. How to use it. Unfold, refold.'

Simple, familiar topics, such as these, afford the best opportunities for inducing children to talk; and nothing is more important in dealing with the little ones from neglected homes.

The Ecole Maternelle in Other Countries

France does not stand alone with regard to nursery schools. In Belgium an école gardienne, as it is called, is attached to every crèche, and is managed on much the same lines as the écoles maternelles.

Germany, Switzerland, Portugal and Hungary all have their maternal schools or kindergartens.

In Hungary[16] they are excellent. Early in the nineteenth century, a Countess of Brunswick, having been much impressed by the infant schools of Owen's follower, Wilderspin, in England, came back to Hungary, and urged the claims of infant education just at the moment when reform was rife there.

A normal school for training infant teachers was founded so early as 1837, and in 1875 kindergartens were recognized by the State as a definite form of public instruction.

By an Act of Parliament, passed in 1891, attendance at a kindergarten is compulsory for all children between the third and sixth years. These schools were dominated at first by the German idea, but by 1899, when Miss Catherine Dodd visited the country, the language, songs, and games used in them were markedly national in character, showing the influence of Hungarian life and history. One game, for instance, represented the shepherds taking care of their herds on the plains, and guarding them from the wolves which came down from the mountains; while another showed traces of the Hungarian struggles with the Turks. Weary soldiers march to fight the Turks. The village rouses into activity; the baker, the winepresser, the housewife, the tailor, and the shoemaker, all set to work to feed, clothe, and house the soldiers.

'I visited a village kindergarten this year [she writes]. The village lay among vineyards in a celebrated wine district on the Danube. In front of the building was a large canvas tent covering a great patch of sand, and here, sheltered from the sun, were fifty bare legged mites playing. They played games which were characteristic of the district. There was a wind game, and the children imitated the wind which blew the boats along the Danube. There was a game of making wine casks. Groups of children formed the cask, and the other children walked round, hammering in imaginary nails; while other children cut down imaginary trees to make the casks. There were one hundred and fifty children in this kindergarten. They were all in charge of one qualified teacher and her little maid servant. Everybody admitted that the staff was small, but they urged that it was a poor district. The town kindergartens are well staffed and fitted up with all necessary apparatus.

'I found a class of five year old children, sitting on benches out of doors under the acacia trees, building with Gift III. They smiled at us and cried out, "Tzten hozta" ("God has brought you"); and they showed the bridges to cross the Danube, the wells to get water on the plains, the mills to grind corn, which they had built.

'All kindergarten teachers play the violin. In the games and songs the teacher is

leader. She marches first, playing her violin, and the children follow, singing. . . .
I spent a day in a kindergarten training school during the examinations. In the
garden we found some twenty girls, with their violins, practising the national
songs of Hungary. They marched round the garden, singing and playing in chorus,
until they were called in to meet the examiner.

'All kindergartens in Hungary must have open playing places shaded with trees.
Children under three may be admitted, but, as the regulation quaintly states, not
in swaddling clothes.'

Though Hungary is the only country where the attendance of
children under five is compulsory, yet we have seen that in all,
except England there is some recognition of State responsibility
with regard to children below school age; and it is clear that
something must be done in this direction before long. It is, therefore, most important that the question should be thoroughly
ventilated.

The proposal made in the Minority Poor Law Report that the
entire supervision of maternity and infancy, and the administration
of whatever public provision is made for these services should be
in the hands of the local health authority has, of course, a very
important bearing on it. This proposal would, if fully carried out,
remove entirely from the domain of the education authority any
public day nurseries or nursery schools which may be decided on.
The common sense view seems to be that throughout the life of
the child its interests should be guarded both by the education
authority and the health authority; but that the province of the
latter, which would at first cover the whole field, would become
gradually more restricted. At the stage when health considerations
are predominant, the local health authority must undertake the
administration, making use of the teachers of the education authority as required; at the stage when educational considerations
are predominant, the administration must be in the hands of the
education authority, making use of the doctors of the health authority as required. In the crèche there should be, as in France, daily
medical inspection, and the management should be chiefly in the
hands of doctors; but even here questions for the educational expert
will arise with reference to the qualification of the staff and the
training of the older infants. In the nursery school, the medical
inspection required will be almost as frequent, but the educational
point of view will need to be rather more adequately represented
in the committee of management.

How this joint action of the local health authority and the local
education authority can best be attained, at all stages of the child's
life, is a question of administration with which we need not meddle
here,[17] but it seems desirable that there should be no sudden break
at any age. The establishment of public crèches, under the direct

control of the local health authority, would be an invaluable supplement to the system of combining the work of health visitors, either paid or unpaid, with that of the medical officer of health and his staff. This system, already successfully established in many parts of London, aims at keeping under observation every infant from the time of its birth by means of friendly visits and advice. As things are at present, a health visitor is often harrowed by the hopeless conditions into which a baby is born, and feels that her advice is little better than a mockery. Mothers are often quite unable, either from poor health or from the dire necessity of bread winning, to nurse their babies or attend to their constant needs; but there are worse cases still where, from sheer lack of any alternative, a new born infant must be left to the tender mercies of a drunken or dissolute mother, whose one precaution is to insure its life.

In cases of this kind, a public crèche, to which the medical officer of health had power to order the removal of any neglected infant, would be a great resource. Such enforced removal would never happen, of course, in the case of any decent home or of any mother who was nursing her child; but as an alternative for the casual minder, the feeble grandmother, or the ten year old sister, it would be invaluable.

The question of payment would have to be settled as in the case of school feeding, after inquiry into the family resources, and need not in any way interfere with the decision of the medical officer. The cases that would come before him may be classified as:–

1. Temporary

Homes even of the best type are liable to be disorganized from time to time by the disablement of the mother or father, or by some other unavoidable misfortune; and the temporary removal of young children to a safe refuge affords invaluable help towards tiding over such a period, while it saves them from the evil consequences of neglect.

2. Wage Earning Mothers

During the first three or four months of an infant's life, the mother might well be restrained by law from going out to work, home aliment being provided in necessitous cases; but as the child grows older, some mothers will certainly desire to return to their work, and provided that they are not in receipt of public assistance for the children, conditional on their devoting themselves to the care of the children, there seems no adequate reason why they should not do so.

3. Homes that have been or ought to be Broken Up

The widower or deserted husband has no choice at present but to pay a neighbor to look after his children, a service often most unsatisfactorily performed; but there are cases even more piteous. Bad health, bad habits, or merely unemployment on the part of the father, slatternly incompetence, or something worse, on the part of the mother, bring about a gradual and hopeless deterioration of the household which renders it unfit for little children to live in. Under such circumstances, it is essential that the medical authority should have power to order their removal to a public nursery, where they will be entirely under the parental control of the State.[18]

Reforms to Work for

1. That the age for compulsory school attendance be raised to six, with a corresponding addition at the other end, making the compulsory period from six to at least fifteen or even older.

2. That the medical officer have power to enforce the attendance at a suitable nursery school of any child under six who is not suitably cared for at home.

3. That every local authority be required to provide adequately for children from three to six in free nursery schools, with sleeping accommodation and ample open air and covered playgrounds, and no teaching of the three R's.

4. That at such schools suitable meals be provided at the expense of the rates, table manners being an integral part of the curriculum.

5. That every local authority be also required to provide boarding schools in the country to serve as convalescent and holiday homes for the children attending nursery schools who are found by the medical officer to need country air, and also for the reception of children removed from their parents by the order of the medical authority.

6. That sufficient accommodation be provided in every district for infants under three in small day nurseries under the control of the local authority, such nurseries to be entirely free.

7. That the feeding of the children at these day nurseries be under direct medical supervision, mothers being encouraged to attend regularly for the purpose of suckling their infants.

8. That in connection with every such nursery there shall be a 'school for mothers,' or 'consultation for nurslings,' where babies may be brought by their mothers for free medical inspection and advice, and where pure and suitable milk will be provided free or at cost price.

Notes

1 Report of the Consultative Committee upon the School Attendance of Children below the age of Five (Board of Education, July 2nd, 1908), p. 12.
2 Ibid. Appendix I. and V.
3 Ibid. Appendix III.
4 Ibid. Appendix III. Memorandum by Dr. Haldane on the air in schools.
5 Ibid. Evidence of Dr. James Niven, Medical Officer of Health, Manchester, pp. 80 and 81. Dr. Niven has since furnished statistics showing that over a period of five years in Manchester the case mortality was substantially the same amongst children attending and those not attending school.
6 Ibid. Evidence of Dr. Kerr and Dr. Hogarth, Medical Officers of the Education Department of the London County Council, pp. 63 and 64.
7 Ibid. P. 57.
8 'Habits, whether they be born in us or are subsequently acquired, constitute man's whole nature, and they are the results of experience or education. Our education does not begin when we commence to learn to read or write, nor does it commence when we learn to breathe or suck. It has been steadily going on ever since our first foundations were laid in the immeasurable past. The education of the infant consists in teaching it how to acquire good and useful habits which are not born in it, and which will enable it to live a complete life, and take full advantage of the opportunities of its surroundings or environment.' – 'Infant Education,' by E. Pritchard, M.A., M.D. (Oxon.), M.R.C.P. (London).
9 Report of the Consultative Committee upon the School Attendance of Children below the age of Five, pp. 90–96.
10 Report of Miss M. B. Synge, published by the Board of Education in July, 1908, together with the Report of the Consultative Committee previously quoted.
11 The French statistics are taken from the Report of the Chief Officer of Public Control.
12 A movement towards a better condition of things has been recently made by the National Society of Day Nurseries, founded in 1906 with the object of assisting local committees and affiliating existing nurseries.
13 For further details consult 'The Nursling' (see Bibliography, page 19), Lecture X., and translator's preface.
14 See Report by Miss May published with that of Consultative Committee.
15 'An Outline of the System of Education in New Lanark,' published, 1824, by Robert Dale Owen (Robert Owen's son); see 'Life of Robert Owen,' by F. Podmore (London: 1906).
16 Report on Hungarian Education, Special Reports, Vol. 8, p. 498.
17 Cf. Minority Poor Law Report (Official Edition), Note on p. 1224.
18 Minority Report of the Royal Commission on the Poor Law, p. 825, par. 2.

A SUMMARY OF SIX PAPERS AND DISCUSSIONS UPON THE DISABILITIES OF WOMEN AS WORKERS (1909)

The Writers of the Papers

Miss Emma Brooke
Dr. Constance Long
Mrs. Ernestine Mills
Mrs. Gallichan (C. Gasquoine Hartley)
Miss Millicent Murby
Dr. Ethel Bentham

INTRODUCTION

The series of papers here summarized was read before the Women's Group of the Fabian Society, during the winter of 1908–9, as a preliminary to the consideration of the problem of women's economic independence under Socialism. They are not to be taken, separately or collectively, as embodying the views of that Group. They were read to elicit opinion and convey information upon matters fundamental to the interests of women as workers. The scheme of work of which they form the preliminary portion is given on the concluding page. The Introduction and the final Remarks are contributed by the Studies Committee of the Women's Group, and embody the general views of that Committee.

By personal economic independence in the present state of society, we mean that a person is in possession of an income sufficient to supply his or her needs, and entirely at his or her disposal. An independent income, as things are, may be derived from private property, or be gained as wages or salary in some occupation. Economic dependence, on the contrary, is the condition of a person who receives the supply of his or her necessaries, in cash or in kind, from another individual, at that individual's pleasure. A woman, for example, is economically dependent when her parents or her husband give her an allowance, or otherwise maintain her; but she is economically independent if she owns private property or earns her own living.

In a socialized community personal economic independence will mean that the individual is recognized as having a personal claim upon the State for a definite share of social wealth. That share may be awarded as salary for social service rendered, or as a special allowance, *e.g.*, child maintenance, sick pay, or an old age pension. In any of these cases, the person thus socially recognized as entitled to an income will be an economically independent person.

Women desire to be thus economically independent, and the Fabian Women's Group has set itself to find out what are the conditions of this economic independence. Is it possible for women to claim it under the same conditions as men, or have they to contend with sex disabilities, which differentiate them economically from men as workers? Young, old, or sick persons are recognized by Socialists as having a valid claim to a share of social wealth, though they are doing nothing to help directly to produce it, because they are disabled by special circumstances. Is a woman, just because she is a woman, to put forward a claim to her personal share of social wealth as a partially disabled person, or are healthy adult women to serve the State as workers, and as workers claim their salaries?

The first question for Socialist women to determine is: of the mental and physical weaknesses attributed to women, which are really natural and inevitable, which are merely imaginary or the unhealthy products of past and present social conditions?

The papers here summarized have been directed to throw light upon this particular question in so far as it is concerned with women when not actually engaged in childbearing.

———

In the following pages the words 'free sexual relations,' 'sexual freedom,' etc., do not mean illicit relations or sexual licentiousness any more than the words 'free trade' mean smuggling, or 'free speech' profanity and falsehood. At present sexual relations are very largely compulsory. Women are compelled to enter into them by the fact that they have no other means of livelihood; and this is as true of lawful relations as unlawful ones. No opinion is expressed or implied herein as to the propriety of any particular form of sexual relation, because it is impossible to obtain any general agreement on that point in a large society of British subjects of divers religions and races. The controversies as to civil marriage without a religious ceremony, marriage of first cousins, marriage of deceased wives' sisters and of divorced persons, not to mention the extreme forms of polygamy which are lawful in the non-Christian quarters of the Empire, make it necessary to avoid all reference to legal and sectarian standards of sexual conduct. There is, however, a practically unanimous agreement that sexual relations should be free: that is, that whatever form they may take, no person should be forced to contract them by pecuniary pressure or any other external force. To be compelled to marry to escape destitution is clearly sexual slavery. To be compelled to eke out an insufficient wage or to supply a lack of any wage at all by the sale of one's person in the streets is only a more miserable degree of the same degradation. No respectable person has yet been found to deny that it is desirable to set women free from such compulsion. The subject does not become controversial until question arises as to what sexual relations between free individuals should be sanctioned by religion, prescribed by law, or tolerated by custom: in short, as to the best form of marriage. These pages stop short of that question. It will be time enough to consider it when there is some real freedom of choice possible for the great majority of women. Meanwhile we confine ourselves to the question of economic liberty.

SUMMARY OF PAPERS AND DISCUSSIONS
(Prepared by Miss Murby)

I. Introductory Paper

On June 25th, Miss Emma Brooke delivered an address, of which an epitome, prepared by the lecturer, follows.

To understand properly what is the inward meaning of the women's movement, it is necessary to throw a backward glance at the last century's phase of that movement. Then the centre of restlessness was amongst unmarried women, who were styled 'redundant' because of their single state. These women undertook their own cause, insisting that their humanity came before their sex, and that they would take their proper place in natural history as *homo* and *sapiens*. The constructive result of their campaign was the winning of the higher education of women and the rush of women into the professions; also, in the course of years, the formation of an improved type of woman generally, a type modified for the better both physically and mentally.

Last century's movement was, however, incomplete as far as women's emancipation went, because it was won by ignoring sex. In spite of the great advance in freedom and scope of life, the stigma attached to sex was not removed. This is exemplified by the way in which the work of even the best and highest women is ignored nationally and misses any national reward. The most glaring example of this sex stigma is the case of Florence Nightingale, who received no national recognition or reward, though by essentially womanly work she revolutionized the manner in which war is carried on.

This century we have arrived at a point where, instead of ignoring sex, we must affirm it, and claim emancipation on the ground of sex alone. To this end, we must abandon all useless comparisons of ourselves and our achievement with men and their achievement, and equally useless comparisons between different types of our own sex. Just as the fabric of manhood is considered to be one and the same from the humblest ploughboy to the most gifted man in the world, so must the fabric of womanhood be considered the same from the humblest mother of the people to the most gifted woman in the world. We must cease to talk of exceptional women or of sex disabilities, and found our claim for complete emancipation upon that special work in the world and for the State which our differentiation from men imposes upon us. This differentiation is the potentiality for motherhood, and is the endowment of every woman, whether realized or not. The stigma attached to our sex is really a stigma attached to this great potentiality, and we can only remove it by beginning with the emancipation of the actual mother.

The State endowment of motherhood has a fascination for the mind as an expedient; but a hasty application of this idea, by men alone, will probably react disastrously on women themselves. Wrongly applied, the State endowment of motherhood may bring the merely functional burden of maternity to press too heavily on individual mothers, and may result in reducing them to a slavelike powerlessness supported by law. This would be disastrous to true motherhood and with the mother, disastrous to the children and the race. Physical maiming of children, mental and moral maiming of children, has been and still is cruelly common, even amongst well-to-do middle class families, where the birth-rate is higher than the mother can bear, and where the home is presided over, in consequence, by a nerve-racked, exhausted woman. The sacrifice of the mother to a physical function is really the sacrifice of the race; and no remedy which does not knit up within it, not merely a security against infanticide, but a security against this maiming and misery of children through the exhaustion of the mother, is either wise or complete.

To save at once the mother and the children, the present writer would suggest that the State endowment should be indirect and be a State endowment of children, because by such an endowment the responsibility of both parents would be engaged.

At the same time, the honorable recognition by the State of the mother's function of maternity would tend to ensure her the respect and protection of her husband, who would be forced to see in her no longer his personal head servant or slave, but a free agent employed in services of inestimable value to the State, which services the State, through the children, recognizes, honors and supports.

By such a recognition the stigma at present attached to all women could not fail – as it seems to the present writer – to be removed; with the possible result that women's work when performed on a larger scale and in other directions would also be better recognized and better remunerated.

Lastly, it is the faith of the writer that the women's movement is really a race movement, and its success essential to the further progress of the race. For this reason, there need be no question to the Socialist woman whether Socialism or the women's movement comes first. The women's problem cannot be truly solved without Socialism, while the success of Socialism itself lies as a germ in the heart of that problem.

———

In the discussion which followed, it was felt that the endowment of the child might still leave the mother in a subordinate position. Dr. O'Brien Harris proposed to supplement Miss Brooke's suggestion by an arrangement under which, while every woman would be trained to some craft, she would be entitled to a continuance of an income equal to that derived from such craft during whatever time she rightly devoted to maternal duties. Supposing her husband's income sufficient for the maintenance of both, so that she gave up her occupation on marriage, then she should be entitled to half that income. And the endowment of the child should in any case be paid by the State, both parents acting as trustees.

Numerous other points were raised, and it was felt that in order to clear opinion on the important issues involved it was necessary to take the whole problem in detail. It fell naturally into two divisions, the first being formulated thus: Can able-bodied women claim economic independence on the same terms as men except when they are actively engaged about their maternal functions? Is the female human being equally capable by nature with the male of sharing in the production of social wealth, material and immaterial? If not, to what extent is she disabled, and why?

The answers to these questions afford the necessary preliminary to a proper appreciation of the problem of women's economic independence under Socialism.

II. Papers on the Disabilities of Women not actively engaged in Child-bearing

Dr. Constance Long opened Division I., Part I., on July 16th with a lecture on the 'Effects upon Mental and Bodily Activities of the Natural Periodic Fluctuations in the Physiological Life of Normally Healthy Women.'

The periodic fluctuations known as menstruation are a normal physiological process, and should not appear as a 'great upheaval of nature.' The process commences at puberty, and the girl enters on her period of adolescence, which lasts about twelve years, full physical maturity being attained at twenty-five years of age, when the reproductive organs are fully developed and the average woman is physiologically ripe for maternity.

Much is said about the dangers of puberty, but actually the greatest strain occurs in the later years of adolescence – from twenty to twenty-five – a point of importance in considering educational matters. Moreover, it must be remembered that the necessary readjustment of the organic balance involves a physical strain during which any inherited defect or constitutional weakness is likely to manifest itself; but the changes of puberty affect both sexes, and although menstruation has been recently urged as a frequent cause of insanity, statistics clearly show that what is known as 'adolescent' insanity affects males more than females.

A similar period of physical stress occurs in women at the other end of the menstrual life, somewhere between the ages of thirty-five and fifty-five; a corresponding climacteric affecting men usually between fifty-five and sixty-five. Here, again, a certain type of insanity is sometimes found, this time affecting women more frequently than men; but Dr. Blanford, speaking from forty years' experience as a mental expert, is of opinion that 'uterine or ovarian disorders are not serious factors in the causation of insanity,' and regards the cessation of the periods as 'a concomitant

110

occurrence, not as having anything to say to causation.' Dr. Percy Smith, of Bethlehem Asylum, and Dr. Mercier concur; and Professor Martin, of Berlin, with vast experience, says that 'healthy women do not run the risk of insanity from their sexual functions, nor are they endangered as to insanity by operations on these organs.'

The menopause occupies roughly from six months to two years, and this length of time naturally gives much opportunity for inter-current diseases to declare themselves; and it is the refuge of the ignorant to attribute any and every ill for the ten to fifteen years round about this epoch to the change, which careless inaccuracy has surrounded with many unnecessary horrors.

Similarly, ignorance and superstition have largely colored our views regarding the menstrual function. It must be remembered that until recently everything on this subject came from men, and almost exclusively from gynaecologists, who, owing to their constant intercourse with pathological women, honestly came to believe that all women were dominated by their menstrual func-tion, and that all women showed in greater or less degree the stigmatic characteristic of uterine disease. Both the medical profession generally and the laity caught up these ideas from the expert; and women readily believed what they were told on such authority, so that now it is extremely difficult to make headway against the exaggerated opinions on this subject. These almost reflect the irrational practices of savage tribes, references to which are common in the writings of travellers and sociologists; and we find amongst the superstitions prevalent in England one referred to in the *British Medical Journal* of 1878, and even supported by some medical men, viz., 'that the touch of a menstruating woman contaminates food.' Dr. Clouston explains this by saying that there is actually decreased efficiency in the preparation of food at this time. One frequently hears the belief expressed that washing the hands in cold water will interfere with the flow, and there is also an idea extant that baths must be discontinued. On this point Dr. Houzel's experience is of interest. He records the fact that the fisherwomen of Boulogne reach a late menopause, on the average at forty-nine and a half years. This condition, which is physiolog-ically desirable, he attributes to the bracing effect of wading in the sea, whether menstruating, pregnant, or suckling, in daily pursuit of their occupation. In an enquiry recently undertaken by the lecturer it was found that amongst five hundred cases, 67.4 per cent. take no baths during the period; 16.2 per cent. take hot baths only; and 9.2 per cent. take cold baths as usual.

Further results of this enquiry tended to show that in the vast

111

majority of cases attendance at school, gymnasia, professional and industrial work was not affected by the function. These results may be supplemented by the conclusions of Miss Alice Gardner, Lecturer at Newnham College, regarding Cambridge students:–

(1) In the case of students who are in normally good health, their time of month during the tripos makes very little difference to their class. Slight feelings of discomfort can be overcome by persons who have sense and self-control.

(2) When people are really delicate their state may have some effect on their place. I think of two cases in which a student took a second class when she *might* have got a first if she had been at her best. In neither of these cases did the disadvantage seriously affect the subsequent career of the student. It was known that she had done *well*, but that, being delicate, she had not shone in her examination.

(3) Cases in which people are really very ill once a month are exceptional and to be treated as such. *One* student had, I remember, to take an aegrotat. It may be better for such people not to take triposes or to give their tripos up if the time is unpropitious. But I think these cases are too rare to affect any general policy.

(4) Neither of us (*i.e.*, Miss Gardner and the Vice-Principal of her college) could think of any case in which the mental strain of the tripos at an unfavorable time had produced bad effects afterwards. This seems important.

(5) As to ordinary intellectual work, it certainly has not seemed to me that students do better or worse according to times and seasons. Of course one is occasionally inclined to put down flabby work to physical delicacy, but I do *not* think that a healthy and sensible person becomes flabby in mind from ordinary physical causes. Work done with a slight additional effort is not necessarily poor work.

Remembering the exceptional strain upon the physical organization at the time of puberty, it becomes an important consideration whether boys and girls are not sometimes enfeebled by putting too great a mental strain upon them in their days of development. The necessity of earning their livelihood by their brains forces many girls in certain social grades to take comparatively stiff examinations, and the pressure of economic conditions leads to their being taken early, and thus we find over-strain just at the period when energies are least to spare. It is quite unnecessary to interrupt education in order that menstruation should be normal; this should rather be adapted so as to admit of justice being done to the body on all physiological points without directing special attention to them.

Whilst uttering a warning against excessive indulgence in sport, especially in matches, Dr. Long reminded us of the dictum of Dr. Kelly, an American surgeon, who stands pre-eminent in the treatment of women's diseases, viz., that nothing has been added to our knowledge to vitiate the conclusion drawn by Dr. Mary Putnam Jacobi in 1875, that 'there is nothing in the nature of menstruation to imply the necessity or even the desirability of rest for women whose nutrition is normal. The habit of periodical rest in them might easily become injurious. Many cases of congestion developed in healthy but indolent and luxurious women are often due to no other cause.' Dr. Kelly speaks highly of the effect of college life on women, and Dr. Long's useful enquiries amongst working women furnish strong testimony to the slight effect on the regularity of their employment which can be ascribed to sexual disability. It must, moreover, be borne in mind that women are at a great economic disadvantage, their rate of pay often entailing a miserable standard of living which may itself be responsible for much of the ill health ascribed to sexual causes.

The well-known empirical character of insurance companies calculations robs their estimate of the allowance to be made for women's health of any value; and the fact that women pay more for less benefit, may possibly only be regarded as a dislike on the part of the companies to give up a remunerative source of revenue.

As regards the effect of sex disabilities in the professional world, neither singers, painters, writers, nurses, teachers, nor doctors furnish any evidence for emphasizing sex disability, though it was recognized that women are often subject to special stress owing to their under payment and overwork; and the need for hygienic education as regards food, clothing, cleanliness, fresh air, exercise and recreation was strongly insisted on.

———

Mrs. Ernestine Mills, on November 3rd, gave some suggestions as to the Origin of the Physical Disability of Women.

The physical weakness of woman is often talked about as if womanhood itself were one long disease and woman a weakly creature to be set apart and specialized for a merely animal and sexual existence. Maternal mortality is regarded as almost necessarily incidental to childbirth, instead of the true fact being proclaimed that in the majority of cases death in childbed is due to dirt, ignorance, and neglect, or to physical defects which are probably the result of some preventable want of bodily development. Whilst woman's mental condition is improving, her physical condition has scarcely been seriously considered. Why is she weaker than man? Has she always been so, and must she always remain so?

Among the lower animals there is not this enormous disparity; they perform without interference with normal habits those functions which to the civilized woman are fraught with more or less prolonged disability and danger. Nearly all the evidence on this subject has been collected and recorded by men, and the account given by Havelock Ellis in 'Man and Woman' as to the effect of sex bias in the results of certain skull measurements, made with a view to proving man's superiority in the possession of the higher intellectual faculties, disposes us to regard as specially significant any facts admitted to tell in favor of women. The difference in the strength of the sexes commences at puberty, and is much increased in civilized woman at the period of childbearing; and this is accepted by many women as a right and inevitable condition. To others, however, it seems desirable to understand both the natural and artificial causes of this process of physical degeneration, when slowly from the strong female animal the weak woman was evolved.

It may be objected that anything which tends to weaken the female would eventually have the same effect on the male; but though this is doubtless the case to some extent, in all forms of life we find sexual dimorphism, that is, the occurrence of characters peculiar, on the one hand, to the male, and, on the other, to the female, sex alone.

The first active efforts towards lowering the strength of women are probably found in the tribal customs of savage races. In almost all such races we find much less difference in size and brain weight of men and women than among civilized races, but in very early days artificial means seem to have been taken to induce or increase the weakness of women. Very widespread and ancient is the evidence of the repressive treatment to which young girls are subjected at puberty. Darkness, starvation, and imprisonment were, and in some places are to this day, the continuous lot of these unhappy creatures for months and even years. Numerous illustrations were quoted by the lecturer, not as isolated instances, but as survivals of customs of apparently universal extension, as traces are found in Alaska and South Africa and amongst races as distinct as the Esquimaux and various Indian peoples. From the

114

Islands of New Britain and New Ireland in 1877 a missionary records the imprisonment of girls from the age of seven years until the full development of the breasts, a period of about five years, during which they are kept in dark cages with very little air, and containing only a small stage of bamboo, on which the inmate had to sit or crouch, there being no room to lie down. They were allowed to leave the cages only once a day to wash in a small wooden bowl placed near each doorway. The initiation ceremonies of the sons of the chiefs of the same tribes are of an entirely opposite character, as usual in records of this kind. Although sometimes subjected to physical pain, boys are in no case confined or restricted as to food, which is, on the contrary, usually supplied more lavishly. In these customs is it not possible that we have the beginnings of the induced physical inequality between the sexes, and that we are influenced to-day by the survival of the fetish? At the time of sexual development more food is required, and the young girl at this period has been systematically starved; and, bearing in mind the strong effect of suggestion on the primitive mind, may it not be that such customs survive in many forms of neurosis and hysteria? It has even been adduced that menstruation is an artificially induced occurrence, and is the result of the over sexing of the human female by the selfish and more excitable male; but little has been done to establish any definite conclusion on the point, though the 'Encyclopaedia Britannica' says that the function 'borders on a pathological change.' Among animals ovulation is not attended by hemorrhage, except in certain cases in captivity or in non-natural conditions. Professor Metchnikoff says 'it is highly probable that the periods, as they exist to-day, are a recent acquisition of the human race.' It is stated that there was once a time when the human race had a yearly breeding season, as is said to be still the case among the Esquimaux. The change which is noted in some species of apes, as, *e.g.*, the mandril, may probably be due to the evolution of memory and the resultant effort to repeat the sensation felt at the yearly breeding season. These considerations, coupled with the fact that amongst all primitive people menstruation is looked upon as something horrible and uncanny, point to it being not altogether a natural occurrence. Havelock Ellis quotes numerous tribal superstitions relating to it, and in the *British Medical Journal* recently it was suggested that, in the interests of their patients, women doctors when menstruating should not enter the wards! Whether the process will ever disappear or be modified is a problem for research workers.

The strength of the primitive woman must have been very great, although she was never so well fed as man. Among the Andomlies, on the Congo, Sir Harry Johnston tells us that the women work very hard as carriers or laborers; and that they are often stronger than the men and more finely developed.

The woman as mother has been persistently and artificially handicapped. It is not many years since the pregnant woman was systematically bled, and only recently have we ceased to starve the newly delivered mother; whilst the not uncommon slight fever after childbirth was treated by bleeding, to the extent of seventy ounces of blood to begin with, and followed by drastic purges.

Huxley, in his 'Lay Sermons,' heralds a change, when he says: 'We are indeed fully prepared to believe that the bearing of children may and ought to become as free from danger and long disability to the civilized woman as it is to the savage.' What is the modern woman doing to bring about this change?

One potent cause of weakness in women they have practised for about three thousand years, *viz.*, the wearing of corsets, the effect of which on the heart and lungs, respiration and circulation, is very disastrous; recent experiments carried on by Dr. Sargent illustrating this conclusively. The same authority also suggests that the weight of the skirt has much to do with the arrest of growth of the legs of girls.

The lecturer quoted illustrations showing the existence of modifications, due to use and environment, to prove that, even considering woman as a domesticated animal, there is no reason why her structure should not be as greatly modified and altered as that of other animals. It is not final, even if it could be proved to be true, to say that one sex is weaker than the other.

Another interesting point raised was that greater differences exist between the sexes in polygamous animals than in monogamous, the difference being presumably caused by the excessive sexual activity of the males.

It is still a common error to confuse the animal instinct of reproduction with the human love which is gradually differentiating our race from its brute ancestors. To the human woman of the future, as opposed to the animal woman of the past, we look for a remedy, for the training of the future generation of men is in their hands; even the number of the future generation of men is in their hands. Though more males are born, fewer survive. This excessive male mortality is due, not to their mothers, but their grandmothers, for this reason: the head of the male infant is at present rather larger and thicker than that of the female, and a potent cause of death in infants is pressure caused by narrowness of the pelvic cavity. This condition is associated with ill development, often due to rickets consequent on improper feeding during the first few years of life. So that when we get a race of women who constrict their bodies in stays, ignorant of the most elementary laws of health, who deliberately appeal only to what is animal in man, and who will not take the trouble to rear their own offspring, not only the health and progress of the race is affected, but the numerical proportion of the sexes. But is it too much to hope that in some far off day women may shake off even the physical results of superstition and ignorance and acquire bodies so perfected that their natural functions may be performed with at least no more difficulty than that experienced by females of other species?

Surely no woman will doubt that this will be to the ultimate advantage of the human race.

––––––––

Mrs. Gallichan (C. Gasquoine Hartley), in her lecture on 'Nature and Nurture: their Effect upon the Physical and Mental Life of Woman,' continued and carried further the ideas embodied by Mrs. Mills. The important question was asked whether the differences between men and women were variations, or modifications acquired through environment? It is possible that the characteristics of the modern woman are merely a veneer imposed by environment on succeeding generations of women, for women are less emancipated from their surroundings than men and far more saturated with restrictive influences. As formulated in Galton's law, every human being has for inheritance a mosaic of ancestral contributions. These may include a certain number of characteristics, which, though latent, may be transmitted to await the liberating power of their appropriate nurture. It may be that woman's awakening at the present time is due to some such deep rooted cause, and that we are now realizing a development which has been long arrested.

We ask whether the male preponderance is a natural and inevitable law, and turn to the life of simple people for a fuller comprehension of our own. Broadly speaking, the work of the world has been separated into two clearly marked divisions; men have been remarkable for the militant, and women for the passive, characteristics of humanity. At a certain period in our development women became inferior, because men acquired superior motor fitness. Motion, being restricted in women and unrestricted in men, gradually determined the characteristic life of each sex. There was nothing arbitrary in this arrangement, which was simply a division of labor. We find amongst the earliest and most primitive peoples that the men had the destructive and slaying part to perform, whilst the women looked after the duties of nourishment; and this division is typical of their activities. Men's efforts were violent, but brief, and they required long rest: women were able to expend more prolonged energy at a lower tension. But woman's part was no less important than man's part. It is said by Professor Otis Mason that 'all the pacific arts of to-day were once woman's province. Along the lines of industrialism she was the pioneer, inventor, cultivator, and organizer.' There is good reason for thinking, too, that the strength of the savage woman was little, if at all, less than the strength of the savage man. They have been known to fight when necessary, and a North American Indian is reported to have said to Hearne: 'Women were made for labor. One of them can carry or haul as much as two men.'

Feminine control over the means of production led to great power, and evidences of this are to be found in the widespread traces of the matriarchate, a form of which is still in existence in certain parts of the world. The change in the status of women cannot, Mrs. Gallichan thinks, be ascribed to the bearing of children. Primarily, it must be attributed to economic causes; secondly, to natural causes, such as man's change of habits as hunting became less necessary or possible; and, thirdly, to the development of the sex *motif.* Man's increasing domesticity found a new interest in woman's sex quality; he desired to preserve her beauty and save her from association with other men. The change from communal marriage to exogamy, or marriage outside the tribe, made the bride a stranger in the tribe to which she was introduced, perhaps speaking another language; and in this way she became absolutely dependent upon her husband, and was regarded as his property. Marriage by capture gave way to marriage by purchase, and thus we find the comparatively modern dowry system and condition of chattel slavery.

History, therefore, seems to show that the condition of woman is a veneer, imposed on her at first by the work of the tribe; and, secondly, by her sexual relations. Woman's withdrawal from labor and her seclusion under the growing value set upon her chastity, resulted in a new type noted for 'feminine weakness.' The menstrual function occasioned contempt, and was regarded as a spell of impurity. Thus was encouraged a phase of parasitism in which women acquiesced, with the result that the conditions of their life were circumscribed and their mental interests limited to personal relationships. Almost everyone of the special characteristics that are to-day ascribed to woman can be traced back to the period of marriage by purchase; whereas when woman was a worker, with free sex relations, we find her strong in body and capable in mind. Marriage by capture or purchase resulted in her dependence, and we note that it was from this time that her humanity was sacrificed to mere femininity.

There is, in conclusion, no final and lasting hope for woman save in economic independence, which, the lecturer holds, can alone free sexual relations from economic compulsion. In the mosaic of woman's inheritance lie dormant many qualities, and in the awakening of these lies our hope for the future.

———

On December 19th Miss Murby spoke on 'Sex and Society: a Few Radical Considerations.' She described the physiological relationships of the male and female elements, and the incapacity of the ovum to develop before impregnation by the minute and intensely active spermatazoon. She took up the relationship of man and woman as typified in these elements, and pointed out how, even assuming that their relative activity and passivity found mature manifestation in the katabolic and anabolic tendencies of the resultant male or female offspring, it was futile to argue that one set of qualities is of more value from a social standpoint than the other. Supposing it to be admitted that 'passivity' is the characteristic of woman, which is far from being invariably the case, yet that 'passivity' constitutes a resistant quality of profound selective value. Enquiries into evolution have shown what effect the need for securing female favor has had upon the development of males, how they have vied with each other in personal adornment, and learnt the arts of song and exquisite expression to gain their ends. Female opposition it is which has more than anything else made man introspective, forced him to pause and take stock of the world, in a word, to realize the value of his time relationship. Hebbel, the great German dramatist, said: 'Woman lives only in the moment; man with head and feet stretched beyond,' which is true in so far that woman makes of this life a home for man, and gives him a sense of the beauty of the present. That has been her function throughout natural history. She has acted as the practical critic of his theories; but, as Mr. Havelock Ellis points out, the sexual selection which operated when the two sexes met on a free natural basis has now given way under economic stress, and not until women realize freedom in this respect will the full value of their selective power again be felt. There is nothing derogatory to woman in accepting this view of her nature. It is not necessary to judge her by the male standard, for the power and nature she owns

are not secondary to man's – he being incomplete without her –
but equal, being co-existent and complementary.

The lecturer also put in a plea for a less individual conception
of love than is common. The birth of love in most persons is the
first dawn of cosmic consciousness, and if at that epoch in life the
attention of lovers were directed more to the vital and communal
significance of the new and surging energies with which they were
charged, the result might conceivably be an intensifying of social
sympathies. Certainly, between the individual man and woman
the narrowing of love to personal issues only was belittling. If
each realized that behind their mutual attraction pressed the whole
strength of past racial life, this universalizing of their relationship
would enhance its dignity, add a new importance to each life, and
assist in uplifting the whole plane of social values. If the share of
women in unlocking some of life's mysteries were generally and
frankly admitted, as privately and in individual cases it necessarily
is, surely there could no longer be any point in regarding them as
a sex in any way inferior to men. Either sex has direct contact
with the great primary stream of life, and derives from it, in
addition to much that is common to both, a certain fund of knowledge and experience which the other can only receive at second
hand.

There seems to be a great risk of women losing the full value
of much championship because of the adoption of a male standard
in judging them. It is admitted that women's physical disabilities
do not interfere with their special function; and this leads the
way to the sound conclusion that if women are criticized, not by
comparison with men, but by their ultimate relation to the vital
scheme, their physical strength will be found fully equal to men's,
which conclusion, moreover, is endorsed by the statistics proving
the greater longevity of women, notwithstanding the extension of
their work into spheres remote from those prescribed by nature.
The same applies mentally. The existence of even a quantitative
difference in intellect in men's favor is more than can be always
admitted, of course; but, as a general rule, the difference between
the minds of men and women is one of type, and the masculine
standard is irrelevant. Even a very slight mental or physical vari-
ation is sufficient to give a bias towards one form of interest rather
than another; and just as a sporting man and a mathematician live
in worlds apart, speak in different languages, and must be judged
on different planes, so does the original bias towards one side or
other of the line of cleavage between the sexes result in a difference
between men and women generally which it seems futile to ignore.
'For woman is not undeveloped man, but diverse.' It is better that

the existence of that diversity should be accepted as part of the basis of our claim for full recognition, rather than time should be wasted over attempts to minimize it. Man can afford to neglect us no more on account of our differences than our resemblances; and, interesting as the ethnographic and historic study of sex relations always is, it must not be forgotten that we were man and woman to start with and shall end the same. Difference existed prior to the explanations now adduced and, it is to be hoped, will continue to exist after all our struggles towards a more enlightened future. Our aim should be not so much resemblance as mutual comprehension, and this will not be fully possible until the irritation caused by the artificial barriers now preventing our comradeship has been removed once and for all.

———

The ensuing discussion produced objections to the argument by analogy with the male and female elements, it being denied that the difference between the reproductive cells of the two sexes involves any necessary difference between the intellectual capacities of the resultant male or female offspring. Dr. Bentham, in particular, questioned any essential or qualitative difference between the minds of men and women, and suggested that any quantitative difference might be ascribed to past unfair influences. Mrs. Reeves thought that the lecturer had treated women's influence in the world in the mass, as due to her unconscious exercise of certain sexual instincts, and that the future would involve a more individual and conscious resistance to male predominance; but as both men and women are the offspring of male and female elements, it must be inherent in both sexes to be capable of becoming perfect in originality, initiative, and force. She held it to be impossible that one sex could be a mass of resistance and instinct and the other be compact of alertness and originality, and looked forward to a period when, from emancipation following the present struggle, we should have acted and reacted on each other, so that the sexes should show a closer resemblance.

The lecturer, in reply, agreed as to there being no sex in brains; but said that there was certainly a difference in the modes of their activity as between men and women at the present time, a fact to which common observation bears witness; whilst women are not to be blamed alone, of course, for the narrow range of their interests. She admitted the blending of the sex qualities, and was in no wise inclined to draw hard and fast distinctions; but closed by insisting on the strength of the position for women when their function is identified with that of the germ cell, provided the equal importance of this element with the male contribution be duly emphasized.

Dr. Bentham followed, on January 12th, with a lecture on 'Sex Differences.' She argued that it is first necessary to recognize the distinction between a fundamental and a secondary sex difference. There are certain physical differences between men and women that we all recognize; and it is maintained by many in theory, and held in an indefinite way by many more, that these outward differences cause and imply a difference in their mental and moral qualities, and that this is not only in degree, but in kind. Close examination of these assumptions reveals a common fallacy, *viz.*, that those peculiarities of which they speak are necessarily and solely related to the sexual nature of men and women. In short, it is implied that the sexual nature of mankind rules all its manifestations of energy. In opposing this conclusion, Dr. Bentham reminded us that, with developing humanity, a larger and larger share of activities have become independent of the sexual nature, until it is not uncommon to find men and women in civilized society with little or no sexual feeling, social citizens though they be. Whether this be a desirable type or not, its existence proves that the influence of the sexual nature on the higher and intellectual life, or even the emotional life, varies enormously from individual to individual, and occasionally almost reaches the vanishing point.

In the very simplest forms of life – in unicellular organisms – there is no differentiation of function or sex. Propagation is effected by the simple division of the cell and of its nucleus into two parts (each exactly like the other), which then become independent. You can say of them either that there is no sex, or that they are wholly sexual; there is no one part set apart for reproductive functions.

But in these single-celled organisms there is also observed 'conjugation,' when two individuals coalesce and each cell and each nucleus divides into two and each half unites with a half of the other to form a new cell. This is asexual since they are exactly similar, but the effect would seem to be a strengthening of the resultant cells by, as it were, introducing new blood.

In somewhat more complex organisms, these cells do not part company when they divide but remain attached to one another and form a kind of commonwealth. Then one can see at once that some cells in a little group will be less advantageously situated for absorbtion of nourishment than others, and so begins a division of labor. By degrees this differentiation of function brings about a differentiation of form, and the cells become modified in most surprising fashion to serve their special purposes. Thus arise skin, bone, teeth, hair, etc. But all the bodies of the most complex animals – including ourselves – originate as simple cells, and in the individual history of each of us, divide and multiply, just as do the cells which exist independently. By degrees, the power of reproduction of the individual becomes restricted to a single set of cells, just as other groups of cells take other special uses, but the power of division remains with the modified cell. Thus a skin-wound is healed over, a broken bone is united, a child becomes an adult by the multiplication of these modified cells; but, for the production of a new organism, the activity of the set of cells specialized for that end is necessary.

The next advance is for the reproductive cells to become somewhat different themselves. In order to reinforce and strengthen the reproductive capacity there is established a difference in kind, and for reproduction, instead of two similar cells meeting, one of each kind is needed.

In most plants, and some animals, such as snails, each individual develops in itself both kinds of cell – that is, male and female. In some plants they are so placed that they can be self-fertilized. In more, in order to provide for strengthening by fresh blood, the one kind of cell becomes very small and light so that it can be moved on insects' legs, by the wind, etc., and thus reach the stationary cells. Snails can act alternately as what we call males and females.

This differentiation of the sexual cells is then complete in certain plants and animals comparatively low in the scale, but obviously makes no difference in the development of other parts of the individual. Nor can one even say of them that one takes an active or a passive part.

The modification of cells to their special purpose is not absolutely fixed in plants. For instance, though the usual reproductive part of plants is the flower, a new individual can be made by budding or cuttings. In such cases cells that have been modified in another direction take on reproductive functions again and form the parts, whatever they may be, which are necessary to the complete individual.

But in the higher vertebrates these powers are quite lost. We cannot bud out new parts; the cells can only multiply their own kind and effect growth or minor repairs. There is no reproduction without the special activity and conjugation of the two kinds of specialized cells, and these two kinds are carried by separate individuals.

In some species – fishes for example – the two kinds of special cells meet outside the bodies of the parents. In birds they meet within, but are immediately deposited without; with a store of food and provision for protection during development. In viviparous animals this protection is given within the parent's body, the food is supplied as it is needed, and the distinctive development of some of the body cells is carried still further to provide for this mechanical necessity. But that the sexual differentiation is carried so far as to affect all cells of the body – those composing skin, intestine, eyes, for instance, or brain and nervous system – is more than we have any right to assume.

So far as we can see, on the contrary, there is absolutely no difference between many of these tissues in male and female. And since, *e.g.*, there is no difference between male and female organs of sight and hearing, why should it be assumed that other parts of the central nervous system, less open to inspection, become so influenced by the development of one separate group of modified cells that an entirely different quality is to be predicated of them?

Such a theory implies the entire subordination in both sexes of intellectual to sexual life, whereas there is just as much evidence in support of the contrary view that the various groups of cells composing systems of the body, in conjunction with the various centres of control in the nervous system, become more and more capable of minding their own business, while the higher brain becomes more and more differentiated and less and less hampered by these separate needs; so that while in the humbler organisms the whole body breathes, reproduces, excretes, the civilized man carries the division of labor to a progressively higher point, and his brain only needs to concern itself in a minor degree with these simple necessities, but has energies to spare for the wider life that distinguishes him from his ancestors. Thus the differentiation of each group of specialized cells will affect that part of the central nervous system which is especially concerned with it rather than the whole; and if this be taken as the point of departure, perhaps the differences between the sexes, which are so much insisted on, may be accounted for as secondary rather than fundamental.

Even were the sexual and mental characters more closely related than is implied if the foregoing argument were accepted, still the specific characterization of the male and female modes of activity as active and passive respectively is not important. The processes of growth involve precisely similar mechanic changes whether in the male or female organism up to a certain point, and it is impos-

124

sible to say how or when sex is determined. Moreover, in the development of the sexual organs those of each sex retain traces of the other. It is, in short, unlikely that a differentiation occurring so late in embryonic life will influence the nature of the organism to so profound an extent as is expressed in the general conception of sexual differences.

What are some of the most notable differences between the sexes at the present time?

Women are supposed to be incapable of abstract reasoning, and dependent on the concrete; without originative capacity, but able to work on ideas presented to them; illogical, and swayed by feeling rather than reason; not to excel in organization, either trusting too much or too little; not accurate, and ignoring detail; narrow in their views, and given to worrying over trifles; wanting in courage and self-reliance, and consequently unwilling to assume responsibility.

But these incapacities are also the failings of men, though perhaps exhibited in greater proportion, and they are counter-balanced by qualities in which women excel. It is often conceded that women are more patient and painstaking; more unselfish and concerned with their employers' interest; more conscientious; and what reason is there to assume that want of enterprise, fear of responsibility, and deficiency in logic, are explicable as sex differences only?

On the contrary, it is far more likely that the effects of conditions and training are accountable, for the surrounding pressure of trifles influences us from our very birth. It has been impossible for women to obtain the invaluable training of free contact with the outer world which gives boys a knowledge of their desires and capacities. Girls can get definite teaching and training in many things, but the *liberty to train themselves* is still lacking; and this is essential for the teaching of self-reliance and the encouragement of initiative.

With regard to physical differences, it should be pointed out that sexual life amongst men is not without its disturbances. They are not gathered into a short period, but they do exist; and it may also be shown that the different incidence of disease on the two sexes is far from furnishing conclusive evidence as to the greater feebleness of woman being a specifically sexual character.

CONCLUDING REMARKS

In conclusion, we may note that the opinion commonly held that women are necessarily inferior to men physically and intellectually was vigorously contested. Miss Brooke laid emphasis on the potentiality for motherhood; but, instead of regarding this potentiality as the foundation of our subordinate position, she adduced it as the very ground on which we are to base our claim for a higher and more satisfactory recognition. Dr. Long deprecated the tendency to morbid exaggeration as applied to normal functions, whilst recognizing the danger to girls as well as to boys if subjected to undue mental stress at periods of development. Mrs. Mills went further. She repeated Metchnikoff's suggestion that the menstrual function is pathological, and was inclined to ascribe woman's weakness to the inherited result of past repression. Mrs. Gallichan endorsed this, showing how the marriage customs and life after marriage with its frequent complete dependence upon men had tended to isolate women and circumscribe their interests. Miss Murby argued that even accepting woman's weakness or the ascription to her of passive qualities, it is not, therefore, necessary to deduce that she is inferior to man; while Dr. Bentham asked for proof that all mental characteristics are necessarily influenced by sex. Since certain faculties of which we can easily judge, such as the special senses, seem to be quite identical in the two sexes, the assumption that sexual development governs all intellectual processes needs much more justification than it has ever received.

The one point on which all our lecturers agreed was the prime necessity for woman's economic freedom, so that her powers may expand to the full extent of her natural ability.

It will be seen that the trend of expert opinion, and the suggestions from various points of view contained in most of these papers and the discussions thereupon, indicate that the natural disabilities of women as workers have been, and still are, absurdly exaggerated. In the case of normally healthy women, at all events while not actively engaged in childbearing, it would appear that sex hindrances should, under fair hygienic and social conditions, be so slight as to be negligible in the majority of occupations. And, in an economically well-organized community, free women would not be obliged to undertake work for which they felt themselves unfit. What such work is the world is not yet in a position to determine. Women have, as yet, advanced too short a distance on the road to freedom to know their own possibilities and limitations. They are only just beginning to investigate for themselves the physical and mental problems that most nearly concern them. In the papers of. Dr. Long and Dr. Bentham special attention is drawn to some of these much needed enquiries, and Mrs. Mills and Mrs. Gallichan suggest other fields equally unexplored by those most vitally interested in the results.

It appears to us that false theories and evil social conditions have been, and largely are, responsible for the actual, as well as for the presumed weakness of women, and that such weakness affords no valid ground for asserting that women should not, in common with men, take their share as productive workers in creating wealth for society and reaping a personal reward.

The next series of papers will deal with this same question as it applies to mothers with young children.

———

Proofs of this Summary have been circulated amongst the members of the Fabian Women's Group for their comments and criticism. The comments received indicate a general agreement with the opinions of the Studies Committee of the Group as expressed in the Introduction and Concluding Remarks.

SCHEME OF WORK

INTRODUCTION

GENERALIZATIONS AND DIFFICULTIES

PART I

DIFFERENCES IN ABILITY FOR PRODUCTIVE WORK INVOLVED IN DIFFERENCE OF SEX FUNCTION.
Division 1. – Natural Disabilities of Women when not actively engaged in Childbearing.
Division 2. – Natural Disabilities of Women when actively so engaged.

PART II

WOMEN'S ECONOMIC INDEPENDENCE IN RELATION TO SOCIAL CONDITIONS.
Division 1. – Women as Productive Workers and as Consumers in the Past.
Division 2. – Women as Productive Workers and as Consumers in the Present.

PART III

PRACTICAL STEPS TOWARDS SUCH MODIFICATION OF SOCIAL CONDITIONS AS WILL ENABLE WOMEN:
(a) Freely to use and develop their Physical and Mental Capacities in Productive Work, whilst remaining free and

fully able to exercise their special function of Childbearing;
(b) Each personally to receive her Individual Share of the Social Wealth.

FABIAN TRACT No. 151
(October 1910)

THE POINT OF HONOUR:
A Correspondence on Aristocracy and Socialism

Ruth Cavendish Bentinck

DEAR CHRISTOPHER,—

My attachment for you personally was, as you know, very great. It is therefore a dreadful shock to me to be forced to recognize a rebel and a traitor in one who was a relation and a friend; but to me it seems demoralizing to remain on good terms with bad people – a man's character being shown by the company he keeps – so I find it impossible to associate with a person of your stamp, just as it would be impossible for me to keep up a friendship with a forger or any other immoral person. Forgive my plain speaking, but I am a plain man and about to speak out my mind for the last time.

I have tried to make every allowance for you. You have always been endowed with an unfortunate disposition, intolerant of anything savoring of restraint, impatient of procrastination, and contemptuous of prudence – which I even recollect you calling a 'ditch-begotten virtue,' an expression which of itself betrays you as an intolerant crank.

The Dangers of Too Much Knowledge

Owing to various deplorable circumstances, and also in a large measure to your own reckless and headstrong disposition, you have, I admit, been brought into contact with many facts which are not generally realized; and these you have only looked at through your own perverted spectacles, which incline you to attribute all those things, which you ignorantly and arrogantly assume to be unmitigated evils, to the defects of our present social system.

As you see, I have taken all the extenuating circumstances into account. I will not even ask how it is that one brought up as you were can so forget our family traditions and the ideals pertaining

129

to his rank as actually to avow himself a Socialist. I have made full allowance for the causes which may have induced you to adopt the mischievous course you are now pursuing. I own you have seen things which at first sight may arouse indignation. Your spirit revolts at what you consider to be 'injustice'; but *is* it 'injustice'? A better balanced mind would penetrate below the surface of things and realize its own inability to define abstract justice.

Sentimentalism in Foreign Policy

For instance, when justice is meted out to some person or persons in Spain or Russia, Egypt or India, you and people of your kidney are apt to jump to the conclusion that it is an 'injustice' because the sentence does not happen to meet with your approval. This frequently leads you into making seditious utterances provocative of endless ramifications of disorder; and yet you know perfectly well that it is not possible for a government office to vouchsafe a reason for its actions, therefore the justification for them does not get published, and many are led astray by misguided and shortsighted sentimentalists who refuse to see any but one side of these questions. You do not consider that the men on the spot have spent their lives in studying the best means of dealing with the native population, etc., and are therefore better able to say what is considered 'justice' in those regions than people who have never been in the country, and cannot expect to grasp the full significance of its problems in the same way as the officials, or even as well as those who go to such places in search of sport.

The Uses of Aristocracy

With regard to our own country, how could it get on without the aristocratic class? Look at the work, often hard, generally tiresome, and always unpaid, which they do on county and district councils, school boards, magistrates' bench, etc., to say nothing of various charities.

Of course there are black sheep in every flock, and I do not deny that the 'smart set' gives occasion for anything that Socialists may say of them; but, after all, they are not many in number, and are mostly aliens or risen from the middle classes, therefore the present argument does not apply to them. I own that many things in England are far from being perfect; but this is the case in every civilized country, and it would benefit no one were I to go and live in some mean and monotonous street amongst the myriads of beings who are degraded beyond redemption in our filthy cities. Most people in our class will do more good by keeping an oasis, where culture and beauty, art and literature, may find a home and not be overwhelmed by the ocean of brutal ignorance and coarse hideosity surrounding us.

That is my ideal and the work my artistic perception prompts me to carry on. There will always be squalor and ugliness enough for you to wallow in, because as fast as you sweep it up in one place it will reappear in another, so long as every individual unit does not 'do his duty in that state of life unto which it has pleased God to call him'; or, in other words, till everyone tidies up his own pigsty before attempting to clean up the farmyard – and if all the pigs did that there would be far less dirt in the world.

The Responsibilities of the Classes

I have a strong belief that the thing nearest one's hand is one's first duty; that we have inherited certain work and responsibilities; and that if we neglect those and plunge into work of our own choosing, we are not doing what God intended, and end in doing more harm than good. As it is, I think most people of our class are honestly endeavoring to tidy up their own corner of the world before trying to tidy other people's. This is the duty which I hope and believe I should endeavor to fulfil were I the meanest mole-catcher on the estate instead of its owner, and I only wish you could say as much instead of spending your time in making discontented and disloyal citizens; for this is a sorry occupation any fool is capable of, though it takes a wise man and a truly religious one to make people happy and contented, each in his sphere.

Do you remember our early days and all the 'secondary gods,' as you were pleased to call them – old Hannah, the stud-groom, the keeper, etc.? They gave you a very good example, for were they not all absolutely contented in their several positions? Would that you had assimilated some of their strong common sense! But your rebellious and predatory instincts were apparent even as a child. I have not forgotten your nocturnal expeditions to the lower gardens nor the fruit you kept hidden in the moat. I know your people pretend to be amused by the words 'robbery and confiscation,' but the aim of the equal distribution of wealth, though in itself ideal, is an object which can only be attained by appealing to man's predatory instincts, and the proposal to despoil one set of people for the benefit of another can only be called 'confiscation,' and, as such, can hardly fail to produce demoralization.

Socialism Demands a Higher Morality

I do not, of course, share the ignorance of those who confound feeble and isolated instances of Communism with Socialism, and I am well aware that Socialism has never been tried by a nation.

131

This in itself proves nothing, though the probability is that the experiment would have been undertaken long ago had there been any reasonable expectation of success; but the success of Socialism presupposes an improvement and elevation in human nature which we are not justified in anticipating: it assumes the complete eradication of all selfish instincts, the surrender of all natural affection, and the grinding down of all degrees of intelligence to a common level. The realization of Socialism suggests a barrack-like monotonous existence in which one set of people will be perpetually watching another to see that no unfair advantage is being taken, a life in which there will be little or no scope for originality or independence, and in which there will be nothing to look forward to, as the incentive to progress will be absent.

And even then the inequality and 'injustice' will remain. To take only one instance. I am less physically attractive than X., although perhaps equally deserving. Why should X. enjoy the privilege of ensnaring the affection of some desirable female, whilst I am spurned?

In the interests of common justice I demand that X.'s classic features and model proportions should be planed down or distended to my own level. X.'s attractive exterior is in no sense due to his own exertions; it represents an unearned increment to which he clearly has no right, and it is only fair that he should be called upon to sacrifice it on behalf of the community of which I am one. This argument applies with even greater force to the opposite sex.

No. If you got your Socialistic State to-morrow and everybody equal and enjoying the same advantages, in six months' time those with brains and intelligence would come to the front and those without them would sink, for the former would take advantage of the latter. The whole idea is so Utopian, so idealistic, so totally unpractical! What man who has had to deal with men and their administration on a big scale has ever been a Socialist? Poets, dreamers, ranters, people with an exuberance of philanthropy and no practical knowledge, people who are dissatisfied with their conditions, those who have sunk to the lowest depths and have nothing to lose – there is your Socialist raw material and I wish you joy of it!

Fatalism

Believe me, the huge fabric of modern civilization is working out its own evolution, and to try to increase the speed of the machine by pouring cans of liquid into it which it is totally unprepared to assimilate, will only result in a shudder of the machine, a spitting out of the liquid, and procedure by evolution as before.

In the vast network of most complicated inter-relations which builds up the civilized world, can you honestly believe that it is possible to straighten out the tangle and have everything nice and smooth, and everyone doing exactly as they should for each other's benefit? The modern industrial world is, alas! so constituted that the conditions you deplore must ever be with us in some form or other, and nothing that you or I can do is capable of altering what may, for all practical purposes, be looked upon as one of nature's laws.

There are other countries besides our own, and the adoption by one nation of a purely Utopian idea would dislocate the whole machine to its own injury; other nations would take advantage of the madness, and the crazy people who had accepted this form of social conditions would be crushed out of existence, for its Socialism would be an *unnatural* state, and therefore doomed to extinction.

Our Nation of Shopkeepers

Great Britain is a kind of vast shop, which either handles and distributes the goods of foreigners, or supplies other countries with its products. The vast majority of the population is employed in distributing or producing these goods, and the sale of the goods is dependent upon their being of the same, or better, value than those which are produced elsewhere. Eliminate competition between British producers, and the value of the goods will diminish and their price increase. What, in that case, would become of the millions of men and women whose labor produces the goods in question?

The British Isles, already overpopulated, are incapable of sustaining the forty-four millions who now inhabit them unless the product of their labor can be exported, and it is impossible to believe that a nation which forbade private profit could compete successfully with rivals who adhered to the system of competition.

It is futile to talk of Socialism as a cure for all ills as long as the world is what it is. You cannot make people subservient to an idea and go against their natural inclinations and interests for the *sake* of an idea.

Classes a Law of Nature

Look at nature; and if you can find a successful state of Socialism among animals or plants, I will take all this back. But until you do, I shall continue to assert that Socialism is not only a waste of your time, but a wicked waste, inasmuch as you are now spending

133

your life in rousing a turbulent and dangerous spirit which, when once called forth, you may find it is beyond your power to allay; and you may yet live to regret your reckless wickedness in appealing to men's baser passions and setting class against class. But I will not enlarge on this theme; I have already written enough to show you how deeply I regret that we have indeed arrived at the parting of our ways, and that in future we must be as strangers to one another.

PONTEFRACT.

———

DEAR P.—

So our divergent opinions have strained your friendship to the breaking point; but mine is still intact, although you call me a philanthropic, idealistic dreamer and a wicked thief appealing to men's baser passions, all in one breath.

Do you remember that legend about the first Norman robber recorded in our line? How he, being about to engage in battle, rode down the lines, reviewing his forces and giving orders? He commanded one of his officers to begin the attack by storming a certain position. This wretched fellow, glancing at the site indicated, replied that it could not be done. Our ancestor lifted his brows. 'What, then, do you suggest?' 'I cannot say,' replied the captain, helplessly. Whereupon, without further waste of time or talk, it is related that our amiable forefather, 'raising his battleaxe, clove his head in twain,' remarking that 'it contained neither courage nor ideas, but only a mouth to eat,' and so rode slowly on down the lines, the matter being of no great importance.

'Toujours l'Audace'

Now that callous old savage was right. If we have neither courage nor ideas, and placidly proclaim our inability to attack and deal with the difficult questions of the day – riding the while decked out in burnished armor, exacting respect from those we imagine ourselves born to lead, and expecting to have our greedy mouths filled with the choicest food the army commissariat has to offer – well, then we deserve to have our handsome, but inefficient, heads 'cloven in twain,' that's all. And yet this is the position you take up when you say 'we cannot alter present conditions.' Is not the present chaotic industrial system of man's own making? If so, it is capable of amelioration, alteration, and eventual reconstruction by man: it is no more a law of nature than that we should wear trousers or tall hats. But it is a natural law that certain people should feel impelled to persuade their fellow men that humanity is capable of attaining something incomparably higher and better than that which it has already reached. But for these restless individuals we should all still be happily engaged in scratching up roots and trapping birds for our meagre sustenance, coloring our bodies with clay as our only artistic effort, lining our foetid caves with dead bracken as our only luxury, and killing one another as our only pastime.

Nowadays these pioneers are styled 'agitators' because they disturb the brain calcifying prejudices which so agreeably numb our intellects, and they, deeming themselves the unworthy little tools God is pleased to work with, consider it is their duty to ensure that the world does *not* remain what it is. They believe mankind is improving steadily, and, at times, even rapidly. So surely as I am like a god compared to palaeolithic man – hairy, bull-necked, long-armed, flat-headed – so surely will the man of one hundred and fifty thousand years hence be as a god compared to me.

Our Intolerable Civilization

Already you are yearning for an improved environment. The thousands of 'mean and monotonous streets,' with their myriads of stunted and misshapen beings, breathing dirt-laden air and thinking with dirt-laden minds, disgust you. Then why tolerate them? Your artistic and fastidious nature prompts you to flee from all that is abominable and shut yourself up on your own estate, surrounded only by people or objects whose companionship and contemplation strike no jarring note; but this does not prove you superior to the struggling millions, toiling in crowded towns under conditions which do not admit of their developing any sense of beauty. I can only admit your claim to excellence when I find your artistic perceptions strong enough to goad you into fighting ugliness outside your walls as well as in, and not acquiescing in its prevalence in your country any more than you would in your individual home.

The Ideals of Aristocracy

You reproach me with forgetting the ideals of our class, but it is precisely these traditions and ideals that have made me a Socialist. The only reason that every intelligent member of our family is not one is due to the fact that most of the others were sent to school young or had these ideals destroyed otherwise.

All things carry within them the seeds of their own dissolution, and aristocracy is no exception to this rule. I maintain that no one, saturated as we were in the spirit of a once proud race, could fail to grow up into an uncompromising Socialist the moment he applied his tenets to modern conditions – unless some powerful influence counteracted his early training.

Let me remind you of the two dominant ideas which were set before us from the beginning.

The Governing Class

Idea No. 1 was that we were unquestionably superior beings. The world was full of inferior beings placed there on purpose to do our bidding and minister to our wants. These inferior beings were good creatures in their way, so long as they did as they were told, behaved respectfully, and were content 'in that state of life' in which God 'had been pleased' to place them. Any inclination on their part to leave this 'state of life' was little short of blasphemy. Any leisure they might have must be spent, not as they chose, but as the superior beings thought best for them, any claim they might make to appreciate art of any sort instantly became a jest. You may still find traces of this lingering in *Punch*: Mary Ann going to a Wagner concert after cooking the mutton, or a blacksmith in a picture gallery, both still serve as side-splitting jokes (though one wonders if any prehistoric beast can still be found to emit simian cachinnations over them). In short, life for these inferior beings was to be a life of hard work, and they ought to enjoy it – but as for enjoying life itself. . . ! That was reserved for the superior beings.

Fight for the Weak

Idea No. 2 was that we must always fight for the weak against the strong, against the oppressor for the oppressed, for the forlorn hope, in the losing cause, and this against all odds and at the cost of any personal sacrifice. If you were one of three hundred on a sinking ship, yours the right to be the two hundred and ninety-ninth person to leave that ship – the proud and enviable position of being the three hundredth belonging to the captain. If adrift in a boat, your honor required that you should do your share of the rowing and do without your share of the food. If lost in the desert with only one tepid water-bottle between three people, it was for you to see to it that the water was only drunk by two and that neither of these two should answer to your name – and so forth.

All children are by nature generous and heroic; they respond readily to such teaching, probably only because it appeals to their artistic and dramatic instincts; but, whatever the cause, they undoubtedly respond. Not that they become little angels revelling in self-denial. We were selfish little brutes and fought like demons; all the same, you remember, we formed a high ideal of what the imaginary person would do or say under any given circumstances, and we made up stories and planned adventures in which this splendid individual did all manner of brave and impossibly quixotic things.

How Children see it

Now you will take note that once these two ideas are thoroughly assimilated, once you have imbued a child with the conviction that it is his privilege to fight for the rights of the down-trodden, and you at the same time place a down-trodden people of his own race under his nose, whose rights he feels he ought to do battle for, then you have already – so far as ethics are concerned – your Socialist to hand! You have only to add a few elementary principles of political economy and you have your practical Socialist up-to-date. The thing is inevitable. Inevitable, too, the fierce resentment I experienced on discovering that the aristocracy were not attempting to live up to their own ideals, dead within them, and out of whose detritus the fungus of pocket-politics now sprouts instead. Inevitable, too, my exultation on finding the old ideals enshrined in the hearts of the people as they prepared to follow the fiery pillar to the promised land.

It is well to remember the 'secondary gods.' They were about as contented as governors of provinces usually are – and we owe them much – especially the great man who kept the cinnamon turkeys and always held his hat in his hand, even when ropes of rain were coming down, so great was his respect for all superior beings, even when they were very small indeed; and the coachman who, when out riding, never forgot his 'place,' but kept so far behind us as to render ordinary intercourse impossible – a pompous proceeding which so enraged us that you recollect we crossed and recrossed the ford after rain, knowing his horse had a fancy for lying down in water and always hoping we might drown him – a pious wish which was once nearly fulfilled, the horse rolling over his leg in a strong current, causing us much terror and hard work in extricating him – still speechless and respectful – from the river bed. Yet this man's abject servility furnished us with our first chance of seeing English people who were not personal retainers. Do you remember the wild gallops to distant villages? the sweets and nuts flung over playground walls to amuse children who surely thought us mad? the poacher? the pastrycook? the gipsies? and all the wonderful people outside the park walls? . . . and now you have shut yourself up and out of England again, and tell me that 'justice' is an attribute I am unable to estimate correctly!

Here we both see the same fact under different aspects. Surely if each man's individual conscience does not revolt at what he personally thinks unjust, there would be no justice at all! The unjust would have it all their own way, whilst the righteous ones sat in a subdued row, twiddling powerless thumbs and softly murmuring, 'What we see appears to *us* cruel and unjust, but let us not oppose it till we are quite certain that we are capable of arriving at a correct definition of abstract justice.' So one might sit gazing contentedly at the Crucifixion. Thus in point of fact many *did* sit. Yet I do not seem to notice that later generations have specially revered those 'well-balanced minds' for the part they played on that occasion.

Roughly speaking, injustice is strength taking advantage of its power to crush weakness. Injustice implies a lack of imagination. 'Justice' should be impartial, but no human being has sufficient imagination to place himself in the position of another so entirely as to be absolutely impartial. For that reason, 'justice' *untempered* by mercy – which is merely the result of imagination – is invariably injustice: a truth which the great Duke of Wellington perceived in that moment when he asserted that 'military law' was no law at all.

The Men on the Spot who Know

You hold that the omniscience of the 'man on the spot' should be taken for granted, and that no action of his should be criticized. In 1567 you would have maintained that the Duke of Alva was right in his treatment of the Netherlands because he had a great knowledge of the world, and that therefore his 'bloody council' was assuredly the best means of dealing with and governing people. You would have maintained that the views of the one hundred thousand artizans who emigrated to England were not worth listening to, and that the 'strength of mind' Alva showed in sending Counts Egmont and Horn to the block was beyond praise. Yet, in spite of his methods of 'dealing with problems on the spot,' his fleet was eventually destroyed, and he was only too thankful to leave a country where he boasted of having executed no less than eighteen thousand men.

In our own days the 'Congo atrocities' were perpetrated by Christians who had 'studied the problems on the spot.' It is the carping spirit inherent in a few people which acts as a necessary restraint on those who might otherwise get drunk on overmuch authority. Their vanity makes them susceptible to public opinion, and they weigh their actions a little more when they know these are liable to be criticized by somewhat exacting compatriots. Lord Acton said, 'Power tends to corrupt, and absolute power corrupts absolutely.' I only object to this wielding of absolute power.

You accuse the 'misguided sentimentalists' of never seeing any but one side of the question. This is indeed true. No matter what paper you take up, you are sure to see 'necessary measures of repression' commended, exhortations to a greater display of 'firmness,' etc.; and all this from panic-stricken, pale-faced persons, wielding pens to order at their dreary desks, and who, never having been on the spot, are no more fit – according to your own theories – to form public opinion than those 'sentimental cranks,' who have, at any rate, the courage of their theories, and who may frequently be found to have formed the same because they have roamed the world in many an unbeaten track.

Patriotism no Monopoly

I dwell upon this at some length because it is a pose of our 'class' to speak as though they had a monopoly of patriotism. If any reform is proposed at home they scream, 'Think of its effect in India!' or 'Do not indulge in parish politics, but remember the susceptibilities of the Fiji Islanders and Basutos!' Well and good; but let an Englishman raise his voice in protest against some arbitrary measure or unfair sentence passed in any of our distant dependencies, let him hint that our country's honor is at stake, and the aristocratic imperialists fling themselves on him at once. He is a 'traitor,' he 'ought to be shot,' and so forth.

If your imperialist carried his 'man on the spot' theory to its logical conclusion, he would believe that only men who have lived with and amongst those they legislate for are capable of knowing what it is they require. In this case the interests of miners would be handed over to those who had themselves worked in mines, and the concerns of cotton spinners to those who had spun cotton. But no; the leisured class fancy themselves born with a sort of marvellous intuition that takes the place of knowledge, and expect everyone to acquiesce in their decrees, when these should in 'justice' only apply to the one and a quarter million people in this country whose interests the deer park dwellers may fairly be said to understand.

Aristocrats as Administrators

You ask me to look at the work done by the upper classes on county councils, as magistrates, etc. It is precisely because I *have* looked that I accuse. They are mostly so unwilling to attack the

139

more serious problems of our time that they even display an occasional activity in opposing those who would. Hence a fitful interest in local matters, usually in order to prevent any progressive measures being enforced, and to guard what they conceive to be their own interests. One hears rich men derided for not giving larger sums to the party funds. On enquiring why a man who appears to take no interest in politics should spend his money thus, the reply is, 'Well, it's a very good form of investment.' This sentence sets one thinking.

Of course, many rich people and numerous captains of industry do excellent work; but I doubt your finding these exceptions invariably belong to the ancient nobility, who, taking it all round, resist most strenuously any attempts on the part of the working man to manage his own affairs. Now I agree that every pig should attend to his own sty, but I see certain pigs attempting to compel other pigs, less fortunately situated, to restrict their energies to attending to the upkeep of the selfish ones' styes, and prevent them from bestowing any attention on their own! I note, in passing, that to my simile of an armed knight proudly asserting his right to lead the attack on apparently invulnerable enemies, you retort with an appropriate comparison concerning swine.

Is Sport Culture?

You suggest that those who feel unequal to the task of fighting our twentieth century dragons are keeping 'culture, beauty and art' alive in some restful oasis. Let us be candid. Do the leisured class fulfil this function? You and I have been associated since our childhood with people who did little when they had money, except spend it on idle ostentation. Their lives were supported in luxury by a host of parasites ministering to their self-importance, and you are well aware that the character and general upbringing of this class tends to produce a highly conventional, ill-informed and narrow-minded type. Our sons are hardly brought up to this duty of 'sheltering culture' or encouraging science in the expensive schools we send them to. The more intelligent may tell you the difference between Lybia and Lydia, or afford some immaterial detail concerning the Hittites, but their ignorance as to the history, laws, literature or geography of the Empire they are taught to boast of is phenomenal. Other contemptible nations may have a history, or even laws. These are beneath our notice. Political economy would be classed as 'rot.' No; games are of paramount importance to the 'governing class,' therefore what the oasis really shelters is 'sport.' Mill said, 'Science takes cognizance of a phenomenon, and endeavors to ascertain its law; art proposes to itself an end, and looks out for means to effect it.' Which of these two processes is going on at the present time in any of the 'oases' known to you and me? Even the cultivated oasite is not clamorous in his demands that others may share in, or be given opportunities for learning to appreciate, those things which are, after all, the only ones that make life worth the living. Surely he may be compared to a man who is being rowed by others in a heavy sea, whilst he sits warmly clad on the dry seat, nibbling *pâté de foie gras* sandwiches, sipping champagne, and occasionally throwing the dripping oarsmen a weevilly dog-biscuit in order that their strength may be kept up sufficiently to go on rowing him! Would you be surprised if some day they heaved him overboard? No; you would do it yourself. We are not so unlike after all, and perhaps our quarrel – if quarrel it be – lies far back in those fruit-stealing days when, having committed every possible crime, you repaired to the billiard-room and practised skilful strokes, whilst I, no less steeped in sin, vanished in the library behind fat tomes on anthropology, whose musty and alluring smell is in my nostrils even now, and whose precepts I never forgot. Your very letter proves a transition in human nature. Here you are, an avowed opponent of my every thought and deed, actually endeavoring to 'make allowances' for me! Time was when the only allowance you would have made would have been one of distance as you aimed a sharp stone at my head, or of quantity as you poured some death-dealing drops in my drink. In these days you find yourself weighing extenuating circumstances in my favor. It is but a short time ago that we burnt heretics and witches at the stake, and starved people to death, and, in some countries, reserved that worst torture of all, the 'Iron Maiden,' for the worst criminals of all, namely, those who desired to improve their country's condition. Some might still wish to see those methods made use of now, but public opinion – which is after all only private opinion in the aggregate – has changed, and, with it, our customs. Even I recollect men denouncing trade unions and declaring that the sooner English workmen imitated the Chinese and learnt to live on a handful of rice the better for them and for the country! What fool would say this now? And this process of amelioration which manifests itself in ever greater tendency towards concerted action and combination would not seem to you a 'despoiling of one set of people for the benefit of another' if you studied the writings of modern economists more carefully.

The Failure of Individualism

The prejudice against Socialism is due to the prevailing habit of looking at all the existing evils caused by an obstinate individualism and then saying: 'That is what Socialism will be, only ten times more so!' At present a cut-throat competition forces selfishness upon us, insecurity and grinding poverty destroy natural affections, and want and destitution reduce millions of intelligences to one common level of devitalized incapacity. The passions – not the reasoning powers – survive. Mournful, barrack-like institutions *are* here now testifying to the failure of a system which denies men security in their own country, and assumes the only incentive to be money – forgetting appetite, not to mention vanity. It is an insult to all the finest minds of any and every epoch to suggest that the alteration of a vicious system would eradicate the wish to excel from our nature. Only we hope to do so in future without materially injuring others. Socialists desire that 'those with brains and intelligence' should 'come to the front,' but they also claim that those less gifted should enjoy security, respect, and leisure as citizens performing necessary labor for the welfare of a grateful community.

You confound natural with fictitious inequalities when dealing with the 'unearned increment' of X.'s physical attraction. We want to enhance natural advantages by giving all equal opportunities of developing mentally and physically to the utmost. Look at our women! See how these fictitious and cruel disabilities now prevent girls – intended by nature to grow into beautiful women – from becoming real 'women' at all – battered, twisted caricatures, with drawn faces and cunning or heavy eyes. The same applies to men. May God forgive you your insolent allusion to 'physical inequalities' which conjures up such visions that, for the moment, I cannot. Socialism being a comparatively new faith, it is remarkable how many of those holding it have already been found in positions where they had to deal with men on a large scale. Dozens of names suggest themselves to me had I the space, but I must confine myself to reminding you that the father of English Socialism, Robert Owen, managed a cotton mill at nineteen, and was part owner of the New Lanark Mills when twenty-eight.

Concerning 'Utopia,' I am tempted to tell you how I once accompanied a motherly primrose dame of high degree when opening a crèche in a foul industrial town. She made a short speech, in which she said a crèche was a temporary measure to palliate temporary evils, but that she hoped for a day when mothers would be enabled to feed and look after their own infants. Every subsequent speaker (they were all millowners!) alluded to Lady T.'s 'Utopian ideas,' with sarcastic smiles. Driving home, the dear woman protested, wearily, 'I've had nine children and attended to each one, and I do assure you that nursing an infant is *not* the occupation I should select in paradise. Men have such odd ideas concerning Utopia.'

Socialism and Competition

But let us turn from her to our old friend Chambers's Biographical Dictionary. Here we see that 'Marx's aim is *not* to propound Utopian schemes, nor even to offer programmes of social reform, but to elucidate an historical process which is inevitable'; and in this you concur, for you admit that the huge fabric of modern civilization is working out its own evolution, only you are annoyed when it betrays a tendency to evolute without consulting you. History shows that it is the backward nations, slow to adopt new ideas and unwilling to evolute, who get into an 'unnatural state'; and that the more advanced ones, having adopted new methods, are obliged by force of circumstances to crush the laggard peoples out of existence. Moreover, if Socialism is impossible, why oppose it so fiercely? As to Socialism eliminating competition between British producers, *would* the value of British goods diminish and the price increase? Gigantic combinations are now, in the interests of private profit, gradually achieving the elimination of competition; and when you find that these amalgamations cause the price of goods to increase, you will also find that your only remedy lies in Socialism. Goods manufactured on a large scale might show better value than those turned out by numerous struggling competitors, with antiquated plant and cheap labor, on a small one. John Bright said that adulteration was a form of competition. Indeed, the dictionary recognizes it as such: 'Adulteration. The act of debasing a pure or genuine article for pecuniary profit by adding to it an inferior or spurious article, or by taking one of its constituents away.'

When you speak of England as 'a kind of vast shop handling and distributing goods,' and appeal to my better nature by asking 'what would become of the millions of men and women whose labor produces the goods in question' if competition were eliminated? my heart remains as the nether millstone, and for obvious reasons. *What becomes of them now?*

A Little Lower than the Angels

Nature shows it is useless to fling all manner of seed at random on a rough bit of ground with some ill-considered remark about 'the survival of the fittest' as one lies down to watch the result. Nor, should you desire to plant an oak for future generations, will it avail you to stick an acorn in the crevice of some wall and tell it that if it is really an acorn it will become an oak anywhere. So it may: a little dwarfish caricature of what might have been one of the most magnificent growths in creation. Yet these incredibly silly things are what we do with the young of our own kind.

You want me to take the example of animals. You have already done so, selecting pigs. I refuse to compare mankind to the rest of the brute creation: till you can show me animals that cook their food, wear clothing that is not an integral part of their bodies but made for them by other animals of their own kind, or sacrifice their lives deliberately, not only for the sake of their own young, but for strangers, or even merely an idea. Even 'those who have sunk to the lowest depths' are capable of dying for another. True, it is difficult for their atrophied brains to grasp an idea. Even if they could, their devitalized natures and anaemic bodies would be incapable of working for it. This explains why *no Socialist has or ever will* come from the slums. All our recruits hail from the artizan or professional classes, men who have known responsibility and had practical experience. The 'submerged tenth,' oddly enough, share your views concerning our faith. They cannot see that ideas *do* rule the world; that men *are* subservient to them, and *will* 'go against their natural inclinations and interests' for the sake of the 'vision splendid' God has vouchsafed them.

Come out of your hole into England once more. Cast away the prejudices which blind you, and you will find a nation of aristocrats forming up swiftly, silently, shoulder to shoulder, in the cold grey dawn, preparing to stem back the great hosts of materialism which have gathered in such force on every side. I entreat you, fight with and not against us, for a long, fierce conflict it will be, during which many will fall; but they shall reckon their lives well lost, dying, as they will, with the ideal ever before them and the sun rising in the East.

Yours,

CHRISTOPHER.

THREE YEARS' WORK
1908–1911

Fabian Women's Group

INTRODUCTION

The Fabian Women's Group has now been in existence for three years. It was formed to concentrate and to promote activities which have now so far developed that the Executive Committee thinks well to issue a general report covering the whole period, from the Spring of 1908 to the Spring of 1911.

The Formation of the Group and its Purpose

The winter of 1908 was a period of activity and unrest amongst women within the Fabian Society as well as outside. The suffrage movement was rapidly growing in volume and force, and encountering increasingly bitter opposition, and many ardent suffragists amongst Fabian women felt that the Society was not keeping pace with a movement to which it had recently committed itself by the insertion of a new clause in its basis. Also thoughtful women everywhere were becoming conscious that much more than a disputed claim for a political right lies behind both the ostensible demands of the woman movement and the opposition to it.

On March 14th, in that year, a little party of Fabian women met in Mrs. Pember Reeves' drawing room to discuss the situation. They resolved to form themselves into a Group with two main objects:– Firstly, to make the equality in citizenship advocated in the Fabian basis an active part of the Society's propaganda and an active principle in its internal organisation; Secondly, to study women's economic independence in relation to Socialism. Mrs. Charlotte Mary Wilson was chosen as Group secretary.

A circular to this effect, containing an invitation to a general meeting, was sent to all the women of the Society. On April 4th, a large gathering assembled in Miss Wallace Dunlop's studio, and resolved to issue the following announcement:–

THE FABIAN WOMEN'S GROUP TO THE MEMBERS OF THE SOCIETY

We have formed a Women's Group, and appealed to the women of the Society to join us on the following grounds:–

Difference of sex function causes, and must necessarily cause, some difference between men and women in mental outlook.

This natural difference has been artificially exaggerated and distorted by the subjection of women.

At the present time there is a rising spirit of revolt amongst women against subjection in all its forms, and against the morbid mental outlook it has engendered in both sexes.

The mainspring of this revolt is the growing consciousness of women that their mental faculties are essentially similar to those of men, whilst the naturally distinctive mental outlook of each sex is equally valuable in social evolution.

In the Socialist movement, the consciousness of common mental faculties and a distinctive mental outlook in men and women, is taking practical shape in the growing desire of women to study and work out amongst themselves the complex problem of their economic independence under Socialism, before contributing their views upon it to the general consensus of Socialist opinion.

The Fabian Society has always implicitly conceded the principle of equality of opportunity between men and women, and has lately put a formal recognition of their equal rights of citizenship upon its basis. It is therefore meet and right that the Fabian should be the first Society to try definitely to define the intimate relation between the two most vital movements of the time, Socialism and Women's Emancipation.

Accordingly, we Fabian women have formed ourselves into a group, to study and discuss women's economic independence in relation to Socialism, and to carry our conclusions into our practical work in both movements.

We also desire to make the theoretical equality of Fabian men and women a working reality within the Society – (i.) by training ourselves in the usages of public life and the organised expression of opinion; (ii.) by securing the representation of the women of the Society upon its Executive in proportion to their numbers, in order that their distinctive mental outlook may find adequate expression in the Society's policy.

The proportion of women to men in the Fabian Society has largely increased within the last two years. When the last Members' List was issued, in Dec. 1906, there were 1,060 members of whom only 234 were women. In April, 1908, there are about 2,000 members, of whom about 600 are women. But of the 21 members of the Executive 17 are men. We have therefore nominated three women candidates in addition to the four women, all members of our Group, who served last year and are standing for re-election.

The following clause was added as an amendment, accepted by the meeting after much discussion:–

With reference to the Society's circular about the proposed Parliamentary Fund, it is suggested that Fabian women seriously should consider whether or no they should contribute to any Parliamentary activity as long as women are as a sex denied the Parliamentary franchise.

Before the next meeting, on May 9th, the numbers of the Group had risen to 159, two more women members had been added to the four already sitting upon the Fabian Executive; arrangements had been made to take part in the suffrage processions organised by the National Union of Women's Suffrage Societies, and the Women's Social and Political Union; and a group banner had been designed and the materials for it presented by Miss May Morris. Its motto is, 'Equal opportunities for men and women.'

PART I
THE GROUP'S WORK IN FURTHERING THE CITIZENSHIP OF WOMEN:

I. Local Government

The Group now proceeded to elect an executive committee, and to organise its work along the two main lines mapped out at its preliminary meeting; practical citizenship and economic inquiry. Whether we achieved any immediate success or not, we were sure that taking such part as is open to women in public business, and in the rough and tumble strife of practical politics, is an indispensable preparation for the full civic rights we claim. Again, looking at the matter from another point of view, the uphill work of practical reform is an indispensable stimulus and corrective, without which economic inquiry can scarcely bear fruit. Seclusion in the world of thought starves the thinker. Therefore our first effort was to start some citizenship work.

Discussion turned upon a suggestion thrown out by Mrs. Sidney Webb. In local government women's citizenship is theoretically recognised, but it is imperfect, ill understood, unappreciated, and little used, whilst the evils crying out for women's intervention are enormous. She urged us to see what we could do in this direction. In response ten of our members volunteered to make inquiries, in as many parts of London, as to agencies already at work, and Fabians and other Socialists who might help in forming local committees, or making use of existing organisations for citizenship propaganda amongst women electors; also in supporting the candidature of women for Local Bodies. A citizenship sub-committee was formed consisting of the executive of the Group, the ten volunteers, and other co-opted members. Mrs. Miall Smith was Chairman, and Miss Ellen Smith Secretary.

The results of this departure were manifold, none of them in exact accordance with the original plan. In some places our members took an active share in initiating or carrying on the work of Women's Local Government Associations, or Women's Circles of the I.L.P.; in others they took part in local affairs in connection

147

with a Fabian group or a Labour organisation; in one or two no scope for action was found.

During the first two years the sum of our collective activities as a Group was occasional help in local elections and the effort of our members to qualify as municipal electors. Several of our members also contested elections as candidates for local bodies; Mrs. Pease and Miss F. Smith for Rural District Councils, and Miss Margaret Smith (Mrs. Stockman) for the Birmingham City Council.

In 1910 several of our members came forward as candidates. Mrs. Miall Smith stood at a bye-election for the St. Pancras Borough Council in May. Mrs. Ackroyd served as a Guardian of the Poor in Croydon. Mrs. Miall Smith was returned for the third time for the Board of Guardians in St. Pancras, and Miss Caroline Townshend stood as one of six Labour candidates for the like office in Fulham. Though she did not get in, the contest helped to carry Minority Report propaganda into the very stronghold of the reactionaries.

Meanwhile we were making preparations for putting forward some Fabian women as candidates at the London County Council election in 1910. From the beginning of our citizenship work this had been our greatest ambition.

With the Progressives we were unsuccessful in gaining adoption for our women. In one constituency the local Selection Committee was afraid of Miss Atkinson, an admirable candidate, because she refused to denounce the Suffrage agitation, though she clearly explained that she did not consider the Parliamentary Franchise a subject relevant to a London County Council election, and that therefore she should decline to enter upon it in her election campaign. We had hoped that Mrs. Miall Smith would be able to contest the election in North Hackney. Unhappily there were many local difficulties, and when it became clear, owing to the opposition to a woman's candidature offered by certain of the Progressives, that Mrs. Miall Smith had no chance of being elected, she generously withdrew frm the contest, that none of the Group's energy might be diverted to a forlorn hope.

Our third London County Council candidate, Dr. Ethel Bentham, who stood in the Labour interest, had at first like difficulties to contend with. She only succeeded in overcoming them by twelve months' steady work in her chosen constituency. As far back as November, 1908, we had consulted with the Central London Branch of the Women's Labour League, with a view to arranging joint action in local government elections. In 1909, by the efforts of this Branch, to which eight or ten of our members belonged, the Women's Labour League in Kensington and

Paddington was revived, with Dr. Marion Phillips as Secretary, and Dr. Bentham was adopted by it as candidate for the constituency. During the autumn a strong election committee was formed from the local Trade Unions, the Kensington and Paddington Trades and Labour Council, and other Labour and Socialist organisations. It was recognised by the Central 'London for Labour' Committee of the Independent Labour Party to which it sent delegates. During the winter a number of successful public meetings were held, and Dr. Bentham was enthusiastically received as Labour Candidate. When the election campaign began, the Group made a splendid response to the appeal for service and financial help. Our members spoke, both indoors and in the open air, canvassed and assisted in office work, some of them coming long distances to do so; others who could not come, did clerical and other work at home. With the assistance of a few pounds from the Fabian Society, the Women's Labour League and one or two private donors, the Group raised the whole of the £135 required for the election expenses. Dr. Bentham obtained 2,724 votes, and aroused genuine enthusiasm amongst her supporters: in fact her defeat seemed an earnest of future victory. Much valuable propaganda both for Socialism and for the cause of women was done during the campaign.

The work thus begun is being continued in North Kensington. Dr. Bentham, being a resident in the constituency, is of course engaged in the social and political work of the district. The Independent Labour Party and Women's Labour League, to which several of our members belong, are very active bodies there, and are especially interested in questions of Local Government. In such matters their interest is the greater because several of them are engaged in Care Committee work, and two of the Kensington Borough Councillors are members of the Independent Labour Party. A successful campaign has just been carried on for better provision by the Borough for consumptives, and a long fight is being waged to obtain more municipal wash-houses. The most pressing need of the constituency is electoral registration in the Labour interest, a need as great for County Council as for Parliamentary elections.

The Fabian Executive, at the Group's request, sent up a resolution to the Labour Party Conference, in January, 1910, in favour of the Local Government Qualification Bill. This measure opens County and Town Councils to candidates qualified by residence. The resolution, the first ever placed by the Fabian Society upon the agenda of the Conference, was successfully carried. The Bill is still amongst the measures awaiting the leisure of the House of Commons.

From inquiries recently made amongst our members, and answered by some ninety of them, we find that twenty-six are qualified as municipal electors; twelve are possible candidates for local bodies; six are serving as school managers and nine on Care Committees; eight are members of Women's Local Government Associations, and three of the London Reform Union, one being a Vice-President.

II. The Suffrage Agitation

The appearance for the first time of a Fabian contingent in the great Suffrage processions of June, 1908, was followed by the systematic mention in the Fabian News of those Fabians who suffered imprisonment or distraint for the Suffrage cause during the ensuing winter. Resolutions of protest against the treatment of Suffrage prisoners were carried by large majorities at the Society's meetings in November, 1908 and 1909, and were sent to the Home Secretary and to the Press. The attitude of the Fabian Society as an organisation making the demand for Women's Suffrage a prominent part of its programme, was recognised by an invitation to send Fraternal Delegates to the London Convention of the International Women Suffrage Alliance in 1909.

In May, 1910, a resolution calling upon the Government to give urgency to 'a measure removing the sex disabilities of women in parliamentary elections' was carried by a large majority at the Society's Annual Meeting. In July the Fabian Conference, on the motion of W. S. Sanders, for the Executive, voted urgency, and unanimously adopted the following resolution, which was sent to the Prime Minister:– 'That this Conference calls upon the Government to grant facilities for the Women's Suffrage Bill, now before the House of Commons, to pass through all its stages during the present session.'

During 1910 the Women's Group took part in five demonstrations in favour of the Conciliation Bill. A large Fabian Contingent, organised by Miss Elspeth Carr, marched in the processions arranged by the Women's Social and Political Union on June 18th and July 23rd. On the latter occasion the Society for the first time had a special Suffrage platform at the mass meeting in Hyde Park. Mrs. Pember Reeves was Chairman, and the speakers were Mrs. Boyd Dawson, Dr. Marion Phillips, Mrs. Margaret Stockman, Dr. Haden Guest, Gerald T. Hankin, George Lansbury and W. S. Sanders. We have to thank the last named for taking an active part in organising the platform. Our banner was also carried in the

Trafalgar Square procession arranged by the London Society for Women's Suffrage on July 9th. The Group sent delegates to the Queen's Hall meeting, arranged by the National Union of Women's Suffrage Societies, and we co-operated with the Professional and Industrial Suffrage Society and the New Constitutional Suffrage Society in organising a meeting at the Memorial Hall on the 11th of November, when Miss Murby spoke as our representative. To our great regret the Trafalgar Square demonstration of the Freedom League was held too early in the Autumn for the Group to accept the invitation officially to take part.

The Group also sent the following resolution to the Prime Minister on June 21st:– 'This business meeting of the Fabian Women's Group urges the Prime Minister to give such facilities as shall enable the Women's Suffrage Conciliation Bill to pass through all its stages in the House of Commons during the present session of Parliament.' Before the last general election the Group sent the following resolution on December 1st to the Fabian candidates, Mr. Will Crooks and Mr. Harry Snell:– 'This meeting calls upon the Fabian candidates, in accordance with the avowed policy of the Society, to urge upon the electors the cause of Women's Suffrage, as of vital importance at the present moment.' Many of our members made their contribution to the Fabian Parliamentary fund dependent upon the candidates' support of Women's Suffrage. Mr. Crooks declared himself an adult suffragist; Mr. Snell laid special stress on the claims of women.

The Group also sent the following resolution to the Fabian Executive on November 22nd:– 'As a general election is approaching, and as before the last general election the Fabian Executive published in the "News" certain paragraphs headed "Advice to Members" which practically amounted to a Fabian election manifesto, and were so regarded in the Press and elsewhere, and as in that "Advice" Women's Suffrage was not mentioned as a matter of importance: This meeting calls upon the Executive to urge upon members of the Society, upon this occasion, the vital importance of the enfranchisement of women, as being, like the representation of Labour, an essential part of that machinery of democracy upon the development of which the sound advance of Socialism is absolutely dependent, and which it is the object of the campaign against the Lords' Veto to strengthen.' In deference to the strongly expressed opinion of its women members, the Fabian Executive put Women's Suffrage first among the special subjects which, after the fight against the Lords, it advised Fabians to press upon the attention of Parliamentary candidates.

Thus it will be seen that during the last three years the Fabian Society has led the way amongst Socialist organisations in pressing the claims of women to citizenship.

The Group numbers among its members the adherents of more than a dozen Suffrage organisations, with every variety of Suffrage policy. As a Group, therefore, we are strictly non-party in our attitude. We act collectively on broad Fabian lines: when occasion serves we press women's claim for equality in citizenship because its recognition is essential to the healthy advance of Socialism.

PART II
THE GROUP'S INQUIRY CONCERNING THE ECONOMIC POSITION OF WOMEN

The Problem

Turning to the other main purpose for which the Fabian Women's Group was formed, we turn from an essential factor in the realisation of Socialism to the subject matter of Socialism itself.

Socialism means to every Socialist the economic re-organisation of Society, whatever he may hold that it should mean in addition. It means the re-organisation of Society on the basis of the collective ownership of the means of production and exchange, and the collective control of industry and distribution. As Socialists we all hold that the community as a whole should be acknowledged the ultimate owner of national wealth, and that wealth production and wealth distribution should be nationally so organised as to bring about the largest and the most equal opportunities in life for each individual in the nation.

Further, Socialists are in general agreement that it is an essential part of this economic re-organisation that everyone should be brought up to work, and be trained for the occupations for which he has aptitude and preference. Socialists also generally agree that every worker should be free to consume as he pleases the share of wealth allotted to him in return for his work, subject only to the restriction that he does not injure the community thereby. In other words, under Socialism the individual will be economically independent, and that personal economic freedom will widen as Socialism develops.

Where in all this do women come in? It used to be vaguely supposed that, as a matter of course, Socialism meant for women what it meant for men. It was forgotten that women's economic position to-day is no more the economic position of men than their political position is that of men. We are only now recognising that if, as Socialism advances, women are to be considered economically as well as politically independent individuals, entitled, equally with men, to equality of opportunity, they have a great deal of leeway to make up.

Unless in the case of an exceptional woman here and there, it was only during the last century that women, timidly began to attempt to break away from paternal and marital control, and to claim individual independence and responsibility. The Married Women's Property Acts were a national acknowledgement of the justice of their economic claim. But the legal right to economic independence does not give that independence to those who neither earn nor inherit an income, and a vast number of women are to-day in that position. They are still the dependents of individual men; as consumers they are under their husband's economic control, whatever the intrinsic value of their unpaid services. The poorest wage-earner, only able to get employment at a capitalist's convenience and at his price, is still free to spend the pittance he or she earns, as he or she likes best: such a worker is economically independent, though within narrow limits. But the wife of the capitalist, or of the best paid of his workmen, is a dependent person, subject to the master of the purse strings, unless she possesses an income of her own by work or inheritance. 'We women are the slaves of slaves,' exclaimed a Socialist workman's wife.

One of the driving forces of the woman movement to-day is the secret resentment of women against this position of economic dependence, and the subjection in which it keeps them. Socialists must recognise that women's economic revolt is not merely against the enslaving economic control of the capitalist, but against the enslaving economic control of the husband. Its conscious expression is limited to-day to comparatively few, but it is a growing force.

Large numbers of women are however forced into the labour market, just as men are forced into it, by sheer necessity. The conditions they find there are often unfit for human beings whether they be men or women; but the women are additionally handi-capped. Usually neither their training for money-earning work, nor their rate of pay, nor their chances of getting the better sorts of work, are as good as those of men. All this they have to contend with, in addition to the disabilities inherent in their function of motherhood; many of these disabilities being artificially and need-lessly accentuated by preventable causes.

No, women are not in the same economic position as men to-day, and cannot advance hand in hand with them towards Socialism, because men have already advanced much further than women towards personal economic freedom. The first fact which Socialists have to face with regard to women is that, whilst as yet comparatively few of them have reached the measure of economic independence attained by men, there is a dawning conviction that its attainment by the womanhood of the nation is the true remedy for various social ills which otherwise seem well nigh irremediable.

With regard to men it is agreed that all measures of reform leading onward towards Socialism should be so framed as to safeguard for each individual man personal economic independence, securing his freedom as a consumer, and tending to place him, as a producer, more and more under the control of the state, of which he is a responsible citizen, instead of under that of individual owners of wealth.

With regard to women, we Socialists have to decide whether or no we will set ourselves to clear the way to individual economic independence for all women on the same terms as for all men. We have to decide whether or no we will further women's claim for paid employment, and fight their battle in the labour market, with the view of strengthening their position and bringing them into line with men in the Socialist advance towards work for all for the equal advantage of all. If the claim for equality of opportunity does not mean this for women, what does it mean? The question is an urgent one for all Socialists, since the trend of every measure of reform on the road to Socialism will be affected by it, and more especially it is a question for Socialist women. It is this inquiry which the Fabian Women's Group was formed to prosecute.

Our First Attempts to Seek a Solution

We did not begin by arranging a course of lectures to preach a doctrine, or prove a point, or even to define the position. We set ourselves first of all to get thoughtful women to tell us what they were thinking and feeling on the subject.

Our first paper was by a Socialist wife and mother, who had herself gained economic independence by her arduous and brilliant work: and we asked her to take 'Women and Work' as her general subject. The special aspect of it she chose was the 'Natural Disabilities of Women.' Women, she held, are predominantly creatures of sex, whose paramount need is a mate and children: and also they are heavily weighted throughout life by physical and mental disabilities unknown to men. Nevertheless their economic independence ought to be secured if only to enable them to mate well and wisely.

This lecture was followed by one from Miss Emma Brooke, urging that the ability for motherhood was in itself a cogent reason why the claim of women to full social recognition, economic and political, should be acknowledged.

After the ground had been broken in these two Introductory lectures, a Studies sub-committee was appointed to direct our inquiry. It consisted of the Group Executive and some co-opted members. Its Chairman was Miss Emma Brooke, and its Secretary Mrs. Charlotte Wilson.

The stress laid on the inevitable disabilities of sex in the first lecture had roused a strong feeling of opposition amongst our members, including some who were themselves mothers. It was felt that an altogether disproportionate importance had been attached to female incapacity for other vocations than motherhood. Our Studies Committee therefore decided to take natural and inevitable sex disability as a preliminary subject, with the object of discovering what women themselves are feeling about it.

Papers Upon the Natural Disabilities of Women as Workers:

Series I. The Disabilities of Women when not Engaged in Child-Bearing

The series was opened by a paper from Dr. Constance Long, who set the physiology of the matter clearly before us. This was followed by a number of papers treating of women's natural disabilities as workers from a variety of standpoints.

Series II. Disabilities of Mothers

The first series was succeeded by a second dealing with mothers in particular. This was opened by an introductory lecture on 'Difficulties' by Mrs. Pember Reeves, followed by a paper explaining the physiology of motherhood, from Dr. Ethel Vaughan-Sawyer. Afterwards we discussed many papers containing the views of various women, most of them mothers themselves. We also had informal talks on the subject.

Summaries of the Progress Made in Our Inquiry

A summary of each series of papers and discussions was printed for private circulation and presented to every member of the Fabian Society. The first summary was edited by Miss Murby, in conjunction with the Studies Committee of the Group; the second by Mrs. Bernard Shaw in the same way.

In their introductory and concluding comments on both Summaries the Studies Committee defined the question at the stage which its discussion had then reached, and epitomised the consensus of opinion on the points raised. There seemed to be a general desire for the economic independence of women, married and single; a general belief that for women who are not mothers occupied with young children, the path to that independence should be paid work; and a general sense that the conditions of domestic toil are detestable to-day, and press even more severely on women than the hardships of the labour market. The paid houseworker, living in, is popularly known as a 'slavey,' except in the upper ranks of the trade; but the mass of married women doing unpaid domestic work are in even worse case, and must remain so until the confusion between sex-relationship and economics, handed down to us from ancient conditions now vanished or rapidly changing, is disentangled.

The further and crucial question of motherhood, as on the one hand a disability to the worker, and on the other a service rendered to the community, was rather touched upon than fully considered in its relation to the Socialist ideal. But the opinion seemed general that there was a tendency abroad to exaggerate the inevitable disabilities of the mother of young children, apart from removable conditions of hardship. Nevertheless the adequate fulfilment of the functions of motherhood, if it is to be accompanied by economic independence for the mother, must be in some form recognised as deserving and requiring economic assistance from the State. The full consideration of this question and of the closely related questions of the maintenance, rearing and training of children, was reserved until the facts of women's economic conditions in the past and in the present had been closely examined. The object of the two first series of papers and discussions had been to throw, as a preliminary, some light on the extent of the natural disabilities inevitable to women as workers, as distinct from disabilities which are a result of existing social arrangements capable of modification and improvement. The greatest stumbling-block we found in our way was that women themselves have not studied the question scientifically in their own interests. The available material is presented by the male investigator with his own unavoidable sex bias.

Conference upon the Natural Disabilities of Women as Workers

In July, 1910, a conference was held at 150, Whitehall Court, upon the two Summaries.

Invitations to send representatives were accepted by the Association of University Women Teachers, Ling Association, Women's Labour League, Women's Industrial Council, Association of Shorthand Writers and Typists, Research Committee of the Christian

Social Union, Association of Sanitary Inspectors, Salvation Army, Association of Assistant Mistresses in Public Secondary Schools, Women's Institute, Headmistresses' Association, Married Women Teachers' Association, National Union of Women Workers, Eugenics Education Society and the Women's Co-operative Guild. Amongst the guests were Miss Lucy Deane, Miss Clementina Black, Dr. Constance Long, Sister Kerrison, Mrs. McKillop, Madame Michaelis and Professor Edith Morley. Expressions of regret at inability to be present were received from Miss Anderson, H.M. Principal Lady Inspector of Factories, Miss Collet, of the Board of Trade, Mrs. Ernest Rhys, Mrs. Karl Pearson, Dr. Ethel Vaughan-Sawyer, Miss Adler, L.C.C., and Miss Alice Ravenhill. Both the afternoon and evening session were largely attended by Group members.

In the afternoon the chair was taken by Mrs. Bernard Shaw, who explained in her opening speech how the Group had been led to begin its investigation of the conditions of economic independence for women by considering their physical and mental disabilities as workers, since this had been the first stumbling-block encountered in the inquiry. The discussion upon the Summaries was opened by Mrs. Matthews (Ling Association), followed by speeches from Mrs. Colonel Moss (Salvation Army), Dr. Marion Phillips, Dr. Constance Long, Miss M. M. A. Ward (Women's Labour League), Mrs. Pember Reeves, Mrs. Greenwood (Women Sanitary Inspectors), Miss Deane (formerly Chief Lady Factory Inspector), Miss Bramwell (Association of Headmistresses), Dr. O'Brien Harris, Miss Fitzgerald (Association of Shorthand Writers and Typists), Miss Sergeant, Miss Young (Shorthand Writers and Typists), Miss Lenn, Mrs. Van Raalte, Miss Williams, and Dr. Bentham.

Miss Murby took the chair at the evening session, which was devoted to 'Certain Fundamental Considerations.' Mrs. Charlotte Wilson and Mrs. Pember Reeves read short papers on 'Work' and 'Motherhood,' and after questions had been answered, the discussion was opened by Miss Clementina Black, whose interesting and sympathetic speech was followed by speeches from Mrs. Van Raalte, Miss Constance Smith (Christian Social Union Research Committee), Miss Waters (University Women Teachers), Miss Atkinson, Miss Mary Phillips (Christian Social Union), Mrs. Fisher, Mrs. Gallichan, Mrs. Stanbury, Miss Peacock, Miss Deane, Dr. Bentham, Mrs. Matthews, and Mrs. Dice. The Chairman, in her concluding remarks, voiced the general opinion of the Group as to the extreme utility of the Conference, the object of which had been to elicit the views and criticism of women interested in the same subjects, but working on other lines. The large amount of sympathy and appreciation which had been shown would encourage us to continue our work, and to pass on with better heart to the very complex inquiry into women's actual share in wealth production which forms the next part of our scheme of study.

The conference closed the preliminary part of our inquiry. We had elicited the opinions of a number of thoughtful women, of very varied experience, upon the urgent need in the interests of national progress for a special study by women themselves of their economic conditions. And we had listened to and discussed the views of many others upon the popular confusion of mind which, at one moment, will exaggerate the extent and distort the nature of the essential disabilities of the female human worker; and at the next moment will ignore those disabilities altogether as regards the social burden imposed upon her. The subjection of women has obscured the primary fact that such disability as capacity for motherhood brings with it is but the negative side of a special ability, the full and healthy development and exercise of which is of absolutely paramount national importance. Henceforth our work is mainly concerned with the abilities, not the disabilities of women in relation to their economic position in the community.

Papers on British Women as Producers and Consumers

SERIES I. BEFORE THE INDUSTRIAL REVOLUTION

At the close of 1909 the Group had already begun to discuss a series of historical papers, dealing with the position of women as workers and as consumers in this country during the ages before the Industrial Revolution. As that past has made our present, it is essential to obtain some idea of how it evolved. Here again we were met by the old difficulty in another form, Women in the past had not counted as individuals. As the individual man gradually emerged as a responsible, economically independent citizen from tribal and mediaeval corporate life, with its concomitants of slavery and of serfdom, the woman remained the adjunct of the man. She was his belonging; a creature attached civically and economically to him and under his control; and industrial history does not deal with her except incidentally. Her work, and its relation to her means of subsistence, are taken for granted and practically ignored by our historians. Consequently at every stage in our national economic development research into original contemporary sources must be made to discover facts about women as workers and consumers. It has taken time to find students to undertake this spade work on new ground. We cannot hope to do more than indicate the immense scope for research it reveals. With all deference to Rogers, Ashley, Toynbee, Hasbach and Cunningham, the economic history of this country from the point of view of the workers, to say nothing of the women workers, has yet to be written. Much new material has been unearthed, and there is no historical research work so important to the Socialist movement on its intellectual side. It is essential to the soundness of our constructive thought.

The historical papers already read before the Group include 'Teutonic Tribal Conditions,' by Mrs. C. M. Wilson; 'Celtic Women,' by Mrs. Ernest Rhys; 'Women under the Manor and in the Guilds,' Miss Mabel Atkinson; 'Types of Women before the Reformation,' Miss Eckenstein; 'Laws and Regulations relating to Prostitution, A.D. 800–1500,' Mrs. Maria Sharpe Pearson; 'Women in the Woollen Industry,' Miss B. L. Hutchins; 'Women in the Linen Industry,' Miss Elspeth Carr; 'Women in the Mining Industry,' Mrs. Tegan Harris; 'Apprenticeship of Girls,' Miss O. J. Dunlop; 'The Tudor Household,' Miss Evelyn Fox. Papers are in preparation on 'The Household and its Industries in Mediaeval Times'; 'Household Activities in the 17th and 18th Centuries'; 'Women in Agriculture since the break up of the Manorial System,' and 'Women as Holders of Property.'

It is intended that the series of Historical Papers shall be concluded during 1911, and an account of them, arranged in chronological order with an introduction, issued as Number III. of the Group series of Summaries.

BRITISH WOMEN AS PRODUCERS AND CONSUMERS
SERIES II. SINCE THE INDUSTRIAL REVOLUTION

Meanwhile we are beginning to consider the next division of our inquiry, the change wrought for women as workers and as consumers by the Industrial Revolution, amid the direct results of which we are living to-day. When this survey has been completed we shall be in a position to estimate the problem before us and make some suggestions as to its solution.

PART III
MISCELLANEOUS ACTIVITIES

Occasional Lectures

Besides the papers which form part of a series in our scheme of economic inquiry, we have had lectures dealing with current topics connected with the aims and interests of the Group. During

1910–11, Miss Clementina Black spoke to us upon 'The Sweated Woman Worker and the Trade Boards' Act'; Lady McLaren on 'Economic Points in the Woman's Charter'; Mrs. Cavendish Bentinck and Dr. Ethel Bentham on the evidence laid before the Divorce Commission; Mrs. Boyd Dawson and Miss Ellen Smith on the evidence collected by our Sub-Committee on Women in Prisons; Mrs. Pember Reeves on an interesting experiment initiated by her, and carried on by one of our Sub-Committees, on 'The Effects of an Allowance to Mothers, under carefully regulated conditions, before and after the birth of a child'; Mrs. Sidney Webb upon the 'Crusade against Destitution as it affects Women'; Miss Eva Gore-Booth on 'A much needed Extension of the Factory Act' and Miss Maud Davies on 'Women Workers in Villages.' We are now looking forward to a lecture by Miss Mary MacArthur upon 'The Industrial Organisation of Women.'

Women's Group Tracts

Our Studies Sub-Committee, in co-operation with the Fabian Executive, is now about to begin the issue of a series of Fabian Women's Group pamphlets. The cover has been designed and presented to the Group by Mrs. Elizabeth Wilson. No. 1, by Miss B. L. Hutchins, deals with Women in Industry; No. 2 will deal with the problem of Domestic Work. No. 3, by Dr. Ethel Bentham, will be upon Education, with reference to the physical and mental capacities of boys and girls. No. 4, drafted from the evidence collected by the Prisons Sub-Committee, will relate to the present penal system as it affects women.

The Fabian Conference

The Group was represented at the Fabian Conference, in July, 1910, by five delegates, Miss Hankinson, Dr. O'Brien Harris, Dr. Marion Phillips, Mrs. Elizabeth Wilson and Mrs. Charlotte Wilson.

The following resolution was placed upon the agenda:– 'That in the furtherance of social reform, Socialists, men and women, should oppose legislation and methods of administration tending to increase the economic dependence of women.' It was proposed by Mrs. C. M. Wilson, who laid stress upon the social dangers inherent in one-sided, piece-meal reforms. In seconding the resolution Miss Atkinson pointed out that it was in no sense an objection raised to the State regulation of industries in the interests of the workers: it was simply a caution against the advocacy of regulations so framed as to increase the dependence of women upon the incomes of men. The discussion showed that the group's point of view was not clearly grasped by some Fabian delegates, but in the end an amendment, proposed by Mr. Sidney Webb, which covered the ground more completely than we had ventured to suggest, was carried with our delegates' cordial agreement. It stood as follows:– 'That in the furtherance of social reform Socialists, men and women, should insist with special care that, in any legislation or methods of administration, any change should take a form which will not incidentally increase the economic dependence of one able-bodied adult person, whether male or female, on any other person.' Dr. Lionel Taylor proposed an additional amendment: 'And further, that attention should be paid to the importance of scientific inquiry, in every case, into the biological and economic effects likely to result.' This again was an enlargement of our original demand gladly accepted by our delegates.

The Royal Commission on the Laws of Divorce

After hearing papers by Mrs. Cavendish Bentinck and Dr. Bentham, upon the evidence given before the Commission during the early part of 1910, the Group resolved to offer its testimony. A Sub-Committee, with Mrs. Dice as Secretary, was formed to collect information from our members, some of whom are women engaged in professional and social work, bringing them into close contact with the most intimate affairs of family life. Dr. Bentham was appointed the Group's representative before the Commission. Her evidence, admirably given, was taken at considerable length by the Commission and well reported in the Press. Her main point was the existing inequalities of the law of divorce as between men and women and as between the rich and poor; and she brought forward telling instances to show how the law now tends to break up family life, to lessen respect for the marriage tie, to increase illegitimacy and prostitution, and generally to degrade social life. Her evidence was received with marked attention, and she was questioned as to the remedies she would suggest. The Group afterwards passed a warm vote of thanks to her for her valuable services.

The International Socialist Congress

Several of our membes were Fabian delegates to the International Socialist Congress in September, 1910, and Miss Murby also represented the Society at the Women's International Socialist Conference which preceded it. In October the Women's Labour League invited the Group to send representatives to a conference to consider the establishment of an International Committee of British Women Socialists. Miss Berry and Mrs. C. M. Wilson were sent as delegates, and suggested that it was the Fabian Society rather than the Group which should be represented on the proposed committee. The Preliminary Committee have therefore sent an invitation to the Fabian Executive which has appointed two of our members, Miss Murby and Mrs. C. M. Wilson, as representatives of the Society.

Women and the 'Right to Work.' Technical Training

The Group is always on the look-out to support Women's claims as workers. In 1909 it brought forward the grievances of married teachers at the Fabian Conference, and in January, 1911, co-operated with the Fabian Education Group in a meeting at Clifford's Inn, where a discussion on the subject was opened by Miss A. K. Williams, the first woman Vice-President of the London Teachers' Association.

In October, 1910, we sent the following resolution to the Post-master-General:– 'That this meeting of the Fabian Women's Group protests against the payment of girl messengers in the Post Office Service at a lower rate than boys for the same work; being of opinion that a Government Department should set an example in the matter of equal pay for equal work for both sexes.'

Apparently the resolutions and protests showered upon the Post-master-General from many quarters have produced their effect, for he has publicly explained that the girls are working shorter hours than the boys and under different conditions, hence their lower wages; also that their employment affords an opening to adult employment on the Post Office staff.

Hearing that the London County Council had established a technical school of cookery at the Westminster Institute, where boys take a three years' course in all the branches of the art, we inquired if the like advantages are anywhere offered to girls, and found that they are not. We therefore wrote to the three women upon the L.C.C. Education Committee, suggesting that the Cookery School should be open to girls as well as boys. Miss Adler and Miss Lawrence replied that this seemed impracticable; the former added that a class for professional women cooks may shortly be opened in connection with one of the Girls' Trade Schools. In her opinion the only way to secure efficient training for women is to give them full advantages in their own institutions; otherwise their interests will be subordinated to those of the men workers.

PART IV
ORGANISATION AND FINANCE

Membership

Any woman member of the Fabian Society can join the Fabian Women's Group. The minimum annual subscription is 1s. Associates of the Society can become associates of the Group at a minimum annual subscription of 2s. 6d. Women who have left the Society, while remaining in sympathy with its principles, can be subscribers of the Group at the discretion of the Committee at a minimum annual subscription of 1s. The Group contained 211 members, 2 associates and 1 subscriber, in December, 1910.

FABIAN TRACT No. 157
(June 1911)

THE WORKING LIFE OF WOMEN

Miss B. L. Hutchins

It is still the custom in some quarters to assert that 'the proper sphere for women is the home,' and to assume that a decree of Providence or a natural law has marked off and separated the duties of men and women. Man, it is said, is the economic support and protector of the family, woman is its watchful guardian and nurse; whence it follows that the wife must be maintained by her husband in order to give her whole time to home and children. The present paper does not attempt to discuss what is in theory the highest life for women; whether the majority of women can ever realize their fullest life outside the family, or whether an intelligent wife and mother has not on the whole, other things equal, more scope for the development of her personality than any single woman can possibly have. The question I am here concerned with relates to the actual position of the women themselves. Is it the lot of all women, or even of a large majority of women, to have their material needs provided for them so that they can reserve themselves for the duties that tend to conserve the home and family?

Let us see what the Census has to tell us on the subject. We find that in 1901 there were in round numbers 15,729,000 men and boys, and 16,799,000 women and girls, in England and Wales. This means that there are 1,070,000 more women than men, and if we omit all children under fifteen there are about 110 women to every 100 men. This surplus of women has increased slowly but steadily in every Census since 1841; that is to say, in 1841 there were in every 1,000 persons 489 males, and 511 females; but in 1901 there were in every 1,000, 484 males, and 516 females.

The disproportionate numbers of women are no doubt partly due to the Imperial needs which compel a large number of men to emigrate to our actual or potential colonies and dependencies. It is impossible to say how many are thus to be accounted for,

164

probably not a very large proportion, save in the upper classes. The Census shows figures for the army, navy, and merchant seamen serving abroad, but if these are added to the population of the United Kingdom the excess of women is still considerable. There seems to be no means of estimating the numbers of men who are absent on private business.

The main cause of the surplus of women seems to be their lower death-rate, and this is popularly accounted for as the advantage resulting to women from their comparatively sheltered life and less exposure to accident and occupational disease. This assumption no doubt accounts for some part of the difference; women do not work on railways or as general laborers, or usually in the most unhealthy processes of trades scheduled as 'Dangerous' under the Factory Act. There can be no doubt either that the death-rate of women has been lowered by the operation of the Factory Act in improving conditions of employment. The death-rate of men has also been lowered, but in a less degree, because although men benefit by improved conditions in the factory just as women do, the proportion of men employed in factories and workshops is small comparatively with women, so many men being employed in transport, building, laboring, docks, etc. These latter occupations so far have obtained very little legal protection from the risks and dangers run by the workers, although many of these dangers are notoriously preventible.

Still it is doubtful whether the lower death-rate of women can be entirely accounted for by the greater degree of protection enjoyed. Women often work longer hours even under the Factory Act than most men do under their trade union; much of the work done by women in laundries, jam factories, sack factories, and others, is extremely laborious. Again, the enormous amount of domestic work accomplished by women in their homes, without outside help, in addition to the bearing and caring for infants and young children, must be equal in output of energy to much more than all the industrial work of women, especially when the rough, inconvenient, and inadequate nature of the appliances common in working-class homes is considered, and the still more painful fact is remembered that the very person responsible for all this work is often the one of the family who in case of need is the first to go short of food.

It is true that more men than women die of accidents. But let us add to the accidental deaths the deaths of women from childbirth and other causes peculiar to women. We find that in 1907 10,895 males died from accidents; 4,890 females died from accidents; 4,670 from causes peculiar to women, 9,560 altogether, about 1,300 less than men. But the total deaths of men in 1907 exceeded the deaths of women by 14,297, an excess more than ten times as great.

There is also the question of age, which is important in connection with the death-rate. The number of boys born is larger than the number of girls, about 104 to 100. The death-rate of boy babies is almost always higher than that of girls, and in 1907 the death-rate of boys under four was higher than that of girls, but the death-rate of boys from four to fifteen was lower than that of girls at the same age; then at fifteen the male death-rate again rises above the female and remains higher at all later ages.

DEATH RATES, 1907, PER 1,000 LIVING

	Under 1 year per 1,000 births	aged 1	2	3	4	under 5	5	10
Males	130	38.4	15.5	10.1	6.9	44.8	3.3	1.9
Females	104	36.2	14.8	9.7	7.6	37.0	3.4	2.0

	15	20	25	35	45	55	65	all ages
Males	2.9	3.8	5.6	9.5	16.9	33.7	94.1	16.0
Females	2.7	3.2	4.6	7.8	13.1	26.0	85.9	14.1

Now if the lower death-rate of girls and women is due to their being taken more care of, how inexplicable are these figures. There is little enough difference in the care and shelter given to boys and girls under four, yet the boys die much faster; between four and fifteen, on the other hand, girls usually are a good deal more sheltered and protected than boys, and less likely to run into dangerous places and positions, yet from four to fifteen the male death-rate is slightly lower than the female. At fifteen when, as we shall see, a very large proportion of girls begin industrial work, the death-rates are again reversed, the male death-rate being thenceforward the higher. Nor does it appear that the death-rate of young women is much influenced by the fact of industrial employment. It is true that in Lancashire, where many women and girls work, the death-rate of women is higher than in England and Wales; but in Durham, where comparatively very few women and girls are employed, the death-rate is higher still.

PERCENTAGE OF FEMALES OCCUPIED

	LANCASHIRE			DURHAM		
	Ages 15	20	25–34	15	20	25–34
Single	78	80	76	40	49	49
Married or widowed	24	25	19	1	2	3
Death-rates, 1907–						
Male	3.3	4.2	6.1	3.8	4.7	5.6
Female	3.0	3.5	5.4	3.7	4.4	6.3

The contrast seems to indicate that it is not the fact of employment, but the conditions, both of life and employment, that are prejudicial to women in these industrial centres, for although death-rates have generally fallen, they are still higher in most of the mining and manufacturing districts, notably in Lancashire and Durham, than the average of England and Wales.

It will be agreed that the greater average duration of life among women is sufficient to account for a large excess number of women over men, over and above the emigration of many young men, which contributes to the same result. The surplus of women is distributed very differently in different districts: it is greater in London and the Home Counties, and also in Lancashire; less in the mining districts and the rural districts; and generally much greater in town than country. In the urban districts women over fifteen number 112, in the rural districts only 102, to every 100 males. This is perhaps partly due to the girls going to towns as domestic servants; for although the percentage of domestic servants is rather higher in the country than in town, the actual numbers are much less, and particular towns and residential urban districts – Bournemouth, Hampstead, and the like – show a very high percentage of servants. But the higher proportion of males in the country must in part be due to the fact that babies born in the country have a better chance of life. Although the number of boys born is greater than the number of girls (it was about 1,037 to 1,000 in 1891–1900, and slightly higher since 1901), the boy babies are on the average more difficult to bring into the world and more delicate for the first few years of life, as is shown by the male infant death-rate being higher than the female. It follows that though boy babies are more numerous at the outset, the girls steadily gain upon them, and at some point in early life the numbers are equal. If infant mortality is high, the surplus boy babies are very soon swept out of existence, and there may be 'superfluous women' even under five years old! But in healthy districts, especially in the country, where infant mortality is low, the boys survive in greater numbers, and exceed the girls in numbers up to the age of twenty; thus in later life the disproportion of women is not so great in the country as it is in towns. This fact constitutes one important reason (among others that are better known) for improving the sanitary conditions in towns. A diminution in infant mortality will tend to keep a larger proportion of boys alive, and thus by so much redress the balance of the sexes. To give an instance: in rural districts of Lancashire the boys under five were 1,018 to every 1,000 girls; in the urban districts, which include many towns with a high infant mortality, the boys under

167

five were only 989 to every 1,000 girls. It is impossible here to give many details on this point, but fuller statistics are given in the *Statistical Journal*, June, 1909, pp. 211–212.

Marriage and Widowhood

But it is evident that one way or another we must face the fact of a large excess number of women, even though we may hope that improvement in the people's life and health may prevent some of the waste of men and boys' life that occurs at present. How are women provided for? Marriage is still the most important and extensively followed occupation for women. Over 5,700,000 women in England and Wales are married, or 49.6 per cent.; nearly one-half of the female population over fifteen.

In every 100 women aged			15–20	......	2 are married.
,,	,,	,,	20–25	 27	,,
,,	,,	,,	25–35	 64	,,
,,	,,	,,	35–45	 75	,,
,,	,,	,,	45–55	 71	,,
,,	,,	,,	55–65	 57	,,
,,	,,	,,	65–75	 37	,,
,,	,,	,,	75	 16	,,

In middle life – from thirty-five to fifty-five – three-fourths of the women are married. In early life a large proportion are single; in later life a large proportion are widowed. Put it in another way. From twenty to thirty-five, only two out of every four women are married, most of the others being still single; from thirty-five to fifty-five, three in every four women are married; over fifty-five, less than two in every four are married, most of the others being already widowed. It is only for twenty years (between thirty-five and fifty-five) that as many as three-fourths of women can be said to be provided for by marriage, even on the assumption that all wives are provided for by their husbands.

As we have seen, women exceed men in numbers, and not only that, but the age of marriage is usually for economic reasons later for men than women, and some men do not marry at all, consequently it is utterly vain to assume that women *generally* can look to marriage for support, and to talk of the home as 'women's true sphere.' Mrs. Butler wrote, now many years ago, that, like Pharaoh who commanded the Israelites to make bricks without straw, 'these moralisers command this multitude of enquiring women back to homes which are not, and which they have not the material to create.' Although about three-fourths of the women in the country do get married some time or other, at any given time fully half the women over fifteen are either single or widowed. Women marry younger and live longer than men, consequently the proportion of widows is considerable, something like one woman in every eight over twenty years old. The largest proportion occurs, as might be expected, at advanced years.

In every 100 women aged 35–45 ...... 6 are widows.

,,	,,	,,	45–55 16	,,
,,	,,	,,	55–65 31	,,
,,	,,	,,	65–75 52	,,
,,	,,	,,	75 73	,,

Occupation

The number of women and girls over fifteen returned in 1901 as occupied was 3,970,000, or 34.5. This figure can only be regarded as an approximate one, as there is little information to show how many of the numerous women who work occasionally, but not regularly, do or do not return themselves as occupied, and even if this information were forthcoming, it is difficult to see how any precise line of demarcation could be devised to distinguish the degree of regularity that should constitute an 'occupied' woman. The figure is again obviously inadequate in regard to women's *work* (as distinguished from occupation), as no account is taken of the enormous amount of work done at home – cooking, washing, cleaning, mending and making of clothes, tendance of children, and nursing the sick done by women, especially in the working class, who are not returned as belonging to any specific occupation.

It is misleading, however, to take the percentage 34.5 as if it meant that about one-third of all women enter upon a trade or occupation.

In every 100 women aged 15 ...... 66 are occupied.

,,	,,	,,	20 56	,,
,,	,,	,,	25 31	,,
,,	,,	,,	35 23	,,
,,	,,	,,	45 22	,,
,,	,,	,,	55 21	,,
,,	,,	,,	65 16	,,
,,	,,	,,	75 7	,,

These figures show what is a very important point to remember, viz., that the majority of women workers are quite young, and this is one great difference in the work of men and women. The Census shows that over 90 per cent. of the men are occupied till fifty-five, and 89 per cent. even from fifty-five to sixty-five. But for women, especially in the industrial classes, the case is different. Their employment is largely an episode of early life. The majority of young working women work for a few years and leave work at marriage, as is shown by the rapid fall in the percentage occupied from the age of twenty-five. It is often stated by social investigators that the prospect of marriage makes working girls slack about trade unions, and indifferent about training. Many girls seem for this reason to fail in some degree to realize their full possibilities or to achieve their full industrial efficiency. In the case of those who do marry, and whose best years will be given to work socially far more important than the episodic employment carried on by them in mill, factory or workroom, this alleged lack of industrial efficiency is not perhaps of much consequence. But although a large proportion of women are married before thirty-five, and as we know, the proportion married is greater in the working classes than among the middle and upper classes, yet it is a mistake to suppose that the mature single woman in industry is so rare as to be a negligible quantity. There are, for instance, nearly a quarter of a million single occupied women between thirty-five and forty-four. They include 88,000 domestic servants, 32,500 professional women (teachers, doctors, etc.), 30,000 textile workers, and 40,000 workers in making clothes and dress. These figures show that self dependence is a necessity for many even at the age when, and in the class where marriage is most frequent. The importance to the single self-supporting woman of a skilled occupation which she can pursue with self-respect and for which she can be decently remunerated, need hardly be emphasized here.

Married and Widowed Women Occupied

The proportion of married or widowed women who are occupied is about 13 per cent., but, unlike the single women, whose percentage of occupation steadily falls as age increases, the percentage of married or widowed occupied is low at first, highest between thirty-five and fifty-five, and then falls to old age.

In every hundred married or widowed women occupied, six are under twenty-five; forty-four are between twenty-five and forty-five; forty are between forty-five and sixty-five; ten are over sixty-five.

The figures in our Census unfortunately do not separate the married or widowed occupied, so it is difficult to estimate from the above figures what proportion falls in to either class, but there can be little doubt that the high percentage of middle-aged women is due to widowhood. Frau Elizabeth Gnauck-Kühne, who has made a very able study of the life and work of German women,[1] tells us that in Germany, of married women only 12 per cent. are occupied, of widowed women as many as 44 per cent. The proportion of occupied widows is probably lower with us, as we have much less small farming, which in Germany is often carried on by women after the husbands' death; but there can be little doubt that the proportion of widows working is higher than the proportion married. In a very interesting passage Madame Gnauck points out the peculiar handicap suffered by a woman who is thus forced to renew industrial activity in middle life. The industrial life of women, she writes, is not continuous, but is split in two. Woman is normally provided for by marriage, let us say, for twenty or thirty years. But marriage is not a life-long provision for the average woman, it is only a provision for the best years of life, those years, in fact, in which a woman is ordinarily most capable of taking care of herself. The husband is, in many cases, swept off in middle life, and in the industrial classes he has usually not had very much chance of saving a competence for his widow. A certain proportion of women, therefore, we cannot say exactly how many, are forced to re-enter the labor market by widowhood, or by other economic causes – illness of the husband, desertion, and so on. Once more the woman appears in the industrial arena, with all the disadvantage of a long period of intermitted employment and loss of industrial experience. Having lost the habit of industrial work, having very usually children to look after and a home to find, she has to compete with girls and young women for wages based on the standard of life of a single unencumbered woman. It may be that the inferior technical skill often attributed to women as compared with men is largely due to this fact, that while a man gives his best years to his work, a woman gives precisely those years to other work, and therefore returns to industry under a considerable handicap. We can hardly doubt that this is a chief cause of pauperism.

The late Mr. Kirkman Gray, in his interesting unfinished work, 'Philanthropy and the State,' wrote:– 'The theory is that the male can earn enough for a family and the female enough for herself. But this theory, even if we accept it as correct, makes no allowance for the fact that every eighth woman is a widow. Here then is the bitter anomaly of the widow's position in the economic sphere. As head of a family, she ought to be able to earn a family wage; as woman she can only gain the customary price of individual subsistence.' The Minority Report of the Poor Law Commission recognizes the same anomaly. 'It is to the man that is paid the income necessary for the support of the family, on the assumption that the work of the woman is to care for the home and the children. The result is that mothers of young children, if they seek industrial employment, do so under the double disadvantage that the woman's wage is fixed to maintain herself alone, and that even this can be earned only by giving up to work the time that is needed by the care of the children.'

Even the Charity Organization Society, which usually inclines to ignore the social aspect of economic hardship and treat every case as merely individual, is forced to recognize the anomaly of the widow's position. 'We must look the poor woman's troubles in the face. . . . She has to do the work of two people; she has to be the breadwinner and go out to work, and she must also be the housekeeper. She has to wash, clean, and cook, make and mend clothes, care for and train her children. Can one pair of hands manage all this? And, secondly, when she goes out to work our poor widow will probably only earn low wages . . . about 10s. a week, and she will certainly not be able to support herself and her family on that.'[2]

The reflection here occurs that the life of women is inseparably connected with the life of men, and we may well pause to ask whether it is necessary so large a proportion of women should be widows at all. There is an excellent saying, that 'we can have as many paupers as we like to pay for.' It has an intimate bearing on the toleration of preventible disease and accidents as well as on administrative laxity in the Poor Law. The comparative mortality figure for the general laborer is more than double that of occupied males generally, and it is true the Registrar-General ascribes some of this mortality to confused returns, but even if some allowance, say 25 per cent., be made on this ground, the excess is still great. A pamphlet by Mr. Brockelbank[3] shows that in 1907 one shunter in thirteen was killed or injured at his work on the railway. The same writer gives reasons for supposing that the published returns of fatal accidents to railway servants fall far short of the truth, only those accidents which cause death within twenty-four hours being reported as fatal.

Many other occupations have a deplorably high death-rate, and it would seem that there is still a good deal to be done in improving the conditions of those workers who are not under the Factory Acts or protected by any effective organization. The protection of women by factory regulation has gone on the lines of protecting the individual woman worker at her work. Surely protection is also needed for the woman at home who sees her husband go off daily to some dangerous trade, where, for want of the necessary technical means for the prevention of disease or accident, he may be killed, maimed, or incur disease, and she and her children be left desolate.

It is notorious that a great deal of industrial disease and many accidents are due to causes largely preventible and within control. A very interesting report was issued last year in regard to dangers in building operations, which affect a large number of men – over a million. The report states that laborers are the principal sufferers from accidents, and have the most dangerous part of the work to do. One trade union secretary stated that 9 per cent. of his members had accidents in 1905. On this scale in eleven years each member would have an accident. Another union official said that a large number of accidents were preventible, and asked for more Government inspection. An employer stated that accidents were, in his belief, largely due to the lack of competent foremen and skilled supervision; he had only had three accidents in thirty years' experience, and attributed this immunity to his engagement of a really competent man. He thought the building trade got into bad odor with the public owing to the tendency to save in wages and put incompetent men to work that needs really expert supervision. Another witness complained that accidents were caused by putting unskilled men to skilled work for the sake of cheapness.

Dr. Young stated before the Physical Deterioration Committee in 1903 that factories contributed to the spread of phthisis, and that he considered that while a great deal had been done to combat the special dangers and diseases incidental to special trades in general industrial conditions, a great deal remained to be done, and legislative interference had by no means reached its limit. From the Registrar-General's report we find that very high rates of phthisis occur among men in early manhood and middle life. In 1891–1900 of the total deaths among men twenty-five to thirty-five, nearly one half were due to phthisis and respiratory diseases. The comparative mortality figure for certain occupations in 1900–02 was as follows:–

	Phthisis	Other Respiratory Diseases
All occupied males	175	78
All occupied males in agricultural districts	125	38
Tin miners	838	653
General laborers	567	268
General laborers (industrial districts)	450	171
File makers	375	173
Lead miners	317	187
Dock laborers	291	161

It is in the light of such figures as these, it seems to me, that we have to study the problem of married or widowed women's work and the pauperism of able-bodied widows and their children. As women become better instructed, better organized, able to take more interest in politics, and especially when they obtain the Parliamentary franchise, it is to be hoped that they will agitate for drastic legislation and stringent inspection in the industries carried on by men and unregulated by Factory Law.

In the mining and industrial counties the death-rate is markedly above that of England and Wales as a whole, and it is somewhat curious that while a great deal of attention has been given to the infant mortality of Lancashire, which is usually explained as being due to married women's employment, much less notice has been taken of the fact that the *corrected* death-rate of Lancashire is even more above the average than is the mortality of infants.[4] In 1907, which was an exceptionally healthy year, the death-rates of Lancashire, though diminished, showed themselves still conspicuously above the average; which can be most simply shown by taking the death-rate for the whole country as 100.

COMPARATIVE DEATH-RATE, 1907

| | General Death-Rate, corrected for age-constitution | | |
	Infants	Male	Female
England and Wales	100	100	100
Lancashire	117	124	126

A large part of this excess mortality, which is not by any means peculiar to Lancashire but can be paralleled in some mining districts and exceeded in the Potteries, is made up of deaths from phthisis and respiratory diseases, which are now considered to be largely traceable to unhealthy conditions of houses and work places, and in very great measure preventible. It is impossible in the limits of this paper to give full statistics, but those who desire further information are referred to the Reports of the Registrar-General, especially the two parts of the Decennial Supplement, published in 1907 and 1908 respectively, which are an invaluable mine of facts and figures, and also to the *Statistical Journal* (*loc. cit.*).

The Woman's Handicap

It is not very easy to summarize briefly the facts of woman's life and employment, which demand a treatment much fuller than is possible within our limits. But there are several points which seem to be of special importance. First, there is the curious fact that women, though physically weaker than men, seem to have a greater stability of nerves, a greater power of resistance to disease, and a stronger hold of life altogether. It is notorious that there are more male lunatics, and very many more male criminals than female, and much fewer women die from alcoholism, nervous diseases, suicide, and various complaints that indicate mental and physical instability, while more women than men die of old age. On the other hand, there are more female paupers and more female old-age pensioners than male, and these facts seem to indicate that women on the whole are handicapped rather by their economic position than by physical disability. We have seen that in this country women are more numerous than men, and that for various reasons they cannot all be maintained by men, even if it were theoretically desirable that they should be so maintained, a point which I am not here discussing. It follows that (quite apart from the question of economic independence as an ideal) economic self dependence is in a vast number of cases a necessity. It is impossible to estimate in how many cases this occurs, but it is safe to say that many women do in fact support themselves and others, and that many more would do so if they could.

Normally working women seem to pass from one plane of social development to another, not once only but in many cases twice or thrice in their lives. We might distinguish these planes as status and contract, or value-in-use or value-in-exchange. All children, it is evident, are born into a world of value-in-use; they are not, for some years at all events, valued at what their services will fetch in the market. At an age varying somewhere between eight and eighteen or twenty the working girl, like the boy, starts on an excursion into the world of competition and exchange; she sells her work for what it will fetch. This stage, the stage of the cash nexus, lasts for the majority of girls a few years only. If she marries and leaves work, she returns at once into the world of value-in-use: the work she does for husband, home, and children is not paid at so much per unit, but is done for its own sake. This accounts on an average for say twenty-five years; then she, in numbers at present unknown, is forced again to enter competitive industry on widowhood. This is what Madame Gnauck has called the 'cleft' (*Spalte*) in the woman's industrial career. The lower death-rate of women is actually a source of weakness to them, in so far as it leaves a disproportionate number of women without partners at the very time when owing to the care of young children they are least capable of self-support, and it increases the competition of women for employment. Their use-value in the home, however great, will not fetch bread and shelter for their children. Professor Thomas Jones, in his deeply interesting report to the

Poor Law Commission (Appendix XVII., Out-Relief and Wages) has been impressed by the pitiful fact that outside work should be forced on women whose whole desire is usually to be at home. He writes in reference to the well-intentioned efforts made by the Charity Organization Society to train widows for self support, efforts which, unfortunately, have not met with much success: 'The widow whom it is sought to train is no longer young. It is rather late to begin. . . . Further, many women are domestic by instinct, and dislike factory life. More important still in explaining failure . . . is the conflict between the bread-winner and the house-mother. Many a mother is distracted during the training time with anxiety for the children at home who may or may not be properly cared for.'[5]

Many serious discourses and amiable sermons are delivered in public and in private on the supreme beauty and importance of woman's influence, the necessity of maintaining a high standard of home life, and the integrity of the family. All this may be true, but for many women it is singularly irrelevant. *Il faut vivre.*

A woman may possess all the domestic virtues in the highest possible degree, but she cannot live by them. Value-in-use is subordinated to value-in-exchange. Mrs. Brown may be much more useful, from the point of view of her family and the community, when she is engaged in keeping her little home clean and tidy and caring more or less efficiently for the fatherless little Browns' bodily and spiritual needs, than she is when fruit-picking, sack-making, or washing for an employer's profit. But the point is that these kinds of work do at worst bring her in a few shillings a week, and the former – nothing at all. In the face of such facts it is absurd to tell women that their work as mothers is of the highest importance to the State. We may hope, however, that public opinion will ere long be convinced that the present system of dealing with indigent widows, as described in Professor Jones's Report, is wasteful of child life, destructive of the home, and cruelly burdensome to the most conscientious and tender-hearted mothers. The truly statesmanlike course will be to grant widows with young children a pension sufficient for family maintenance, on the condition that the home should be under some form of efficient inspection or control to ensure the money being properly laid out and the children cared for.[6] In the case of those women who are not naturally adapted to an entirely domestic life and prefer to work for themselves, it might be arranged that some portion of the pension should be diverted to pay a substitute. These cases would probably not be numerous, but it is as well to recognize that some such do exist.[7]

Socialists will not fail to realize that the case of the mother of small children forced under a competitive system to do unskilful and ill-remunerated work and neglect the work that is all-important for the State, viz., the care and nurture of its future citizens, is only an extreme instance of the anomaly of the whole position of woman in an individualist industrial community. This is not a place to enter on a discussion of the lines on which the economic position of women may be expected to develop under Socialism. I desire here merely to emphasize the importance of the distinction between value-in-use and value-in-exchange which seems to me to lie at the root of the whole social question; but most especially so as regards women. Our present industrial system, and therewith largely our social system also, is continually balanced perilously on the possibility of profit. Production is directed, not towards satisfying the needs and building up of the character of the nation's citizens, but merely towards what will yield most profit to the individuals who control the process. Except to the extent of the regulations of the Factory, Public Health, and Adulteration Acts (often inadequate and imperfectly enforced), it makes no difference at all whether the objects produced are useful or poisonous, beautiful or hideous, whether the conditions are healthy or dangerous, ennobling or degrading; profit is the only test. The special anomaly of the woman's position is that while the pressure of social tradition is continually used to induce her to cultivate qualities that, so far from helping, are a positive hindrance to success in competitive industry, yet when circumstances throw her out into the struggle there is little or no social attempt made to compensate her for her deficiencies. Her very virtues are often her weakness.

No sane person can argue that adaptability to the conditions of profit-making industry can afford any test of a woman's merit *quâ* woman, yet it is all that many women have to depend on for their own and their children's living. The position ought at once to be frankly faced that women's work at home is service to the State, and it may be hoped that ere long some practical step may be taken to put in force the Minority Report suggestions regarding allowances to widows with young children.

Notes

1 'Die Deutsche Frau.'
2 'How to Help Widows,' by A. M. Humphrey, p. 1. (Published by the Charity Organization Society.)
3 'A Question of National Importance.' (Hapworth and Co., 1909.)
4 See Corrected Death-Rates in Counties. Registrar-General's Report for 1907, pp. 12–20, cf. p. 14.
5 Poor Law Commission, Appendix, Vol. XVII.
6 See Minority Report Poor Law Commission, Part I., p. 184 (Longmans' edition).
7 I am not here alluding to cruel, depraved, or drunken mothers. In those cases children should obviously be entirely removed from the mother, and she herself dealt with penally or curatively, as may be deemed advisable.

FABIAN TRACT No. 158
(July 1911)

THE CASE AGAINST THE CHARITY ORGANIZATION SOCIETY

Mrs. Townshend

The Charity Organization Society Blocks the Way

It is surprising to find that the most strenuous opposition to almost
every scheme for social betterment comes from a body of people
who are devoting their lives to that very purpose. Why have
charity organizers resisted and denounced the proposals of General
Booth's 'Darkest England' scheme; of Mr. Charles Booth's Old
Age Pensions scheme; of all the various schemes for providing
meals for hungry school children; of the Old Age Pensions Act of
1908; of every scheme for 'school clinics'; of every scheme for
providing for the unemployed? Why did they object to the
proposals of the Minority Report of the Poor Law Commission,
the most masterly scheme ever brought forward for co-ordinating
the forces against destitution, the very object they have themselves
in view?[1]

Those of us who are keen that the public sense of responsibility
should be awakened with regard to destitution must feel that this
opposition on the part of 'charity experts' is of the utmost importance, and I want if possible to trace it to its source and to see what
it has to do with the organization of charity.

'The Greatest of These is Charity'

And first of all, what do we mean by charity? It is hard to say
how much the Christian laudation of the virtue has to answer for.
The current misinterpretation of the thirteenth chapter of the
First Epistle to the Corinthians has set a seal of merit and respectability on free gifts that becomes very mischievous if it serves to

179

accentuate the human weakness of preferring impulse to science and generosity to justice.

When the question arises as to whether it is better to fight destitution out of the rates by means of a series of preventive measures aimed not at results but at causes, or on the other hand, to leave it to be dealt with, so far as possible, by free will offerings administered by volunteers, those beautiful familiar words form a very real handicap in favor of the obsolete and more slipshod alternative. But how much of the virtue that 'vaunteth not itself' is really to be found in the modern subscription list?

Charity and Commercialism

As long as the ties between men were largely personal, as long as production took place in the workshop of the craftsman and the household of the lord of the manor, almsgiving was a natural healthy expression of human love and sympathy. As such it is still to be found among the poor. One sees sometimes in the slums a certain generous happy go-lucky community of interests which comes far nearer to the charity that 'suffereth long and is kind' than any that can be organized. The virtue still inheres in such rash and ill-considered acts as the hasty adoption of motherless children or the sharing a scanty meal with a starving neighbor, but it tends to be squeezed out by the machinery of investigation that becomes necessary, if almsgiving is to be placed on a scientific basis.

The beneficence of to-day is not to be blamed because the element of love has evaporated from it. The loss is inevitable. It is due to the complexity of modern life, to those dissociating forces that have reduced all mutual service to a basis of cash payment. The swiftly rising tide of industrial change, sweeping away all the old landmarks of service and responsibility, has left a chasm between rich and poor. A capitalist class with a civilization of its own cannot enter into the everyday life of the wageworker, who lives from hand to mouth, with habits, necessities, and pleasures entirely different.

It is this separation that cuts at the root of charity, severing the outward act from the inward grace. Robbed of close personal contact, the relationship of giver and receiver is bound to lose its beauty.[2] I can without loss of dignity accept help from a friend who loves me, but not from a stranger. Among the rich the warm impulse to help a friend in distress is replaced by a sentimental pity for seething humanity, and the act of devotion or loving service by a donation to a charitable institution; while among the poor, glad acceptance of friendly aid in time of need is apt to degenerate into cringing dependence, for gratitude is not a wholesome emotion unless it be vitalized by love. All the specific defects with which we are familiar – misdirection, waste, overlapping, professional parasitism – arise out of this separation.

Origin of the C.O.S.

It was to fight these evils that the C.O.S. was founded. By the middle of the nineteenth century England, having outstripped her neighbors in industrial change, had become enormously rich. The contrast of the wealth of the capitalist class and the poverty and insecurity of the worker had become pronounced, and the blood money of charity flowed freely in an ever increasing stream.

But thoughtful people were becoming dissatisfied with charitable methods and results. In the later months of 1860, a time of much poverty and distress, sundry letters to the *Times* gave expression to this feeling and led to the formation of the 'Society for the Relief of Distress,' which aimed at establishing a more personal relation between giver and receiver and a more careful administration of charity. In March, 1868, Mr. Hicks, a member of this society, brought forward a proposal for establishing a central board of charities, to classify them, analyze and compare their accounts, and present an annual report. In June of the same year the 'Association for the Prevention of Pauperism and Crime' was founded, with the Rev. Henry Solly as Hon. Secretary, Lord Shaftesbury, Lord Lichfield, and many other well known people as members. This society, though it began by aiming at big constructive schemes, such as that of employing 'waste labor on waste land,' gradually decided to limit its work to organization and propaganda. A paper read by Dr. Hawksley on December 17th, 1868, seems to have brought about this decision. It was issued as a pamphlet, entitled 'The Charities of London and Some Errors of their Administration, with Suggestions of an Improved System of Private and Official Charitable Relief.' Dr. Hawksley estimates the total annual expenditure in London on the repression of crime, relief of distress, education, and social and moral improvement, at over seven millions, but points out that little good was being done by the expenditure of this great sum, because neither poor law nor charity aimed at *preventing* destitution. His recommendations are practical and far reaching. They include a central office for the control and audit of charities and for the inspection of annual reports, and a large staff of voluntary district visitors to carry out the necessary investigation of cases and applications. These suggestions formed the starting point of the C.O.S. 'The movement began,' writes Dr. Hawksley, in a letter dated October 22nd, 1892, and quoted in an editorial article on the origin of the society in the *C.O.S. Review*, 'with Mr. Solly and the Association for the Prevention of Pauperism and Crime, and after a laborious existence of some months ended in accepting Lord Lichfield's suggestion to concentrate all our forces on charity organization, etc., as proposed in my pamphlet.'[3]

The Object and Methods of the C.O.S.

are thus stated in its 'Manual':–

'The main object of the society is the improvement of the condition of the poor. This it endeavors to attain (1) by bringing about co-operation between charity and the poor law, and between charitable persons and agencies of all religious denominations amongst themselves; (2) by spreading sound views on charitable work and creating a class of almoners to carry them out; (3) by securing due investigation and fitting action in all cases; (4) by repressing mendicity.'[4]

With regard to No. (1), it must be admitted that the society has met with no marked success. London charities are still unorganized and new bodies, called 'Guilds of Help' and 'Councils of Social Welfare,' are springing up to attempt once more what it has failed to accomplish.

Valuable Work of the C.O.S.

With regard to (2), (3), and (4), it has been more successful. There is no doubt that its influence on public opinion has been very important and, to a large extent, excellent. 'The repression of mendicity' appealed forcibly to the well-to-do classes. The hideous inconvenience to the public at large of street begging and of the begging letter ensured a welcome for any proposal for putting a stop to such nuisances, especially one which issued from high benevolence and claimed to further the well being of the destitute. The views and methods of the society, though they never became really popular, were listened to with respect; and it has certainly done a great work in training public opinion concerning the duties and responsibilities connected with almsgiving and in initiating orderly and efficient methods of social work. It has checked well meaning muddlers, has taught how to sift for helpable cases, and how to choose the right modes of help. It may lay claim to initiating in England the reign of the enquiry form and the 'dossier.' Even the country parson and the district visitor are falling into line, while many of the paid investigators for Royal Commissions and the London County Council have owed their efficiency to its training.

The society's want of success as an organizer of charity may perhaps be accounted for by the fact that it soon found itself largely occupied in the actual bestowal of relief, thus entering the lists with the various benevolent societies which it had set itself to investigate and to organize, and offering a concrete example of the actual working of those rules and principles on which the verdicts of the society were based. These soon became a strict and clearly formulated creed.

Principles of the C.O.S.[5]

1. Full investigation into the circumstances of the applicant to be undertaken in every case.

2. No relief to be given that is not adequate, that cannot hope to render the person or family relieved self-supporting.

3. No relief to be given to cases that are either so 'bad' in point of character or so chronic in their need as to be incapable of permanent restoration.

4. All 'hopeless' cases, however deserving, to be handed over to the poor law.

This creed, which, like all sets of working rules, arose out of temporary conditions, many of them badly needing alteration, has gradually acquired a kind of sacred character, and a strange structure of social theory has been built on it that is almost grotesque when compared with everyday experience.

The very excellence of the society's work has served to make this theory more mischievous, for it comes before the public backed by the honored names of devoted workers.

Fundamental Errors of the C.O.S.

I. – LIMITATION OF STATE ACTION WITH REFERENCE TO DESTITUTION

The first step towards organization seemed to be to draw a clear line between the province of the State in dealing with destitution and that of private charity. Unfortunately the early leaders of the society stumbled in taking this first step, and their initial blunder, never having been corrected by their followers, has tainted all the valuable work which they proceeded to set on foot.

They misread the facts that lay before them. They stoned the prophets of their own day and built the sepulchres of those who had preached to their fathers. In other words, they neglected the signs of the times (easy for us to read in the light of the years that have elapsed since 1869), such signs as the agitation for public education, for the decent housing of the poor, and for factory legislation, and they harked back to the decisions of the wise men of 1834. They failed to see that laissez faire was giving way all along the line before the phenomena of modern capitalism. They stuck to the theory of individual independence and of the danger of State interference in a world where man-made laws were enabling the rich to grind the faces of the poor. So long as the relative amounts of rent, interest, and wages were believed to be beyond human control, generosity in the rich, fortitude in the poor, seemed indeed the virtues called for; but those very investigations incidental to the careful bestowal of charity must have brought to light a gross disparity of distribution, a hideous waste of national resources that no charity could stem or cure. If only the leaders of the society had recognized this, had seen that the efficacy of charity for the redress of social grievances was at an end, and that the time had come when the community as a whole must shoulder its responsibilities, the C.O.S. might have begun work of great national importance in preparing the way for modern social legislation. But they did not see this. Habitually oblivious of any department of State action except the Poor Law, they saw merely that the more humane and the more lax of poor law administrators were overstepping the limits which had been legally assigned to them, and they traced the increase not only of pauperism, but also of destitution, to this relaxation of the principles of 1834. These principles – that the poor law should be a stern measure, seeking not the prevention, but merely the relief, of dire necessity, and that the condition of the pauper should never be 'more eligible' than that of the lowest grade of self-supporting laborers, however insufficient for decent life that might be – they were prepared to adopt without modification, in the belief that the diminution of poverty which followed the reforms of 1834 is to be traced exclusively to those reforms, and that similar results might be confidently expected from a return to them. The exclusive importance attached to this one period of history and to this one among many possible causes for the improvement which took place at that time is very characteristic of C.O.S. thought as we know it. It is interesting, therefore, to discover from the writings of Dr. Hawksley, to whom rather than to any other single person the origin of the society is due, and from those of Dr. Devine, the Secretary of the New York C.O.S., that these particular views have no necessary connection with the organization of charity. Dr. Devine, in the 'Principles of Relief,' points out that there were many changes going on in the thirties to which the improvement of the people may have owed quite as much as to that stricter administration of the poor law on which so much stress has been laid.[6]

Dr. Hawksley goes still further, expressing the warmest disapprobation of the reformed poor law, 'which in spirit sought to deal with destitution only in its completed state – it did not attempt the prevention of pauperism by seeing that the children of the dependent, or the idle, or the vicious, were trained for industry and virtue – it did not entertain the question of individual merit or demerit, but it adopted a uniform system of relief which was to be so ingeniously balanced that, on the one hand, its recipients might be prevented dying of starvation or want of shelter, but, on the other hand, that the kind and mode of the relief should be so hard, painful, and humiliating, that none but the very helpless and hard pressed should seek for it. The system was to be a test, and the idea was that if you drive away poverty out of your sight, you would cure it, as if the charnel house could be changed by screening it with a whited sepulchre. The system did not contemplate visiting "the fatherless and widow in their affliction," but it set itself up in the broad way of misery and destitution, and to every applicant, as a rule, it refused the recognition of any domesticities. It treated with contempt the humanizing influences of hearth and home, and with stern voice, pointing the way to the dreary portal of "the House," it said: "Enter or depart without aid." The result has been the creation of an abject, miserable race.'[7]

The society that Dr. Hawksley was to some extent instrumental in founding has departed widely from these views. Its members have fully agreed with him that paupers are 'an abject and miserable race,' but instead of attributing this, as he did, to 'maladministration,' to the fact that grudging relief was given instead of treatment and that it was given too late, only after destitution had set in, they attributed the evil results of poor relief entirely to the fact that it was given by the State, ignoring altogether the very different results of other forms of State action.

Instead of recognizing that the poor law was already obsolete and was bound to become more anomalous with every succeeding measure of social legislation, they accepted it as immutable and made it the corner stone of their system. Their line of argument was very singular. They admitted that the poor law was demoralizing; that its action was merely palliative, not restorative; that at best it could only prevent the worst horrors of destitution, but could not prevent its occurrence and its recurrence; and yet they never proposed any change in the application of public funds! They insisted that private funds should always be expended with a view to prevention and cure, but that public funds should be strictly reserved for those who were already in the last stage of destitution, and therefore already beyond curative measures.

Taking for granted that State action must demoralize, they assigned to private charity the task of preserving from pauperism all those persons or families whose need was only temporary or accidental, or easily remediable, especially where such need was accompanied by good character and record.

It is interesting to find this limitation of State action in a book published in 1868 by Mr. Charles Bosanquet. He was not one of the group who started the society, but he was an early member of it and became secretary in 1870.

'It would not be difficult,' he says, 'to classify cases between the poor law and voluntary charity. The former would take the ordinary chronic cases, the latter, perhaps, some of the more deserving chronic cases, but especially those temporary cases which, it might be hoped, judicious help would save from sinking into pauperism.'[8]

Whether Mr. Charles Bosanquet was or was not the first to introduce this system of classification into the C.O.S. creed, there is no doubt that he continued to preach it after he became secretary and that it has taken a permanent place. 'It is an essential difference between charity and the poor law,' he writes, 'that the former can direct its energies to preventive and remedial action. As the poor law is bound to give necessary existence to all destitute persons, charity is only doing the work of the law if it take up such cases without special reason.'[9]

An authoritative statement of the same view is to be found in the introduction to a recent number of the very valuable Charities Register and Digest which is published annually by the society.

'The claim for poor law relief rests, it may be broadly stated, upon the destitution of the claimant. . . . On the threshold of the question then we see the boundary lines of charity and the poor law. To charity it is not a question of primary importance whether a person is destitute or not. For it destitution is no test. It has more chance of helping effectually if a person is not destitute. It has to prevent destitution and indigence. It may have to supply actual necessaries, but to place the poor beyond the reach of need or to prevent the recurrence of need is its true vocation. It is unlimited in its scope and gives as a free gift. From the point of view of the poor law the question of destitution is all important. It is the passport to relief. Its administration is tied and bound with restrictions. Its supplies are drawn from a ratepayers' trust fund. Its main purpose is not to prevent or remove distress, but to alleviate it. It is a stern alleviative measure. It helps only when it must; charity always when it wills.'[10]

It is singular that in these utterances, and hundreds of similar ones that could be adduced, the charity organizers give no reason (other than the present condition of the law) for this hard and fast distinction between the principles which should guide public and private administrators in dealing with destitution. Presumably they think the reasons *sautent aux yeux*, but surely much might be said for entirely reversing their decision. The prevention of destitution implies that we should search out those who are on the downward road and arrest their progress before they become 'destitute.' Such action demands a many-sided and far-sighted policy, for the roads that lead to destitution are many and gradual. It demands a considerable outlay, producing distant and not always obvious results. Above all, it demands disciplinary powers.[11] Where are we to look for the statesman who will co-ordinate and maintain such a policy, for the Exchequer to supply capital for such a purpose, for the authority to wield such powers, if not the Government of the country? And yet, according to Dr. Loch and Dr. Bosanquet, this is precisely where we are not to look.

If they wished to lay down a hard and fast rule, one might have expected that it would be that great remedial and preventive measures should be left to the national and local executive, the collective wisdom of the nation, while private charity should concern itself with the pitiable, but apparently hopeless cases, should indeed humbly take up the work of palliation with instruments of love and religion and personal self sacrifice that the State can with difficulty command, as, in fact, the Salvation Army and the Church Army profess to do. On the contrary, their decision is, as has been shown, exactly the reverse; charity is to be remedial, the State is to confine its action to palliation.

This decision accords perfectly, no doubt, with facts as they are. It is a statement of the theory behind the existing poor law, but in the writings of the charity organizers there is acceptance and approval as well as statement. Dr. Bosanquet emphasizes and explains that approval in his essay on 'Socialism and Natural Selection' 'We should never forget,' he says, 'that the system,' i.e., State 'interference,' 'is a necessary evil, nor ever handle our national initiative, whether through the poor law or through more general legislation, so as to relieve the father of the support of the wife and children or the grown up child of the support of his parents. We should raise no expectation of help or of employment invented ad hoc which may derange the man's organization of life in view of the whole moral responsibilities which as a father he has accepted.'[12]

A good example of the actual mischief wrought by this pernicious doctrine that public action weakens private resource is to be found in the C.O.S. attitude towards the agitation for school clinics. The absolute futility of school inspection unless followed by treatment is obvious. At least fifty per cent. of the children in our schools are suffering from defects which, if not dealt with, will seriously handicap them in after life. These defects require treatment from a nurse under medical supervision. It is simply ridiculous to suppose that the mother of a family living on a pound a week in two rooms can find leisure to take her child suffering from adenoids to a distant hospital, can wait for it to recover consciousness, and then bring it back, still bleeding, in a public omnibus; that she can afterwards superintend the breathing exercises that are as important as the operation, or if the child's ears are affected, can spend half an hour daily in syringing them. The position becomes still more impossible if a second child requires spectacles and a third has decayed teeth to be stopped or extracted; yet such a case is not impossible or even unusual. It is perfectly clear that if the men and women of the next generation are to start life with a fairly sound physique, the preventive measures which are taken for the rich man's child in the nursery must be taken for the poor man's child in the school.

Advice, nurses, nursing appliances must be provided collectively, since it is a sheer impossibility that they can be provided in the home. The Education Department, the medical profession, members of care committees, and even county councils outside of London, are beginning to see that the difficulty can be met only by means of medical centres in connection with the schools. One might expect that a society whose aim is 'the improvement of the condition of the poor' would guide public opinion towards such a conclusion. We find instead that the C.O.S. has been acting, as usual, not as a pioneer, but as a powerful, though fortunately insufficient, brake.

At this last stage of the controversy (March 21st, 1911) nothing authoritative has been issued by the society. In default of it we may quote from the Occasional Paper on 'The Relief of School Children' (No. 8, Fourth Series). Such measures 'teach him' (the child) 'to look to outside help for the things he has a right to expect from his parents, a lesson he will not be slow to remember when he himself is a parent. The child needs before all things in the present day to learn the lessons of self-reliance and self-respect.'[13]

And from an essay of Dr. Bosanquet's entitled 'The Social Criterion': 'Granting a complete system of inspection at schools and of sanitary supervision through the health authorities and advice from health visitors, the normal mode of medical attendance should be for the wage earner as for ourselves, attendance by his family doctor, whom the head of the family chooses, trusts, and pays. On a provident system this is in many places successfully arranged, to the complete satisfaction of the doctor and of the patient. When, however, we should go to the specialist or to expensive nursing homes, the wage earner will be referred by his family doctor to the appropriate hospital or infirmary. . . . Thus the division of labor is properly maintained, the all important relation of trust and confidence between the family and the family doctor is not interfered with, the general practitioner's position is secured, and the hospital also is secured in the acquisition of interesting cases and in the fullest exercise of its powers of helpfulness.'[14]

With regard to proposals for free medical treatment, Dr. Bosanquet says: 'Such a policy is calculated to ruin the medical clubs and provident dispensaries, and to substitute visits of an official who, however good, is not the people's choice for the family doctor whom they like and trust and pay.'[15]

This question of school medical treatment is for the moment, perhaps, more under discussion than any other question of social reform, and for that reason affords the most striking example of the C.O.S. policy of obstruction; but that policy is perfectly consistent and perfectly general in character. It erects a barrier in the face of every attempt to lighten that pressure on the wage-earner which results from existing industrial conditions.

II. – That Unearned Income Injures the Poor but not the Rich

Another arbitrary assumption of the charity organizers is that for any man to enjoy any benefits which he has not definitely worked for and earned is injurious to his character. The naïveté with which they take this for granted is really preposterous when one remembers that nearly all the more respectable and refined members of the community are themselves living chiefly on wealth which they have not earned. One begins to wonder how those of us whose income is derived from dividends have any independence of character left. Dr. Bosanquet points out that the recipient of charitable help is injured because it comes miraculously and not as the natural result of personal effort;[16] but what effort do I make in connection with my dividends from the North Eastern Railway, and what can be more miraculous than my waking up one morning to find that certain shares that were worth £100 yesterday are now worth £105?

Dr. Bosanquet must really find some other reasons for objecting

to doles, unless he is prepared to return to the ancient canon law
with reference to usury.

III. – 'CHARACTER IS THE CONDITION OF CONDITIONS'[17]

The third grave error in C.O.S. theory is like the first, in that it
arises out of the acceptance of human arrangements as if they were
heaven-sent and unchangeable.

Accepting the individual ownership of land and capital and a
competitive wage system – all with exactly the same limitations
and mitigations that are to-day in force, and no more – as the
inevitable basis of society, the charity organizers are driven to an
easy optimism that sees a satisfactory opportunity open to every
virtuous worker, and looks forward with composure to a future
when the working class, having been taught thrift, industry, and
self-control, will do its duty in that state of life to which modern
industrial processes shall call it.

Poverty, even extreme poverty, seems to them unavoidable.
'Destitution,' says Dr. Loch in his last book, 'cannot disappear.
Every group of competing men is continually producing it.'[18] Not
to abolish destitution, but to improve 'social habit,' should be, he
thinks, the aim of the philanthropist. It is for this reason that he
looks coldly at all recent schemes for social betterment.

'The remarkable and well known investigations of Mr. Charles
Booth and Mr. Seebohm Rowntree, which have stirred public
thought in many circles, were, in our judgment,' he says, 'faulty
from this point of view. They were not analytical of social habit,
but of relative poverty and riches. They graded the population
according as they were "poor," or "very poor," or above a poverty
line. Their authors aimed at marking out such a line of poverty,
forgetful, as it seems to us, of the fact that poverty is so entirely
relative to use and habit and potential ability of all kinds, that it
can never serve as a satisfactory basis of social investigation or
social reconstruction. It is not the greater or lesser command of
means that makes the material difference in the contentment and
efficiency of social life, but the use of means relative to station in
life and its possibilities. Nevertheless, in these investigations it was
on the possession of means that stress was laid. Hence the suggestion that the issue to be settled by the country – the line of social
reform – was the endowment of the class or classes whose resources
were considered relatively insufficient.

'But to transfer the wealth of one class to another, by taxation
or otherwise, is no solution of social difficulty.'[19]

For a clear statement of the opposite view we cannot do better
than turn to the writings of Dr. Devine, General Secretary of the

New York C.O.S., and thus discover that the views of Dr. Loch are not inseparable from the aims of the society. 'I hold,' says Dr. Devine, 'that personal depravity is as foreign to any sound theory of the hardships of our modern poor as witchcraft or demoniacal possession; that these hardships are economic, social, transitional, measurable, manageable. Misery, as we say of tuberculosis, is communicable, curable, and preventable. It lies not in the unalterable nature of things, but in our particular human institutions, our social arrangements, our tenements and streets and subways, our laws and courts and gaols, our religion, our education, our philanthropy, our politics, our industry and our business.'[20]

Even more definitely Dr. Devine, towards the end of the same book, expresses the view 'that distress and crime are more largely the results of social environment than of defective character, and that our efforts should therefore be directed toward the changing of adverse social conditions, some of which can be accomplished only by the resources of legislation, of taxation, of large expenditure, or by changes in our educational system, or in our penal system, or in our taxing system, or even in our industrial system.'[21]

If we turn to the writings of Mrs. Bosanquet, perhaps the most popular exponent of what we are accustomed to look on as the C.O.S. view, we find that though she is more willing than Dr. Loch to admit the drawbacks of extreme poverty, yet she is equally certain that the aim of the philanthropist should be to stimulate the energy and improve the character of the sufferers, rather than to make any change in 'adverse social conditions.'

'How can we bring it about,' she asks, 'that they (i.e., "those whom we may call the very poor") shall have a permanently greater command over the necessaries and luxuries of life? The superficial remedy is that of gifts. . . . But this is a policy which has no tendency to remove the evil. . . . The less obvious, but more effective, remedy is to approach the problem by striking at its roots in the minds of the people themselves; to stimulate their energies; to insist upon their responsibilities; to train their faculties. In short, to make them efficient.'[22]

'Wherever there are people in want,' she continues, 'there lies the possibility of a new market and an increased demand for workers. The key necessary to open it is the efficiency which will enable them to buy by their services, what before they only needed.'[23]

This theory – that the root of the problem must be sought in the minds of the people themselves; that the key to the industrial impasse of unemployment is the efficiency of the worker; that, in short, the poor need not be poor if they choose to exert themselves;

and that the only way effectually to help them is to drive home their personal responsibility – is indeed the keynote of the C.O.S. philosophy; and yet, we may remark in passing, that, as in the case of the first 'error,' it is markedly absent from the utterances of the actual founders of the society.

The Rev. Henry Solly, in his address on 'How to Deal with the Unemployed Poor of London,'[24] alluding to recent riots in Wigan, quotes from the *Spectator* for May 2nd, 1868: 'Five hundred lives ought to have been taken in that town rather than five hundred laborers should have been robbed by violence and with impunity of their labor, rather than the law should have been made ridiculous and authority contemptible,' and adds: 'True, most sorrowfully and unanswerably true; but what about the responsibility resting on owners of property in the neighborhood for allowing twenty thousand colliers to live in a state of semi-barbarism? What about the responsibility of persons of property and education in this metropolis, if the question of preserving the reign of law and order were to be decided some day by slaughtering five hundred miserable semi-savage fellow citizens in the streets because we would not adopt remedial and preventive measures in time?'

We find the same frank acknowledgement of collective responsibility in Dr. Hawksley's address already quoted from: 'When we think,' he says, 'of the suspended murderer, let us ask ourselves whether we took pains to educate and train him for virtue and usefulness; and if we have not, let us bow our heads and be silent in the overwhelming sense of our responsibility. Or when we view the sad state of the poor – their overcrowded and filthy dwellings, the foul air, the bad and adulterated food, the disproportion between the present expenses of living and the wages that such darkened minds and feeble bodies can earn – let us again be mute and grateful that our own state is better, let us remove these stumbling blocks in the way of health and virtuous industry. Before we venture to judge these people, let us rather ask ourselves how much more are we to blame than they.'[25]

Nothing could be further removed from the tone of virtuous superiority which characterizes the writings of later exponents of C.O.S. views, and yet these two men may be said to have first formulated the aims of the society.

It may perhaps be claimed that the new theory is due to experience, that it is founded on poor law statistics and on the observation of C.O.S. investigators, who find that there is nearly always some moral defect associated with cases of dire poverty.

The argument from poor law statistics may be ruled out at once. It is simply misleading to speak as if pauperism and poverty were interchangeable terms. Pauperism can be diminished, or even quenched altogether, by a change in the poor law which would leave poverty just where it was.

The fallacies that underlie the other argument are a little more subtle. First, the ancient fallacy of 'any and all.' One may say with truth to the last dozen people who compose the queue outside the pit door of a crowded theatre, 'if you had been here half an hour earlier you would have got good seats,' but if one says it to the whole crowd it is obviously untrue, for the amount of accommodation remaining the same, the number of disappointed people would also remain the same. In Mr. Hobson's words, 'the individualist argument by which our charity organization thinkers seek to show that because A, B, or C in a degraded class is able, by means of superior character or capacity, to rise out of that class, no one need remain there, contains the same fallacy. It assumes what it is required to prove, viz., that there are no economic or other social forces which limit the number of successful rises. It assumes that every workman can secure regularity of employment and good wages . . . and that all can equally secure for themselves a comfortable and solid economic position by the wise exertion of their individual powers. Now if there exist any economic forces, in their operation independent of individual control, which at any given time limit the demand for labor in the industrial field . . . these forces, by exercising a selective influence, preclude the possibility of universal success. All economists agree in asserting the existence of these forces, though they differ widely in assigning causes for them. All economists affirm the operation of great tidal movements in trade which for long periods limit the demand for labor, and thus oblige a certain large quantity of unemployment. The C.O.S. investigator naturally finds that the individuals thrown out of work in these periods of depression are mostly below the level of their fellows in industrial or in moral character, and attributes to this "individual" fact the explanation of the unemployment. He wrongly concludes that if these unemployed were upon the same industrial and moral level as their comrades who are at work, there would be work for all. He does not reason to this judgment, but, with infantile simplicity, assumes it.'[26]

We find a similar assumption underlying the argument with regard to underpayment in 'The Strength of the People.' Mrs. Bosanquet takes for granted that payment is determined by quality of work, and concludes, quite logically, that the cure for a man's poverty is to make him do good work. To a casual observer the argument receives some support from appearances, as in the case of unemployment, for just as the unemployed are usually less steady and skilful than the employed, so is the sweated worker less efficient than the well paid worker.

To conclude that efficiency would secure good wages is, however, quite unwarrantable, for wages are determined in a state of free competition not by the intrinsic value of the work, but by the relative needs of the worker to sell and the employer to buy. Unfortunately, however, though good work does not always secure good wages, bad wages will usually produce bad work. 'The father of a family who receives eighteen shillings a week and pays seven shillings for lodging cannot, if he also feeds his wife and children, either remain or become a very good workman. Before he can do better work he must be better paid. Mrs. Bosanquet thinks otherwise. Efficiency and, consequently, prosperity might, she appears to believe, be enforced upon the poor by the withdrawal of such help as is now accorded them. . . . The hunger and hardship of their daily lives do not furnish an adequate spur, but perhaps despair might do so. We seem to hear Mrs. Chick exhorting the dying Mrs. Dombey "to make an effort." '[27]

This attempt to abolish sweating by improving the sweated worker is on a par with that perennial crusade against prostitution, which consists in 'rescue work' and the inculcation of personal chastity, leaving entirely out of consideration the economic conditions which give rise to prostitution. Both are attempts to eradicate social evils by improving the moral character of their victims, *without arresting the causes*, and therefore both are as useless as Mrs. Partington's mop.

But even if we grant that efficiency is the true cure for sweating or, to put it more broadly, that a man's social position depends on his character, we have still to consider what his character depends on. Does it not depend largely on his physique, his upbringing, and his general surroundings? Even if we admit that all energetic individuals may make satisfactory lives for themselves, how can we expect that the requisite moral energy shall be generated in the environment of poverty? It may be true, as Dr. Bosanquet says, that material conditions are largely independent of 'the energy of the mind which they surround,' but it is at least equally true that the energy becomes impossible under certain material conditions. The driving force of individual effort is a realization of higher wants. How are these wants to grow in such an atmosphere?

It is indeed hard to understand how this theory that the moral elevation of the masses must precede in point of time all successful reforms of environment can have survived the impact with fact which C.O.S. methods imply. With the slum child before their eyes, born with low vitality, reared by ignorant and poor parents, breathing bad air, wearing foul clothes, tormented with vermin, how can they assert that the problem is a moral one, that 'in social reform character is the condition of conditions'?[28] 'Only give scope of character, it will unfailingly pull us through.' Of course material improvements will be of no use unless they react on character, but have we any reason to suppose that they will fail to do so? Is it not likely that the child bred in cleanly habits will wish to be clean, and, in general, is not the way to raise the standard of living to accustom the young to higher ways of life? Even if it is true that character is the most important element in social reform, it is equally true that habit is the most important element in the formation of character, and habits of life are conditioned by environment.

But in all this talk about character it is well to consider whether the characteristics on which Dr. Loch and his followers lay so much stress are the most important for the future of our country.

It has been said that the C.O.S. holds a brief for the independence of the workers. Certainly this is the virtue on which these writers chiefly insist. The constantly recurring argument against old age pensions, against school feeding or school clinics, is that such State aid will tend to relax the effort to be entirely self-supporting. The C.O.S. ideal is that every head of a family should provide for his children, and even for his collateral relatives if they happen to be incapable of providing for themselves. 'That terrible pressure of the poorer upon the poor, which Mr. Booth regards as so serious an evil, appears to Mrs. Bosanquet[29] an element of hope and strength. Morally the charity of the poor to one another is undoubtedly a beautiful thing; economically it is assuredly one of the causes that increase and aggravate poverty, and such diminution of pauperism as is produced by the maintenance out of the workhouse of an aged or sick relative may, in the long run, lead to the destitution of a whole family. The last result of such maintenance may, if widespread, be far more nationally expensive than if all the sick and aged were supported out of the public purse.'[30]

But apart from the question whether it is cheaper for us to support the sick and the aged or to bind that burden exclusively on the wage earner, it remains for us to enquire whether a thrifty, calculating habit of mind, a tendency to count the cost to the uttermost farthing before giving way to a generous or aesthetic impulse, to prefer always the solid necessaries of life before its joys and delights, to limit one's outlook to the material wellbeing of oneself and one's blood relations, whether such a disposition is the one and only basis of national prosperity. What becomes of the graces of life under such a régime, what becomes of the search after beauty and knowledge, what becomes of that training in corporate action on which all successful administration depends and of the sense of human solidarity which lies at the root of citizenship?

But now, apart from theory, let us test this statement as to the all-importance of character by what we see around us. Is it true or is it not true that a man's personal character determines the comfort and wellbeing of himself, his wife, and family? If so, the agricultural laborer at twelve shillings a week, whose family cannot have clean skins, clean clothes, and enough to eat, must be a worse man morally than the fox hunting squire who is his landlord, and the house mother, toiling early and late to keep her children decent, a worse woman than the squire's wife waited on by five servants.

Is it true or is it not true? If not, then not character, but the accident of birth is the condition of conditions, together with the laws and customs of the time and country into which a man is born.

Now these laws and customs are after all of human origin. We, the governing classes, are responsible for them. The C.O.S. philosopher appears to think that they are God ordained and came down from heaven ready made, but does not attempt to reconcile such a view with his studies of history and of the varying laws and customs of different countries at the present time.

Social conditions are amenable to human action. In a democratic country laws and customs are modified by public opinion acting on and through the Government. What becomes then of this terror of State interference, with its debilitating effect on individual character? It stands revealed as a satisfaction with social conditions as they exist at the present time in England and a dislike to any proposed modification of them. 'We like things very well as they are. We have much and you have little; but you must cut your coat according to your cloth, as we do. If you are very thrifty, very sober, very industrious, if you put off marrying till you have insured your life and built yourself a really nice cottage with a bath room, and put by a nice little annuity for your old age, there will still be time for you to produce two or three strong healthy sons to work for our children. We may go to our clubs, our dinner parties, and our theatres, but you must not frequent the village alehouse. We may send up our sons for scholarships at Oxford, but you must pay out of your hard earned wages for any higher education that your children may desire. You must pay your rates and taxes as we do. There is no reason why we should bear a disproportionate amount of the burden; for though our wealth is greater, more is expected of us and our needs are greater. Any attempt, however, on your part to secure for yourselves any special return for your expenditure is most mistaken. It is true that the vast sums spent on the army and navy provide convenient and respectable careers for the less brilliant of our sons; while the more brilliant can obtain official posts at home or in India, well paid out of public money. It is true that it is the streets where we live that are well lighted and paved out of the rates, but this is all as it should be, and any attempt on your part to have your children fed when you are out of work or medically treated at the public cost is most ill judged. School meals and nursery schools would relieve your wife of part of her unceasing toil and might enable her to keep your home and your children cleaner, while school clinics might make a vast change in the health and wellbeing of the coming generation and in the future of our country; but what are these advantages compared with the sacredness of individual responsibility and of family life? It is the duty and privilege of every man to organize his life in view of the whole normal responsibilities which as a father he has accepted, and any State assistance which interferes with that duty and privilege is a cruel kindness. So important is your individual independence that it must not be jeopardized even to improve the health and save the lives of your children. It is better for England that her citizens should grow up crooked, diseased, and undersized than that they should believe in mutual aid and learn to look upon State funds as common funds, to be wisely administered for the common good.'

Such, in plain words, is the C.O.S. attitude towards poverty. So stated the theory sounds offensive and absurd; but when we meet with it interwoven with high sounding philosophical phrases and also with the record of many years of unselfish and benevolent effort, we are apt to be hoodwinked as to its real character. There is, moreover, insidious attraction for the well-to-do in this notion that destitution is but the natural working out of human character. If the present condition of affairs suits us, much satisfaction is to be derived from the assurance that any alteration of outward conditions, any change in human laws or institutions, would be worse than useless. The theory thrives and spreads among our upper and middle classes because it strikes root into the indolence and self-satisfaction of an easy and sheltered life.

Notes

1 For their own answer to these queries, see 'The Social Criterion,' Dr. B. Bosanquet. Blackwood.
2 It may be mentioned here that the C.O.S. does all it can to prevent almsgiving from becoming purely impersonal by sending to each donor a report on the cases helped by his subscription and enabling

him to take some interest in their individual circumstances. But this artificial contrivance for generating sympathy at a distance, away from the sights and sounds and smells of destitution, is far from restoring the ancient community of feeling.

3 'Origin of the London C.O.S.,' *C.O.S. Review*, No. 94, October, 1892. See also 'Philanthropy and the State,' B. Kirkman Gray, Appendix to Chapter VIII.

4 'Relief and Charity Organization,' Occasional Paper No. 8, Third Series C.O.S. Papers.

5 Cf. 'Principles of Decision,' C.O.S. Paper No. 5.

6 See 'Principles of Relief,' Professor Devine, pp. 276–7. The Macmillan Co.

7 'The Charities of London,' etc., T. Hawksley, M.D. Published by the Association for Preventing Pauperism and Crime, London, 1868.

8 'London: Some Account of its Growth, Charitable Agencies, and Wants,' by C. B. P. Bosanquet, M.A., Barrister-at-Law, pp. 199–202. Hatchard, 1868.

9 'History and Mode of Operation of the C.O.S.,' C. B. P. Bosanquet.

10 Introduction to Annual Charities Register and Digest, 1909, 'On the Functions of the Poor Law and Charity.' Cf. 'Charity and Social Life,' C. S. Loch, p. 319. Macmillan, 1910.

11 The experiments already tried in the operations of the Local Health Authority, the Local Education Authority, and the Local Lunacy Authority have been – in marked contrast with the Poor Law – highly promising in their success.

12 'Aspects of the Social Problem': XVI. 'Socialism and Natural Selection,' Dr. B. Bosanquet, p. 304.

13 Occasional Paper C.O.S. No. 8, Fourth Series.

14 'The Social Criterion,' a Paper read by B. Bosanquet, M.A., I.L.D., November 15th, 1907, before the Edinburgh C.O.S., p. 23.

15 Ibid. p. 24.

16 'The point of private property is that things should not come miraculously and be unaffected by your dealings with them, but that you should be in contact with something which in the external world is the definite material representation of yourself.' 'Aspects of the Social Problem,' p. 313.

17 'Aspects of the Social Problem,' Dr. Bosanquet, Preface, p. vii.

18 'Charity and Social Life,' C. S. Loch, p. 393. Macmillan, 1910.

19 Ibid. pp. 386–7.

20 'Misery and its Causes,' E. T. Devine. Macmillan & Co., 1909.

21 Ibid. p. 267.

22 'The Strength of the People,' Helen Bosanquet, p. 114. Macmillan, 1902.

23 Ibid. p. 115.

24 'How to Deal with the Unemployed Poor of London, etc.' Paper read by the Rev. H. Solly at the Society of Arts, June 22nd, 1868, which brought about the formation of the 'Association for the Prevention of Pauperism and Crime.'

25 'The Charities of London, etc.,' T. Hawksley, M.D. Read at a meeting of the Association for Preventing Pauperism and Crime, December 17th, 1868.
26 'The Crisis of Liberalism,' J. A. Hobson, p. 205.
27 'Sweated Industry,' Clementina Black, p. 155.
28 'Aspects of the Social Problem,' B. Bosanquet, Preface, p. vii.
29 See 'The Strength of the People.'
30 'Sweated Industry,' Clementina Black, p. 155.

FABIAN TRACT No. 162
(February 1912)

FAMILY LIFE ON A POUND A WEEK

Mrs. Pember Reeves

Who are the poor? Are only those people counted poor who are driven to sleep on the Embankment or to throng the casual wards? Or does the term cover all cheap labor? If so, at what wage does poverty begin? Attention is often diverted from the condition of an individual or of a class by the perfectly accurate announcement that there are 'plenty of people worse off than that,' to which statement would probably be added the generally accepted formula that the poor should be divided into the 'undeserving' and 'deserving.' Deserving of what? Nobody likes to say 'of sufficient pay for the work they do.' And yet if they do not deserve that, what do they deserve?

It is the purpose of this tract to describe the resources of London working men and their families when the wages range between 18s. and 24s. a week. These men are often somebody's laborers, or they may be carters, horse-keepers, porters, railway carriage washers, fishfryers, and perhaps one may be a borough council street sweeper on half time. They are in regular work and receiving a regular wage, which means that they are not in any sense casuals, though they suffer at times from unemployment and live in the dread of it. Whole streets are inhabited by this class of family. They 'keep themselves to themselves' with as much anxiety and respectability as the dwellers in a West End square. They generally live in the upper or lower half of a small house, for the whole rent of which either they or the other family are responsible to the landlord. A kind of sordid decency is the chief characteristic of their horribly monotonous streets. Mile after mile of them, every house alike except for the baker's or greengrocer's shop at the corner, they cross and recross, broken occasionally by big thoroughfares where trams, omnibuses, and public houses are. A church, a chapel, or more often a school, makes a welcome oasis in the architectural desert. The ordinary visitor seldom finds access to these houses, where the people are jealously respectable and make no claim on any charity or institution other than the hospital.

The Cost of Houseroom

How does a Lambeth working man's wife with four children manage on a pound a week? If ordinary middle class persons were to attempt the calculation, they would stop with a sense of shock and come to the conclusion that everything, from rent to food, must be very cheap in Lambeth. Now is this so? The chief divisions in a twenty shilling budget are rent, insurance, light and heat, food. To begin with rent, a good unfurnished room in Lambeth, measuring twelve feet by fifteen feet, costs 4s. a week. A house of eighteen rooms, with storage for coal, with hot and cold water system, and sinks and waste pipes throughout, can be obtained in Kensington, rent, rates, and taxes included, for £250 a year. If the tenant of this house paid 4s. a week for every twenty square yards of his floor space, he would, roughly speaking, pay £385 a year. But if he paid 4s. a week for the same amount of cubic space that the Lambeth man gets for his 4s., the West End householder would pay about £500 a year instead of £250. These figures are approximate, but they are calculated from real instances. Add to this that the large house has better air, greater quiet, and healthier surroundings. The man who pays a rent of 7s. or 8s. in South London may be paying over one third of his income, for which he may get three tiny rooms in a four roomed dwelling, with a mother or other relative occupying and paying for the fourth room. The living room may be ten feet by eight feet, and three of its walls may be pierced by doors, the room itself being the passage way to the back yard. Two slightly larger rooms are bedrooms. A family of eight persons divides into two parties, four elder children sleep in one bed in one room, while the parents and two younger children sleep in the other. The four elder children go, perhaps, to three different schools. When one of them brings home measles from its school measles go round the bed; when another brings home whooping cough from its school the same course is pursued by whooping cough. The afflicted children are kept away from school, but the baby and the two year old, who are both teething, have no chance of escape. The distracted mothers do what they can, but in many cases the rooms are terribly damp, and in many the chimneys smoke continually. The convalescence of the children – if they do convalesce – is difficult and prolonged. For one third of his income then the man with £1 or 22s. a week cannot afford space enough for health. His wife may have to carry

201

all her water upstairs and, when it is used, carry it down again. There is no storage for coal; perhaps no room for the humblest mailcart for the baby. Add to this that as likely as not the walls are old and infested with bugs, which defy the cleanest woman, and can only be kept under by constant fumigation and repapering. It is obvious that the well-to-do man for less than a third of his income can afford a better bargain than this for the housing of his family.

Coal is another necessary which the poor cannot afford to buy economically. The woman with 20s. a week must buy by the hundredweight. She pays from 1s. 4d. in the summer to 1s. 7d. or 1s. 8d. in the winter. The same quality of coal can be bought by the ton in Kensington for less than 1s. per cwt. in the summer and for 1s. 1d. in the winter. Gas also is dearer by the pennyworth than by the 1,000 cubic feet.

Certain kinds of food can be bought cheaply in Lambeth Walk of a Sunday morning – meat which would not be saleable on Monday – vegetables in the same plight. But sugar has risen as ruthlessly for the poor as for the rich, milk has done the same, and even the tinned milk which is separated before being tinned, and which is the only milk a woman with 20s. a week can afford, is now a halfpenny more a tin. Bread is no cheaper in Lambeth than in Kensington, but the Lambeth woman buys hers at the shop because she is then entitled to the legal weight, whereas the 'delivered' bread of the West End is known as 'fancy' bread by the trade and is generally under weight.

Insurance for Funerals

Insurance in Lambeth (up to the time of writing) means burial insurance. The middle class man does not need to pay out something like a twentieth part of his income in order to provide for the possible burials in his family. The poorly paid working man is driven to this great expense for two reasons. First, he is likely to lose one or more of his children, and the poorer he is the more likely he is to lose them; second, the cost of a funeral, including cemetery fees, is out of all proportion to his means. It is generally supposed that poor people, rather than miss the delight of a gorgeous funeral, will dissipate money which ought to be spent on rent or food or thrift. As a matter of fact undertakers in Lambeth or Kennington will bury an infant for the sum of 28s. or 30s. This includes the cemetery fee of 10s. An older child will cost according to size, a child of three perhaps £2 5s., until the length of the body is too great to go under the box seat of the funeral vehicle, when a hearse becomes necessary and the price leaps to something like

£4 4s. At a later stage the cemetery fee goes up. Under these circumstances the poor man has as alternatives burial by the parish and insurance. It is the insurance which is the extravagance – not the way he manages his funerals. But his fear of being made a pauper or of being driven to borrow the price of a child's funeral keeps his wife paying a weekly sum, varying with the number of children, of from 6d. to 1s. or even over. One penny a week from birth barely covers the funeral expenses at any age in childhood. Adults commonly pay 2d. a week. A peculiar hardship which often befalls the poor man is that, owing to periods of unemployment, his payments are interrupted and his policies may therefore lapse. His children are at those times less well fed and more likely to die, and he may quite well be driven to the disgrace of a pauper burial after having paid insurance for many years. Burial by the parish is taboo among the poor. It is no use arguing the case with them. The parents fiercely resent being made paupers because of their bereavement. Moreover they consider the pauper burial unnecessarily wanting in dignity and respect. They say that as soon as have the parish they would have the dustman call for their dead. The three years' old daughter of a carter out of work died of tuberculosis. The father, whose policies had lapsed, borrowed the sum of £2 5s. necessary to bury the child. The mother was four months paying the debt off by reducing the food of herself and of the five other children. To reduce the food of the breadwinner is an impossibility. The funeral cortège consisted of one vehicle in which the little coffin went under the driver's seat. The parents and a neighbour sat in the back part of the vehicle. They saw the child buried in a common grave with twelve other coffins of all sizes. 'We 'ad to keep a sharp eye out for Edie,' they said; 'she were so little she were almost 'id.'

The following is an account kept of the funeral of a child of six months who died of infantile cholera in the deadly month of August, 1911.

The parents had insured her for 2d. a week, being unusually careful people. The sum received was £2.

	£	s	d
Funeral	£1	12	0
Death certificate	0	1	3
Gravediggers	0	2	0
Hearse attendants	0	2	0
Woman to lay her out	0	2	0
Insurance agent	0	1	0
Flowers	0	0	6
Black tie for father	0	1	0
	£2	1	9

This child was buried in a common grave with three others. There is no display and no extravagance in this list. The tips to the gravediggers, hearse attendants and insurance agent were all urgently applied for, though not in every case by the person who received the money. The cost of the child's illness had amounted to 10s. – chiefly spent on special food. The survivors lived on reduced rations for two weeks in order to get square again. The father's wage was 24s., every penny of which he always handed over to his wife. Until burial can be made an honorable public service there seems to be no hope of relief in this direction for the family living on any sum round about £1 a week.

How the Budgets were obtained

In order to explain how the family budgets given further on were obtained, it is necessary to state that an investigation has been carried on for three years by a small committee formed of members of the Fabian Women's Group. The investigation has for its object observation of the effect on mother and child of proper nourishment before and after birth.

To further this enquiry it was found necessary to take down each week in writing the whole family expenditure for that week. The budgets thus collected began before the birth of the child and continued until that child was a year old. The names of expectant mothers were taken at random from the out-patient department of a well known lying-in hospital. Only legally married people were dealt with because the hospital confined itself to such persons. The committee decided to refuse cases where virulent disease in the parents might outweigh the benefits of proper nourishment, but it was considered that moderate drinking on the part of the parents would probably be a normal condition and must therefore be accepted. As a matter of fact, tuberculosis in some form or other was found to be so common that to rule it out would be to refuse almost half the cases. Respiratory and tuberculous disease was therefore accepted. With regard to drink, on the contrary, only one instance did we find of a woman who drank. A few men were supposed to take a glass, but in every case but one they faithfully rendered over to their wives the agreed upon weekly allowance. Out of fifty cases taken at haphazard this is a good record.

As may well be imagined, the visitors did not find accounts in being. The women 'knew it in their heads,' they said, but to write it down was absurdly impossible. Gradually, however, the interest grew, and with patience a few weeks generally saw some kind of record of the family expenditure. The first attempts taught the investigator far more than they taught the mother. A book was supplied to each woman, and week after week she entered in it every penny she received and spent. Wednesday was the great day when, with her floor scrubbed and her hair as tidy as she could manage, she disentangled these accounts with the aid of the visitor. Her spelling was curious, but her arithmetic was generally correct. 'Sewuitt. . . 1²/₁' was as serious an error as the figures often knew. 'Coul . . . thruppons' is Lambeth for 'cow-heel . . . 3d.' Seeing the visitor hesitate over the item 'yearn . . . 1d,' the offended mother wrote next week, 'yearn is for mending sokes.' Eight women were found who could neither read nor write. Sometimes they had only forgotten, and were capable of being coaxed back into literary endeavour, but in a few stubborn cases the husband came to the rescue, and in three, eldest sons or daughters, aged ten or twelve, were the scribes. One wrote in large copperplate, 'peper . . . apeny,' which threatened to remain ambiguous till his return from school. Fortunately the mother had a burst of memory. Another entry, 'earrins . . . too d' gave a lot of trouble, but turned out to mean 'herrings . . . 2d.' A literary genius of thirteen kept her accounts as a kind of diary, part of which ran as follows.

'Mr. D, ad too diners for thruppence, wich is not mutch e bein such a arty man.'

Pages of this serial had to be reduced, though with regret, to the limits of ordinary accounts. Many of the women enjoyed their task, and proudly produced correct budgets week after week.

A typical budget is that of Mrs. X. Her husband is a railway carriage washer, who earns 18s. for a six days week and 21s. every other week when he works seven days. He pays his wife all that he earns. There are three children. The two budgets were taken on March 22nd and March 29th, 1911.

A 21s. WEEK.

	s.	d.	
Rent	7	0	
Clothing club	1	2	for two weeks.
Insurance	1	6	for two weeks.
Coal and wood	1	7	
Coke	0	3	
Gas	0	10	
Soap, soda	0	5	
Matches	0	1	
Blacklead, blacking	0	1	
	12	11	

Left for food 8s. 1d.

	s.	d.
11 loaves	2	7
1 quartern flour	0	5½
Meat	1	10
Potatoes and greens	0	9½
½ lb. butter	0	6
1 lb. jam	0	3
6 oz. tea	0	6
2 lb. sugar	0	4
1 tin milk	0	4
Cocoa	0	4
Suet	0	2
	8	1

Average per head for food 1s. 7½d. a week, or less than 3d. a day all round the family. But a working man cannot do on less than 6d. a day, which means 3s. 6d. a week. This reduces the average of the mother and children to 1s. 1¾d. or less than 2d. a day.

AN 18S. WEEK.

	s.	d.
Rent	7	0
Coal and wood	1	7
Gas	0	10
Soap, soda	0	5
Matches	0	1
	9	11

Left for food 8s. 1d.

	s.	d.
11 loaves	2	7
1 quartern flour	0	5½
Meat	1	9½
Potatoes and greens	0	9
½ lb. butter	0	6
1 lb. jam	0	3
6 oz. tea	0	6
2 lb. sugar	0	4
1 tin milk	0	4
Cocoa	0	4
Suet	0	3
	8	1

Average per head for food 1s. 7½d. a week, or less than 3d. a day.

In the same street lives Mrs. Y, whose husband is a laborer who works at Hackney Marshes, a long way off. He earns 24s. and gives his wife 19s. 6d. His fares cost 3s. 6d. a week. There are three children. Date of visit October 25th, 1911.

	s.	d.
Rent	7	0
Insurance	0	7
Calico club	0	6
Coal club	1	0
Soap, soda	0	4½
Gas	0	8
Blacklead and blacking	0	1
Mangling	0	2
Wood	0	1
1 yard flannelette	0	2¾
Hearthstone	0	0½
	10	8¾

Left for food 8s. 9¼d.

	s.	d.
7 loaves and 7 loaf bottoms	2	7½
½ quartern flour	0	2¾
Meat	2	9½
Potatoes and greens	0	10
1 lb. butter	0	10
½ lb. tea	0	7
3 lb. sugar	0	7½
Fish	0	3
	8	9¼

Average for food per head 1s. 9d. a week, or 3d. a day.

Mr. Y. is rather a bigger man than most Lambeth workers, and requires at least 4s. a week spent on his food. Hardly too large an allowance for a working man. But that reduces the average spent on the rest of the family to 1s. 2¼d. a week per head or 2d. a day.

The housekeeping allowance is often all that the man earns. The wife either allows him a few coppers for fares, or not, as she can afford. Where the wage is regular, but below £1 a week, this is usually the case. A man with 24s. will keep 2s. or 2s. 6d., and will dress, drink, smoke, and pay fares out of it. A very usual amount for a man to pay his wife is 20s. a week. It almost looks as though there were an understanding that, where possible, that is the correct sum. The workman earning 20s. a week often pays it all over to his wife. If his wages rise to 22s. he goes on paying the 20s. and keeps the extra money. Given, then, the 20s. a week it entirely depends on how many children there are, whether the family lives on insufficient food or on miserably insufficient food – whether the family is merely badly housed or is frightfully crowded as well as badly housed.

To illustrate this, here are the budgets of three women with varying numbers of children, each of whom is allowed 23s. a week – an amount which generally means that the husband is earning about 25s. In one of these cases this is so, but in the other two it will be noticed that the 23s. is the whole family income. In spite of this, and in spite of the fact that it is above the average allowance, the amount spent a week per head on food falls to 1s. 1¼d. all round when there are six children. If 3s. 6d. be spent on the man, the average for the woman and children is 9¼d. per week.

Mr. A, horsekeeper, wages 25s., gives wife 23s., three children born, three alive, five persons to feed. March 24th, 1909.

	s.	d.
Rent	6	6
Insurance	0	10
1 cwt. coal	1	6
Lamp oil	0	5
Boots	1	6½
Soap and soda	0	4
Wood	0	2
	11	3½

Left for food 11s. 8½d.

	s.	d.
11 loaves	2	6¼
Meat	3	11
Potatoes	0	10
Greens	0	2½
1 lb. margarine, 1 lb. jam	0	9
8 oz. tea	0	8
2 tins milk	0	6
2 lbs. sugar	0	4½
½ quartern flour	0	3
Bacon and fish	0	11
Rice	0	3
Suet	0	2¼
Pot herbs	0	4
	11	8½

Average for food per head a week 2s. 4d. or 4d. a day.

Mr. B sells on commission, earns about 15s., boy earns 2s., girl 6s., wife gets in all 23s., five children born, five alive, seven persons to feed. July 6th, 1910.

	s.	d.
Rent	7	6
Insurance	0	7
½ cwt. coal	0	7½
Gas	1	0
Boots	2	6
Soap and soda	0	4¼
Hat	1	0¾
Saved	0	2¼
	13	9¾

Left for food 9s. 2¼d.

	s.	d.
9½ loaves	2	3
Meat	2	6
Potatoes	0	7
Greens	0	2½
1 lb. butter	1	0
7 oz. tea	0	7
1 tin milk	0	3½
3 lbs. sugar	0	6¾
½ quartern flour	0	2½
Bacon	0	4½
Cornflour	0	2½
Currants	0	1½
½ lb. cheese	0	3½
	9	2¼

Average for food per head a week 1s. 3¾d. or 2¼d. a day.

Mr. C, carter, wages 23s., gives wife 23s., seven children born, six alive, eight persons to feed. April 21st, 1910.

	s.	d.
Rent	8	6
Insurance	1	0
1 cwt. coal	1	6
Gas	0	11
Boots mended	1	8¼
Clothing club	0	6
	14	1¼

Left for food 8s. 10¾d.

	s.	d.
14 loaves	3	2½
Meat	2	0¼
Potatoes	0	9
Greens	0	3
2 lb. margarine	1	0
4 oz. tea	0	4
No milk		
4½ lb. sugar	0	9
½ quartern flour	0	3
No bacon		
Dripping	0	4
	8	10¾

Average for food per head a week 1s. 1¼d. or almost 2d. a day.

In these three budgets the women housed their families as well as they could and economized in food when the family increased. The rooms were as large and light as they could get – inadequate and bad, of course, but not specially dark or damp. Mrs. B needed less coal in July, so she laid out extra money on clothes. She always saved, if it were only a farthing. It is curious to note how with the larger family the first set of expenses goes up and the amount left over for food goes down. On the whole these families were about equally housed. The first two women have so far reared all their children. Mrs. C has lost one. Compare this result with the second and third of the following budgets, where the women economized in rent in order to spend more on food.

Mr. D, emergency 'bus conductor, wages 4s. a day, four or five days a week, five children born, five alive. August 25th, 1910.

	s.	d.
Rent	9	0★
Insurance	0	7
½ cwt. coal	0	8
Gas	0	4
Soap, soda	0	2
Matches	0	1
	10	10

★Three light, dry, airy rooms at top of model dwelling.

Left for food 6s. 6½d.

	s.	d.
10 loaves	2	3½
Meat	1	8

	s.	d.
Potatoes	0	6
Vegetables	0	2
1 lb. margarine	0	7½
6 oz. tea	0	6
2 tins milk	0	6
1½ lb. sugar	0	3½
	6	6½

Week's average per head for food 11¼d. or 1¾d. a day.

Mr. E, fishmonger's assistant, wages 24s., seven children born, four alive. March 24th, 1910.

	s.	d.
Rent	5	6★
Insurance	0	7
1¾ cwt. coal	2	3
Gas	1	0
Starch, soap, soda	0	5
Wood	0	1
Newspaper	0	1
	9	11

★Two fair sized, but very dark, damp rooms in deep basement.

Left for food 12s. 7½d.

	s.	d.
10 loaves	2	3½
Meat	5	2
Potatoes	0	6
Greens	0	4
1 lb. butter, 1 lb. jam	1	3½
8 oz. tea	0	8
6½ pints fresh milk	1	1
2½ lb. sugar	0	5¼
½ qrtn. flour	0	2¾
Bacon	0	6
Currants	0	1½
	12	7½

Week's average per head for food 2s. 1¼d. or 3¾d. a day.

Mr. F, carter, wages 22s., nine children born, four alive. July 14th, 1910.

	s.	d.
Rent	4	6★
Insurance	0	8½

	s.	d.
1 cwt. coal	1	6
Lamp oil	0	8
Starch, soap, soda	0	5
Boot club	1	0
Clothing club	0	6
	9	3½

*Two tiny rooms in very old one storey cottage below level of alley way.

Left for food 10s. 8½d.

	s.	d.
11 loaves	2	6
Meat and fish	3	0
Potatoes	0	8
Vegetables	0	5
1 lb. margarine, 1 lb. jam	0	10½
8 oz. tea	0	8
1 tin milk	0	3½
4 lb. sugar	0	10
1 qrtn. flour	0	6
Bovril	0	6½
2 lb. rice	0	4
Salt, pepper	0	1
	10	8½

Week's average per head for food 1s. 9½d. or 3d. a day.

All the children in these three families are delicate. Perhaps there is a worse heredity in the case of Mrs. D's children than in the other two. Mrs. D, who had only 17s. 4½d. to spend and a child more to spend it on, paid 3s. 6d. more in rent than Mrs. E, and 4s. 6d. more than Mrs. F. She spent less on coal and gas than either of the others – even taking into account that July is a warm, light month. She spent less on cleaning and nothing on clothes. She fed her family – her husband, herself and five children – on 11¼d. a head a week. All her children were living.

Mrs. E, who lives in very damp, dark rooms, has to spend heavily on coal and gas to keep them warm and lighted. Even for the time of year she takes an unusual amount of coal. She spends more on cleaning, and takes in a Sunday paper. She had 22s. 6½d. to spend, and was able to allow 2s. 1½d. a week a head for food. She has lost three children.

Mrs. F economizes in food as well as rent, and spends 1s. 6d. a week on clothing. She has lost five children.

Each of these families had lived a very long time in the rooms described. The three women were clean, hardworking, and tidy to a fault. The men decent, kindly, sober and industrious. The comparison of the two tables seems to show that air, light and freedom from damp are as necessary to the health of young children as even sufficient and proper food. In fact, the mother who provided good housing conditions and fed the family on 11¼d. a head per week, did better for her children than the mother who lived in the underground rooms – spent plenty of money on coal, and fed her family on 2s. 1¼d. a head per week. The poor mother who economized on both food and rent in order to clothe decently did worst of all.

Another budget which compares interestingly on this point with Mrs. F's is that of Mrs. G. She has slightly over 20s. a week, sometimes a few pence over, sometimes more than a shilling over. She houses her children better than Mrs. F does, and spends much less a week on food. She has reared all her six children.

Mr. G, printer's laborer, wages 24s., six children born, six living. He goes a long distance to his work and is obliged to spend on fares. Date of budget, September 20th, 1911.

Mrs. G.	s.	d.
Rent	8	0
Insurance	1	8
¾ cwt. coal	1	0
Gas	0	11
Starch, soap, soda	0	5
Boot club	1	0
Clothing club	0	6
Boot laces	0	1½
Matches	0	1
Blacking	0	0½
	13	9

Left for food 7s. 11d.

	s.	d.
14 loaves	2	11
Meat	2	0
Potatoes	0	6
Vegetables	0	4
1 lb. margarine	0	6
No tea		
2 tins milk	0	7
2 lb. sugar	0	5
1 qrtn. flour	0	5

	s.	d.
Salt	0	1
Pot herbs	0	2
	7	11

Week's average per head for food 1s.

Mrs. F.	s.	d.
Rent	4	6
Insurance	0	8½
1 cwt. coal	1	6
Lamp oil	0	8
Starch, soap, soda	0	5
Boot club	1	0
Clothing club	0	6
	9	3½

Left for food 10s. 8½d.

	s.	d.
11 loaves	2	6
Meat and fish	3	0
Potatoes	0	8
Vegetables	0	5
Margarine and jam	0	10½
8 oz. tea	0	8
1 tin milk	0	3½
4 lb. sugar	0	10
1 qrtn. flour	0	6
Salt, pepper	0	1
Bovril	0	6½
2 lb. rice	0	4
	10	8½

Week's average per head for food 1s. 9½d.

It will be seen that Mrs. G spends a regular 1s. 6d. a week on clothes, the same amount that Mrs F does. She has 21s. 8d. to spend, where Mrs. F has 20s., but she has six children, whereas Mrs. F has four. She spends 3s. 6d. a week more on rent, and certainly houses her family better, having three small, inconvenient, crowded, but fairly light, dry rooms, in place of Mrs. F's terrible little abode. She buys cheaper bread and flour, and spends but 1s. a week a head on food. She has lost no children, whereas Mrs. F has lost five. It is not to be supposed that the surviving children of Mrs. F, or the children of Mrs. G are robust and strong. Poverty has killed Mrs. F's five weakest children and drained the vitality of her four stronger ones. Poverty has prevented any of

Mrs. G's children from being strong. The malnutrition of school children, which was so conspicuously mentioned in the published report of Sir George Newman, Chief Medical Officer of the Board of Education, seems to be explained by these budgets. The idea that mothers who have to feed man, woman and children on 1s. a head a week can do anything else than underfeed them must be abandoned. But it is also evident that the mothers who in desperation try economizing in rent in order to feed better are doing unwisely.

The question of food values is much discussed in connection with ignorance and extravagance on the part of the poor. It is possible, of course, that a shilling, or elevenpence farthing might be laid out to better advantage on a week's food than is done in the foregoing budgets. But superior food value generally means longer cooking – more utensils – more wholesome air and storage conveniences than can be commanded by these women. To take porridge as an instance. When well cooked for an hour and eaten with milk and sugar, most children would find it delicious and wholesome. But when the remainder of last night's pennyworth of gas is all that can be allowed for its cooking, when the pot is the same as that in which fish or potatoes or meat are cooked, when it has to be eaten half raw without milk and with but a hint of sugar, the children loathe it. They eat bread and dripping with relish. No cooking is required there, for which the weary, harassed mother is only too thankful – so they almost live on bread and dripping. A normal menu for a family of seven persons living on £1 a week is as follows:–

Breakfast for seven persons.

1 loaf; 1 oz. dripping or margarine; ¼ oz. tea; ½ oz. sugar; ¼d. worth tinned milk.

Dinners.

Sunday, 3 lb. meat; 3 lb. potatoes; 1 cabbage.
Monday, any meat left from Sunday, with suet pudding. The father on weekdays taking a chop or other food with him to work.
Tuesday, Thursday, Friday, Saturday, suet pudding, with treacle or sugar, or gravy and potatoes.
Wednesday, 1 lb. meat and potatoes stewed with onions.

Tea for seven persons.

1 loaf; 1 oz. dripping or margarine; ¼ oz. tea; ½ oz. sugar; ¼d. worth of tinned milk; Saturday evening may see a rasher or a bloater for the man's tea.

215

It will be noticed both from the budgets and from this menu that tinned milk is the only milk which the mother can afford. Each of these threepenny tins bears round it in red letters the words 'This milk is not recommended as food for infants.' Nevertheless it is the only milk the infants get unless their mother can nurse them. If the mothers are able to nurse they always do for two very convincing reasons – it is cheaper – it is less trouble. But the milk of a mother fed on such diet is not the elixir of life which it could be, and which, under different conditions, it should be. Very often it fails her altogether. Then the child is fed on tinned milk. When it is fractious, because it is miserably unsatisfied, it is given a dummy teat to suck or a raisin wrapped in a bit of rag. This is not because the mother is ignorant of the fact that she could nurse much better if she took plenty of milk, or that if her child must be brought up by hand it were better to feed it from the M.B.C. milk depôt. It is because milk usually costs 4d. a quart, and just now costs 5d., and either price is prohibitive. The milk depôt feeds a new baby for 9d. a week till it is three months old, when 1s. 6d. is charged. The price rises regularly till it reaches something like 3s. at the age of a year. In a family where the weekly average is 1s., or even 1s. 3d., 1s. 6d. cannot be devoted to the new baby without cutting down the average for everybody else. So baby often has 'jest wot we 'ave ourselves.' It is all there is for him to have.

Meals and Manners

The diet for the other children is chiefly bread, with suet pudding for a change. Often they do not sit down for a meal; it is not worth while. A table is covered with newspaper and as many plates as there are children are put round with a portion on each. The eating of this meal may take ten minutes or perhaps less. The children stand round, eat, snatch up caps and hats, and are off to school again. Breakfast and tea are, as often as not, eaten while the child plays in the yard or walks to school. A slice of bread, spread with something, is handed to each, and they eat it how and where they will. In some cases the father comes home for a meal at some inconvenient hour in the afternoon, such as half past three or four or five. This may mean that the children's chief meal takes place then in order to economize coal or gas and make one cooking do. This is not because the mother is lazy and indifferent to her children's well being. It is because she has but one pair of hands and but one overburdened brain. She can just get through her day if she does everything she has to do inefficiently. Give her six children, and between the bearing of them and the rearing of them she has little extra vitality left for scientific cooking, even if she could afford the necessary time and appliances. In fact one woman is not equal to the bearing and efficient, proper care of six children. She can make one bed for four of them, but if she had to make four beds, if she had to separate the boys from the girls and keep two rooms clean instead of one, if she had to make proper clothing and keep those clothes properly washed and ironed and mended, if she had to give each child a daily bath, if she had to attend thoroughly to teeth, noses, ears, and eyes, if she had to cook really nourishing food, with adequate utensils and dishes, and if she had to wash up these utensils and dishes after every meal, she would need not only far more money, but far more help. The children of the poor suffer from want of light, want of air, want of warmth, want of sufficient and proper food, and want of clothes, because the wage of their fathers is not enough to pay for these necessaries. They also suffer from want of cleanliness, want of attention to health, want of peace and quiet, because the strength of their mothers is not enough to provide these necessary conditions.

Clothing

It is easy to say that the mothers manage badly. If they economize in rent the children die. If they economize in food the children may live, but in a weakened state. There is nothing else that they can economize in. Fuel and light are used sparingly; there is no room for reduction there. Clothes hardly appear in the poorer budgets at all. In the course of fifteen months visiting, one family on 23s. a week spent £3 5s. 5½d. on clothes for the mother and six children. Half of the sum was spent on boots, so that the clothes, other than boots, of seven people cost 32s. 9d. in fifteen months, an average of 4s. 8d. a head. Another family spent 9d. a week on boots and 9d. a week on clothes in general. There were four children. Other families again only buy clothes when summer comes and less is needed for fuel. Boots are the chief expense under this heading, and few fathers in Lambeth are not able to sole a little boot with some sort of skill. Most of the body clothing is bought third and fourth hand. How it is that the women's garments do not drop off them is a mystery. They never seem to buy new ones, and yet the hard wear to which the clothes are subjected ought to finish them in a month. It is obvious that clothing can hardly be further reduced. Remains insurance. It has been shown that steady, hardworking people refuse to have their dead buried by the parish. If they should change their attitude to this question and decide to economize here, it is difficult to imagine the state of mind of the 'parish' when confronted by the problem.

How then is the man on a pound a week to house his children decently and feed them sufficiently? How is his wife to care for them properly? The answer is that, in London at least, be they never so hardworking and sober and thrifty, the task is impossible.

But there is a large class who get less than a pound a week. There is also a large class who get work irregularly. How do such people manage?

A small proportion of the cases undertaken in the investigation, from ill health and other causes, fell out of work. Their subsequent struggles afford material with which to answer this question.

Mr. H, carter, out of work through illness, gets an odd job once or twice in the week. Wages 24s. when in work. Six children born, five alive.

July 7th, 1910, had earned 5s. 5d.

	s.	d.
Rent	goes	unpaid
Insurance	lapsed	
Coal	0	2
Soap, soda	0	4
Gas	0	6
Matches	0	1
Blacklead	0	0½
	1	1½

Leaving for food 4s. 3½d.

	s.	d.
9 loaves	2	0¾
Meat	0	9
Potatoes	0	3
Vegetables	0	1
Margarine	0	1¾
3 oz. tea	0	3
Tinned milk	none	
1½ lb. sugar	0	3
Dripping	0	6
	4	3½

Or an average per head for food of 7¼d. a week, or 1d. a day.

July 14th had earned 15s. 10d.

	s.	d.
Rent (two weeks)	11	0
Insurance	lapsed	
Coal	0	2
Gas	0	5

	s.	d.
Soap, soda, blue	0	4½
Wood	0	0½
	12	0

Leaving for food 3s. 10d.

	s.	d.
7 loaves	1	7¼
Meat	0	6
Potatoes	0	3½
Vegetables	0	1
Margarine		—
4 oz. tea	0	4
Tinned milk		—
1½ lb. sugar	0	3
Dripping	0	6
1 lb. jam	0	3¼
	3	10

Or an average per head for food of 6½d. a week, or less than 1d. a day.

Mr. I, bottle washer, out of work through illness, wife earned what she could. Wages 18s. when in work. One child born, one alive.

August 10th, 1910. Mrs. I had earned 2s. 6d.

	s.	d.
Rent	went	unpaid
Insurance		lapsed
Coal		—
Lamp oil		—
Soap, soda		—
	nothing	

Mrs. I was told by infirmary doctor to feed her husband up.

	s.	d.
3 loaves	0	8¼
Meat	1	1
Potatoes	0	3
Vegetables	0	0¾
3 oz. tea	0	3
1 lb. sugar	0	2
	2	6

Average per head for food 10d. or 1½d. a day.

219

August 17th. Mrs. I had earned 3s. 6d.

	s.	d.
Rent	went unpaid	
Insurance	—	
Coal	0	4
Lamp oil	0	2
Soap	0	2
Firewood	0	1
	0	9

Mrs. I still feeding her husband up.

	s.	d.
4 loaves	0	11
Meat	1	0
Potatoes	0	2
Vegetables	0	1
1 oz. tea	0	1
1½ lb. sugar	0	3
Margarine	0	3
	2	9

Average per head for food 11d. or 1⁴/₇d. per day.

When Mr. I could earn again, his back rent amounted to 15s. He found work at Finsbury Park, he living south of Kennington Park. He walked to and from his work every day, refusing to move because he and his wife were known in Kennington, and rather than see them go into the 'house' their friends would help them through a bad spell. People in that class never write, and to move away from friends and relations is to quit the last hope of assistance should misfortune come. Mr. Y, who works on Hackney Marshes while living at Kennington, is another instance of this. A fish fryer who had to take work at Finsbury Park declared that he walked eighteen miles a day to and from his work.

Mr. J, carter out of work through illness, took out an organ when well enough to push it. Wages 18s. when in work. Six children born, six alive.

Those children who were of school age in these three families were fed once a day for five days a week during term time. None of the children were earning. The three women were extremely clean and, as far as their wretched means would allow, were good managers. It is impossible to lay out to advantage money which comes in spasmodically and belated, so that some urgent need must be attended to with each penny as it is earned. After a certain point of starvation food must come first, though before that point

is reached it is extraordinary how often rent seems to be made a
first charge on wages.

Jan. 26th, 1910, Mr. and Mrs. J had earned between them 9s.

Feb. 2nd,	,,	,,	,,	,, 7s.
Feb. 9th,	,,	,,	,,	,, 8s. 10d.
Feb. 16th,	,,	,,	,,	,, 9s.
Feb. 23rd,	,,	,,	,,	,, 7s. 6d.

	Jan. 26th		Feb. 2nd		Feb. 9th		Feb. 16th		Feb. 23rd	
	s.	d.	s.	d.	s.	d.	s.	d.	s.	d.
Rent	5	6	3	0	5	6	5	6	3	6
Coal	0	6	0	6	0	4	0	6	0	6
Wood	0	1	0	1	0	1	0	1	0	1½
Lamp oil	0	1	0	1	0	1	0	1	0	1½
Soap, soda	0	2	0	2	0	2	0	2	0	4
	6	4	3	10	6	2	6	4	4	7
Leaving for food	2	8	3	2	2	8	2	8	2	11
Average for food per head a week in holidays	0	4	almost	5	0	4	0	4	0	4½

It is an undoubted fact that the great majority of babies born to
this class of parent come into the world normal as regards weight;
rosy fat little creatures who should flourish and thrive in decent
conditions. At the end of a year they show many signs of delicacy
most of which have been created by lack of warmth, lack of air,
lack of light, lack of medical care, lack of food. It seems certain
that could these children have what is necessary to a healthy child
they are capable of growing up into healthy men and women.
Baby clinics, school clinics, free public baths, free public wash-
houses would seem to be but the beginning of a scheme of national
care for the nation's children. The argument that the conditions
described in this tract are useful in that they kill off the sickly
children and allow the stronger to survive is an argument which
is not followed by its supporters to a logical conclusion. The
conditions which kill a weak child drain and devitalize strong
children. For every one who dies three or four others live to be in
need later on of sanatorium or hospital, or even asylum. It would
surely pay the nation to turn its attention to the rearing of its
children. It is no use urging that parents are drunken, and lazy and
vicious; where that is true all the more do their children need
protection and care; in fact, they only have to be drunken and lazy
and vicious enough, for their children to be boarded out by the
local authority, and four shillings paid weekly for their food alone,
a sum undreamed of by the ordinary decent mother on a pound a
week. If the parents, with all the strength, with all the industry,

with all the thrift, with all the anxious care shown by these budgets, can only lodge their children as they do, and feed them as they do, what is the use of appealing to the parents for what only money can procure, money being the one thing they have not got? If this rich and powerful nation desires to have strong, healthy children, who are worthy of it, what is to prevent it? There is no reason why the school children should suffer from malnutrition, or why an unusually beautiful summer should kill off the babies like flies.

What Can be Done?

The remedy for this state of things is not easy to devise. Advance is likely to be made along two lines where it has already begun – the growing demand for a national minimum wage and the responsibility for the nation's children which is being increasingly assumed by the State. Trade boards are a beginning, piecemeal and tentative, which should make a starting point for a strong effort to attain a national minimum wage throughout the kingdom. It would be comparatively simple to define a fair wage for the individual worker. In Fabian Tract No. 128, 'The Case for a Legal Minimum Wage,' the difficulties and limitations, as well as the advantages, of that bed of Procrustes, a family minimum wage, are very fully dealt with. But, after all, the whole question raised by these budgets is one of children. A wage which was a tight fit for three children would be miserably inadequate for six or seven. Add to this that there is no certainty that the wage earner, man or woman, would always spend the whole wage upon actual necessaries. If amusements, however innocent, were brought into the budget, something already in it would have to go. Very moderate drinking would upset the balance altogether. It is not reasonable to expect working class men and women never to spend on other things than rent, insurance, clothing, firing, and food. Middle class people do not expect from themselves such iron self-control. Children, once an economic asset, are now a cause of expense, continually increased by legislation, which tends more and more to take children and young persons out of the labor market. The State, which has wisely decreed that children shall not be self-supporting, has no more valuable asset than these children were they reared under conditions favorable to child life instead of in the darkness and dampness and semi-starvation which is all that the decent, hardworking poor can now afford. Any minimum wage which is likely to be wrung from the pockets of the employing class during the next few years would not affect the question raised by the earlier budgets in this tract where the wage is already over £1 a week. Therefore, along with a strenuous demand for a national minimum wage, advance must be made on the line already laid down by the State in its provision of free and compulsory education for its children and in its statutory endorsement of the principle of school feeding. The establishment of school clinics, which is a step likely soon to become general, ought to be followed by a national system of compulsorily attended baby clinics. It is obvious from official reports already laid before the public that by the time they can be received into a national school many children have already suffered for want of medical attention. The doctors in charge of baby clinics knowing that what a hungry, healthy infant wants is milk, and being confronted week after week with the same hungry infants gradually growing less and less healthy as their need was not satisfied, would collect and tabulate in their reports an amount of evidence on the subject which would revolutionize public opinion on the question of the nation's children and their needs.

If men, already in steady receipt of wages as high as any minimum wage likely to be attained for years to come, can only feed and house their families after the strictest personal self-denial, as these budgets show, the State, if it is to concern itself with its most vital affairs, should recognize its ultimate responsibility for the proper maintenance of its children. That this responsibility might eventually take the shape suggested in 'The Case for a Legal Minimum Wage,' for the children of widows or unmarried women, is quite possible. Some form of child maintenance grant might be placed in the hands of parents who, as joint administrators, would be answerable for the well-being of their children. It would be easy to discover through the clinics whether this duty was in each case being efficiently performed. A child, presented happy and well cared for, would be a sufficient guarantee, and a child whose condition appeared to be unsatisfactory would be noted and all necessary steps would be taken to secure its welfare. The country has faced the dead weight of Old Age Pensions; it is not impossible that the creative and repaying task of building up the nation's youth should be collectively undertaken.

FABIAN TRACT No. 163
(May 1913)

WOMEN AND PRISONS

Helen Blagg and Charlotte Wilson

(DRAFTED BY MISS HELEN BLAGG AND MRS. CHARLOTTE WILSON
FROM MATERIAL COLLECTED DURING 1910–11 BY A COMMITTEE
OF THE FABIAN WOMEN'S GROUP, WHICH ALSO INCLUDED MISS
ATKINSON, MRS. BOYD DAWSON, MRS. MAPPLEBECK, MRS. RUTH
RIDSDALE, MISS ELLEN SMITH.)

PART I. – DEVELOPMENT OF THE ENGLISH PENAL SYSTEM

Introduction

Women suffer under the criminal law and its administration as
men do and in other ways besides. In order to understand what
specially relates to women it is necessary to consider our penal
system as a whole. The penalty of imprisonment is now its central
feature; but the predominance of the prison is a comparatively
new thing, coincident with the growth of our present economic
conditions, and as they change it seems likely to cease. The instinct
of self-preservation in a community is the source of all penal
systems; but that instinct has intermingled with a variety of
passions, and striven to explain and express itself by very dissimilar
ideas and methods at different periods in our history. Fragments
of all of these compose the underlying strata of our penal system
to-day.

Revenge and Restitution

The original form of punishment was retribution – an eye for an
eye and a tooth for a tooth – really the fundamental childish instinct
of hitting back when struck. Later, as an alternative to retribution,
came the idea of restitution, that is of payment in money or kind

224

for personal damage done or for goods appropriated. In Anglo-Saxon customary law each man and each part of á man had a price, which was paid as compensation direct to the injured person and his kin. Later his lord and his king demanded compensation as well. Ultimately the State annexed the whole in criminal cases on the plea that the wrongdoer had broken the king's peace. An attenuated remnant of the ancient custom of restitution has come down to us in the form of fines, and of the damages and costs awarded in civil cases. But it is believed by some criminologists that a return to the old idea, recast to suit modern conditions, might be a valuable agency in the reform of the criminal.

Revenge and Expiation

Ideas of revenge and restitution have been allied from time immemorial with that of expiation. The wrongdoer must be made to atone for his crime by undergoing some form of personal suffering. Under the influence of mediaeval theology revenge and restitution merged in the expanding force of this ancient doctrine till it became the dominating factor in criminal procedure. Hanging, burning, beheading, dismemberment, crushing, branding, ducking, whipping, mutilation, the stocks, and the pillory were favorite modes of punishment in England almost down to modern times. Banishment from city, village, guild, or hundred, which often meant in the Middle Ages outlawry[1] and starvation, was succeeded early in the seventeenth century by transportation to our plantations across the Atlantic, the transported being sold as servants to free settlers.[2] After the revolt of the American Colonies Australia was substituted for America as a dumping ground for our convicts, male and female; and the plight of most of them there in 'hulks' or 'factories,' in chain gangs, or as 'assigned servants,' was little better than that of servitude in the plantations.[3] Transportation finally came to an end in 1867 with the refusal of West Australia to receive convicts.

Up to the beginning of the last century death or transportation were the usual forms of punishment even for trivial offences. A child might be hanged for stealing a pocket handkerchief. But since 1838 the death penalty has rarely been exacted for any offence save murder.[4] Since 1868 executions have taken place in private. In earlier times they were public, and people used to make up parties to see criminals hanged.

Little mercy was shown to women in the matter of punishment; indeed burning, one of the most cruel of deaths, was a frequent penalty for their offences. A woman was burnt for coining in 1789. The penalty was abolished the following year. A woman was flogged through the streets of London for the last time in 1767. Whipping for female offenders was finally abolished only in 1820.

Whilst the idea of expiation dominated society mere imprisonment was too mild a final penalty for anything but debt or lesser political offences. Gaols were fever haunted, pestiferous dens, sometimes underground, where men, women, and children awaiting trial or execution of sentence were fettered and huddled promiscuously together. They got food and drink by bargaining with their gaoler, who received no wages, but made his living out of the prisoners and could retain them in bondage until they paid him. There were also Houses of Correction for rogues and disorderly persons and the Bethlehem Hospital (Bedlam) for obstreperous lunatics, where the public paid to go on Sundays to see the insane, like animals in the Zoo, behind the iron bars of their cages.

Deterrence and the Reform of the Criminal

A note of coming change was struck during the eighteenth century. The Society of Friends in America and in England were pleading against the death penalty, and urging that room for repentance be given to the criminal; while Howard[5] and Bentham were formulating schemes of punishment which might deter from crime, whilst reforming instead of merely torturing the evil doer. The agency they proposed was imprisonment in isolation, and the cellular penitentiary at Millbank was built in 1816 to try an experiment for which, however, public opinion was not yet ready. For more than thirty years Millbank was the white elephant of prison reform.

The movement initiated by Romilly and Mackintosh for the substitution of the penalty of imprisonment for those of death or barbarous misusage, progressed side by side with the efforts to improve the state of local prisons initiated by Howard, and carried on by Elizabeth Fry, Nield and Buxton and their Society for the Reform of Prison Discipline. The reforms it strove to effect were the classification and separation of prisoners, at all events of the sexes; a bed for each person, if not a separate cell; some attempt to preserve health; the appointment of prison chaplains and the moral instruction of prisoners; continual and arduous employment; the use of fetters only as an 'urgent necessity'; and female officers for female offenders. For many years the reformers were ridiculed as 'ultra-humanitarians' endeavoring to 'pamper the criminal classes,' but they succeeded in provoking a series of Parliamentary enquiries and some enactments, which, like the efforts of the eighteenth century, remained a dead letter until public opinion overtook legislation.

General progress, including the establishment of a regular police force in 1829, and the more efficient lighting of towns, combined with the abandonment of the worst barbarities of our criminal law, resulted in a gradual diminution of crime. This reassured the public, and when the Australian Colonies made their first resolute stand against transportation in 1840, England was ripe for a new development of the penal system.

The building of the model prison at Pentonville, with 520 separate cells, was followed by the promulgation by Sir George Grey, Home Secretary 1846–52, of a new scheme, in which the prison was the main agency for dealing with all classes of criminals – except those condemned to capital punishment or let off with a fine. (1) A limited period of separate confinement in a penitentiary or local prison, accompanied by industrial employment and moral training. (2) For long sentence prisoners hard associated labor at a public works prison. (3) A ticket-of-leave, curtailing the sentence of well-behaved industrious convicts, but leaving them under police supervision. National uniformity in the discipline and diet of local prisons was finally secured by the Prisons Act of 1877, which placed gaols throughout the country under the jurisdiction of the Home Secretary with Prison Commissioners (Prison Board) under him, and Prison Inspectors. Thus the ideal of a method of punishment which should deter by its severity, while reclaiming the criminal by its moral suasion, has been reduced to practice and subjected to the test of experience for nearly three-quarters of a century. Those most convinced of its necessity will hardly contend that it has justified the high hopes and noble enthusiasm in which it originated.

The Modern Point of View

The scientific study of criminal psychology and pathology and of social conditions in relation to crime, combined with an enlarging sense of collective responsibility, has made the twentieth century thoroughly impatient of the results produced by the penal reforms of the nineteenth. The statistics of recidivism (i.e., the recurrence of convictions of the same person) demonstrate failure to reclaim the individual, whilst the inadequacy of deterrence is suggested by high premiums against burglary and larceny, by country roads infested with rogues and vagabonds, streets with prostitutes, drunkards and pickpockets, hotels and clubs with cardsharpers and 'kleptomaniacs,' and commercial centres with swindlers and embezzlers, most of whom never come within the reach of the law. It is scarcely needful to add that women suffer even more than men from this continuance of social insecurity.

Modern criminologists regard the attempt to combine aims so incompatible as deterrent punishment and a serious attempt to reform the criminal as the makeshift of a period of transition. The path of penal reform is seen to lie towards the prevention of crime by removal of causes, the classification of criminals for the purpose of dealing with them in the manner most for their own interest, as well as for the public good, the protection of society by the segregation, under beneficent conditions, of the insane, the deficient and the hopelessly anti-social, and the systematic effort to restore the erring to mental health by humane curative and educational treatment.

These proposals of reform are based on an alteration in our view of the incidence of personal responsibility, and the part played by the individual will in conduct. The old idea of penal as of educational discipline was to crush and break; the modern idea is to fortify and build up force of character. Kropotkin, writing twenty-two years ago of his own experience gained 'In Russian and French Prisons,'[6] drew attention to weakness of will and a natural but misdirected desire for approbation, as common characteristics of criminals, whose show of dangerous anti-social energy is often a result of sheer desperation; and his opinion has been confirmed by our best English observers. The remedy indicated by modern thought lies in a development of the personal sense of responsibility for self-direction, which can only exist where scope is afforded for some freedom of action and opportunity given for the exercise of bodily and mental powers. The old idea was that the collective force of society should be used to suppress the will and stultify the faculties of every person of whose activities custom or authority disapproved. The modern idea is that the collective force of society should be used to stimulate and support the exercise of individual will power under a sense of personal and social responsibility, and to make every effort to strengthen and restore it where it is enfeebled or lost, combined of course with opportunity for the free exercise in a useful and healthy direction of such powers as the individual may possess. In a word our present inclination towards a positive rather than a negative method for the solution of such social problems as destitution, ignorance or sickness is extending likewise to the treatment of crime.

Such changes would involve nothing less than the abolition of our present prison system, and the movement towards them is as yet but partial and tentative. Our judicial and administrative authorities are aware that the present state of things is by no means satisfactory, but they are still befogged by the idea of safeguarding us by means of punishment as a deterrent, if not as an expiation. They are still trying to reconcile this attitude with the partial adoption of methods likely to be effectual in forestalling crime by preventing its causes and in humanely reclaiming the criminal or gently rendering him innocuous. The two radically incompatible points of view clash at every step, and consequently our latest reforms tend to be halting, inadequate and self-contradictory. Nevertheless they are paths leading up to the coming change.

PART II. – PRISONS

The prison being the main penal agency of recent times most men and women who come under our criminal law are to be found within its walls. Though the death penalty still stands on the statute book for offences other than murder, it is many years since it has been so applied. The present method of inflicting it is less cruel,[7] and even for murder there is a growing tendency to extend the limits of the mental irresponsibility or extenuating circumstances which permit incarceration to be substituted for hanging, e.g., in cases of maternal infanticide.[8]

The Prison System

Solitary confinement as a part of imprisonment was first introduced by Sir James Graham as Home Secretary in 1842, with the intention that it should be accompanied by definite training. Till 1898 each long-sentence prisoner underwent this confinement, at first for eighteen and afterwards for nine months; it was then reduced to six months, and now to only one for those condemned to hard labor or penal servitude.[9] In the case of women it is only undergone by convicts (New Rules, July, 1910). Silence is however insisted upon during associated labor and exercise. A prisoner is supposed to speak and to be spoken to only by officials, and then as little as possible.

Penal servitude was devised in 1853 as a substitute for transportation. It has been applied since 1891 to all prisoners (convicts) with sentences of three years and over. These convicts are employed in associated labor, the men in public works, in building, quarrying, farm work or trades; the women in baking, bookbinding, sewing, knitting, tailoring, mattress making, twine making, gardening, cooking, washing, and general service for the prison. There is but one convict prison for women, that at Aylesbury. Only forty-two women convicts were admitted during 1910–11, of whom thirty-two are classified as 'recidivists' and ten as 'star' prisoners.[10]

Solitary confinement takes place first in the local prison, in which those with shorter sentences spend their whole time.

Local prisons, in which far the larger number of women are confined, usually accommodate both men and women prisoners in different wards; and, generally speaking, there is one prison to each county. A number of unsuitable local prisons were closed by the Prisons Acts of 1877 and 1898, but in many places there is still room for much improvement in sanitary and other arrangements.

The court, on passing a sentence of imprisonment without hard labor, may direct the prisoner to be treated as an offender of either the first or second division. In the absence of direction he or she is treated as a prisoner of the third or ordinary division, with or without 'hard labor.' The first division implies detention merely, the second penal discipline much mitigated. Besides short sentence prisoners in these three divisions, local prisons contain those sentenced to death, those awaiting trial, and those imprisoned for debt, all kept separately and under special rules. There is also a star class for first offenders of good previous character who are willing to give respectable references.

In local prisons a matron, and at Aylesbury a lady superintendent, has charge of the women's side. Since the revelations of the suffrage prisoners in 1908–9, a medical woman Inspector of Prisons has been appointed.

Hard labor for a man means labor in solitary confinement, but for a woman associated labor for the same length of time daily (six to ten hours excluding meals), unless the doctor objects, 'regard being had to any advice or suggestions from the Visiting Committee or Discharged Prisoners Aid Society.'

In both local and convict prisons there is a system of marks for industry and good conduct, whereby prisoners may earn remission of sentence and also various privileges attained by stated grades and a gratuity before discharge.

Convicts are classed in three categories:–

A. Ordinary, including (1) star class, as in local prisons; (2) intermediates i.e., other first offenders; (3) recidivists.
B. Habitual offenders sentenced to preventive detention, who can earn privileges and also gratuities to spend in prison, but not remission of sentence.
C. Long sentence prisoners, who after serving ten years and earning all privileges ordinarily possible, may earn special privileges and gratuities, together with remission of sentence.

The prison staff consists of a governor, doctor, chaplain, and their assistants, and of warders. There are also warders in the prison hospital, ministers and priests who visit Nonconformist and Roman Catholic prisoners, and skilled instructors. There is a visiting committee of local magistrates for local prisons, and a board of visitors appointed by the Home Secretary for convict prisons, also unofficial ladies' visiting committees and societies which aid discharged prisoners.

Prison regulations[11] are alike for men and women, with the exceptions here noted. Women prisoners are dealt with by female officers and a female officer accompanies any male official, even the governor, when he visits the women's quarters.

'The labor of all prisoners shall, if possible, be productive, and the trades and industries taught and carried on shall, if practicable, be such as shall fit the prisoner to earn his livelihood on release'; but 'a prisoner may be employed in the service of the prison,' and short sentence women are so employed, as technical instruction cannot usefully be given to them.

A man over 16 and under 60 condemned to hard labor sleeps on a plank bed without a mattress for the first fortnight, but a woman is allowed a mattress.

All non-technical instruction is under the control of the chaplain, and must include reading, writing and arithmetic, and religious exhortation, for which purpose the chaplain often visits the cells. The prison library consists of books sanctioned by the commissioners (in convict prisons by the directors). During the first month prisoners may only read books of instruction – religious and secular.

'Prisoners who do not do their best to profit by the instruction afforded them may be deprived of any privileges in the same way as if they had been idle or negligent at labor,' or be punished according to the general rules. (Regulations in Cells, 1911.)

The main difference between men and women is in diet. All females are allowanced with juveniles. Males over 16 have larger rations.

Analysis of Dietary in Local Prisons

Diet A. For all prisoners sentenced to less than four months, during the first seven days of imprisonment. Bread (men 8 oz., women 6 oz.) and gruel (1 pt.) daily for breakfast and supper. Dinner: Bread (men 8 oz., women 6 oz.) and porridge (1 pt.), or potatoes (8 oz.) or suet pudding (men 8 oz., women 6 oz.).

Diet B. After first seven days for whole term if not exceeding four months. Bread and gruel (same amounts as A) daily for breakfast and supper for women, porridge substituted for gruel for men's supper. Dinner: Bread (6 oz.) and potatoes (8 oz.) daily, together with soup (1 pt.), or cooked meat (men 4 oz., women 3 oz.), or suet pudding (men 10 oz., women 8 oz.) on two days a week each. Beans (men 10 oz., women 8 oz.) and fat bacon (men 2 oz., women 1 oz.) on the remaining day.

Diet C. After first four months for rest of term. Breakfast: Bread (8 oz.) and porridge (1 pt.) for men, bread (6 oz.) and tea (1 pt.) for women. Supper: Bread and cocoa in the same relative amounts. Dinner: As in Diet B, slightly larger quantities of potatoes, suet pudding, meat or beans being given.

Juvenile prisoners may, in addition to the above diet, be allowed milk, not exceeding one pint per diem, at the discretion of the medical officer, and one pint of porridge in lieu of tea for breakfast.

The dietary for convicts is like C, but somewhat more varied, and sweet things are not excluded.

'The diet for special classes of prisoners, viz.:– (a) Prisoners on remand or awaiting trial who do not maintain themselves, (b) Offenders of the First Division who do not maintain themselves, (c) Offenders of the Second Division, (d) Debtors, shall be Diet B; provided that they shall receive for breakfast one pint of tea in lieu of gruel, and for supper one pint of cocoa in lieu of porridge or gruel; and that when detained in prison more than four months they shall receive C Diet at the expiration of the fourth month.'[12]

Women, like men, are punished for offences against prison discipline by close confinement, by three days on bread and water, or a longer period on low diet in special cells on a plank bed. They may be put in irons but not flogged. Punishments are awarded by the governor or the visiting committee under strict regulations. Prisoners may make complaints to either of these authorities. If a prisoner takes advantage of the privilege, such boldness is said often to result in loss of marks or privileges.

A mother may keep with her an infant at the breast until it is nine to twelve months old.

Such in rough outline is the existing prison system as applied to both sexes.

The Prison System as it Appears to Those Immediately Concerned

The Prison Commissioners every year issue a report which shows how seriously they take their responsibilities and how anxiously they endeavor to make the best of a system which they still look upon as inevitable. Prison officials whilst holding office are debarred from publishing their views, but on retirement inspectors, governors, doctors, matrons, and chaplains have done so. Their testimony is, intentionally or unintentionally, amongst the most damning evidence against things as they have been and still are.

'The working of prison systems, whether at home or abroad,' says Dr. Morrison, late Chaplain at Wandsworth Prison, 'teaches us that any person, be he child or man, who has once been in prison is much more likely to come back again than a person who, for a similar offence, has received punishment in a different form.' – 'Crime and its Cause.'

The experience of prisoners themselves is necessarily rare and difficult to obtain. Very occasionally an unfortunate more able to express himself than most publishes such a book as 'Five Years Penal Servitude, by One who has Experienced It.' Amongst these the splendid and terrible 'De Profundis' and 'Ballad of Reading Gaol' of Oscar Wilde stand alone. Occasionally a political prisoner like Michael Davitt publishes a thoughtful appreciation of what he has observed. When anyone who has experienced imprisonment does speak it is to condemn the system.

'Penal servitude,' said Michael Davitt in 1885 ('Leaves from a Prison Diary') 'has become so laborate that it is now a huge punishing machine destitute, through centralized control and responsibility, of discrimination, feeling, and sensitiveness; and its non-success as a deterrent from crime and complete failure in reformative effect upon criminal character are owing to its obvious essential tendency to deal with erring human beings, who are still men despite their crimes, in a manner which mechanically reduces them to a uniform level of disciplined brutes.'

Women in Holloway

Since Elizabeth Fry described the 'hell above ground' at Newgate few women have written of prison from close personal observation. No female prisoner recorded her experiences until suffragists in large numbers were sent to Holloway (1907–11). Their criticisms are therefore worthy of careful consideration even on that ground alone. The letters or statements of twelve women are here quoted. All are first hand and carefully verified.

FIRST EXPERIENCES SUMMARIZED

Received into prison from the van the prisoners are stripped, deprived of all personal possessions, even a name – henceforth they are known by number only – bathed, and dressed in prison clothes, each one wearing clothes exactly similar to those of every other female prisoner of the same division. The second division wear green, the third brown, of like texture. The dress has been very much improved during the last two years by the woman Inspector of Prisons. Until 1910 the outfit was that in use by the working classes of 1860, but it is now chosen with a view to hygiene and to the individual needs of the prisoners. A cloak is provided, which may be kept in the cell as an additional wrap. One handkerchief (a duster) is allowed each week, and only one towel is provided.

DAILY ROUTINE

Called at 5.30–6 a.m. Breakfast, about 7 (one rarely knows the exact time). Chapel, 8.30. Associated labor (under skilled instructors for long sentence prisoners). Exercise (about one hour). Dinner, about 12 o'clock. Associated labor. Supper, 5 p.m.

The cell door is then closed for the night and, except in the case of serious illness, is not allowed to be opened again until the next morning. The prisoner may read until the light is turned out (about 8.30), or may go to bed directly she has eaten her supper. All prison work has been taken from her and she is allowed to do no work for herself, nor are mothers with infants allowed to make the baby's clothes.

Between rising and chapel the bed has to be made, the cell scrubbed, and all tin utensils polished. Associated labor under instruction includes needlework, dressmaking, laundry work, or gardening. The rule of absolute silence is in force the whole day.

When out at exercise the prisoner must walk all the time, to stand still or to sit down is not allowed, unless under special medical permission. On Sunday the prisoner attends chapel twice and, unless she is allowed out for exercise, is confined to her cell the rest of the day, no work being done.

FOOD AND HYGIENE

'The food may be sufficient to ward off the actual pangs of hunger, but the monotony of the diet amounts, after a time, to positive torture.'

'The food is scanty, the ventilation totally inadequate; the result is to make prisoners dull and stupid, unfit to earn their living when they come out, yet the reason that many are there at all is chiefly from their inability to earn an honest living.'

'The food of third division prisoners consists of gruel of no flavor whatever, and of the consistency of paste, and coarse brown bread. This is served at 7 a.m. and 5 p.m. At mid-day meat and potatoes are served. I believe the food allowances are worked out so that if they are all consumed a sufficient quantity of the various necessary foodstuffs is taken. But it is now generally admitted that food consumed with a sense of distaste cannot be assimilated, and the bad air and lack of exercise, and the fact that the meals are taken alone, naturally reduce the prisoners' appetites so that they cannot eat the uninviting food, or if they do so, it is of little use to them. Moreover the bread is so hard and dry and is so irritating to the stomach as frequently to set up gastric disorders, so that few of the women can eat half the amount supplied. Therefore it will be readily seen that the women are habitually underfed, their vitality is low, and they are an easy prey to all diseases.'

Many other prisoners speak of the prevalence of diarrhoea, which is very weakening, and, with prison conditions, is most inconvenient and distressing in every way. The 'convenience' supplied in the cell is totally inadequate, and even if it be of a proper size and does not leak, the fact that it remains unemptied from evening till morning is, in case of illness especially, very insanitary and dangerous to health. 'Lavatory time' is permitted only at a fixed hour twice a day, only one water-closet being provided for twenty-three cells.

'I slept in one of the ordinary cells, which have sliding panes, leaving at the best two openings about six inches square. The windows are set in the wall high up, and are 3 by 1½ or 2 feet area. Added to this they are very dirty, so that the light in the cell is always dim. After the prisoner has been locked in the cell all night the air is unbearable, and its unhealthiness is increased by damp. The cells are washed at six in the morning, and the corridors are washed at the same time. In spite of the fact that any adequate through ventilation is impossible, owing to the height of the windows and the small area that opens, the prisoners are locked into the cells again at seven for breakfast, so that they sit in a wet cell and are forced to breathe the evaporating moisture which cannot escape. A great number of the prisoners suffer from chronic catarrh, and anyone with a tendency to consumption could hardly fail to contract the disease.'[13]

In this connection it must be borne in mind that when mental and physical vitality are at a low ebb and impressions from without few and monotonous, the physical facts of existence loom gigantic in the mind and physical discomfort may cause mental agony, especially if the suffering is inflicted by others against whose will the victim has no appeal. Enforced privations produce exactly the opposite of the spiritual uplifting, sometimes a result of voluntary asceticism.

DISCIPLINE AND ITS EFFECTS

A matter on which the suffrage prisoners lay much stress is the inhuman way in which the wardresses address the prisoners, and the lack of all human intercourse between them. This was explained by an official in the prison service as being necessary in order to avoid any possibility of favoritism, and to avoid jealousy among the prisoners. To maintain order among such a hetero-geneous collection of rebels as a crowd of prisoners, it is found necessary to accustom them to obey a sharp word of command.

'The prison system is not calculated to reform criminals. It induces deceit above all things – the rule of silence being one that everybody breaks whenever possible. It reduces people to mere numbered machines, thus doing away with any sense of personal responsibility. It suppresses all initiative and undermines all self-reliance, whereas I take it that the desirable thing is to build up a sense of self-reliance and respect, and to encourage people to have a stronger sense of individual responsibility towards the rest of mankind.'

'The whole system is one to destroy anyone's self-respect and moral control.'

'I observed the gradual hardening of certain of the prisoners who were quite obviously full of grief and shame on arrival. . . . The principal effect of the prison system as it now exists seems to me to be the destruction of self-respect and initiative. I believe many of the wardresses who come into closer contact with the prisoners than any of the other officials, take what opportunity they find of urging the women to a better way of life, but since the system works in the other direction, their influence cannot be very great. The wardresses are as much prisoners as we are.'

'To be continually in disgrace; to never hear a kindly tone or a word of encourage-ment, is sufficient to crush those who are already weak, and who have fallen in the battle of life. . . . There is an atmosphere of fear and suspicion throughout a prison that weakens the character and engenders deceit.'

'Every endeavor is made to render the life dull, monotonous and dreary; all the surroundings are as hideous as human ingenuity can make them, the food unappetizing, and the whole tone brutalizing and hardening.'

Punishments

'When you are put into the punishment cell[14] you feel as if you were absolutely cut off from the rest of the world, the echoes of footsteps along the stone corridors, the banging and locking of doors become so magnified as to have a gruesome and horrible effect on your nerves.'

'Hour after hour, day after day (seven days) I spent sitting on the wooden bed, doing nothing, hardly thinking, staring into vacancy. I could well imagine the loneliness, silence (for two doors close this cell), darkness and cold, sending women mad. The horror of it is still with me, and night after night, unable to sleep, I go through it all again. . . . I tried walking about to obtain exercise, but the cell echoed so weirdly and horribly I was obliged to desist.'

This prisoner was in 'close confinement,' i.e., no exercise, chapel, or anything that takes a prisoner out of her cell is permitted.

'The punishment cell is longer and higher, though not so wide as the ordinary cell. . . . The furniture consisted of two shelves in one corner, a wooden bed three inches high with wooden pillow, also fixed into the ground, with the top and one side against the wall, and a tree trunk clamped into the wall was the only seat. A few tin utensils, every one of which leaked. . . . The cell was damp, and any water spilt took days to dry up.'

Most prisoners complain of want of ventilation, especially in punishment cells, but one says:–

'The punishment cell is bitterly cold and very draughty. And all punishment cells are very dark, light only shining in on bright days, and in the middle of the day.'

Handcuffs, another form of punishment, are described as

'A brutal torture, especially when placed behind, as the arms have to be forced back and twisted before they can be fastened, and they are fastened in such a manner as to give cramp; after a time your arms are dead and numb.'

As to the infliction of punishments the same prisoner says:–

'The way the punishments are dealt out by the visiting magistrates is really too callous. The sentences, you know, are already arranged before they have heard your side of the question.'

Punishments may be given for not completing the task set. In undetected cases of incipient insanity or imbecility, the effect of such punishment is too hideous to contemplate.

What wonder then that the women who go to prison become hardened criminals, and that the problem of the female recidivist haunts the brains of the conscientious commissioner?

The root of the matter seems to be insufficient opportunity for individual treatment, and the effort to draw out the best that is in each prisoner. Goodness, kindness, humanity are crushed out by the deadening life. The high grim walls, the iron bars, the hard bed, and all the bare surroundings are but outward signs of the essential fact of the absence of love and beauty. In the piteous words of the 'Ballad of Reading Gaol':–

'For neither milk-white rose nor red
May bloom in prison air;
The shard, the pebble and the flint,
Are what they give us there:
For flowers have been known to heal
A common man's despair.'

236

PART III. – CRIMINALS AND CRIME

I. – Relative Statistics for Men and Women[15]

According to the last Annual Report of the Prison Commissioners the number of prisoners received under sentence in His Majesty's Prisons amounted to 186,395 during the year, a decrease of 13,870 from the year before (p. 4). Some of these moreover were committed several times during the year, so that this total is in excess of the actual number of fresh offenders received. The total numbers in custody during the year were 194,037 males and 42,581 females in local prisons, and 4,559 males and 164 females in convict prisons (p. 29).

AVERAGE DAILY POPULATION OF PRISONS 1910–11 (p. 5)

	Males	Females	Total
Local	14,596	2,386	16,982
Convict	3,195	114	3,309
Borstal	508	27	535
State Inebriate Reformatories	24	54	78˙

Note that the number of women prisoners is very much smaller than that of the men. Nevertheless records of recidivism show that of the males a percentage of 58.8 only had been previously convicted and as many as 77.2 of the females (p. 17).

These figures seem to lead to the following conclusions:– Either (a) Crime among women, while confined to a much smaller class than among men, proceeds from an ineradicably unmoral nature; in other words, those women who commit crimes are much worse morally and therefore less reclaimable than men criminals; or (b) Prison treatment is better suited to men than to women, reforming a percentage of 41.2 of them, while only 22.8 of the women are deterred from committing further breaches of the law; or (c) Owing to the state of public opinion imprisonment affects the future social and economic life of women more adversely than that of men, and further crime results from bad company, poverty and despair.

The period of detention and the method of treatment naturally affect the whole question.

PERIODS OF DETENTION IN LOCAL PRISONS[16]

The total number of prisoners committed to local prisons from ordinary courts during 1910–11 was 166,230. (Males 130,350, females 35,880.) The length of sentences was as follows:–

	Males	Females
Over 2 years	3	0
Over 18 months and under 2 years (inclusive)	235	11
Over 12 months and under 18 months	1,044	33
Over 3 months and under 12 months	7,967	1,143
Over 1 week and under 3 months	74,896	21,606
1 week and under	46,205	13,087

Thus it will be seen that while the majority of prisoners of both sexes are convicted for three months or less, the average length of sentence is even shorter for women than for men, and only 44 women out of 35,880 were convicted for twelve months during the year.

The Prison Commissioners[17] give a 'typical case' of a girl of 20 committed for a month or less thirteen times in two years for prostitution, vagrancy or indecency. The Lady Inspector says of such cases 'a stream of bright, childish girls passes in and out of the prisons many of whom are in the power of older and worse people than themselves. . . . In spite of their dreadful experiences they do not differ greatly in (natural) mental and physical development from the better class girls who are growing happily at school and hockey-field while they are qualifying as prison habituals.' Their stunted minds, she continues, are gradually perverted, enfeebled or unhinged unless they can be removed from the influences that are destroying them, but short sentences for purposes of educational treatment are well-nigh useless.

AGES OF CONVICTED CRIMINAL PRISONERS COMMITTED TO LOCAL PRISONS ON CONVICTION DURING THE YEAR ENDED MARCH, 1911

	Male	Per centage of total	Female	Per centage of total
Under 12	—	—	—	—
12 to 16	32	—	2	—
16 to 21	10,380	7.0	1,163	3.2
21 to 30	36,555	27.7	7,831	21.8
30 to 40	36,626	27.8	12,569	35.0
All ages	131,746	—	35,949	—

The question of the age incidence of crime is important. It appears from these statistics and others that the age incidence is higher in women than in men. The proportion of youths to girls under 20 is about nine to one, the number of men between the ages of 20 and 40 are much the same, but far the largest proportion of women criminals are aged from 30 to 40. (Appendix V, p. 67).

DIFFERENCES IN THE NATURE OF CRIME[18]

		Convictions on Indictment	Summary Convictions and in default of Sureties	Total
(a) Offences against the person (murder, wounding, cruelty, including cruelty to and neglect of children, assault and immoral offences)	Males	939	9,067	10,003
	Females	84	1,877	1,961
(b) Offences against property with violence (burglary, robbery, etc.)	Males	2,475	—	2,475
	Females	36	—	36
(c) Offences against property without violence (chiefly larceny, stealing and fraud, including forgery)	Males	4,626	16,234	20,858
	Females	412	2,575	2,987

The above table gives the figures for the three main divisions of serious crime. The most noticeable fact in it is the comparative rarity of crimes of violence among women; except for cruelty to children, including neglect,[19] the proportion is markedly less than amongst men. It may also be taken as a certainty that there is a much smaller skilled professional criminal class among women than among men. There are few professional criminals in class (a); probably the largest number, chiefly men, belong to class (b).

A barrister tells us that in his many years' experience at the criminal bar, practically all women convicted of indictable offences are (1) prostitutes or (2) married women convicted of neglecting their children through drink, or (3) domestic servants who have succumbed to their peculiar facilities for stealing clothing or jewellery; usually girls in poor households and themselves physically and mentally below par. Of these three categories prostitutes are immensely the largest, from 85 to 90 per cent. of the whole. 'It would be almost true to say that indictable crime among women is confined to women who are prostitutes. This is, I fancy, the main explanation of the greater irreclaimability of women criminals.'

It is interesting to compare these facts with those of the older system before penal servitude took the place of transportation for long sentence prisoners. From 1787 to 1837, 43,506 men and 6,791 women were transported to New South Wales, and 24,785 men and 2,974 women to Van Dieman's Land from 1817 to 1837. The largest consignment in any one year occurred in 1833, when 2,310 men and 420 women were sent to New South Wales, and 1,576 men and 245 women to Van Dieman's Land. The evidence before the Select Committee[20] stigmatized the conduct of the women convicts as being 'as bad as anything could well be.' They were 'ferocious,' 'drunken and abandoned prostitutes,' 'more irreformable than male convicts.' When assigned as servants 'from negligence they turn to pilfering, from pilfering generally follows drunkenness, and from drunkenness generally debauchery, and it is very rare indeed, that a woman remains a few months in service before she goes to the factory for punishment.' 'The proportion of women reformed is much smaller than amongst men,' but 'those who have good mistresses turn out well.' In some places convict women servants could only obtain some sort of protection from brutal ill-usage by prostituting themselves. (Evidence of Rev. Dr. Ullathorne, Vicar-General of New Holland). Women convicts 'contaminated all around them, and it was impossible to reform them,' 'they are so bad that settlers have no heart to treat them well,' nevertheless, marriage sometimes reformed them. (Evidence of P. Murdock, Superintendent of Emu Plains).

The comparison of these observations upon the results of a bygone method with observations upon the methods of to-day seems to indicate that whilst women are less likely to become criminals, they react still more disastrously than men under penal severity; also that there is an intimate connection between prostitution and crime amongst women.

II. – Causes of Crime

It must be borne in mind that 'crime' is an arbitrary legal term. 'There is an enormous mass of so called crime in England which is not crime at all. . . . Eighty-three per cent. of the annual convictions, summarily and on indictment, followed by committal to gaol, are for misconduct that is distinctly non-criminal, such as breaches of municipal byelaws and police regulations, drunkenness, gaming, and offences under Vagrancy Acts';[21] also the peculiarly feminine offence of prostitution.[22]

The large proportion of brief sentences (p. 14 infra) are in themselves enough to indicate the triviality of the offences, and, as Major Griffiths says, 'the question will arise some day whether it is really necessary to maintain fifty-six local prisons, with all their elaborate paraphernalia, their imposing buildings, and expensive staff to maintain discipline in daily life and insist upon the proper observation of customs and usages, many of them of purely modern invention.' He might have added 'or of dubious social value.' We have nearly always some men and women in our prisons who are there for zeal in social reform or individual experiment distasteful to custom or to the powers that be, though the future may regard it as harmless or even acclaim it as beneficial.

Turning to crimes of more serious character, one of the most important determining causes appears to be mental disease or defici-

240

ency. Besides the considerable number of criminals certified insane before conviction there is an even larger proportion found to be insane on reception in prison or at some period during imprisonment.

The Report of the Medical Inspector for 1910–11[23] gives the number of prisoners certified insane in local prisons during the year as 136, of whom 121 were males and 15 females.

We select the following as typical cases:—[24]

Age	Degree of Education, Standard	Occupation and Offence	Sentence	Supposed Cause
27	I	Servant, neglecting children	3 months hard labor	Recurrent melancholia (puerperal) due to trouble
35	Nil	Rag Sorter. Drunk and Disorderly	1 month hard labor	Melancholia, due to intemperance
28	IV	Dressmaker. Prostitution	1 month imprisonment	Insane on admission. Melancholia, due to stress
29	Imperfect	Laundress. Burglary	3 years penal servitude	Recurrent mania, probably congenital

Congenital mental deficiency appears in the statistical table as the main cause of insanity leading to crime. Other causes appearing with regularity are alcoholism, epilepsy and syphilis. Among criminologists hereditary predisposition is also generally accepted as an operative cause.

The congenitally feeble-minded form a much larger proportion of the prison population than actual lunatics. During 1910–11 'the number of prisoners formally recognized as being so feeble-minded as to be unfit for the ordinary penal discipline was 359 in local prisons and in convict prisons 120.'[25]

In this class must also be included the moral imbeciles, chiefly congenital. Here is a typical instance:—[26]

No. 1191, aged 27, education imperfect, a hawker, who committed an indecent assault, sentenced to three months hard labor, was found on reception to be of 'unsound mind' in the form of 'congenital mental deficiency, moral,' from 'congenital syphilis.'

Again, there are a certain number of mentally unusual persons, possibly of exceptionally brilliant gifts, who need special conditions to develop healthily, and not obtaining them may become criminals. Add to these, and to the mentally unsound and deficient, all those normal persons who are goaded or led into crime as a result of preventible social causes, such as extreme poverty, or negligence and misusage in youth, and a very small proportion of our criminal population remains to be accounted for as individuals by nature so anti-social as to be a perennial danger to their fellow men.[27]

PART IV. – PATHS OF CHANGE

It is abundantly evident that the causes of crime above indicated have their root deep in our existing social organization. Any adequate preventive measures must be inextricably bound up with such wide issues as security of employment, a living wage, housing and sanitation, and national responsibility for the nurture and training of youth, for the care of the feeble and sick in body and mind, and for the prevention of destitution.

Furthermore, the difficulties created by existing law are, as the Prison Commissioners observe, 'well-nigh insuperable.' Our Common Law is an obscure tangle of custom and precedent; our confused mass of Statutes, Bye-laws and Regulations, sometimes actually provocative in character, is bewildering to the most astute of lawyers, and incomprehensible to the plain citizen.

These large issues can be but alluded to here, gravely as they affect the causes of crime. We pass to the attempts now being made to transform the penal system itself from a mechanism aiding and abetting the manufacture of criminals, into an agency for the prevention of crime and the reclamation of the erring.

A burning question of the moment is the length of sentences. If crime is to be prevented by effectively segregating or reforming criminals they must be put, and kept for some considerable time, under skilled care and supervision, directly they first begin to go wrong; but to inflict long sentences of punitive imprisonment for trivial offences is sheer cruelty. Here lies the crux, and the nation for the nonce is Mr. Facing-both-ways. Nevertheless many changes now in progress are heading straight for the transformation of definite terms of rigorous imprisonment apportioned to the heinousness of the offence into indeterminate terms of humane institutional or external treatment apportioned to the needs of the offender. Such changes fall mainly into two divisions. (1) Further classification and correlative specialized treatment, accompanied by mitigation of the hardships of imprisonment in general. (II) Improvements in official administration.

I. – Classification and Special Treatment

THE PROBATION SYSTEM

The probation system, 'a system of liberty under supervision,' originated in Massachusetts, U.S.A., about 1880, for children, and has now been adopted in at least nineteen of the States. It was recommended strongly at the Prison Congress at Buda Pest, September, 1905, and by the Probation of Offenders Act (1907) came into force in England, January, 1908. By this Act an offender may be discharged, and enter into recognizances to be good behavior, being liable to be called upon for conviction and sentence at any time during the next three years.

The system properly worked is primarily educational rather than punitive. It is an elastic combination of officialism and phil- anthropy and therefore depends for its success mainly on efficient administration. The offender is usually placed by the magistrates under the control of a specified probation officer, who has to be obeyed, who may make compulsory regulations, and who reports monthly to the magistrate. In America, in places where it is worked to great perfection, 70 to 90 per cent. of successes are claimed for the system.

It appears from the criminal statistics for the year 1909 that 8,962 persons in England and Wales were put on probation under the Act, of whom only 624 had subsequently to appear for sentence. Of these 133 were discharged, and only 184 were ultimately sentenced to imprisonment, the others (307) being variously dealt with – in many cases sent to homes or reformatories. Of the total number placed on probation 6,862 were males and 2,100 females. Amongst the females 394 were less than 16 years old, 665 between 16 and 21, and 1,041 above that age.[28]

In its main idea the probation system is almost a return to the law of Anglo-Saxon England, in many ways superior to our own, where the community, i.e., the hundred or the kindred was held responsible for the good behavior of the individual. Modern society is too complicated for an exact return to this idea, but under the Probation Act the community deputes its duties to its representative, i.e., to the probation officer, because that is the best way in which, as a society, it can fulfil its duty to the unfit. And the probation officer who understands the duties of the office will see that the family, i.e. the parents or guardians are made to fulfil their duties. In the case of young offenders the parents quite as much as the children are 'put on probation.' Working through the family and the home this system gives the unfortunate a strong friend from outside who can often provide education and training and employment. It is better than prison from the economic as well as from the humane point of view, for the offender is not removed from work in the outside world, so need not be main- tained by the State, nor is the wage earner's family thrown upon the Poor Law. There is no criminal taint, no loss of status, no association with other offenders; on the contrary in the most successful cases the whole tone of the home is raised. The system aims at making both the unit and the family more useful to society.

To do all this successfully the probation officers must be experienced men and women with insight and tact. They must combine force of character and firmness with gentleness and sympathy. In London existing agencies, such as Mr. Wheatley's St. Giles's Christian Mission, the Police Court Mission of the Church of England Temperance Society, and the Church and Salvation Armies, undertake the greater part of the probation work, in which, on the whole, they seem to have great success. There is, however, room for development and improvement in the system, especially in two directions:–

> (a) Pressure brought to bear on magistrates, especially in country districts, to make use of the Act and, except for the very gravest offences, to refrain entirely from sending to prison any first offender or any juvenile adult for so short a time as to be ineligible for effective Borstal treatment.
>
> (b) Improvement in the training, salary, and status generally of the probation officer, and the appointment of a larger proportion of women.

It seems possible in the future that an increasing number of men and women with a wide outlook and greater culture may find in this work their true vocation. In the United States of America it is often taken up by settlement workers.

REFORMATORY AND INDUSTRIAL SCHOOLS

When all possible use has been made of the probation system, there will still remain a certain number of boys and girls who are homeless or 'incorrigibles.' Such children are now sent to industrial schools and reformatories. By the Children Act of 1908 reformatory is to be preferred to prison for all young persons (fourteen to sixteen years), no one under sixteen is to be sent to penal servitude, and sentence of death may not be pronounced on anyone under sixteen. Practically, therefore, imprisonment is abolished for all girls under sixteen, and for juvenile adults (sixteen to twenty-one) the Borstal system is now in force.

BORSTAL SYSTEM

Amongst the 10,380 male and 1,163 female juvenile adults convicted during the year 1910–11, 489 males and 35 females were selected for treatment in Borstal institutions.[29]

The system is so called from the village of Borstal, near Rochester, where the primary institution stands. The ruling principle is training – physical, mental, and manual. Much use is made of physical drill, of work in the open air, of lectures, of music, instruction in skilled trades, and education generally, and of progress from grade to grade. The upper grade, 'Blues,' dine in a large hall, sleep on spring mattresses in dormitories, and play cricket or football on Saturday afternoon. The food, though plain, is plentiful, and apparently appetizing. There is nothing degrading in the routine; on the contrary, everything is uplifting. The inmates do not show the same recidivist tendency as ordinary prisoners because they have been taught to desire 'something better.' The Governor of Borstal reports 82 per cent. of his boys as satisfactory, and of the 303 youths discharged last year only 13 have been reconvicted. Since July, 1909, this institution has ceased to rank as a prison, and two similar institutions for youths have been opened, as well as one at Aylesbury for girls. They are not meant for first offenders, but to reclaim young people of really bad character. Those in Borstal last year averaged about three previous convictions apiece.[30]

OFFENCES OF BORSTAL INMATES, 1910–11

	Males	Females
Against persons	11	1
Against property with violence	219	—
Against property without violence	214	—
Malicious injury to property	6	1
Other offences	9	33

Sentences of twelve months are insufficient to reclaim young hooligans who on arrival are practically below the normal, physically and mentally. Sometimes it takes eighteen months to make any impression. 'There are many boys here whose wits are dulled by neglect and bad treatment, and this is the first time they have experienced a combination of kindness and discipline.'[31] Two years is the minimum useful sentence, and three is far better; but last year 150 of the Borstal boys were sent for less than two years. The Medical Officer is more and more struck by 'the importance of physical unfitness as a determining factor' in the downfall of these youths.[32] The feeble minded or incorrigibly vicious are not retained in Borstal institutions.

Employment: 11 needlework, 8 cleaners and jobbers in and about the prison, 7 gardeners. It is hoped to add training in laundry work and cooking. The Borstal girls like hard manual labor better than sewing, and 'it is surprising to see the vigor they put into rough work. They are full of energy and apparently tireless.' They enjoy drill and gardening, and the medical officer notes the marked effect of physical exercise in improving not only the physique and carriage, but 'mentally their power of attention and concentration.' The chaplain has been teaching history, geography and other general subjects, and finds the girls 'quicker and more elastic mentally,' 'with much improved powers of observation and thought.'

AYLESBURY BORSTAL FOR GIRLS, 1910–11. (STARTED IN AUGUST, 1909)

In custody at the beginning of the year	23
Received during the year	35
Recommitted (forfeiture of licence)	2
Total	60
Released during the year	34

Average age 18 years and 7 months. Education – 12 had reached Standard IV, and two Standard VII at school. None were wholly illiterate. (The majority of Borstal youths had been in Standards II and III).

'A minimum of three years is needed to eradicate bad habits of want of self-control and inconsequence caused by years of bad environment,' but only five of the girls were committed for this period, and 12 of them for less than one year.'[33]

MODIFIED BORSTAL RULES IN LOCAL PRISONS

This experiment began in 1900, and by the Prevention of Crimes Act (1908) all juvenile adults (16–25 years in this case), except those sentenced to less than one month or more than three years, are dealt with, as far as possible, on Borstal lines under the superintendence of a Special Borstal Committee.[34] Those sentenced to more than four months are sent to special collecting centres. During 1910–11 there were 1,810 juvenile adults treated under modified Borstal rules in local prisons, and of the 651 discharged from special centres, 56 per cent. are known to be doing well, and only 8 per cent. are known to have been re-convicted.[35]

PRISONERS AID AND AFTER-CARE ASSOCIATIONS

Under the Borstal system every case is carefully followed up after leaving the institution by the Borstal Association. There are also voluntary committees, certified by the Home Office, for prisoners' aid at most local and convict prisons. A sum of £7,500 was recently assigned by the Chancellor of the Exchequer for the development of this work in relation to convicts, and since April, 1911, after care for them has been undertaken by one central agency called the 'Central Association for the Aid of Discharged Convicts,' which represents the Government and various Prisoners' Aid Societies, including the Church and Salvation Armies, and the Borstal Association.[36] It will henceforth exercise supervision over the discharged convict. The hated ticket-of-leave system is abolished. A prisoner who has earned a licence which entitles him or her to remission of sentence, is removed from all connection with the police, as long as he or she behaves properly. The Central Association has been at work too short a time for any result to be chronicled, but it should be remembered that the work of obtaining employment, lodging, etc., for discharged prisoners, and giving them encouragement to make a new start is quite as important as that of the probation officer. In this work women are taking a large share.

PREVENTIVE DETENTION

The habitual criminals who, under the Prevention of Crime Act, 1908, constitute the special convict class (B) should rather be termed 'professionals.' The special treatment wa intended for those 'competent, often highly skilled persons who deliberately, with their eyes open, preferred a life of crime and knew all the tricks and turns and manoeuvres necessary for that life.' By the new rules (February, 1911) the criminal presented by the police to the Director of Public Prosecutions for preventive detention, must be over thirty years of age, have already undergone a term of penal servitude and be charged anew with a substantial and serious offence. Convicts under preventive detention cannot, except by special licence from the Home Secretary, earn any remission of sentence. Instead they earn special privileges in prison, where they are kept under separate rules. Since the Act came into operation 250 males and 3 females have been received in this class.[37]

The experiment is of great interest to criminologists and penal reformers. It is a test of the curative effect upon healthy but anti-social persons of prolonged segregation, and also of segregation under conditions deliberately intended not to produce suffering, but to reform.

The Home Office has also recently been endeavoring to mitigate the suffering of imprisonment for convicts in general. The monotony for long sentence prisoners is relieved by periodical lectures and concerts. The Commissioners in their latest report mention with gratification the pleasure (Oh, shades of our grand-parents!) which the convicts take in these entertainments. Aged convicts have been placed in a special class and allowed some comforts.

INEBRIATES

'Over one-half of the women and nearly one-third of the men sentenced to imprisonment in this country are committed for drunkenness, and repeated convictions in both cases, and especially in the case of women, constitute one of the saddest and most unprofitable features of prison administration.'[38] The Inebriates Act of 1908 was an attempt to separate habitual drunkards from other offenders for curative treatment. It provided for the establishment of two classes of institutions, certified reformatories and state reformatories. Any person convicted of drunkenness four times in one year may be detained in one of these institutions for a period not exceeding three years. Those with a three years sentence are usually liberated at the expiration of two years and two months, and if they break out again are sent back to finish the remaining ten months.

The scheme as hitherto administered has turned out a costly failure. The cures are few, the drawbacks many. A woman, for instance, may be liberated to find her home broken up and herself alone and adrift. Two cases were reported recently of women who within three months of their discharge from an inebriate reformatory were re-committed in a state of pregnancy and remained comfortably housed until after confinement, when they were once more allowed to depart, their fatherless babies being sent to a children's home. Such a system is obviously faulty both from the moral and economic point of view, and many magistrates are refusing to make further use of inebriate reformatories. The state reformatories at Warwick (men) and Aylesbury (women) were intended for drunkards convicted of other crimes but have become scrap-heaps for the 'weak-minded, degraded, and more or less irresponsible' persons found unmanageable in certified reformatories. The Medical Inspector of Prisons has some grave words to say of the danger to society of losing all hold over these unfortunates 'simply because a sentence happens to have expired.'[39] The period of detention in such cases should be indeterminate, and the inebriate on release should be placed in the charge of a probation officer. Mental deficients should not be classified or treated with inebriates, but permanently segregated with those afflicted in like manner.

Alcoholism is pre-eminently a 'crime' that can only be effectually checked amongst the poor, as it has been amongst the rich, by a change both in conditions and in opinion. Imprisonment is worse than useless as deterrent or cure. So are fines as at present levied upon family necessities rather than upon the offender's drink money. Possibly home treatment under the care of a probation officer, combined in some cases with compulsory work or physical drill, might give the best chance of reformation to many delinquents in their noviciate.

THE MENTALLY UNSOUND

About 400 feeble-minded prisoners[40] are received by local prisons each year. 'For the last four or five years a record has been kept of their convictions, etc., and there are now nearly a thousand individuals on this register,' writes the Medical Inspector of Prisons, in his report for 1909–10. In 1910–11 he says 'the distressing feature of conviction and re-conviction of weak-minded prisoners shows no abatement'; and the Commissioners again urge their removal from prison to special institutions under medical care.

An attempt is being made to segregate males of unsound mind (not certified lunatics), sentenced to penal servitude, at Parkhurst Convict Prison, and to study them carefully. The medical officer reports 120 convicts classified as weak-minded, and 27 others under observation. The following extracts from his report need no comment.

Classification of 120 weak-minded convicts: – Congenital deficiency with epilepsy 10, without epilepsy 36, imperfectly developed stage of insanity 26, mental debility after attack of insanity 13, senility 3, alcoholic 9, undefined 23.

List of crimes for which they have been sentenced to penal servitude: – False pretences 1, receiving stolen property 2, larceny 24, burglary 13, housebreaking 19, blackmailing 1, manslaughter 5, doing grievous bodily harm 2, wounding 7, shooting 3, wilful murder 10, rape 2, carnal knowledge of little children 8, arson 17, horse stealing 3, killing sheep 1, obstruction on railways 1, unnatural offence 1.

Of these 62 committed their first crime before the age of 20, and the total number of convictions against the whole 120 feeble-minded convicts amounts to 91 penal and 1,306 other.[41]

At Aylesbury the feeble-minded convict women are also segregated in a special ward (daily average 12 during 1910–11).

There is, however, as yet no legal enquiry before conviction as to the pathological cause of crime, and these hapless creatures are still subject to penal discipline in convict prisons, and are discharged when their sentence is served; whilst in local prisons they still drift ceaselessly in and out. It is a crying social need to retain under permanent humane supervision beings whom it is as cruel to punish as it is dangerous to society to leave to their own devices.

IMPRISONMENT IN DEFAULT OF FINE

In cases where a fine is imposed time should always be given for its payment.[42] In 1910–11, of the total number received on conviction 84,885 (or 50 per cent.), 60,386 males and 24,499 females, were committed in default of fine. Obviously there is every reason to avoid sending persons to prison who fail to pay fines through poverty, and who might do so if given a reasonable period in which to earn or borrow money. To refuse them time is economically unsound, and increases the disparity of treatment of rich and poor. It should be noticed that there is not the same law for rich and poor in this matter, for the fine is imposed in proportion to the offence committed, and not to the income of the offender. A fine of 10s. to a work girl travelling without a ticket would equal £10 or even £1,000 to the careless rich committing the same offence, though the penalty imposed would be nominally the same; and, as a matter of fact, in many cases, the girl would go to prison, which entails her moral and economic ruin, while the rich man would not even be caused a momentary inconvenience by the payment of his fine.

AWAITING TRIAL

It is obviously advisable to avoid any association of the potential criminal with criminal surroundings. Children's Courts are a move in the right direction. It is a regulation of the Children Act, 1908, that the trials of boys and girls under fourteen must be held in a court separated by place or day from that used for adult offenders. Children must also now be kept apart from adult offenders during detention; but it is very undesirable that young girls and boys should be kept in gaol on remand for long periods, 'awaiting trial,' as is now the case, even though ultimately they may not be committed to prison. There can be very little distinction in the mind of a girl as to whether she is technically undergoing a sentence of imprisonment, or only awaiting a trial at which she may be acquitted, especially as her treatment in gaol differs comparatively little from that of a convicted prisoner. She obtains that familiarity with the inside of a prison which above all things ought to be avoided.

The whole system of rigorously confining accused persons in such a manner as to cripple their mental activity will presently be recognized as an arrant injustice.

The classification of offenders and the break up of the prison into a series of specialized institutions and services to deal with various classes has begun, but the movement has still far to go.

II. – Improvements in Administration

THE NEED FOR SPECIAL TRAINING

Changes of method such as those above indicated carry with them a need for the special training of officers of all grades connected with the penal service. There are now two grades for wardresses as for warders, and a training school for female officers has been formed at Holloway, where probationers are to be taught hygiene and Swedish drill, and some of them educated as technical teachers. There is no reason why the profession of prison wardress should not rank as high as that of trained hospital or asylum nurse. What is needed is that a woman, with a vocation like that of Florence Nightingale, shall come forward and show by her example that work in prisons is of equal importance with the tending of the sick, or the care of the mentally afflicted.

The post of prison doctor cannot satisfactorily be held by one who practises outside, as it requires very special study and training in pathology and mental science, and should give scope and work enough for a full-time post. In America criminal laboratories are being established for research into the pathology of crime. There are in this country men well equipped to undertake such work, and if, at the same time, statistics could be collected on scientific lines, much might be done towards elucidating the problem of recidivism. These laboratories could be utilized as lecture centres for the training of prison officials. At present only the medical officers are required to have any scientific training at all, and it is quite possible that even they have never studied criminal pathology or psychology. Public opinion should be educated to require at least as much scientific knowledge and special experience from prison officials as from the head and staff of a lunatic asylum.

The absence of specialized preparation for dealing with the delicate and difficult problems of criminal psychology is even more painfully apparent on the bench than amongst prison officials. Admirably efficient as the English judge usually is in eliciting evidence and procuring a just verdict, when he comes to consider the sentence, he is nearly always as complete an amateur as the average magistrate, who knows nothing of criminology or of prison life. Moreover, the whole bias of the English law of criminal evidence (which at every point insists on accentuating the facts of the particular crime and not drawing inferences from the ante-cedents of the criminal) handicaps the judge. He is led thereby 'to make the punishment fit the crime,' whereas the whole work of reform is to make it fit the criminal. Most of our judges are either 'merciful,' which means they revel in short sentences, or 'stern,' which means they give flogging when they can. The judge's work might well stop when the verdict is found, and sentence be passed, after careful, unhurried consideration of the record both of the case and of the criminal, by officials whose experience and expert training is of another sort.

THE NEED FOR WOMEN OFFICIALS

It is exceedingly desirable that women should be on the medical staff of prisons where women are confined. The medical woman Inspector has already done much to improve the conditions of women prisoners, and it is greatly to be hoped that this appointment will be followed by those of other women as medical officers as well as inspectors. The office of spiritual or moral adviser also is one which some women are particularly well qualified to fill in a prison. Again, in a woman's prison it seems desirable that the governor should be a woman. In the small local prison at Aigle, in the Rhone Valley, a woman is governor in charge of both men and women prisoners; why not at Holloway or Aylesbury, where all prisoners are women? And why is not one at least of the Prison Commissioners a woman?

Women are already employed in this country in the detective service. When the whole police force is employed more extensively in the prevention than the detection of crime, as it surely will presently be, women's help will be increasingly needful. A women's auxiliary to the police force, as already in operation in Germany, would be invaluable.

Undoubtedly where girls or women are concerned in cases connected with indecency or immorality the courts might well be cleared of all men, except those officially concerned, as is done in children's courts; but if any of the public are allowed to remain, the court should not be cleared, as is now the case, of all women. It is obviously unfair in such cases that a woman should be obliged to give evidence or to be tried alone before a general audience of men. It would be an advantage if it were made compulsory for a police court matron or woman probation officer to be in charge of young women offenders to prevent their contamination by hardened criminals, and to be present when their cases are tried. It has been suggested that there should be special courts for women as for children, but these will hardly serve any useful purpose unless there are women magistrates and the women's auxiliary to the police force to deal with women and children, innovations which would do more than anything perhaps for the reform of police court procedure, especially as it concerns women and young persons. It seems probable that women would be more likely than men to understand and to enter into cases concerning their own sex. The same qualities which have made women invaluable in poor law, educational, and municipal administration, and in the large and increasing amount of voluntary work which they are doing in connection with prisons, are likely to make them invaluable on the magistrates' bench.

It is probable that in the future women will be appointed as judges and magistrates, as well as summoned to serve on juries; and this is, in our opinion, a consummation most devoutly to be wished in the interests of society.[43] There is no path of change along which women are more particularly concerned to press forward than that which leads them to an official share in judicial procedure and in the administration of the penal system.

Notes

1 Outlawry, i.e., being out of the king's protection, is still a possible penalty for crime; abolished for civil cases 1879. Pollock and Maitland, 'History of English Law,' Vol. I., p. 49, note. For imprisonment in the Middle Ages and penalties incident to exile, Ibid., Vol. II., pp. 516–8. Banishment from the village was practised in Scotland in the nineteenth century. Andrews, 'Old Time Punishments,' p. 114.

2 'White Servitude in Virginia' (Ballagh); 'Slavery and Servitude in North Carolina' (Bassett). Johns Hopkins University Studies, xiii. and xiv.

3 See Report of Select Committee on Transportation, 1838.

4 1,601 persons were condemned to death in 1831; in 1910–11 only 25.

5 Howard first called attention to the subject in his 'State of Prisons in England and Wales,' 1777. Mrs Fry started the 'Association for the Improvement of Female Prisoners in Newgate' in 1817. Like Howard she afterwards carried on a widespread agitation for prison reform at home and abroad.

6 Page 354.

7 A jerk causing instant death by breaking the neck is said to have been first tried as a substitute for slow suffocation by hanging in 1760.

8 Three females were condemned to death during 1910–11, but in each case the sentence was commuted. – Report of the Commissioners of Prisons, Part I, p. 103.

9 Recidivist convicts serve three months in solitary confinement, now called 'separate.'

10 Report of the Commissioners of Prisons and Directors of Convict Prisons, 1910–11, p. 78.

11 The following particulars are taken from the 'Prisons Rules for Local and Convict Prisons in England, issued 1898, and revised to December, 1903,' compared with later administrative orders and the experiences of prisoners down to 1912.

12 Ibid.

13 Next to heart disease the most frequent causes of deaths in prison are

pneumonia and phthisis. – Medical Report of Commissioners, 1910–11, Part I., p. 40.

14 The reference here is to 'special' cells for refractory prisoners.

15 Reference, unless otherwise stated, is to 'The Report of the Commissioners of Prisons and the Directors of Convict Prisons for the year ended March, 1911,' Part I.

16 Ibid, p. 64.

17 Ibid, pp. 11 and 34–6.

18 Statistics brought together from same Report, Tables pp. 104–7.

19 During 1910–11, males convicted summarily and otherwise for cruelty to children 870, females 675. Compare proportion with that for common assault, males 4,416, females 821. Ibid.

20 From 'Report from the Select Committee on Transportation communicated by the Commons to the Lords, 1838.'

21 Major A. G. F. Griffiths, H.M. Inspector of Prisons 1878–96, article 'Prisons,' Encyclopaedia Britannica. For Major Griffiths's larger works see Bibliography. Compare Kirkman Gray, 'Philanthropy and the State,' pp. 161–4.

22 8,642 women were sent to local prisons for this offence during the year March 1910–11; 6,013 of them in default of fine. During the same year out of the 123,172 males and 35,378 females received into local prisons, 3,614 males and 149 females were sentenced as disorderly paupers, 2,115 males and 134 females for neglect to maintain a family, and 926 males and 44 females for stealing or destroying workhouse clothes and other offences against the Poor Law. Under the Vagrancy Acts 20,988 males and 1,061 females were sentenced for begging, and 5,087 males and 381 females for sleeping out of doors. During this year altogether 60,386 males and 24,499 females were imprisoned simply in default of payment of fine, and 17,437 as debtors or under civil process. 910 males and one female were committed under the Game Laws. Report of Commissioners of Prisons, Part I., pp. 28, 109–10.

23 Ibid, pp. 28, 42.

24 Ibid, Appendix 18, Table D. pp. 130–143.

25 Ibid, p. 28.

26 Ibid, pp. 132–3.

27 As an example of such take the poisoner Palmer, as described by Sir James Fitzjames Stephen in 'A General View of the Criminal Law of England,' p. 272.

28 Criminal Statistics for 1909, pp. 166, 167, Table 4, III.

29 Report of Prison Commissioners, Part I., 1910–11, p. 24.

30 Ibid., Part II., p. 192.

31 Ibid, Part II., p. 200, from Report of Governor of Feltham Borstal Institution.

32 Ibid, Part II.

33 Ibid, Part II., pp. 188–90, Report of Officers of Aylesbury Borstal.

34 Age limit for males 16–21; females sentenced for less than one month are eligible.

35 Ibid, Part I., p. 25.
36 Ibid, Part I., pp. 100–1.
37 Ibid, pp. 113–6.
38 Report of Prison Commissioners, 1908–9, Part I.
39 Report of Prison Commissioners, 1910–11, Part I., p. 57.
40 Medically certified as 'unfit for prison discipline'; many have hitherto been uncertified.
41 Ibid, Part II., p. 219.
42 This is one of the reforms which the Home Secretary promised in 1910 to inaugurate at once.
43 A measure qualifying women to exercise judicial functions is now before the Norwegian Parliament. In Mrs. Wolstenholme Elmy's pamphlet, 'The Criminal Code in Relation to Women,' 1880, the cause of the disuse of the ancient 'jury of matrons' is described.

FABIAN TRACT No. 175
(June 1914)

THE ECONOMIC FOUNDATIONS OF THE WOMEN'S MOVEMENT

M.A.

The Spiritual Aspect of the Women's Movement

PURELY economic causes are never sufficient to account entirely for any great revolt of the human spirit. Behind every revolution there lies a spiritual striving, a grasping after an ideal felt rather than seen. Most emphatically is it true that there is a social impulse independent of economic conditions, which has over and over again asserted itself in the demand for the emancipation of women. All the greatest seers and prophets have insisted on the equal value of men and women, and on the right of women to control their own lives. Four centuries before Christ, Plato claimed that in the life of the State women, as well as men, should take their place; and in all the records of Christ's conversations, which the Gospels have handed down to us, there is not one hint that he advocated that subordination of women on which his disciples later on insisted. In Rome also, at the Renaissance, and at the time of the French Revolution, powerful voices were raised in denunciation of the subjection of women.

These demands were, however, only sporadic. At most they affected a small class. It was not until the nineteenth century that the demand of women for political, economic, and educational freedom was heard among any considerable mass of the people. This extension of the demand for emancipation was due to economic changes, to those alterations in human control over environment which are associated with the substitution of mechanical power for human energy in the making of commodities, and with the development of powerful and smoothly working machines in place of human hands and simple tools.

The economic foundations of the women's movement

The Effect of the Industrial Revolution

Probably when Hargreaves invented his spinning jenny, and when Arkwright established his first cotton mill, in which the power of water took the place of the easily wearied arms of humanity, they had no conception of the fact that they were preparing the way for the greatest revolution in human society which has ever taken place since man learnt the use of fire. Yet nothing less was the truth, for then first men learnt how to utilize for their service the energies of the universe without previously absorbing them into their own bodies or into the bodies of domesticated animals in the form of food. Before the end of the eighteenth century man did indeed use water power on a small scale for grinding corn, and the capricious force of the wind for the same end and for propelling sailing vessels. But the energies of steam and electricity and petrol were lying dormant or running to waste all around him, while he sweated at the forge or the loom, and was hauled slowly over badly made roads by the straining sinews of horses. Now throughout human society inanimate forces are at work, harnessed at last successfully to the service of man, shaping iron and steel plates, setting to work looms and printing presses, propelling enormous trains of waggons, urging leviathan ships across the ocean.

Before this mighty revolution, whatever alterations man wanted made in his world must be made through his own physical exertions; now he sets to work the energies of his environment to remould that environment according to his needs. From himself there is demanded merely the brain work of planning and directing and the nervous strain of tendence on the marvellous machines. It is true that in our badly arranged social system (all of whose concepts of property, contract, wages, and labor are still adjusted to the pre-machine era) the increased control over nature has brought but little advantage to the mass of the workers. But the full effects of the substitution of inanimate for human energy have not yet been seen, and will ultimately work themselves out into conditions of life vastly different from those which we know at present.

Women Before the Industrial Revolution

Of all the changes introduced by the industrial revolution there is none greater than the alteration brought about in the position of women. Many people believe that it was only in the nineteenth century that women began, on a large scale, to work for their living. There could be no greater mistake. All the evidence goes to show that before the eighteenth century women, with few exceptions, worked as hard and as long as men did. In the sixteenth century women not only helped their husbands in farm work, but they toiled at spinning and carding of flax and wool as a by-industry of their own. Few nineteenth century women could work harder than the wife of a sixteenth century husbandman, whose duties are thus described by Fitzherbert, writing in 1534:

'First swepe thy house, dresse up thy dysshe bord, and sette all thynges in good order within thy house. Milk thy kye, suckle thy calves, sye up thy mylke, take uppe thy children and array them, and provide for thy husband's brekefaste, dinner, souper, and thy children and servants, and take thy part with them. And to ordayne corne and malt to the myll, and bake and brue withal whanne nede is. And meet it to the mill and fro the mill, and se that thou have thy measure again beside the toll, or else the miller dealeth not truly with the or els thy corn is not drye as it should be. Thou must make butter and cheese when thou maist, serve thy swyne both morning and evening and give thy poleyn [i.e., poultry] meat in the morning; and when tyme of the year cometh thou must take hede how thy hennes, duckes, and geese do ley, and to gather up their eggs, and when they wax broodie to set them there as no beasts, swyne, or other vermin hurt them. . . . And when they brought forth their birds to see that they be well kept from the gleyd, kites, crowe, polecats, fullymarts, and other vermin. And in the beginning of March or a little before is tyme for a wife to make her garden, and to gette as many good seedes and herbes as she canne, and specially such as be good for the pott and to eat. And also in March is tyme to sowe flax and hemp . . . but how it should be sown, weded, pulled, rippled, watered, washen, dryed, beaten, braked, tawed, heckled, spon, wounded, wrapped, and woven, it needeth not for me to show, for they be wise enough. And thereof may they make shetes, bordclothes, towels, sherts, smocks, and such other necessaries; and therefore let thy distaff be always ready for a pastime, that thou be not idle. . . . May fortune sometime that thou shalt have so many things to do that thou shalt not well know where is best to begin. . . . It is convenient for a husband to have shepe of his owne for many causes, and then maye his wife have part of the wool to make her husband and herself some clothes. And at the least way she may have the locks of the sheep either to make clothes or blankets and coverlets, or both. And if she have no wool of her own, she may take wool to spyn of clothmakers, and by that means she may have a convenient living and many tymes to do other works. It is a wife's occupation to wynowe all manner of corns, and make malt, to wasshe and wrynge, to make haye, shere corn, and in tyme of nede to helpe her husband fyll the muckwain or dungcart, drive the plough, to load hay, corn, and such other. And to go or ride to the market to sell butter, cheese, milk, eggs, chekyns, capons, henns, pigs, geese, and all manner of corns. And also to bye all manner of necessary things belonging to the household, and to make a trewe reckoning and account to her husband what she hath paid. And if the husband go to the market to bye or sell, as they oft do, he then to show his wife in like manner.'[1]

About two hundred years later a realistic Scotch novelist makes his hero write thus of his second marriage:

'I had placed my affections, with due consideration, on Miss Lizy Kibbock, the well brought up daughter of Mr Joseph Kibbock, of the Gorbyholm . . . whose cheeses were of such excellent quality that they have, under the name of Delap cheese, spread far and wide over the civilized world . . . The second Mrs Balquhidder that was had a genius for management . . . for she was the bee that made my honey. There was such a buying of wool to make blankets, with a booming of the meikle wheel to spin the same, and such birring of the little wheel for sheets and napery, that the manse was for many a day like an organ kist. Then we had milk cows and the calves to bring up and a kirning of butter and a making of cheese. In short, I was almost by myself with the jangle and din . . . and I for a time thought of the peaceful and kindly nature of the first Mrs Balquhidder with a sigh; but the outcoming was soon manifest. The second Mrs Balquhidder sent her butter on the market days to Irville, and her cheese from time to time to Glasgow to Mrs Firlot, that kept the huxtry in the Salt Market; and they were both so well made that our dairy was just a coining of money, insomuch that after the first year we had the whole lot of my stipend to put untouched into the bank.'[2]

The Family as the Economic Unit; Marriage an Industrial Partnership

These extracts – and many like them could be quoted[3] – show clearly that before the industrial revolution women took a full share in industrial work. The basis of their work, however, was quite different from what it is today. Speaking generally, before the industrial revolution the economic unit was the family, and not the individual. So much was this the case, that in the censuses of 1811, 1821, and 1831 it was assumed that all the members of the family would practise the same occupation. Much of the work done by women in the family was of a domestic nature for the immediate service of their husbands and children, and not for profit. In technical language it was the production of use values, and not of exchange values. This can be illustrated from the inventory of the furniture of a middle class house at Brook, near Wingham, in 1760, which is preserved in an auctioneer's catalogue in the British Museum. The equipment of the establishment included a bolting room, where were kept 'one large neading trough, one meal tub and sieve, and one quilting frame'; a bottle house, which contained, among other things, 'one brine tub, one syder stock and beater, one pickling trough'; a milk house, where were kept 'milk keelers, churns, a butter board, and a butter printer.' In the 'larder' were 'pickling pans and stilling tubs'; in the brew house 'a mash tub, five brewing keelers, and one bucking tub' (whatever that may have been).

But it would be a mistake to assume that women never worked for profit. The second Mrs Balquhidder obviously did. It is common to find a woman carrying on the farm or shop of her husband after his death, and the farmer's wife, who has been already described, was her husband's working partner in his business enterprise as well as his housekeeper and servant. In fact, before the nineteenth century marriage was an industrial partnership as well as a relation of affection. The women worked, and worked hard, contributing much to the wealth of England, which was sold in her markets. This situation must have served to modify considerably the harshness of the common law, which decreed the husband's entire control of his wife's property. Fitzherbert's husbandman, depending as he did on his wife's energy in poultry yard, garden, and spinning room, would not be likely to insist upon his legal rights to take absolute possession of her earnings. And in one way the law recognized the wife's partnership. A husband could not leave his property entirely away from his wife. The widow's ancient right to one third of her husband's property was only abolished in England by the Reform Parliament,[4] that Parliament which was called together on the basis of the Franchise Act, which for the first time introduced the word 'male' into the qualifications of the parliamentary elector.

The Alteration of the Economic Basis of the Family

Before the industrial revolution, then, the household was, as a general rule, the unit of industry, and women worked in it as members of the family for the production of exchange as well as of use values. Now what was the effect of the industrial revolution on the position of women in relation to these economic activities of the family? Briefly, the answer is that the introduction of machinery, by taking work out of the home and establishing the factory, the railway, and the mine as the organs of industry, broke up the family as an economic unit and diminished the amount of production for use carried on within the home. Brewing, baking, butter-making, spinning, weaving, even – to a large extent – the making of clothes, have ceased to be activities of the family; and increasingly housewives are finding that it is cheaper and more convenient to hand over jam making, laundry work, even window cleaning and floor polishing, to agencies that exist independently of the home. This is an inevitable development. Modern machinery and the use of artificial sources of power immensely cheapen production, but they can only be used by organizations bigger than the family group. So that the economic basis of the family has altered more within the last hundred years than in the whole course of Christian civilizaton preceding that time.

Inevitably this has reacted on the position of women, whose relation to the family was always closer than that of men; and the changes in the nature and aspirations of women, which have developed in the nineteenth century, are very largely, though not entirely, due to these altered economic conditions.

The Changed Position of Women

But different classes of women were affected very differently. Among the wealthier people attempts were made to preserve the subordination of women to the family unit, although the economic justification for that dependence had ceased. Among the poor the necessity for the women's contribution to the family income was so strong that they were drafted into the new forms of industrial life without any consideration of their powers or capacities. To put it shortly, parasitism became the fate of the middle class women, ruthless exploitation that of the working class women. The latter were absorbed in large numbers by the new factories, as were also the children, who equally had worked as parts of the family unit; and the first stage of machine production saw the women and children workers cruelly and shamelessly sacrificed to the demands of profit.

The Exploitation of the Working Women

There is no need to repeat this oft told story, but it may be pointed out that the previous close relation of the women and children to the family unit had rendered them incapable of asserting themselves against the powers of capital and competition. And the low wages which they received made them dangerous rivals of the men and no longer co-operators with them. No one during the first agitation for the Factory Acts seems to have realized that the general labor of women and children pulled down the wages of men. The conditions became so bad that dead in the face of a public opinion more strongly individualistic than has ever been the case either before or since, the State was forced to constitute itself the established guardian of the women and children, and to bring into existence all the machinery of the Factory Acts, by which, first in the textile industries and in mining, later on in all branches of machine production, and still later in practically the whole field of industry, an attempt was made to preserve women and children from the degradation and suffering due to over long hours and work in unsanitary conditions. The problem is, of course, not yet fully solved. In the industrial world the cheap labor of women is continually threatening new industries. Since these women believe themselves inferior to men, and since most of them expect to marry early and regard their occupation only as a makeshift, they are naturally willing to work more cheaply than men, and so constitute a perpetual menace to the masculine standard of life, while they themselves are subjected to conditions unfit for human beings. It cannot be wondered at that under these circumstances many social reformers regard the work of women outside the home as an evil development. For women in the industrial world are frequently forced to be blacklegs. Moreover, the conditions of modern large scale industry are determined not by the needs of the human beings who work in it, but by the demands of the machinery, and are therefore often unsuitable for women (equally so, in all probability, for men). In the early days of the movement for State regulation of industry, that innovation on the doctrine of *laissez faire* which then prevailed was justified on the ground that women were not free agents. Men, it was asserted, could and should stand out for themselves against the power of their employers. The State ought never to interfere in the wages contracts formed by its citizens among themselves, but women and children were not citizens. They were weak, ignorant, easily exploited. Further, they represented in a special way the human capital of the nation. The men might be used from generation to generation and the life of the race would still continue, but a nation which lived upon the labor of its women and children was doomed to degeneration.

The Parasitism of the Middle Class Women

In this view there is, of course, a truth which must never be forgotten. But it ignores another part of the problem, that which confronted the other class of women. The middle class women had so awful and so bitter an experience that for a time they were quite unable to appreciate the need of State protection for women.

The result for them of the introduction of machinery was altogether opposite to the effect produced upon the industrial women. As the economic functions of the family diminished, the daughters of lawyers, doctors, wealthy shopkeepers, and manufacturers did not work out new forms of activity for themselves. It would have been against the dignity of their fathers and brothers to permit them to do so. Moreover, it would have diminished their chances of marriage, and would have involved a breach with the people who were nearest and dearest to them. They remained within the family group, occupied in the insignificant domestic duties that still remained and in the futilities of an extraordinarily conventional social intercourse. Dusting, arranging the flowers, and paying calls were the important duties of their existence. The married middle class woman had indeed, as wife and mother, a definite place and important responsibility, though the decay of household activities and the growing habit of living in suburbs, quite apart from the man's business, lessened at every point her contact with the social world and cut even her off more than had ever been the case previously from intercourse with the spheres of industry and commerce. But the unmarried woman, forbidden during her years of greatest vitality and strongest desire for new scenes and fresh interest to find any channels for her energies, save those of 'helping mamma' and 'visiting the poor,' suffered intensely from the inactive parasitism forced upon her. Exploitation brings great suffering; but suffering as acute, though more obscure, is experienced by those whose growing powers and growing need for human contacts are damned within them by an incomprehensible social fiat, resting really on conditions that had passed away a generation earlier. The only escape from this enforced inactivity and dependence was through marriage. The middle class woman, in fact, was regarded solely from the stand-point of sex. There was no way by which she might satisfy her natural wish to use the welling energies within her other than by becoming the mistress of a household. Naturally, therefore, she often regarded 'to be settled' as an end to be aimed at, quite apart from the personality of the man who offered to make her his wife. And the irony of the situation was that to the finer spirits who refused to acquiesce in this degradation of love to the economic plane, there was no other alternative than an existence which became 'that useless, blank, pale, slow-trailing thing' of which one of Charlotte Bronte's heroines so bitterly complains.

The Surplus of Women

As the nineteenth century wore on other tendencies came into play which further increased the hardships of middle class women. The presence of a surplus of women in the middle classes made itself more and more apparent. Probably the cause of this is the emigration of young men, rendered necessary by our enormous colonial development; but it may be that some other and more subtle cause is at work. Exact statistics are difficult to give, as our statistics are not based on class distinctions. But certain conclusions can be drawn, as Miss Clara Collet first pointed out, from the distribution of unmarried males and females over certain ages in different boroughs of London, which to some extent are peopled by different classes of the community. The following table shows how striking the difference is, and how the surplus of females tends to accumulate in the better off districts. Some have urged that these surplus females are really domestic servants. But the number of female unmarried domestic servants over thirty-five is comparatively small.

Number of unmarried males and females between the ages of thirty-five and fifty-five in three wealthy and three poor London boroughs, as given in the Census of 1911.

	Males	Females
Hampstead	1,559	4,655
Kensington	2,785	11,395
Chelsea	1,414	3,688
Woolwich	1,861	1,526
Shoreditch	1,689	1,004
Bethnal Green	1,635	1,320

Putting the same facts in another way, for every 100 unmarried men between thirty-five and fifty-five there are in Hampstead 291 unmarried women of the same ages, in Kensington 409, and in Chelsea 260; while in Woolwich to every 100 unmarried men of these ages there are 81 unmarried women, in Shoreditch only 59, and in Bethnal Green 81.

We can cite also an article by Miss Hutchins in the *Englishwoman*, June, 1913, in the course of which she says: 'Another means of comparing the prospects of marriage in different social strata is by comparing the proportion of single women in the age group 25–45 in rich and poor districts respectively. In making this comparison we must allow for the numbers of domestic servants, who of course very considerably augment the proportion of single women in the wealthy residential districts. The following table shows that, even if we subtract all the domestic indoor servants from the single women in the age group (which is over-generous, as a small but unknown proportion of them are certainly married or widowed), the single women in Hampstead, Kensington and Paddington are a considerably higher proportion than in Stepney, Shoreditch and Poplar. These districts have been 'selected' only in the sense that they were the first that occurred to the writer as affording a marked contrast of wealth and poverty.'

Number and proportion of single women and domestic indoor servants in every 100 women aged 25–45 in certain London boroughs. (Census of 1911).[5]

	Number	Per cent. of Women aged 25–45	Difference of percentage
HAMPSTEAD			
Single Women	11,483	57.3	24.7
Domestic Servants	6,534	32.6	
KENSINGTON			
Single Women	21,967	56	21.8
Domestic Servants	13,431	34.2	
PADDINGTON			
Single Women	13,711	46.6	24.5
Domestic Servants	6,473	22.1	
POPLAR			
Single Women	4,406	19.5	17.3
Domestic Servants	506	2.2	
SHOREDITCH			
Single Women	2,923	18.1	15.9
Domestic Servants	340	2.2	
STEPNEY			
Single Women	7,158	18.4	15
Domestic Servants	1,207	3.4	

This table also brings out the extraordinary difference between the proportions of women of the most marriageable period of life married in rich and in poor districts. The same fact is illustrated by the following table, comparing the number of married, single and widowed women among the population living 'on private means' and among the general population. The comparison is suggested by Miss Hutchins, but the table used by her in the *Englishwoman* cannot be reproduced here as the new Census does not give the information in the same way.

Number and percentage of single, married and widowed women over 20 years of age in the population living on private means and in the general population in England. (Census of 1911.)

	Living on Private Means		General Population	
	Number	Percentage	Number	Percentage
Unmarried	136,705	46.5	3,448,442	30.2
Married	23,724	8.1	6,610,173	57.9
Widowed	133,698	45.4	1,364,715	11.9
Total	294,127	100	11,423,330	100

No doubt the figures in this table are distorted by the number of widows who owe their private means to their widowhood, but even allowing for this it is remarkable to discover that the percentage of married women in the general population is so much greater than in the population living on private means.

But statistical evidence is really not necessary. All hostesses and organizers of middle class social functions know well that one of the constant difficulties with which they have to contend is the over supply of women.

The Salaried Middle Class

Another new element in the position of the middle class woman arises from the fact that her men relations tend to become salaried officials in place of independent merchants and employers. This means not only that the women can no longer take part in the economic activities of their men relations, but that, in the event of the death of the latter, their position is far more precarious. A business or a shop goes on even after the death of a husband or father who established or inherited it, but when a salaried official dies his family are altogether deprived of the support which he afforded them.

Can He Afford to Get Married?

And again, if a wife is no longer of any direct economic value, if, on the contrary, she is an expense, then men, in many cases probably with reluctance, must defer marriage until they can afford that luxury. To a middle class man before the industrial revolution, as indeed to the men of the working class at present, marriage was not a thing 'to be afforded.' A wife was a partner, bringing to the relation of wedlock economically, as well as in other and more emotional ways, as much value as she received. But the middle class bachelor contemplating marriage today realizes that he must be prepared to double, or more than double, his expenditure, while his wife adds nothing to the income. Therefore he defers marriage, finding often an outlet to his emotions in other directions (it would be interesting to endeavour to trace the relation between prostitution and the use of machinery), and the girl who should be his mate withers unwanted in the 'upholstered cage' of her parents' home. Therefore in the nineteenth century the middle class woman had fewer chances of marriage, was less needed in the family life if unmarried, and was liable to find herself when that family life came to an end through the death of a father or brother stranded resourceless on the world.

The Tragedy of the Surplus Women

It is heartrending to think of the hidden tragedies which these sociological changes brought in their train, the mute sufferings of the women, who, unmated and workless, felt themselves of no value or importance to the world around them. What wonder that in the end a revolt came, and women insisted that in the great world of human activities outside the family they, too, must have place and power. Some echo of this unhappiness found its way into the literature of the Victorian era. Charlotte Bronte utters it in the repinings of poor Caroline Helston.

'Caroline,' demanded Miss Keeldar, abruptly, 'don't you wish you had a profession – a trade?'

'I wish it fifty times a day. As it is, I often wonder what I came into the world for. I long to have something absorbing and compulsory to fill my head and hands, and to occupy my thoughts.'

'Can labor alone make a human being happy?'

'No; but it can give varieties of pain, and prevent us from breaking our hearts with a single tyrant master torture. Besides, successful labor has its recompense; a vacant, weary, lonely, hopeless life has none.'

'But hard labor and learned professions, they say, make women masculine, coarse, unwomanly.'

'And what does it signify whether unmarried and never-to-be-married women are unattractive and inelegant or not? Provided only they are decent, decorous, and neat, it is enough. The utmost which ought to be required of old maids in the way of appearance is that they should not absolutely offend men's eyes as they pass them in the street. For the rest, they should be allowed, without too much scorn, to be as absorbed, grave, plain looking, and plain dressed as they please.'

'You might be an old maid yourself, Caroline; you speak so earnestly.'

'I shall be one; it is my destiny. I will never marry a Malone or a Sykes, and no one else will ever marry me.'[6]

'Look at the numerous families of girls in this neighbourhood: the Armitages, the Birtwhistles, the Sykes. The brothers of these girls are every one in business or in professions. They have something to do. Their sisters have no earthly employment but household work and sewing; no earthly pleasure but an unprofitable visiting; and no hope in all their life to come of anything better. This stagnant state of things makes them decline in health. They are never well, and their minds and views shrink to wondrous narrowness. The great wish, the sole aim, of everyone of them is to be married. But the majority will never marry; they will die as they now live. They scheme, they plot, they dress to ensnare husbands. The gentlemen turn them into ridicule; they don't want them; they hold them very cheap; they say – I have heard them say it with sneering laughs many a time – the matrimonial market is overstocked. Fathers say so likewise, and are angry with their daughters when they observe their manoeuvres. They order them to stay at home. What do they expect them to do at home? If you ask, they would answer, sew and cook. They expect them to do this, and this only, contentedly, regularly, uncomplainingly, all their lives long, as if they had no germs of faculties for anything else. A doctrine as reasonable to hold as it would be that the fathers have no faculties but for eating what their daughters cook, or for wearing what they sew.'[7]

The same restlessness, unconscious as it usually was of its cause, was expressed even more fully by George Gissing in that wonderful book, 'The Odd Women.' But to most people the elderly spinster was no more than an occasion for mocking, and yet the same people were most bitter against the women who demanded the right to work, the right to education, and the right to enter politics, those three demands of the disinherited women of middle class Victorian England.

The First Feminist Movement

The first feminist movement emerged into the open at the time of the Reform Bill of 1867. If its origin is grasped, its peculiar characteristics will be easily understood. It was on the whole a demand of elderly unmarried women for the right to freer activities, as the alternative to an impracticable ideal of marriage and motherhood for every woman.[8] Therefore it is not astonishing that these early feminists tended on the whole to ignore differences of sex, since those differences had been made the pretext for condemning them to a condition of parasitism, against which a healthy human being was bound to revolt. It was natural enough that these pioneers of the women's movement should insist upon their likeness to men, should demand the right to the same education as men received and the entrance to the same professions as men followed. In their revolt against the degradations which sex parasitism had brought in its train, it was not unnatural that in their dress and bearing they should neglect the grace and charm which a normal man will always desire in women. It was not unnatural either, when they found a section of the public advocating in industry special protection of women by law, that they should regard this as another form of the masculine exclusiveness from which they themselves suffered, so that to them the right of a woman to be a doctor and the right of a woman to work underground in a mine should present themselves as similar demands. Being but middle class women, influenced by the progressive ideals of their class, they were mostly Liberals, and to their special dread of the exclusion of women from human activities, other than those conditioned by sex, was added the strong individualism of the Liberalism of the period. Therefore they naturally set themselves in opposition to the demand for factory legislation, and there arose in consequence misunderstandings between two sections of reformers, the echoes of which have persisted to our own time.

Its Attitude towards Marriage

The attitude towards marriage of these early feminists has also been much misunderstood. There were, no doubt, a certain number among them who were indifferent or opposed to marriage; but most of them found themselves driven into hostility to normal family relations, mainly because these were used as an argument to convince them that the alterations in the position of women which they desired were impossible. When a woman, struggling for education and the right to work for herself, was met by the objection: 'If you learn Greek or if you become a doctor no one will marry you,' is it astonishing that she answered, 'I don't care if no one does'? Moreover, as has been already said, the pioneers came mostly from the class of 'superfluous women.' They knew well that marriage was far from being the certainty or the likelihood which their opponents always assumed it to be. The alternative for them was not work *or* marriage, but work and money of their own *or* a spinstered existence in their fathers' houses. Therefore, naturally most of them put out of their minds, with what bitterness few people have realized, the possibility of marriage and motherhood, and turned instead to develop their own intellectual and spiritual forces, devoting themselves to public work and to the struggle for that independent living which is so sweet to the woman who has revolted against parasitism.

Economic Independence

Few men understand what importance the modern middle class woman attaches to her economic independence. To men the right to earn a livelihood does not present itself as a hardly won and cherished privilege, but as a tiresome necessity. They may have earned an income with difficulty, but, at least, when they earned it it was theirs to spend as they would. But many women, even wealthy women, dressed in gorgeous raiment, with servants and horses and carriages at their command, never know what it is to be able to spend a guinea on the gratification simply of their own tastes. The money that they receive comes from father or husband, and must be spent as father or husband approve. Workers in the feminist movement are perfectly familiar with the well-dressed and prosperous looking woman who declares, 'Yes, I quite agree with you. I have often thought these things myself, and I wish I could help, but my husband does not approve of Women's Suffrage, and I have no money except what I get from him.'[9] The life of the professional woman is often toilsome and often lonely, but the power of self-direction and self-activity which economic independence brings with it counts for much, and few women who have realized what sex parasitism means, and have succeeded in emerging from it will ever willingly return to it.

The Two Sections of the Women's Movement

So, at the present time there are two main sections in the modern women's movement – the movement of the middle class women who are revolting against their exclusion from human activity and insisting, firstly, on their right to education, which is now practically conceded on all sides; secondly, on their right to earn a livelihood for themselves, which is rapidly being won; and, thirdly, on their right to share in the control of Government, the point round which the fight is now most fiercely raging. These women are primarily rebelling against the sex-exclusiveness of men, and regard independence and the right to work as the most valuable privilege to be striven for.

On the other hand, there are the women of the working classes, who have been faced with a totally different problem, and who naturally react in a different way. Parasitism has never been forced on them. Even when the working class woman does not earn her own living in the world of industry – though practically all the unmarried girls of the working classes do so – her activities at home are so unending, and she subconsciously feels so important and so valuable, that she has never conceived of herself as useless and shut out from human interests, as was the parasitic middle class woman. What the woman of the proletariat feels as her grievance is that her work is too long and too monotonous, the burden laid upon her too heavy. Moreover, in her case that burden is due to the power of capitalistic exploitation resulting from the injustice of our social system. It is not due, or not, at least, to any considerable extent, to the fact that the men of her class shut her out from gainful occupations. Therefore, among the working women there is less sex consciousness. Evolving social enthusiasm tends to run rather into the channel of the labor revolt in general than into a specific revolution against the conditions alleged to be due to sex differences. The working woman feels her solidarity with the men of her class rather than their antagonism to her. The reforms that she demands are not independence and the right to work, but rather protection against the unending burden of toil which has been laid upon her. A speaker at a working women's congress said once, 'It is not work we want, but more love, more leisure to enjoy life, and more beauty.' These facts explain the relative lukewarmness of working class women in the distinctively feminist movement, and one of the possible dangers of the future is that the working class women in their right and natural desire to be protected against that exploitation which the first development of machinery brought with it, should allow themselves to drift without observing it into the parasitism which was the lot of middle class women. If the exclusion of married women from all paid work were carried out; if the unmarried women were at the same time prevented from following all those occupations which reactionary male hygienists choose, without adequate investigation, to assume to be bad for women; if at the same time the growth of the public supply of schools and other agencies for the care of children were to go on and the number of children in each family were to continue to diminish; if the home, by reason of the development of machinery and large scale production, were to lose all those remaining economic activities which are carried on within it, then working women might come to live through the same experience as the middle class women have already known.

Sex-consciousness among Working Women

But changes are proceeding in this situation. The consciousness of their rights and wrongs as a sex is arising among the working class women. They are beginning to see the possibility that even in the fight against capitalist exploitation, on which the men of their class are now entering, their specific interests may be overlooked. The shocking disregard of the needs of women by the Insurance Act has given them a clear proof of this. The great calamity against which the working class woman needs insurance is the death of her husband and bread winner; yet it is commonly stated that in the bargain with the big insurance societies the Government simply threw overboard the plans for a form of insurance which would make more secure the position of widows and orphans. Again, the home-staying working class woman finds that the Government cares little for her health, and makes practically no provision for her care should she fall ill, save in the one case of maternity benefit, and that, by curious irony, was originally to be paid to the husband and not to herself, save where the woman was herself a wage earner. Moreover, the development of social legislation is throwing heavier burdens on the working woman, and is yet making scant provision for her special needs. There are clubs, lectures, holidays provided for men, for boys, for young girls; but for the married woman how little is done? A few schools for mothers, still mainly supported by private charity, in the poorest districts is about the sum total; yet all the while it is she who bears the burden of the insurance paid by her husband, for it comes in nine cases out of ten out of her housekeeping money. It is she who has to send the children to school clean and tidy and has to keep the great appetites of growing boys satisfied; it is she who is regarded as responsible for buying inflammable flannelette, for not providing fireguards or separate cradles for the babies, and whatever else a Government of men may choose to impose on her. So that there is appearing also among the working women an understanding of the fact that their interests are not altogether safe in the hands of men, though the working class women will never probably arrive at the intense consciousness of sex antagonism which characterizes some sections of the middle class feminists, and is due to men's callous disregard of their claims as human beings.

Changed Views among the Middle Class Women

At the same time among the middle class women, too, the situation is altering. Many of them are realizing that to earn their own living is not always the joy it had appeared at first, for the living may be so meagre as to provide, at the cost of perpetual toil, only the merest food and shelter. Although the number of girls among the middle classes who are working for their living is steadily increasing, every now and then one comes across a young woman who finds the rigor of her work and the fierce competition too much for her, and hastens back gladly to the parasitic shelter of her relatives' roof. The lower sections of professional women, in short, are coming to understand the possibilities of exploitation, and are dimly beginning to feel rather than to comprehend the fact that work may be so monotonous and so ill-paid that even their human qualities, and much more their feminine attractiveness, will be beaten out of them in the process of earning their living.

And among the whole community the growth of collectivist feeling is bringing us to realize that State regulation of the conditions of labor is a necessity, and therefore we seldom find now among the feminists that embittered opposition to factory legislation which caused so many difficulties in the seventies and eighties. It is realized on all hands that the position of women in industry is not an exceptional one; that men, too, need protection against over-long hours of work, low wages, and insanitary conditions; and that, therefore, women are not accepting an inferior position in demanding the intervention of the State to secure for them suitable conditions of work.

They Want both Work and Marriage

An even more momentous change is occurring in the attitude towards marriage. The first generation of feminists did not so much oppose marriage as ignore it; but there is now coming into existence a second generation of advanced women, few at present, but destined to increase. Most of them know nothing at first hand of the old struggles. They have gone to high schools and colleges, and education has come to them as naturally as to their brothers. Many under the care of feminist relatives have been carefully trained to win the economic independence for which their mothers and aunts agonized in vain. And now these younger women find themselves face to face with a new set of problems. The fierceness and bitterness of the old struggles caused the first set of feminists to put the question of marriage and the supposed special disabilities of their sex altogether on one side. To-day many of these elder women, looking at their young relatives in receipt of independent incomes, doing work that is of real value to the world, and enjoying in such matters as foreign travel, theatre and concert going, and the cultivation of friendships a degree of freedom which they had longed for as unattainable, wonder what difficulties the young women of to-day can possibly have to contend with. But there are fundamental human instincts which can be disregarded only for a time. The problem of the modern professional woman is that she is forced to reconcile two needs of her nature which the present constitution of society make irreconcilable. She wants work, she wants the control of her own financial position, she

273

wants education and the right to take part in the human activities
of the State, but at the same time she is no longer willing to
be shut out from marriage and motherhood. And the present
organization of society means that for most women the two are
alternatives. In almost all occupations the public acknowledgement
of marriage means for a woman dismissal from her post and
diminished economic resources. This is the case in practically all the
Government posts: women civil servants, including even factory
inspectors and school inspectors, are compelled to resign on
marriage. Even the women school medical officers of the L.C.C.
are now forced to sign a contract stating that they will retire on
marriage,[10] and although the same rule is not so strict in private
business, there, too, it is rare for married women to be employed.
Most women, that is to say, can only continue to preserve that
economic independence, so keenly appreciated and won by such
fierce struggles, on condition of compulsory celibacy and, what to
many women is far worse, compulsory childlessness. Against this
state of things a revolt is beginning which so far is barely articulate,
but which is bound to make itself heard in public before long.
What women who have fully thought out the position want, is
not this forced alternative between activity in the human world
and control of their own economic position on the one hand and
marriage and children on the other, *but both*. The normal woman,
like the normal man, desires a mate and a child, but she does not
therefore desire nothing else. Least of all does she desire to sink
back into a state of economic dependence and sex parasitism.
Women do not want either love *or* work, but both; and the full
meaning of the feminist movement will not develop until this
demand becomes conscious and articulate among the rank and file
of the movement.

Can Child-bearing Women Earn their Living?

Now there can be no denying the fact that this demand will raise
many difficulties. Some writers, chief of whom is that extraordinarily suggestive and interesting American, Charlotte Perkins
Gilman, assume that with improved conditions of household
management and the development of large scale housekeeping and
publicly managed crèches and nursery schools it will be possible
even for childbearing women to continue to earn their own living
in such a way that they will be able not only to keep themselves
during this period, but to contribute their share towards the
bringing up of children, and this without any injury to the children.
To the writer this seems a very optimistic attitude. It may, perhaps,
be practicable for a few exceptional women, who possess sufficient

ability to earn large incomes and have sufficient energy to endure, without breaking down, the twofold strain of working for a living and bringing children into the world. But it is obvious that for the vast majority of women regular work on exactly the same terms as those which men now submit to in office or factory is most undesirable for women during at least six months of the pre-natal and post-natal life of each child. If the child is to be nursed by its mother, as it should be, probably in most cases an even longer period of rest should be taken. The common sense of mankind knows well that just as increasing civilization leads to an increasing protection of children, so, too, it should mean more care for young mothers. During the child-bearing years the welfare of the child should have the precedence over all other consider-ations. But this does not mean that the woman need be incapaci-tated for earning her own living during her whole married life. It is not marriage that prevents a woman from working. On the contrary, the married woman who is leading a normal and healthy life is likely to do better work and be a more satisfactory person than the spinster. The real hindrance is not marriage, but mother-hood. Most people assume that the two are identical; but should absorption in maternal duties extend over the whole of married life? The days have gone past (one hopes never to return) when the married woman had a child every one or two years during the whole of the fertile period of life. The modern family, it seems probable, will not consist in the future of more than three or four children, and even if one made the assumption[11] that the woman should devote herself entirely to the care of the children until the youngest reached school age, there would still remain many years of her life during which she would be strong and fit for work. Indeed, one of the most pathetic sights of to-day is the middle aged woman whose children have ceased to afford her complete occupation. They are absorbed in school life and in the training for their future occupations. The husband, too, gives up his time to his work and his sport, and the woman of forty or fifty, still at the height of her maturity, stronger perhaps, and certainly wiser, than she was in her youth, is left stranded by the current of life, with no interests outside her family; whilst by the family the necessary task of being 'company to mother' is resented and evaded.[12] How much happier would such women be if, when their children no longer needed all their time, they could return to activities outside the household; and how much richer would humanity be if it could avail itself of the services of such women. A type might come into existence, of which only one or two instances have yet appeared, of mature women who, as girls, had

worked for themselves and known what human life, as opposed
to sex life, meant; who then had lived through the normal feminine
experiences of being sought in marriage, loved, and made mothers
of children; and who, ripened and enriched by these experiences,
returned in middle age to the activities of the world, knowing –
because they have lived through – both sides of life. How enormously valuable such women would be in education and in the
medical profession, where, indeed, even now a few of them may
be found.

The Problem of the Future

So, then, the problem before the future is to secure for women
freedom and independence, the right to control their own destinies,
and yet to make it possible for the same women to be wives and
mothers. The solution of this problem will not be easy. It cannot
be attained through the methods advocated by either of the schools
of thought that now hold the field; neither by the feminists of the
more old fashioned sort, on the one hand, who simply demand for
women the same rights as men possess, ignoring all the inevitable
differences of sex; nor, on the other hand, by those who believe
that sex is the only characteristic of women that matters, and
disregard in her the human nature that she shares with man.
Neither independence alone nor protection alone will meet the
case. The whole problem is still so new that it is perhaps best to
be cautious in dealing with it, and to avoid committing oneself
too soon to any specific solution.

Women in Unpaid Public Work

It may be that some women after the days of active motherhood
are past will find a sufficient sphere in unpaid public work of
various kinds, though at present our electoral laws shut out in
practice the vast majority of married women from membership of
all our public bodies except the less important ones.[13]

The Legal Claim to Half the Husband's Income

But it would be unreasonable to insist that the older married
woman as a whole should be confined to unpaid activities of this
specific kind. Moreover, the objection which many of the noblest
women feel to an undefined dependence on a husband would not
be met at all by this suggestion, and we should find that if marriage
means the complete relinquishment of a cherished occupation
many of the finest women will refuse to marry. Some thinkers
advocate that the difficulty should be met by giving to the married
woman a legal claim to half her husband's income, and making

her jointly responsible with him for the necessary expenditure on the family. There will be cases where the care of the household and children takes up the whole of a woman's time, in which such an arrangement would be quite legitimate, and it may be that it should be a possible legal settlement for those who care to adopt it. But it certainly should not be compulsory on all married couples. In the first place, it would obviously increase the tendency to evade legal marriage, and so would defeat the very purpose which it has in view. Again, dependence is not any the less dependence if definite legal provision is made for the endowment of it. Moreover, it would endow childless women equally with the child-bearing women, and it would continue the endowment during the years when the woman might reasonably return to ordinary economic activities. Therefore (although there will be cases where women will be supported by husbands who can afford to do so, and so will be set free either for the parasitic activities of fashion, sport and charity, or will use their leisure and freedom to carry on work for which no financial return may be expected, such as scientific research or the agitation for social reforms), yet the whole line of development should be in the direction of decreasing and not increasing the legal right of woman to be kept by the man, save when child-bearing and child-nurture are in question.

The Endowment of Motherhood

Now, these are really specific activities of the greatest possible importance. No act of citizenship is more fundamental than the act of bringing into the world and protecting in his helpless infancy a new citizen, and therefore the most reasonable solution of the problem, though it may not be applicable in every case, is that women during the period when these activities must absorb their whole energies should be supported by a State endowment, but that this State endowment should not continue longer than the time during which they are so absorbed, and that at the end of that time they should be free to return to their former vocations.[14]

Such a system would at one blow solve innumerable difficulties. If childbearing is protected by the State, it would not be unreasonable for the State to impose on the women who are possible mothers certain restrictions with regard to the activities which they may follow. Moreover, if the husband is no longer solely responsible for the support of his wife and her children, marriage will become easier among precisely those classes where we desire to encourage it. At the same time, if the dependence of women on marriage disappeared, and with it the inevitable accompanying subordination of their own wishes to their husbands' marital demands, we should establish the most reasonable check on the increase of the population, namely, the woman's natural dislike to excessive and unwished for childbearing. That decline of the birth rate among the classes with the highest standard of comfort which exists at present would be checked by the greater facilities for marriage, yet, on the other hand, there would be no danger of the too large families which are due to the dependence of women, and which give rise to over population. At present the distribution of children presents the same inequality as the distribution of wealth; some people have far too many at the same time that others have too few. Another problem which would in time disappear is the inequality of the wages of men and women. The great argument which now weighs with the popular mind in favor of this inequality is the alleged fact that most men have dependants, while most women have not. Unfortunately, this is by no means always true; and, moreover, this theory overlooks the fact that in a certain number of instances, at all events, women compete with men, and therefore if a lower level of payment is established for women, they will drive the men out altogether, as they have done in typewriting, and are in process of doing in elementary school teaching. What we want to work towards is a system whereby all adult human beings not incapacitated by some specific cause shall work for their living and be paid for it, no distinction of sex being made where similar work is done by men and women. Then the young, the aged, and those adults who for some special reason are unable to earn their living, should be supported by the State from the surplus funds available when rent and interest have been absorbed by the community; a system of which we have already made a beginning in old age pensions on the one hand, and maintenance scholarships on the other. And among the most honored and respected of all those endowed by the State should be the women who are rendering to it the greatest possible service, that, namely, of ushering into the world its future citizens. But their reward for this service should only cover the time when their maternal duties prevent them from taking any part in industry.

This is coming to be realized more and more clearly as the ultimate ideal of the feminist movement, and what we have to do at present is, while not straining our adhesion to it unduly in the face of the conflicts of the present situation, to attempt no changes in the law which will make our ultimate attainment of it impossible; so that we should watch very carefully any development which may result in intensifying the dependence of women outside the child-bearing years. It cannot be denied that the demands of some eugenists who are unable to believe that the necessary protection for motherhood can be given save through absolute dependence on a husband may make in this direction, and the increasing tendency of local authorities and government departments and of some philanthropic employers to exclude women from employment simply because they are legally married is equally a danger.

Socialism and Feminism

It will be seen that these changes in the status of women cannot come about in our present individualistic society. In the first place, under the existing state of competition in business a woman who drops out for the childbearing period can hardly expect to be reinstated, and the world will probably honestly have to face the fact that certain readjustments, not otherwise desirable, must be made in order that the mother may not be penalized in her later economic life by reason of her motherhood. Even among elementary school teachers to-day a married teacher who frequently demands leave of absence because of her approaching confinement finds herself at a serious disadvantage. The absence and subsequent return of the married women to their work will no doubt be inconvenient, but the inconvenience must be faced, and the women as far as possible be placed at no disadvantage, if we are to put a stop to our present practice of the deliberate sterilization of the ablest and most independent women.[15]

Such a system could be deliberately and consciously introduced into the public services; it could be imposed on private enterprise by factory legislation, though with much greater difficulty. But it is the development of Socialism, and that alone, which can make it possible throughout the whole fabric of society for the normal woman to attain her twin demands, independent work and motherhood. It is only Socialism which can make the endowment of the women during the maternal years a possibility, that endowment being one of the first charges on the surplus value or economic rent which the State will absorb; and until the State has made itself master of the land and the capital of this country, it will not have an income big enough to enable it to provide adequate endowments for the childbearing women. Therefore it becomes clear that the only path to the ultimate and most deep lying ends of the feminist movement is through Socialism, and every wise feminist will find herself more and more compelled to adopt the principles of Socialism. But the wise Socialists must also be feminists. The public spirit of willingness to serve the community which will be necessary if the Socialist principles are to work must be inculcated into children from their earliest days. Can they be so inculcated by women who know nothing of the activities of the world beyond the four walls of their homes? Women, too, must be citizens and fully conscious of the privileges and duties of their citizenship if Socialism is to be attained. Not least among the duties of that citizenship should be what Plato long ago demanded of his women guardians:- that they should bear children for the service of the State.

Notes

1 Fitzherbert's 'Book of Husbandry.' English Dialect Society. 1882.
2 Galt. 'Annals of the Parish,' Chapter VI. Pages 38–9 of edition in Routledge's Universal Library.
3 'The staff consisted of the general manager, John Dalton; a collier, who prepared the charcoal from the brushwood of the neighboring forest; a 'blomesmyth,' or 'smythman,' in charge of the 'blomeharth'; and a 'faber,' working at the stryng hearth . . . The employment of the wives of the foreman and smith lends an air of domesticity to the little settlement. The wife of John Gyll, the 'blomesmyth,' seems to have been a general factotum, sometimes helping her husband or the laborers, then working at the bellows. At first her employment was intermittent and her payment irregular, but later she seems to have settled down to fixed employment at a regular rate of a halfpenny a blome, i.e., a weight of fifteen stones of thirteen pounds each.' 'Durham County History,' Vol. II., p. 279, quoting Account Roll of John Dalton, first Durham ironmaster (about 1410).
4 Dower Act, 3 & 4 Will. IV., c. 105.
5 Miss Hutchins's original figures, which were taken from the Census of 1901, have been brought up to date.
6 'Shirley,' Chapter XII.
7 'Shirley,' Chapter XXII.
8 Lydia Becker, one of the earliest agitators, is reported to have replied to a married woman, who said that she, too, would like a vote, 'My dear, a good husband is much better worth having than a vote.'
9 The personal experience of the writer will illustrate this point. She was once staying with the wife of a millionaire, and was going on after her visit for a walking tour with a friend in the Lake district. Mrs D., when she heard of the plan, said: 'Are you two going off by yourselves just where you like? That must be delightful. All my life I have never been able to do that kind of thing. Before my marriage I had to go where mamma said, and now, of course, Mr D. always decides about our holiday.' Many a wealthy lady is as much subservient to the whims of her husband as though she were one of his upper servants, which, indeed, in many cases, she is, with the difference that they have holidays and she has none.
10 As these pages pass through the press, the desirability of requiring women doctors to retire on marriage is again being raised on the L.C.C.
11 The writer is not prepared to admit that this assumption is true in

every case, or indeed in many cases. Many women who can *bear* splendid children are not necessarily fit to care for all the details of their health and rearing, and in many cases it would be well that the mother should return to her normal occupation as soon as ever the child no longer required to be nursed every two or three hours, and should use her earnings to pay for the skilled care given in crèche or nursery, resuming charge of the child in the non-working hours. But that this is possible cannot yet be considered as established beyond a doubt.

12 See the serial story 'Won Over,' which appeared in Mrs Gilman's magazine *The Forerunner* during 1913.

13 I am indebted to the Secretary of the Women's Local Government Society for the following note on the electoral laws as they affect the position of married women on public bodies:

For candidature for county and town councils in Great Britain it is necessary to have an electoral qualification, and the candidate's name must appear either on the burgess roll or on the list of county electors. In England and Wales (outside London) married women are in general excluded from standing, as they are not entitled to have their names placed on the register. The Qualification of Women (County and Borough Councils) Act, 1907, removed the disabilities of sex and marriage in regard to candidates, but it did not amend the statute law which demands that candidates for county and town councils shall be electors. Married women can stand in London for the County Council, as the London County Council Electors Act, 1900, gave parochial electors the right to vote for the County Council.

In Scotland and Ireland women owners, women lodgers and women service voters are entitled to be registered, and therefore to stand for county and town councils. In England and Wales these three classes of women cannot have their names placed on the register.

Since 1894 in England and Wales, and since 1898 in Ireland, there has existed a residential qualification alternative with the electoral qualification for the following local government bodies:

ENGLAND AND WALES	IRELAND
Metropolitan Borough Councils.	Urban District Councils.
Urban District Councils.	Rural District Councils.
Rural District Councils.	Boards of Guardians.
Parish Councils.	
Boards of Guardians.	

It is in virtue of this residential qualification that at least two-thirds of the women guardians in England and Wales are now serving, and at the triennial elections for Metropolitan borough councils last November three-fourths of the women candidates were qualified by residence only.

In Scotland the school board is the only local authority for which the residential qualification is available. A change in the law is urgently needed in all three countries, so as to permit of an alternative residential qualification for candidates to all local government bodies.

It should be observed that even where there is no legal barrier against the candidature of married women for local bodies, few married women can in practice stand where it is necessary for candidates to be electors, as married women seldom have qualifications as occupiers or owners, their houses being naturally hired or possessed by their husbands.

The new President of the Local Government Board has undertaken to introduce a Bill abolishing some of these anomalies.

14 It is neither possible nor desirable that we should at this stage adopt a dogmatic attitude as to the length of time during which an expectant and nursing mother should be freed from ordinary industry and be supported by a State grant. It will certainly vary from industry to industry. No pregnant woman should follow any occupation where the lifting of heavy weights is necessary or the raising of her arms above her head (obviously ordinary house work should be one of the first industries to be barred). On the other hand, most doctors advocate light out-door occupations. Women during these periods need work and interests and activities quite as much as the single or childless women: especially do they need what is now often denied them – some amount of social life. It would be easy under a properly organized state of Socialism to set aside excellently appropriate work for expectant mothers, and the State maintenance might then only need to cover a few weeks.

15 Cf. Shaw, 'Man and Superman,' p. 220. 'Mr Graham Wallas has already ventured to suggest, as Chairman of the School Management Committee of the London School Board, that the accepted policy of the sterilization of the school mistress, however administratively convenient, is open to criticism from the national stockbreeding point of view.'

FABIAN TRACT No. 178
(March 1915)

THE WAR, WOMEN, AND UNEMPLOYMENT

The Women's Group Executive

Many social problems have presented themselves to us in a fresh light and in changed relations in consequence of the experience brought by war. One of these problems is that of woman's economic position in this country.

Two aspects of that position are discussed in the two separate parts of this Tract. The first is the immediately practical question of the present wide-spread distress among women workers owing to lack of employment. The second is the helplessness of woman in face of the now pressing economic needs of the nation, owing to her lack of training and want of experience in business and organization.

PART I. – UNEMPLOYMENT AMONG WOMEN WAGE-EARNERS, AND HOW TO DEAL WITH IT

We are only now slowly coming to realize that 'unemployment' in industry affects women as well as men, and often differently from men. How often do we not still find the state of the labor market treated as if it were solely a matter of the relative supply of and demand for *men*? If not many men are out of work, Government officials, Ministers of the Crown, and newspaper writers take it for granted that all is well. The Board of Trade Monthly Index Number (based on the unemployed members of certain trade unions), and the statistical return of unemployed among the trades coming within Part II of the Insurance Act, are quite commonly accepted as fairly measuring the amount of distress from unemployment. Yet the three million persons covered by these two returns include scarcely any women. There is no Index Number with regard to women's unemployment. Hardly any statistics are published about it, or, when published, they are hardly ever given

283

anything like the same prominence as those relating to men. The result of all this is that the great and terrible distress suffered by women wage-earners thrown out of work, whether owing to ordinary trade depression or to dislocation of war, and the consequent suffering to those whom these women wage-earners are helping to support, are very largely overlooked.

It is, perhaps, partly in consequence of this lack of statistical information about unemployment among women that the measures taken to prevent, or mitigate, or relieve unemployment nearly always result in benefit to men. Thus, when it is thought advisable to prevent unemployment by increasing the amount of work put in hand by town councils and other local authorities, it is always in men's trades that the additional volume of employment is created – the town council expedites some work of building, or drainage, or paving, or painting and decorating in order to take on men at wages. When distress becomes acute, the 'relief works' started by the Local Distress Committee, such as road-making, or digging, or tree planting, are nearly always for unemployed men.

What is often forgotten, too, is that statistics with regard to the industries in which men are employed may give quite a wrong impression as to the state of employment in those trades in which women are engaged. Thus, during the months of September and October, 1914, when only a relatively small percentage of men were registered as unemployed, largely owing to the enormous number taken into Government pay or employed on municipal works, the percentage of women thrown out of work and standing idle without wages *was at least three times as great*. Yet the small percentage of men registered as unemployed was constantly being cited during that period as evidence that things were going on quite well, and that no exceptional measures were required. If as large a percentage of men had been registering as unemployed as there were women thrown out of work much more energetic steps would have been taken.

In the following pages we shall seek to prove the need for definite and distinct consideration, both by Government and the local authorities, not forgetting local relief committees of all sorts, of the needs of the women wage-earners who are unemployed, and to explain what ought to be done to help them, together with the part which might and should be taken in this matter by women themselves.

Who are the Women Wage-earners

Few people realize to what an enormous number the women wage-earners have grown in the United Kingdom. Never before have

we had such a host. From the 1911 census we learn that no fewer
than 4,830,734 females of ten years and upwards were engaged 'in
gainful occupations' in England and Wales alone. This total of
close upon *five millions of working women and girls* excludes all those
wholly engaged in unpaid domestic work at home. About 80,000
out of the total are working employers; about 313,000 more are
'individual producers' working on their own account; the
remainder, comprising the vast majority, are serving for salaries
or wages. It is high time that we realized that industrial wage-
earning is not an exceptional thing for women. More than half the
entire female population of these islands between the ages of 15
and 25 is thus at work for hire. In fact, the great majority of British
women are wage-earners during some part of their lives; at the
most employed age 70 per cent. are employed.

Here are the 'gainful occupations' at which the bulk of approximately five millions in England and Wales were working in 1911:–[1]

	Domestic service (indoors)	1,260,673
	Cotton manufacture	372,834
	Dressmaking	333,129
	Teaching (all branches)	211,183
	Local Government (including Police and and Poor Law Services	176,450
Net totals in industries or services.	Wool and Worsted manufacture	127,637
	Tailoring	127,527
	Drapery	110,955
	Inn or hotel service	110,506
	Agriculture	94,841
	Printing, bookbinding and stationery	87,609
	Grocery	58,935
	Boot and shoe making	45,986
	National Government	34,089
	Medical and nursing	87,699
Totals in Occupation Tables.	Art, music, drama	49,998
	Laundry	167,052
	Metal trades	101,050
	Charwomen	126,061

If the female workers of Scotland (593,210) and of Ireland
(430,092) be added to those of England and Wales, the total reaches
6,877,338. By 1915 the number of women and girls working for
gain in the United Kingdom must have risen to over six millions.

It may be worth while to add a statistical estimate – the most
accurate that can be framed until the Board of Trade deigns to
give as much attention to women as to men – of what such of
these women earn as belong to the manual working wage-earning

class, omitting the professionals, such as doctors, artists, teachers, journalists, managers, clerks, and municipal or national Government officials, and to compare their earnings with those of men of the manual working wage-earning class. The estimate includes the value of board and lodging, when supplied, and of all extras, but deducts an estimated percentage for unemployment, holidays, and short time.

Table prepared for the Fabian Women's Group by Mr Sidney Webb showing estimated earnings of Employed Manual Working Wage-Earners in the United Kingdom in the year 1912:

MALES

Class	Numbers	Average earnings in full week, including emoluments.		Average Wages Bill for a full week.	Yearly Wages Bill.*
		s.	d.	Million £	Million £
Men in situations:					
Below 15s.	320,000=4%	13	0	0.12	10
15s. to 20s.	640,000=8%	18	0	0.58	27
20s. ,, 25s.	1,600,000=20%	22	6	1.80	85
25s. ,, 30s.	1,680,000=21%	27	6	2.31	109
30s. ,, 35s.	1,680,000=21%	32	6	2.73	128
35s. ,, 40s.	1,040,000=13%	37	6	1.95	92
40s. ,, 45s.	560,000=7%	42	6	1.20	56.5
Over 45s.	480,000=6%	50	0	1.20	56.5
Men in situations	8,000,000=100%	30	0	12.00	564
Casuals	700,000	12	0	0.42	18.5
Adult males	8,700,000	28	4	12.42	582.5
Boys	1,900,000	10	0	0.95	44
All males	10,600,000	25	3	13.38	626.5

Average earnings per adult employed manual working man throughout the year
$\frac{582.5}{8.7}$ £66.95, or £1. 5s. 9d. per week.

*Allowing five weeks for short time, sickness, involuntary holidays and unemployment.

FEMALES

Class	Numbers	Average earnings in full week.		Average weekly Wages Bill for a full week.	Yearly Wages Bill (net, as above).
		s.	d.	in £100,000.	£
Women in situations:					
Below 12s.	1,000,000	9	0	450	21,150,000
12s. to 15s.	1,500,000	13	0	975	45,825,000
Over 15s.	500,000	17	0	425	19,975,000
Women in Situations	3,000,000	12	4	1,850	86,950,000

Casuals	100,000	3	6	17½	822,500
Adult women	3,100,000	11	7	1,867½	87,772,500
Girls	1,500,000	7	6	565	26,550,000
All females	4,600,000	10	7	2,432½	114,322,500
Total Wages Bill					£740,875,500

Average earnings per adult employed manual working woman

throughout the year $\dfrac{87.772}{3.1}$ £28.31, or 10s. 10½d. per week.

NOTE. – The difference between 4,600,000 (the estimated number of female manual working wage-earners in 1912) and 6,000,000 (the estimated number of women and girls gainfully occupied in 1915) is to be accounted for partly by the increase in numbers between 1912 and 1915, but mainly by (a) the women employers; (b) the women working on their own account in industrial occupations; (c) the women and girls gainfully occupied but non-manual working wage-earners, such as doctors, artists, teachers, journalists, managers, clerks, local and national government employees. Domestic servants are included as manual working wage earners.

The estimate allows for an average of five weeks' wages lost in a year through short time, sickness, involuntary holidays, and unemployment. This 'ordinary' amount of unemployment, though it makes a big hole in a woman's scanty wages, is not that about which we are now concerned. What is serious is the continued inability to get another situation, prolonged perhaps for many weeks; the weary search for a vacancy that takes the very heart out of a woman; the drain on the scanty savings so difficult to accumulate, which brings her face to face with the worst that fate can have in store for her.

How to Prevent Unemployment

The first thing to be done, when prolonged and widespread unemployment is imminent or apprehended, is to seek to prevent it. In this case prevention is ever so much better than cure. If private employers are beginning to turn off their 'hands,' it is the duty of public employers – that is to say, the Government Departments and the various local authorities – to do all that they can to increase their own staffs. When there is a falling off in the amount of employment in the way of trade, whatever work or service useful to the community can be undertaken by the public authorities ought then to be deliberately undertaken. Labor should be engaged at the standard rates of wages in the ordinary way, with the object of maintaining undiminished, as far as possible, the total volume of wage-earning employment. Nor need we be too careful that the augmentation of public employment is exactly in those particular crafts or specialized occupations in which a diminution of private employment is likely to occur. Coincidence in this respect, in so far as it is practicable, greatly facilitates matters, and it is not suggested that discharged clerks or jewellers can become navvies or cooks; but in the ever-changing tides of the vast labor market, the broadening of any channel has an effect in carrying off some of the flood, and of thereby relieving the pressure elsewhere. Any increase in demand for labor, by lessening the number of possible competitors, helps indirectly every kind of labor that is seeking employment.

This policy of actually preventing unemployment by augmenting public employment, in order to counterbalance the diminution of private employment – a policy quite distinct from that of letting people fall into unemployment and then providing 'relief works' on which to set them to work just because they are unemployed and in distress – is now what is advised by the political economists. It has been definitely adopted as the policy of the State. In the Development and Road Board Act, 1909, it was expressly laid down by Parliament that, in creating employment under that Act, the Commissioners were to 'have regard to the state of the labor market'; the implication being that they were to do little when trade was good, and as much as possible when trade was bad.

In August, 1914, when so much unemployment was caused by the war, we saw the various Government Departments (such as the Office of Works in particular) under the direct instructions of the Cabinet, frankly recognizing the public responsibility for preventing as much unemployment as possible, and racking their brains to discover what work they could put in hand. Finally, we had the Local Government Board quite explicitly enjoining this policy on the local authorities as a general principle.

'Obviously the best way to provide for persons thrown out of their usual employment as a result of the war is to provide them with some other work for wages. . . . Where the demands of the normal labor market are inadequate, the committee should consult the local authorities as to the possibility of expediting schemes of public utility, which might otherwise not be put in hand at the present moment. Whatever work is undertaken by local authorities . . . should be performed in the ordinary way. . . . The men engaged . . . should, of course, be paid wages in the ordinary way.' – (Circular P.R.D. 7, August 20th, 1914.)

Note the words 'the men'! Unemployment among six millions of gainfully occupied women and girls needs to be prevented just as much as unemployment among the fourteen millions of gainfully occupied men and boys, and no doubt the Local Government Board meant their advice to be taken as regards both sexes equally; but, unfortunately, those in charge of our Government Departments and those who run our town councils are almost exclusively men. When they put in hand schemes for increasing the volume of public employment, what is thought of is, practically always, employment for men. This, of course, comes easiest to them; and, moreover, few unemployed women wage-earners have even a municipal vote.

Women should see to it that, when unemployment is threatened, or has actually occurred, this policy of augmenting the volume of public employment is applied in the case of women, as it is in the case of men. The local authorities ought everywhere to be pressed to increase their staffs of women and girls, as some partial set-off to the new employment that they seek to provide for men. As there were no fewer than 176,450 women and girls in the Local Government service in England and Wales alone in 1911, the addition of only five per cent. (or one for every twenty already employed) would mean that nearly 9,000 unemployed women would be taken off the labor market. What town councillors are apt to do, if they are not reminded of women's needs in this respect, is rather to leave accidental vacancies unfilled among their women teachers or clerks, so that the staff falls off by five per cent. or more, and unemployment is actually increased.

We ought to urge on the borough and urban councils – also upon the county councils – that, in times of trade depression, they should take special care that their staffs of women and girls (teachers, typists, clerks, inspectors, health visitors, nurses, asylum attendants, charwomen, school cleaners, lavatory attendants, etc.) are kept at full strength, and, wherever occasion arises, promptly increased. We should press for the fullest possible number of learners or probationers to be taken on in every department, so that an increased number of women might be trained for higher work; that, for instance, all possible opportunities should be taken to increase the numbers of scholarships for girls, girl student-teachers, and female teachers in training; that additional training colleges and hostels should be established; that the number of probationer-nurses in the public health hospitals and workhouse infirmaries should be augmented; we should insist that the elementary school staffs of women teachers should be increased – at any rate to the extent of all the trained teachers available, even taking on at once the whole year's supply leaving college in July – so as to effect the very desirable reform of reducing the size of the classes, wherever accommodation permits; we should demand that the opportunity be taken to introduce, among the council's staff, women sanitary inspectors and women health visitors; or to increase their number if already instituted, up to the limit of the local requirements.

We might very well press the local police authority (in London,

289

the Home Secretary; in the City of London, the Corporation; in counties, the Standing Joint Committee; in boroughs, the Watch Committee) to appoint the police matrons who are so urgently required at all police stations. Why should they not appoint, too, some women as police constables, in order that they may be employed in various directions where they are more suitable than men? In the United States no fewer than twenty-five cities have now one or more 'policewomen,' Chicago having twenty, whilst Baltimore, Seattle and Los Angeles have five each, Pittsburgh four, and San Francisco and St. Paul each three. Canada, too, is beginning to utilize its women as police assistants, Vancouver setting the example in this direction. In at least thirty-five towns in Germany women police assistants have been appointed; in Mainz, Munich, Dresden, and ten other towns, they are appointed by the State and municipal authorities. Women police have also been appointed in Austria, Denmark, Holland, Norway, Switzerland and Sweden. Even in England, in order to meet the conditions arising from the war, women are now serving on the patrols organized by the National Society of Women Workers, and as voluntary police-women organized by the Women's Freedom League, but they are not appointed on oath, and, therefore, have no power of arrest; moreover, the work is of a voluntary character. The police patrol work has already been abundantly justified, and should be extended in many directions. Police and military authorities alike are welcoming, and in some cases asking for, this co-operation on the part of women. If women can do the work, why withhold either the official status or the pay? The latest published report of the Commissioner of Metropolitan Police, for 1913, reveals the fact that London, at all events, employs one paid woman police officer, whose business it is to take the depositions of women and children in certain cases. By this time it may be hoped that there are more than one. In Southampton two women police constables were appointed in January, 1915.

Again, the local education authority might well take this opportunity to keep back from the overstocked labor market as many as possible of the girls about to leave school at thirteen or fourteen, and secure to them a year or two more educational training, wherever possible of a technical character. To enable such girls to abstain from wage-earning, it would be necessary to provide them with maintenance whilst under training. This it is within the legal powers of the local education authority to do by awarding them maintenance scholarships, carrying not only full education but also a payment of the necessary few shillings a week. The number of such scholarships for girls compares very unfavorably with that for boys.

The idea might be carried further. It would be distinctly advantageous if the local education authority would, at times when women are exceptionally unemployed, offer maintenance scholarships pretty freely to selected girls of sixteen or eighteen, who are willing to put themselves under training, either for any skilled craft at which they could eventually get employment, or for sick nursing, for which there is a rapidly growing permanent demand; or, indeed, for any of the higher openings for women. A patriotic education committee might be moved to agree to such a proposal by offering special scholarships to the daughters of 'men at the front,' or of killed or wounded.

The present provision of technical education for girls by local authorities is extremely inadequate. In London, since 1904, trade schools have been established for limited numbers of girls, including, at present, schools for dressmaking, ladies' tailoring, millinery, upholstery, trade embroidery, corset and lingerie making, waistcoat making, cookery, domestic service, laundry work and photography; but outside London trade schools for girls hardly exist. At Manchester and Plymouth schools for dressmaking have been established, though in the former city there is provision for only twenty-four students; Reading has a school for domestic economy, the Birmingham education authority has lately opened a school for the training of girls as children's nurses, and the Brighton education authority has just decided to start a school for laundry work. This exhausts the list.

Trade schools apart, in the recent general development of technical instruction under the auspices of the Board of Education and local education authorities, whether by means of evening classes or of 'vocational training' in secondary schools, there has been a strong tendency to confine the instruction of girls, other than intending teachers, to housecraft and needlework, or else preparation for clerical work, or, in evening classes, dressmaking.

Now is the time to provide more schools and more classes teaching new trades and promoting efficiency in trades already followed, which will make women competent wage-earners in the future. To this end it will be essential to provide a large number of scholarships with maintenance grants for girls, which grants would help to educate parents in the idea that immediate employment of a boy or girl on leaving school is detrimental to his or her future welfare, and that the school age must be raised so as to secure an adequate and thorough training in some trade or profession. Why should there not be opportunities for women to enter certain skilled and lucrative trades in which at present provision is made only for men? Further, it is necessary to convince parents and local authorities that an educational training would be valuable in avocations not heretofore supposed to require it. A shop assistant, for example, would find her work more interesting, be more efficient, and be able to command better pay if she had a sound knowledge of the nature and provenance of the goods she sells.

Again, the local health committees should certainly see to it that the maternity centre and baby clinic, which every town needs, is at once started and developed. In this connection the sanction given by the Local Government Board for the training and employment, at fourpence per hour, either from relief funds or otherwise, of a staff of 'mothers' helps' or 'sick room helps' to visit the homes of women who are sick or being confined, in order to keep their households going, should certainly be utilized.

Local insurance committees should lose no opportunity to press for a beginning of the scheme for the home nursing of the sick, for which Parliament voted the money in the summer of 1914. The Insurance Commissioners do not want to take action on this decision of Parliament, and they are pleading for delay on grounds of economy and shortage of nurses. But unless a start is made with the training of probationers there will never be enough nurses. The sick need the nursing as much now (and are costing the approved societies as much through lack of nursing) as they did when the House of Commons passed the vote. The Government should be pressed on this matter.

Furthermore, local authorities should find and directly provide work at wages for unemployed women, analogous to the new buildings or the additional furniture by which these authorities can relieve the labour market as regards men. We ought to see to it that local authorities do not postpone any orders for uniforms, asylum clothing, or other garments; they should rather take the opportunity to increase stocks. They can sometimes properly take on a few women in the sewing rooms of the asylums or other institutions. Many women clerks and secretaries who are unemployed might be given work in public libraries. In February, 1913, 59 women were employed in the public libraries of eight metropolitan boroughs, and 314 in those of provincial towns, including 114 in Manchester. The women assistants who are thus employed are of various grades, and the salaries are from £1 a week, rising to 25s., and from £80, rising to £130. The work is particularly suited to women, and if more women were members of public library committees, it is reasonable to believe that the appointment of women librarians would be more frequent. It may not be generally known that women can be co-opted as additional members of such committees.

The local education authority might equip all the children at school with gymnasium and swimming costumes, and see to it that none went without warm socks or stockings and strong boots. But much more might be done. An immense improvement in the health and educational progress of the children in the elementary schools might be effected if local education authorities would start a 'school uniform' for boys and girls respectively; that is to say, suitable underclothing, together with a tasteful and hygienic dress of simple pattern, not necessarily identical in cut or color, but analogous to that adopted in some of the best boarding schools for the children of the wealthy. This would necessitate a free gift of the new clothing, at any rate in the poorest schools or to any parents requiring it. But it would be the means of getting rid of the insanitary layers of dirty wool and of the 'rags and tatters' to which so many of the children are now condemned. What a splendid use might thus be made of a time of unemployment to put the whole school population, even the whole of the children in any particular town or village, into clean and healthy and beautiful clothing!

It may be needful to induce local authorities and other large consumers ordering supplies of clothing as above suggested to give their orders to other firms than those which formerly monopolized the supply, since such firms are in some cases exceptionally pressed by orders from the War Office and our allies, e.g., firms supplying the clothing and boots required for soldiers are working day and night. The Government stated last November that they have spread their orders for khaki amongst two hundred firms, apart from local contracts.

Why We Cannot Set the Unemployed Women to Commercially Productive Work

It is frequently urged that the Government, or the local authorities or relief committees, should open workrooms for unemployed women, and set them to produce any of the ordinary commodities for sale in the market. Thus, at the outbreak of the war in August, 1914, various philanthropic ladies started workrooms in which they employed women at wages *to make garments for sale*. Sometimes they importuned the War Office for contracts for shirts which would otherwise have been given to the usual contractors. Sometimes they begged their friends to give them orders instead of buying at the shops. Sometimes they sold the product to the wholesale dealers, who would otherwise have given out the work among their usual sub-contractors and home workers. Thus, the work done in these philanthropic workrooms was only *diverted from the ordinary channels of trade*. Absolutely no good was done to

293

women as a whole. During that very month shirtmakers and tailoresses and dressmakers were being discharged all over the kingdom, or being put on 'half time,' because the orders which would ordinarily have been given in the usual course of trade were being greatly reduced.

A similar mistaken policy used to be pursued as regards women by the Central Unemployed Body for London, the authority for creating employment under the Unemployed Workmen Act, 1905. For unemployed men this body quite rightly avoided competition with employment in the ordinary course of trade, and put the men to work at useful tasks not yielding any commercial value and not sold in the market. For unemployed women, however, owing to some economic blundering at the Local Government Board which has never been explained, the Central Unemployed Body conducted between 1908 and 1914 sewing rooms for unemployed women, where garments were deliberately made for sale in the market, where the utmost possible output was insisted on at the lowest possible cost, and where the enterprise was ostensibly run on commercial lines. The result can only have been to throw other women out of work. Moreover, the workrooms naturally failed even to make the profits they aimed at, and incurred considerable loss.

All such action is, from the standpoint of doing something for the unemployed, a clumsy error, which ought not to be repeated, whether by local authorities, by relief committees, or by benevolent people. To engage women in productive work of ordinary commercial character, which is merely substituted for other production, does nothing more than put some women into work at the cost of throwing others out of work. The total demand for labor is not increased. The Local Government Board now recognizes the mistake it made between 1908 and 1914, and new women's workrooms of the Central Unemployed Body were, in October, 1914, ordered to be run on quite different lines from the old ones.

New Trades for Women

It may be asked, why should not the women take up new trades, in which they might produce for sale, and make their employment commercially self-supporting, without throwing other persons, or at any rate not other women in the United Kingdom, out of work? There is every reason why this should be done, *if and wherever it is possible*. But experience shows that there are great difficulties in the way. It needs no little ingenuity to discover any new manufacture or service that is both practicable and profitable. It is not easy to obtain the services of someone possessing the necessary managerial skill and the business knowledge that is required. It is often difficult to overcome the inertia and resistance of the ordinary wholesale trader or shopkeeper through whom the product has to be sold. The railway rates are found to make both the bringing of the raw material and the selling of the finished product very costly. Lastly, the women workers themselves require to be trained to the new occupation.

Such experiments are difficult, but there is every reason why they should be tried.

The pulping of fruit, with a view to its preservation and bottling or canning in jelly form, was started in September, 1914, at Studley Horticultural College, under the Board of Agriculture, by the aid of a grant from the Development Commissioners. The plant cost about £750, and the necessary working capital for the purchase of fruit, etc., amounted to £500. The women were engaged at regular wages by the aid of a grant from the National Relief Fund. No information is yet available as to the commercial results.

The bottling of fruit may be practicable in some districts where fruit would otherwise be wasted. This can sometimes be set up in a small way by zealous volunteers, and made to cover the wages given to the workers. But it is practicable only for a short period in especial localities, and cannot be regarded as a trade. The drying of vegetables for sale in a form in which they can be preserved was also started in Warwickshire in September, 1914. This cost £800 for plant and £300 for working capital. Dried vegetables have hitherto been supplied from the Continent. They are used for export and for the supply of the troops, as well as for ordinary consumption.

The revival of the ancient home industry of hand-knitting is to be commended, in so far as it supplies the market with goods of better quality, for which there is a genuine permanent demand, or goods not otherwise obtainable, such as the special sea-boot stockings knitted by 'trawler' women.

Foreign branches of trade in fancy leather, stationery, and metal ware may, with great advantage, in future employ women in England.

The exodus of foreigners from the country should give considerable scope for English women in cookery, as waitresses, and in several of the higher branches of the catering trade if the embargo of sex be withdrawn. And the withdrawal of more than a million Englishmen from civil life has unavoidably left vacancies which duly qualified women must be found and trained to fill. The Report of the Board of Trade on the state of employment in the

United Kingdom for December, 1914, mentions an increase of 25 per cent. in the employment of women in London banks since the war, and the existence of a similar state of things in some other city employments. In the Post Office also women are working in what were formerly men's departments; they are also entering the grocery trade as shop assistants, acting as lift attendants, finding increased employment in metal work, e.g., in Vickers-Maxim's shops, and undertaking artistic work hitherto done by men in the printing trade.

The making of toys and dolls, in substitution for those formerly obtained from Germany, was started last autumn in various quarters. The Women's Emergency Corps and some branches of the National Union of Women's Suffrage Societies, in particular, have managed to employ a number of women in this way, utilizing the taste and artistic skill that they possess. A large factory on ordinary business lines is now being started at Burton on Trent, and one (The Goblin Toy Factory) has already been started in Reading. It will ultimately employ 1,000 women, many of them skilled workers with artistic training, the majority ordinary factory hands. Handloom weaving has been suggested as an occupation in which women might find commercially remunerative work in the production of articles of special quality, for which a demand has revived. The artistic handicrafts generally, it has been suggested, might be revived with the same purpose.

No experiment in this direction ought to be discouraged. In particular, we should be on the look out for any opportunity for the development of talent or the exercise of taste among women thrown out of work in their own mechanical or monotonous trades. There is now an opportunity to enlarge the field of women's activities, and to fit them to take in future a share in a larger variety of paid occupations, and also, it may be hoped, a fair chance to win and keep a place amongst the better remunerated workers. But we must bear in mind that it is not enough to obtain orders from friends and sympathizers. It is of no use, *as provision for unemployed wage-earners in distress*, to suggest occupations (such as poultry farming, or indeed any other farming, or running a tea-room or keeping a shop) which may, at best, *afford a livelihood as employers* to individual women able to command considerable capital. For the purpose of doing something for the unemployed women wage-earners the question must be honestly faced of whether in the proposed new trade there is (i) a continuing demand, (ii) from entirely uninterested purchasers, (iii) at a price sufficient to cover all the expenses of production, and (iv) of a volume sufficient to find lasting employment at all seasons of the year for a substantial number of women wage-earners, or regularly at certain seasons as an alternative trade. Unless these four questions can be answered in the affirmative, the proposed 'new trade' is a sham, a philanthropic fad, really only another form of charitable relief, or at best a temporary makeshift.

What can be Given to the Unemployed – Doles or Training?

A certain amount of unemployment among women wage-earners can be met by the development of new trades for women, but we cannot hope instantaneously at a time of crisis to provide in this way for the great mass of girls and women – to be numbered literally by the hundred thousand – now thrown out of employment by any severe depression of trade. There they are, in every large town in greater or smaller numbers, myriads of seamstresses and dressmakers of every grade, of tailoresses and milliners, and all the miscellaneous workers on articles of dress; factory operatives of all grades from the 'box' and 'jam' and confectionery 'hands,' the packers and labellers and bottlers of every conceivable commodity; the workers in jute, and wool, and silk and worsted, right up to the 'four-loomers' in the cotton weaving shed; the charwomen and office cleaners; the typists, the book-keepers and the clerks; the nursery governesses and the 'companions,' all find their chances of employment contracting through no fault of their own. What are we to do for them?

There are two answers. The first is the voice of despair – Give them alms.

The Evil Policy of Doles

This is the easiest of all devices, the eagerly adopted remedy of the charitable, the 'cheapest' way of getting the unemployed off the momentarily stirred consciences of the well-to-do. But, as everyone knows who has tried it, the distribution of money amongst those in distress– though we have perforce to resort to it in hard times if we are too stupid or too lazy or too unconscientious to find anything better – is the worst of all methods of relief, demoralising alike to giver and recipient. Hardly any character is strong enough to stand up against the subtle corruption of dependence on alms. The dole is practically never adequate for maintenance; it is never to be relied upon, and consequently never admits of provident housekeeping; yet the mere expectation of it deadens all exertion, initiative and enterprise in seeking new employment. The unaccustomed idleness, with its evil loitering and inevitable gossiping, is especially demoralising to women used to regular employment. Finally, there is the tragic dilemma of the 'scale.' If the weekly dole is large enough for really adequate maintenance in full health and vigor, it will be (as the nation has with shame to confess) considerably in excess of the earnings of women at work in half the women's trades; and it is not in human nature to resist the temptation of letting slip the chances of employment that involve an actual loss of income. If, on the other hand, the dole is made less than women actually earn at their work, it means slow starvation.

The Policy of Training

The more sensible practical alternative to employment that is commercially productive is not doles but another kind of employment – employment of an educational character. Those women and girls whom we find it impossible to place in situations in the ordinary way, whom we cannot, even temporarily, take into our augmented municipal employment, and for whom we fail to discover new trades, we can at any rate set to work at their own improvement. The provision of 'maintenance under training' for girls and women is a plain matter of justice. Far less has hitherto been done for the technical training of girls than for the training of boys. There are far fewer scholarships (of all sorts, at all ages) available for girls than for boys. And in the war emergency of 1914, the Government, for its own purposes, applied to the million and a quarter unemployed men the principle of 'maintenance under training' on a gigantic scale, taking them into army pay, and providing them with clothing and boots and complete maintenance, whilst it trained and drilled them into the utmost physical and military efficiency. Nothing analogous to this was done for the three or four hundred thousand women thrown out of work, though they were just as much in need of physical and sometimes of professional training as the men, and the nation, also because of the war, was in urgent need of trained workers.

What Kind of Training

When it is sceptically asked what kind of training could be given to unemployed wage-earners, and whether the women are not too old to learn, we become conscious of the amount of prejudice that lies behind the doubt whether it is of any consequence whether women are properly trained or not! As a matter of fact the problem of providing training for unemployed women offers fewer difficulties than the corresponding problem with regard to men.

In the autumn of 1914 the Central Committee on Women's Employment, formed by the Queen to devise schemes (Miss Mary Macarthur, Hon. Secretary), worked out plans in some detail for exactly this work,[2] to which the seal of Cabinet approval was given. It was laid down, as a fundamental condition, that the work to be done 'should not compete in any way with ordinary industry,' and that 'it should be of such a nature as to maintain or improve the efficiency of the unemployed women.' What was aimed at was 'education or technical training or instruction.' This might, where possible, take the form of instruction in the processes of new trades. It might, on the other hand (and this was found more generally practicable), take the form of instruction in the making and renovation of clothing of all kinds, from cutting out to finishing. It was found that hardly any of the unemployed wage-earning women were competent at domestic dressmaking and needlework, even for their own requirements; and of course hardly any of them proved to be able to dispense with instruction as to reshaping and renovating their own garments and hats. Every kind of mending and adapting furnished many useful lessons.

Simple domestic economy was also taught with great success. Practical cookery, home laundry work and even the elements of domestic hygiene and infant management could be made subjects of instruction. All this naturally requires organizing, and involves the engagement of competent, skilled instructresses in the different subjects – thus finding suitable employment for such persons who are themselves out of work – and these engagements have, of course, to be at comparatively high rates of pay. The Government rightly insisted, through the Central Committee on Women's Employment, that no attempt must ever be made to beat down the standard rates, whether of forewomen or instructresses, cooks or charwomen.

But the training given was by no means all of domestic utility. Workers already belonging to a skilled trade, or anxious to train for a skilled trade, were grouped for a special course of trade instruction provided by the local education authority, after consultation with the women's department of the Labor Exchange as to local demand for skilled workers.[3] About 150 girl clerks were sent to educational institutions to learn foreign languages; 30 ex-factory girls, by their own desire, were sent to train in market gardening [an experiment reported in January, 1915, as very successful]; some elder women were trained as sick-room helps for laid-up mothers of families. In January, 1915, the committee were giving grants to 55 work and training rooms (about 4,158 workers), carried on by local representative committees, and had 27 more under consideration, whilst their own experimental schemes were occupying and training 1,000 women, besides the 2,000 employed through their contracts branch or by the Central Unemployed Body for London.

299

The experience of the autumn of 1914 by no means exhausts the possibilities of providing training for unemployed women. The problem need not always be dealt with on wholesale lines. When time permits, the cases should be considered one by one, and each girl or woman provided with the individual training best suited to her needs. In a large city the number of women thrown out of work in the different branches of the dressmaking and tailoring trades would allow of the selection of those suitable in age and otherwise to be sent to technical classes that would qualify them for the more skilled and more highly paid branches of their trades, from which they would otherwise remain all their lives excluded. Even three months expert technical training will often start a young woman in the progress from a mere 'hand' at 8s. or 10s. a week into a machinist or a waistcoat-maker, who will presently be making twice or thrice that wage. In the crafts at which women already find employment, such as upholstery and bookbinding, most of them never get a chance of rising to the more skilled grades, at which some women earn relatively good wages. Even a few months instruction would put some of these excluded ones on an upward move. There are thousands of women who gain a living by cooking or laundry work, but there is constant scarcity of really trained cooks and an unsatisfied demand for the higher grades of laundry workers. Some of the unemployed women should be picked out for thoroughly expert technical instruction in these relatively well-paid occupations. Indeed, there seems no reason why selected women should not be put through the necessary training for dairy and other agricultural work,[4] for sick nursing, for dispensing, for midwifery, for the work of health officer and sanitary inspector, even for the understaffed medical profession, where there is such urgent permanent need for women's services, while so many suitable girls, who have had a good secondary education, cannot afford the needful five years of training. Once the idea is grasped that the best way to spend the time of unemployment is in training, and that the best form of provision for the unemployed for whom we cannot find situations is maintenance while they are being taught, there are endless opportunities of instruction and improvement to be discovered.

Experience, alas! shows that it is very difficult to get this principle of 'educational training and maintenance' into the heads of town and county councillors and members of local relief committees, male or female. In the autumn of 1914 the Central Committee on Women's Employment seems to have found it expedient to compromise with those members of the Cabinet and those mayoresses and other 'committee ladies' who did not 'hold with' education, and were always hankering after some way of 'getting the women to work'! In order to satisfy this yearning for 'production,' it was found expedient to allow part of the time to be devoted to 'making things in which it was difficult to pretend that the workers were in any way benefiting, either by acquiring new skill or by otherwise improving themselves.' It was then necessary, if this misguided waste of time had to occur, to see to it that the work of the women, at any rate, did no harm in putting other women out of work. It was therefore sternly insisted on that under no circumstances were supplies to be sent to the soldiers or sailors for the diminution of the War Office or Admiralty orders, and that the produce was never to be sold in any way. What was produced had to be given away to the very poorest, who could not possibly have otherwise been purchasers. In this way a number of women were kept at work making maternity outfits and articles of clothing for gratuitous distribution. As the women learned nothing by this work, and were thus in no way aided to obtain better employment than heretofore, whilst the commercial value of what they produced was inconsiderable and, of course, enormously below what was paid to them in maintenance, this plan of making things for the poor is not to be recommended. It ought only to be a concession to the ignorance or prejudices of the committee when the members cannot be made to see reason.

Payment or Maintenance

It is obvious that what the women receive who are thus given training or instruction, or who are put to work, not at their own trades, in producing maternity outfits or garments for gratuitous distribution, is not in the nature of wages, and much misunderstanding is caused when that term is used for it. What ought to be provided for those unemployed for whom we fail to find productive work is not wages, but *maintenance until situations at wages can be discovered for them.* We want to get them back to regular wage-earning – if possible in a higher grade of work than that which they left – at the earliest possible moment.

What can properly be paid as maintenance? The Central Committee on Women's Employment decided, after careful consideration, that the amount could not safely be put at more than 10s. a week as a maximum for women over eighteen, and for this sum five days attendance (or forty hours) at the educational institution or women's training centre (or women's workroom, as it was sometimes less aptly termed) should be required. Where tramway fares or other travelling expenses have to be incurred, the amount of these might be added. It is desirable that dinners and teas should be supplied on the premises, where convenient, at a very small charge, the women taking it in turns to be taught the very best way of preparing these meals. The maintenance allowance of 10s. a week is, of course, for the woman alone. Whenever she has children, or other dependants, a separate allowance for their maintenance, according to the approved scale, is supposed to be made by the local relief committee. For girls between sixteen and eighteen thrown out of work, and in attendance at the training centre, an allowance of 1s. a day was suggested.

These amounts are far lower than could be wished, and they were much complained of by hasty critics. But there can be no doubt that the decision of the Central Committee on Women's Employment was right; and it is to be noted that it received the unanimous endorsement, after careful consideration, of the War Emergency Workers' National Committee, representing the Labor Party, the Trades Union Congress, and the principal women's trade unions. It is absolutely essential, if maintenance is to be offered to the 5 or 10 per cent. who are unemployed, that this should not actually be more than what is being earned as wages by the 90 or 95 per cent. who are still at work. If a person, merely by becoming unemployed, could get more money than by continuing at work, experience shows that there is real danger of the provision that we are striving to make for the involuntarily unemployed being swamped by a rush of workers throwing up their jobs to get the larger income. Ten shillings a week is little enough. But, unfortunately, there are many hundreds of thousands of women whose wages are less than this sum. Indeed, it was found necessary to add that where a woman habitually earned less than 10s. a week at her work, she must be restricted to fewer than five days a week attendance, so as to prevent it being so attractive to her that she would be in no hurry to get again into employment. It is, of course, of the utmost importance to raise the deplorably low wages common in women's employment; but it is of no use trying to do so by giving more to unemployed women for maintenance than they can earn as wages when they are at work. What we have to secure is an extension of the Trade Boards Act to all trades in which less than (say) 30s. a week is paid to man or woman, and such a raising of the legal minimum wages fixed under that Act as will secure a much higher standard of life than the humbler grades of workers are now permitted to enjoy.

The Dependants of Women Workers

One main cause why public opinion is so careless of the sufferings of wage-earning women is that few persons realize the extent to which the female members of the family amongst the working classes contribute to the family income. It is quite untrue, as is commonly supposed by men of all ranks and by most women in the middle and upper classes, that women workers differ from men workers in having no one to support by their exertions but themselves. Although everyone knows cases of daughters in domestic service who are sending money home regularly, or of factory girls, living at home, who are paying part or all of their wages to their parents, or of married women going out to work, or taking work at home, to help to supply the needs of the family, few persons deduce anything from these facts. Few realize that when large numbers of women workers are unemployed it means a great increase of poverty in working-class homes throughout the country, as well as the distress of the unemployed women themselves.

A careful statistical enquiry of the Fabian Women's Group, extending over thousands of cases, in practically the whole range of women's occupations, showed that *about half* the women wage-earners canvassed were supporting, wholly or partially, either children or parents, or brothers and sisters, or disabled husbands or other dependant relatives. Among laundresses, over 75 per cent. were so contributing; among cotton weavers, 66 per cent.; among needlewomen, 60 per cent.; among domestic servants, 53 per cent.; and among nurses, 52 per cent.

Among women who have received a university education the returns showed 43 per cent. as helping to support others; and in a similar investigation undertaken among themselves by the women employees in the Post Office, 42 per cent. of the women of over ten years service were returned as contributing to the support of others.

From enquiries in a very poor neighbourhood in Outer London among some 750 workers, the majority of whom were girls of about 16–18 years of age, with an average wage of 7s. a week, 84 per cent. were shown to be entirely supporting themselves, and nearly 62 per cent. contributing to the family income over and above their own cost of living.

In Northampton and Warrington particulars have been obtained from cards kindly lent by Dr. Bowley, which contained the results of an investigation made by him into some 1,300 working class households, in which are over 600 female workers, 30 per cent. of whom may be said to be contributing to the upkeep of the family. In both these towns the family wage is fairly high.

From information supplied by the Women's Industrial Council, it was found that out of 578 married women working in gainful occupations, only 53 were not self-supporting, that 97 (or 16.78 per cent.) were the sole support of the family, and that at least 64 per cent. were contributing to the support of their children. In an article on 'Working Class Households in Reading,' Dr. Bowley says that in 609 households canvassed, 'The statistician's normal family of man (at work), wife (not working), and three dependent children only occurs thirty-three times' (*Royal Statistical Society's Journal*, June, 1913).

The fact that, as is ndicated by the above examples and figures, a large proportion of th six million women workers must provide for dependents, is of the greatest importance. *It means that probably at least two millions of gainfully occupied women are responsible for the maintenance, wholly or in part, of others besides themselves.* This is one more reason, and a crucial reason, why serious attention should be given by the Government and by the public to the conditions of women's employment and the needs of unemployed women.

PART II. – WOMEN AND THE CONTROL OF INDUSTRY AND SUPPLY

There are many causes, besides the carelessness of the public, why women's unemployment and the resultant distress commands so little attention. Everywhere the economic position of women is changing with the times, and not only do men fail to grasp the fact and its implications, but women do not understand their own present position themselves.

In England – the European country where agrarian and industrial life has most completely changed during the last hundred and fifty years – the anomalies and contradictions of women's economic position lie thickest. Hence the war crisis caught British women at a peculiar disadvantage. They had in readiness no trained and organized expeditionary force to join issue at once in the economic battle. They were quite unprepared to step into the breach caused in the normal economic life of the nation by the diversion of the energies of increasing numbers of men from the creation of wealth to its destructive expenditure. For nowadays Englishwomen, with very few exceptions, normally take no effective part in directing the business life of the country.

How British Women are at a Disadvantage

In France, in Germany, in Austria, in Galicia, where a large proportion of the population is engaged in agriculture, and where small peasant holdings still abound, women, deprived of their menfolk, have been able to carry on the work of producing food for their people at large as well as for their own families. It is an occupation in which, mind and body, they have been accustomed to take active part. The business of the small holding is as much theirs as their husbands', and many of them also do seasonal field work for wages, e.g., in the beet fields. Therefore, when the withdrawal of the men left them wofully shorthanded, these women were able *to direct their own labor* and to meet the economic strain by gallant exertions. In August the French Government appealed to the women of France to keep agriculture going and to feed the army, and splendidly they have done it. Never have corn harvest and vintage been more successfully gathered in the undevastated districts.

No such simple course of action has been open to the women of England. We have now few small holdings. Women have gradually been dropping out of all share in farm management, even in their ancient kingdom, the dairy, and in the south scarcely any women are now even seasonally employed in agricultural work. Our great-great-grandmothers would have had little difficulty in exerting themselves to supply the serious shortage of labor dreaded by our farmers; but, as things are, the help south-country women could give would be wholly unskilled, and farmers are demanding that little boys, who at least have some idea of farm work, shall be taken from school to do it.

Agriculture is no longer our main industry or source of supply, but Englishwomen are also at a tremendous disadvantage with regard to all the great industrial and commercial undertakings upon which our national maintenance depends. They have next to no part or lot in the organization, direction, and control of these enterprises, though by millions they are employed in them. In France women normally take an active share in the management of a family business, and therefore when the invasion of 1914 called fathers, sons, and husbands to the colors, many mothers, daughters, and wives could and did carry on the concern, thus materially helping to minimise the stagnation and dislocation resulting from the war. But amongst our seven million women in gainful occupations very few indeed have the business knowledge and experience to carry on successfully even the smaller trades. Except those in domestic service – the most unorganized and chaotic of industries – most of our female workers for gain are simply units in the vast army serving male employers; and, with few exceptions, they are as helplessly ignorant of the business management and finance of the enterprise they serve as of the larger economic conditions determining their employment.[5] What part, for instance, do women take in the business management and direction of the cotton industry, in which the majority of skilled operatives are women? Englishwomen are as eager to help their country as are Frenchwomen, but they have lost touch with the guidance of its economic life; consequently an appeal from the English Government to any female section of our industrial population, such as that᾽addressed by the French Government to the women agriculturists of France, would be sheer farce. Our six millions of gainfully occupied women have little or no control over the arrangements conditioning their occupations. Amongst the too few women trade unionists and the handful of women serving on Trade Boards business aptitude is very slowly developing, but amongst women born in the employing classes – except, perhaps, amongst small shopkeepers – the tendency has been to ignore business, even a business carried on by the men of the family, and girls who have entered of conscious purpose upon a breadwinning occupation have usually launched forth in some other direction.

Family and National Housekeeping

If this be the case with regard to the seven million gainfully occupied, it is equally applicable to the millions of unpaid British women occupied in organizing consumption in detail, each in her separate household. At least half of these have no grasp, often scarcely the vaguest conception, of national housekeeping or the relation of their own unit with national supply. Our wholesale distribution, like our great industries, is organized and directed by men; women have been content to remain in ignorance of its larger aspects, to say nothing of controlling them. Consequently, like their gainfully occupied sisters, millions of 'home makers' have no knowledge enabling them intelligently to help their country at an economic crisis, or to deal with the economic distresses of the workers of their own sex, who supply or serve them. Here, however, the light is beginning to dawn – and again, as amongst the wage-earners, the solution is coming from the toilers themselves.

Some three million married working women belong to the co-operative movement, probably about half being actual shareholders, while the remainder are wives of shareholders. In industrial co-operative societies distribution is controlled by the people for the people. In some towns it is already customary for women to attend the quarterly business meetings of the societies, and thus take their share in the control of these societies, which do a trade of nearly £80,000,000 annually. There is a slowly growing movement for placing women on the management committees of societies, and there are now eighty-nine women on fifty-six of these committees, including some of the largest, such as Leeds, with nearly 50,000 members, Manchester, Bristol, etc.

The distributive societies have combined to form the English and Scottish Co-operative Wholesale Societies, doing a trade of £28,000,000 annually. Women are beginning to be sent by their societies as delegates to the business meetings of these societies and thus gain a knowledge of wholesale trading.

The war has proved conclusively the value of the co-operative societies to the consumers. In the panic at the outset they refused in most cases to raise prices, meeting the demand by supplying only the weekly amounts their members were accustomed to purchase. By this action the general rise of prices in capitalistic shops was checked to a considerable extent.

The Co-operative Wholesale Society was able to give valuable information to the Government as to stocks and prices by which they were able to check the statements of capitalistic traders.

In co-operative societies goods are sold at the ordinary market prices, and the surplus, which in capitalistic trade goes as profit to the shareholders, is divided amongst the purchasers in proportion to their purchases, after paying a fixed interest on capital.

By joining a co-operative society and attending its business meetings every woman can obtain a knowledge of distributive and wholesale trading and can share in its control. To enable themselves to do this more intelligently, London members of the Women's Co-operative Guild are attending classes on distribution and supply.

At the universities also, some few girls are seriously studying the economics of supply and its control in relation to consumption. Still the fact remains that British women have much ground to traverse before they can take their proper place as effective members of the greatest industrial community in the world.

Women and the Control of Capital

Another aspect of the economic position of Englishwomen is the curious anomaly that, in spite of their lack of control over industry, supply and the conditions of employment, a large amount of wealth is now entirely at their personal disposal. A British woman, married or single, be she the mistress of hundreds of thousands of pounds, a small shareholder in a co-operative society, or a post office depositor, a physician in large practice, or a charwoman at half-a-crown a day, has now a complete legal control over her possessions and earnings. Like a man, she is free to spend her income and manage her own affairs as she pleases. She need not consult her husband or anyone else; and of course she has the legal and moral responsibilities of an economically independent person. The war subscription lists are a current illustration of the large amount of money thus at the disposal of women.

This money owned by women is part of the capital financing British industry and commerce. Yet the economically independent women of to-day seem to have less practical control over the work supplying national necessities than had, for instance, the working mistress of an English farm in the eighteenth century; though in those days a married woman had no legal right to keep or spend even her own earnings without her husband's consent. Since the decline of agriculture and of the system of domestic industry, and the advent of production and distribution on the grand scale in this country, our women seem to have dropped the slender guiding rein they once held in matters economic. Indeed in the textile industries, when the female 'hands' followed their work from home to factory, the female directing brain was already atrophied. Whilst women have continued to crowd into paid employment, they have failed to obtain any grip of the new forces directing our complex business life, despite the great increase of their personal economic freedom and the opening out of ever widening opportunities of education and of work

Why Women Have Stood Outside Modern Business Life.

It is not a natural lack of aptitude for business in the female brain: witness the organizing and administrative ability manifested by many women at the head of institutions, schools, societies, and large households, and the capacity and initiative shown in the present crisis by so many who in suffrage and other women's societies, or as trade union or co-operative guild organizers, have gained experience in conducting business on their own responsibility. Neither is it lack of intellectual grasp: witness the brilliant achievement of women who take economics as a university subject. Yet many a man has initiated, organized, and directed a flourishing business concern with far less opportunity than many women get, or might get if the normal, average, modern Englishwoman, especially in the employing classes, had not developed the habit of holding herself aloof from business and even the management of her own affairs.

This attitude in the women of the employing, and now of many of the employed, classes seems to have arisen as the direct result of the great Industrial Revolution, which so completely altered our economic life. One of its results was the supremacy of money, so that, instead of the old system of production for use and exchange

The war, women, and unemployment

in kind, supplies were bought and products were sold to an ever increasing extent, and personal wealth was capitalized for machinery and wages. This capitalization of wealth, in the then state of the law with regard to married women's property, meant that the control of capitalist production fell entirely to men. Sir Frederic Eden, in his monumental work on the 'State of the Poor,' in 1797, opines that married women had grown slack in working to provide their share of the family income because of the injustice of the law which deprived them of the disposal of their own earnings. Whether he was right or not about the poor, there was probably a great deal of truth in his suggestion as applied to the wives of the growing classes of large farmers and manufacturers. The great industries separated not only work, but the control and direction of work, from home activities. Husband and wife no longer consulted over the details of daily occupations in pursuit of common interests centring round the homestead, and, moreover, the growing wealth of the middle classes made it less and less necessary for the whole family to work.

Superabundance of wealth fostered the idea that it is 'genteel' and 'womanly' for the women of a family to live in more or less idle and ignorant dependence on the income and exertions of its men, an idea as foreign to the English farmers, craftsmen, and small traders of the eighteenth century as to the laboring folk. Gradually it spread from the upper to the middle classes, and thence downward. To women it was enervatingly easy, and men encouraged and approved it, partly from kindliness, partly because it flattered their vanity, partly from an inclination to dominate, and a delusion of self-interest.

Ever since the modern awakening of womanhood began, the feminine outlook on the economic side has been confused by two opposite currents of social feeling and opinion: the downward current toward gentility, which regards paid work for women as a miserable necessity for the poor and the unfortunate, and even now has by no means wholly spent its force; and the upward current toward conscious recognition of the right and duty of all women, as of all men, to work and to be fairly remunerated. This second current is still mainly individualist in tone, and still splits on the obstacle of marriage, and its course is as yet by no means clearly defined; but the shock of the war, with its revelation of their lack of control over the economic forces that sway national life, has been a rude awakening for intelligent Englishwomen. They feel that their present economic position is an anachronism, and are bitterly conscious of failure and shortcoming; perhaps never so bitterly as when men are praising their zeal in knitting

309

'comforts,' whilst they are becoming more and more aware that thereby they have been taking bread out of their unemployed sisters' mouths. Suppose for a moment that the share of control once possessed by women in the textile industries – a share so real that for centuries statutes dealing with the cloth trade explicitly included clothiers of both sexes – had developed with the industry, instead of perishing utterly a century or more before the Industrial Revolution. Our Government might in that case have been able to make, in the present emergency, just such an appeal to English-women as the French Government made to the women of France. It might have appealed to our women clothiers to carry on one of the industries most essential to the well-being alike of the troops and of the civil population, whilst the men who usually shared in the work went forth to fight. And our women cloth manufacturers might then have organized the absorption into the growing needs of the trade of every unemployed woman capable of the work required.

After the War

Alas for the might-have-been! But the future is our own, and already it bristles with challenge. When the war is over the question of women's employment and unemployment will become more difficult and more acute than now. Not only will there be many young widows, but a considerably larger proportion of the girls of the rising generation than of the young women of to-day will be, not only fatherless and brotherless, but husbandless and child-less. Are girls of the upper and middle class to continue to grow up work-shy and unskilled? Is employment to be open to them and to the daughters of the manual workers only in certain limited directions? Is it to be confined to the lower grades of trade and industry? Are the wages of women always to remain inadequate to their needs? Or will the women of Britain rise to the occasion and insist on a thorough technical training for girls of all classes? Will they declare that a little instruction in baby-craft, and house-craft, and needlework at elementary and secondary schools will not meet the case of women who must earn a livelihood? 'Vocational training' of this sort will not fit our ablest girls to win their way to a place in the direction of national industry, or to influence its future developments. Yet, that they should do so is, above all else, the need of to-day, and will be still more the need of to-morrow. Women must make up their minds to meet it. Business men must be persuaded to train a daughter as they would a son to help and to succeed them. Girls must be taught to manage their own affairs, and expected to do so. Mothers must grasp the fact that henceforth women are called to take active part in the business life of the country, not merely to work for a living if they cannot catch a husband, and that they must be trained accordingly.

To meet the future on the economic side it will not suffice for women to obtain Parliamentary Enfranchisement and adequate representation on Local Governing Bodies. It will not suffice for them to obtain free admission to the middle and upper grades of the Civil Service and of Municipal Employment; it will not suffice that large opportunities of a professional career in the Medical and Health Services, and other honorable and profitable callings, are opening before girls able to take advantage of them. None of these important things will suffice to put the economic position of our womanhood upon a sound basis, unless women in general alter their whole attitude towards business, and conceive it to be their bounden duty, and an act of social service, not merely to study economics, but to set and accustom themselves to take an active share in the practical administration of business and industrial enterprise. There are indications that this drastic change is already beginning to take place – a splendid enthusiasm, a tentative activity in many directions is stirring amongst women. When it takes definite and permanent shape, and not until then, will the problems of women's employment and unemployment be adequately dealt with.

Summary

We have seen that the unemployment among women wage-earners demands consideration independently from that among men; and that it ought to be prevented, as far as practicable, by the same increase of public employment to balance the decrease of private employment. Local authorities ought to take all possible steps to increase the number of the women and girls for whom they provide either wages or scholarships. The opportunities for immediately increasing the volume of public employment are less easy to find in the case of women than in the case of men. Other provision for unemployed women has accordingly to be made. We should strive to set going new trades for women. Apart from this difficult task, we must provide, for the women still unemployed, *not productive work of commercial character* which would result only in throwing other women out of work, but *maintenance under training*. All sorts of training might well be provided, and the experience of the Central Committee on Women's Employment in the autumn of 1914 affords valuable guidance. The fullest standard rates of wages should be paid to all persons employed (forewomen, instructresses, clerks, typists, charwomen, etc.). What is

311

provided for the unemployed women themselves is not wages but
maintenance. This cannot safely be put at more than the women
habitually earn, and the sum of 10s. per week, for five days attendance, is found to be as much as can be given without risk of
the whole experiment being swamped. Separate provision must,
however, be made for travelling expenses and for the maintenance
of dependants. Women workers have others dependent upon their
exertions to an extent at present unrecognized, and their unemployment is a widespread source of destitution.

Women's employment, its conditions, its remuneration, its
vicissitudes, should be the vital concern of women; not only when
their own livelihood is involved, not merely as a matter of philanthropic interest, but because it is essential to the well-being of the
womanhood of the country, and therefore of the whole people,
that women should take an intelligently active share in the economic life of the nation. Though so large a proportion of British
women work to produce our wealth, though so many are occupied
in organizing its consumption in detail, and so many own a
considerable share of it, women have failed to take their proper
part in skilled labor and in the responsible direction of industry
and supply. The economic crisis of 1914 has revealed this failure.
For women, as for men, the war has brought a call to be up and
doing.

Notes

1 Valuable summary tables of the occupations of women in England and
 Wales, prepared by Miss Wyatt Papworth and Miss Dorothy Zimmern,
 are published by the Women's Industrial Council. Price 6d.
2 Memoranda on Schemes of Work for Women Temporarily Unemployed Owing to the War, issued by the Central Committee on
 Women's Employment, 8 Grosvenor Place, London, S.W. (W.E.R, 2,
 3 and 4).
3 The London Juvenile Advisory Committee is issuing a pamphlet
 showing which are the trades which, owing to the war, are needing an
 increased number of learners. (Board of Trade, Labor Exchanges and
 Unemployment Department, Queen Anne's Chambers, S.W.)
4 The Board of Agriculture is actively organizing classes for women and
 girls in butter-making and other branches of dairy and other work
 connected with agriculture.
5 See figures of women working employers for England and Wales, p.
 3. Both mistresses and servants are now beginning to make some
 attempts to organize domestic work in accordance with modern economic conditions.

FABIAN TRACT No. 185
(March 1918)

THE ABOLITION OF THE POOR LAW

Beatrice Webb

For everything there is an appropriate time. There is a time to work and a time to play; a time to eat and a time to sleep. In the politics of the Labour Movement there is a time for speech and a time for action; a time for the declaration of our widest principles and purposes and a time for achieving particular reforms that are part of our programme. Now is the appointed time for securing one valuable and far-reaching improvement in our social organisation, which will put an end to much suffering and demoralisation, and open up the way to further emancipation. Now is the time when a determined effort by Trade Union Branches, Trade Councils, Co-operative Societies, the Women's Co-operative Guild, the Women's Labour League, Socialist organisations, and other progressive bodies from one end of England to the other would secure nothing less that the total and complete

Abolition of the Poor Law

This has been recommended by a strong Government Committee, in which the Labour Movement was represented by Mr. J. H. Thomas, M.P. (National Union of Railwaymen), and myself. The Government is prepared to carry it promptly into law against all vested interests if the people declare themselves emphatically enough. The proposal is now submitted for the verdict of 'public opinion.'[1] It is the business of every section of the Labour Movement to express itself upon it promptly, loudly, and energetically. We can, if we like to take the trouble, at one blow, get rid not only of the Workhouse, the 'Stone Yard,' the Casual Ward, and the Board of Guardians, but also of the demoralising Poor Law itself, and of the very idea of 'pauperism.'

What the Poor Law Is

The English Poor Law, which dates from 1601, was in its time a notable expression of the right of the individual in distress to be helped by the community, and of the duty of the community to rescue from want even the weakest of its members. But the Poor Law and its administration became subject to grave abuses, which were drastically cut down in 1834. Unfortunately the system then adopted was one of limiting the public assistance to the 'relief of destitution'; of refusing to help until 'destitution' had set in; and of a rigid 'deterrence' of all applications for relief by (a) making 'pauperism' a disgrace; (b) treating applicants harshly and discourteously; (c) surrounding the relief by deliberately unpleasant conditions, such as 'the offer of the Workhouse' and the imposition of penal tasks like picking oakum or 'the Stone Yard.' The result has been that the Poor Law is universally hated. The Workhouse, even when humanely managed, is looked on with detestation. The degrading treatment of homeless wayfarers in the Casual Ward is furiously resented by all honest travellers. The unemployed have repeatedly refused to be relegated to the tender mercies of the Boards of Guardians. Men sometimes go to prison rather than seek Poor Law relief. Every year a few starve to death rather than accept the Poor Law Guardians' bitter bread. Yet in many a rural district there is no other shelter for the homeless, no other place for the sick, no other maternity hospital, no other refuge for the orphans, and no other asylum for the feeble-minded, no other home for the helpless aged than the General Mixed Workhouse in which they are all interned.

'CITIZENS, NOT PAUPERS'

Meanwhile there has been growing up, especially under the Town Councils of the most progressive great cities, another system of meeting our needs, not as paupers, eating the bread of charity, but as citizens, supplying ourselves collectively with what would be beyond our reach as individuals. Through the Local Education Authority we provide for our children, not only schools and teachers, but also books for them to read – if they are ailing, also medical treatment – if they are hungry, even food. Through the Local Health Authority we provide hospitals for such of us as are ill, and help in maternity and infancy, not as a matter of charity, but as a matter of the public health, in which all citizens, rich or poor, are equally concerned. Through the Old Age Pensions Committee we issue pensions (as yet far too small in amount, and beginning too late) to such of us over seventy as are in need of them, as a matter not of favour but of legal right. In all these and many other municipal services there is no 'stigma of pauperism,' and nothing disgraceful. When we need this help we are dealt with, not as paupers, but as citizens. And whilst the Town Council administration is very far from perfect, this is found to be much the most successful way of dealing with the cases. The municipal hospitals, the municipal schools, the municipal arrangements for maternity and infancy have been proved to be far and away more successful in preventing disease and death, and illiteracy, than the rival Poor Law institutions – not because the Poor Law institutions are always badly managed, but because they have to be run, even by the kindest and most efficient Board of Guardians, under the cramping and demoralising Poor Law, and subject to the minutely restrictive regulations of the Poor Law Division of the Local Government Board.

Waste of Money

Another result is, in most of the populous cities, a terrible waste of public money in the duplication of institutions and overlapping of services. The Boards of Guardians provide everywhere, in one way or another, for maternity and infancy, for children needing schooling, for the sick and infirm, for the feeble-minded and lunatics, for the aged, and for the able-bodied unemployed – provided that these come under the definition of 'destitute.' The Town Council has its own arrangements for helping the mothers and infants irrespective of destitution, runs its own set of schools, has its own doctors and nurses, administers its own hospitals, sanatoria and asylums, issues pensions to the aged, and even (through the Distress Committee) provides for the able-bodied unemployed. This double set of services and institutions for the same classes of people is wasteful and extravagant. It means an unnecessary multiplication of inquiries and officials. One or other – either the Poor Law system or the municipal system – must go. Which shall it be?

What the Committee Recommends

The 'Local Government Committee of the Ministry of Reconstruction' proposes that –

(a) The entire Poor Law, with all the Orders of the Poor Law Division of the Local Government Board, the whole system of 'deterrence,' and all 'taint of pauperism' should come to an end;

(b) The Workhouse, the 'Stone Yard,' and the 'Casual Ward' should be abolished; and

(c) The Boards of Guardians should cease to exist.

It is proposed that all the buildings and other property of the Poor Law Authorities should be handed over (with proper adjustments for differences of area and for debts) to the directly elected Town and County Councils, to be made use of for the services already administered by their Education, Health, Asylums, and other Committees, in whatever way these Councils find most convenient.

All the present officers of the Poor Law Authorities would either be offered situations at least equivalent in value to those they now hold, or else be liberally compensated for loss of office or for any diminution of emoluments of all kinds.

The Poor Rate would no longer be levied.

Thus the whole Poor Law system would be wound up and finally got rid of.

But we must take care that all the people now dealt with under the Poor Law are provided for, without disturbance or the break of a single day, not only as well as they now are, but better; and that their legal right to maintenance is preserved.

Let us first consider the case of the County Boroughs, the eighty-two large towns like Manchester and Birmingham, which are now wholly governed by their directly elected Town Councils.[2]

The Sick and Infirm

It would be the duty of the Town Council, acting through its Health Committee, to take under its care, and to provide for under the Public Health Acts, along with those whom it already looks after, all the sick and infirm persons (including maternity and infancy and the aged needing institutional care) whom the Board of Guardians now provides for. The Health Committee would enlarge its present staff of doctors, nurses, and health visitors under its chief medical officer; and would increase its institutional accommodation (probably by using for this purpose some of the buildings transferred to the Council) so as to be able to merge among its existing patients, without any distinction according to poverty or riches, all the various classes of sick and infirm persons now in the Poor Law institutions. The Health Committee need not interfere with any voluntary hospitals already existing in the town, although it would probably wish to enter into mutually advantageous arrangements with these hospitals for particular cases or classes of cases. Nor is it suggested for the moment that there need be any change in the work of the Local Insurance Committee or in that of the doctors on the panel. Any reform of the Insurance Act must be left to the future.

The Children of School Age

It would be the duty of the Town Council, acting through its Education Committee, to make, under the Education Acts, all provision required for the children now under the Poor Law who are able to attend school. Already most of these boys and girls attend the Council's schools; but some of them are in residential (Poor Law) schools or 'Cottage Homes,' and where these exist they would be transferred, subject to proper adjustments for difference of area, to the Council, and become part of its ordinary educational machinery, available without distinction for all orphans and other children needing board and lodging as well as schooling. Other 'pauper' children are now in 'Scattered Homes,' which would equally pass to the Council. Others are 'boarded out,' and would likewise be henceforth arranged for by the Council. No child would henceforth be a pauper.

The Persons of Unsound Mind

It would be the duty of the Council, acting through its Asylums Committee (together with its Mental Deficiency Committee, if this exists separately), to make all the necessary provision for persons of unsound mind, including idiots and the feeble-minded, whether or not they are formally 'certified' under the Lunacy or Mental Deficiency Acts (though without any power of compulsorily detaining those not so 'certified'). The Asylums Committee would, therefore have to increase its institutional accommodation – not necessarily on the present expensive scale of regular lunatic asylums – so as to provide proper homes and treatment for the feeble-minded and mentally deficient folk now herded together in the General Mixed Workhouses. Some of the Poor Law buildings to be transferred to the Councils could doubtless be adapted to this purpose. All persons of unsound mind would be freed from the 'stigma of pauperism,' and would be properly treated without distinction of class in respect of their unfortunate mental infirmity, and not in respect of their poverty.

The Unemployed

Under the Poor Law there is nothing for the able-bodied man who seeks in vain for employment, except what is really imprisonment in the Workhouse – it may be, under worse than prison conditions, in an 'Able-bodied Test Workhouse.' If the labourer tramps away in search of work he finds shelter only under degrading conditions in the Casual Ward. Only in extreme distress will the Poor Law Authorities provided employment outside the Workhouse, and then only at stone-breaking or other valueless labour, not at wages, but on a starvation pittance. So futile and disgraceful is the Poor Law system with regard to the able-bodied that even the Conservative Government of 1905 had to abandon it, and by the Unemployed Workmen Act to set up Distress Committees (and in London the Central Unemployed Body), working in conjunction with the Borough Councils. But these Distress Committees, which organise 'relief works' and 'farm colonies,' are cramped in their powers. They are empowered neither to prevent the occurrence of unemployment by regularising the total demand for labour, nor yet find situations at wages for the unemployed, nor yet to provide 'maintenance under training' for the unemployed, nor yet, frankly, to admit the demand of the Labour Party's 'Right to Work' Bill.

What is now proposed by the Government Committee is that the whole business of dealing with the unemployment problem in each town should be placed, with new statutory powers, in the hands of the Town Council, which will be required to appoint a 'Prevention of Unemployment and Training Committee,' *on which 'Organised Labour' is to have a special right to be represented.* This committee will be expressly empowered to prevent the occurrence of Unemployment by keeping the total demand for labour in the town as far as practicable at a uniform level; to find situations for men and women; to provide maintenance and training for any who are unemployed; to provide village settlements if required; to assist towards migration or emigration of families wishing to move elsewhere; and generally to do whatever can be done to deal satisfactorily with the difficulty. As the Workhouse, the Casual Ward, and the 'Stone Yard' will have come to an end with the Poor Law itself, there can be no reversion to these barbarisms.

This is a most important reform. One of its most important features is the right to be conceded to 'Organised Labour' to be specially represented on the committee. The Trades Council and the Trade Union Branches must see to it that this representation is effectively given, as, by explicit order of the Government, it has been given on the Local War Pensions Committees, by the Trades Council (where it is fully representative) or the principal Trade Union Branches in the locality *being allowed to nominate their own representatives.*[3] Where this is not done, and the Town Council chooses what it considers to be 'representatives of Labour' (as happened by a blunder of the Ministry of Food in the Food Control Committees), the result is nearly always failure. The Trade Unions must insist, therefore, on Labour having the right to nominate its own representatives on the 'Prevention of Unemployment and

318

Training Committee,' as the Government intends and desires that it should do.

Home Assistance

There remains the large class of persons in need, for whom the best form of help is a weekly payment to 'maintain the home.' The widows with young children, the old people who can get decently looked after, the men and women crippled by chronic disease, the workers left temporarily without resources through some misfortune – how harshly and cruelly they have often been treated by the Poor Law Guardians, sometimes by the direct instigation of the Poor Law Division of the Local Government Board, in pursuance of the policy of always 'offering the Workhouse' and trying to prohibit all Outdoor Relief.

This is now to come to an end. The Poor Law Orders, including the Outrelief Regulation Order, will drop. There will be no question of Poor Relief. There will be no Workhouse with which to threaten the applicants. The Town Council is to appoint its own committee, the 'Home Assistance Committee,' which is, under new statutory powers, to be responsible for granting 'Mothers' Pensions' to widows, under the name of 'home assistance,' for all cases which can best be helped in this way. This committee is to seek admission to suitable hospitals for those who are sick and who need to go to hospital; to procure admission to appropriate boarding schools for orphan and other children requiring this; to see that the old people and the chronically afflicted, and the feeble-minded are properly cared for; to become the guardian of orphan and deserted children; and to look after the interests of all the families who come to it for help. This 'Home Assistance Committee' is to be concerned only with 'maintaining the home,' and – this is very important – is specifically not to have any institution of its own which it might be tempted to use as an alternative!

The County Council

In this way all the people now looked after by the Boards of Guardians under the Poor Law as paupers would henceforth be looked after as citizens by the Town Council itself through its several committees.

The same system would come into force in the administrative counties, with some necessary adjustments. In London, for instance, it is proposed that all the Poor Law buildings should pass to the London County Council, and that all necessary institutions for the sick and infirm, the persons of unsound mind, and the

orphan and deserted children should be maintained by that Council
– the Metropolitan Asylums Board and the Central Unemployed
Body ceasing to exist, as well as the Boards of Guardians – whilst
the Metropolitan Borough Councils would take over, under their
own Health Committees and their own medical officers of health,
the present outdoor medical staffs of the Boards of Guardians, and
set up their own 'Home Assistance Committees' to grant 'home
assistance' and 'maintain the home.' The London County Council
would undertake by its 'Prevention of Unemployment and
Training Committee' the whole responsibility for preventing the
occurrence of Unemployment by keeping the total demand for
labour in London as far as practicable regular from year to year
and throughout each year; and for providing in the most suitable
way for the unemployed. And, in order to equalise the burden as
between rich districts and poor, it is proposed that two-thirds of
all the expenditure of the Metropolitan Borough Councils under
these heads should, under proper rules, be repaid by the London
County Council. In this way the poor districts would no longer
be crushed by such heavy local rates, to the advantage of the richer
districts.

In the Administrative Counties other than London much the
same sort of arrangements are proposed. But all the places having
50,000 population which are not County Boroughs will, for this
purpose, have the same complete independence as if they were
County Boroughs. This meets the need of such places as
Tottenham and Willesden and Rhondda. The children of school age
will be provided for by the Local Education Authority, whatever it
is. The persons of unsound mind will be dealt with by the Asylums
Committee of the County Council. The County Council will
set up 'Prevention of Unemployment and Training' and 'Home
Assistance' Committees, and these, aided by District Committees
in the different localities, on which the local councillors will sit,
will look after all the cases. With regard to the provision to be
made for the sick and infirm (including maternity and the aged
requiring institutional care), it is suggested that the responsibility
should be with the County Council, and that it should at once
submit a scheme, showing how it proposes to make the necessary
provision for all the various needs for all parts of the County. If
any Borough or Urban District which is important enough to be
a Local Education Authority very much desires to be independent
as regards this new and enlarged Health service, and can show
itself prepared to make proper provision without delay at the
expense of its own rates, it is suggested that it might (under proper
conditions of co-operation with the County scheme) be allowed

to run its own hospitals and homes for the infirm aged, its own scheme of maternity and infancy care, and its own medical and nursing service. But no district is to be allowed to 'contract out' in order to be free to neglect its duty.

Such, in summarised form, is the plan for the breaking up of the Poor Law and the abolition of pauperism, which the Government is understood to be prepared to put before Parliament *if public opinion demands it.* Of its advantage to the poor, and also to the nation as a whole, it is unnecessary to speak. Three questions are asked about it.

Can the Councils Do All the Work?

The answer is: Yes, easily, if the councillors set about it properly, and so organise their business that the elected representatives do the work of representatives, and do not attempt – a fault of many a councillor – to take upon themselves work which ought to be done by the salaried municipal officials, whom the elected representatives ought only to appoint, supervise, and direct. The existing Education, Health, and Asylums Committees will not find their work seriously increased merely because the numbers under their care have grown. But two new committees must be manned (the 'Prevention of Unemployment and Training Committee' and the 'Home Assistance Committee'); and there will be, under the other committees, additional institutions to be looked after by new sub-committees. The need for more men (and especially for more women, and for both men and women of experience in the special work to be done) must be faced. The number of councillors cannot usually be increased with advantage or without making the Council itself too large for efficiency. There seems no alternative but to give the Council power to add to each committee a minority from outside the Council. This resort to unelected persons is sometimes thought to be against Democratic theory. But, after all, the Council itself has still the decision. The committee or the sub-committee can act only under the Council's orders. What is more important, this plan of Co-optation, within due limits, is found to work well. It has long been of great use in most large towns in the case of Libraries and Museums Committees. It was at first strongly objected to in the case of the Education Committee, but after fifteen years' trial very few Education Committees would now wish to abandon it. It would be of considerable value to have some representatives of the Local Insurance Committee on the Health Committee. The same thing would be of great assistance to the Asylums Committee, which has everywhere a most burdensome task, for which many of the councillors can with difficulty find time. And, in the case of the Prevention of Unemployment and Training Committee, *it becomes of very special value if it enables the Trades Council and the principal Trade Union Branches in the district to nominate their own representatives to this Committee.* If only for this reason alone, Organised Labour should think twice before it condemns the suggestion.

Will It Raise The Rates?

The reform ought to lower the rates, not raise them. The General Rate for the Town or County Council's expenditure will necessarily go up; but, on the other hand, *the Poor Rate will cease altogether.* There will have to be more spent in proper provision for the sick and on maternity and infant care; but, on the other hand, the present extravagant duplication of institutions and multiplication of officials will come to an end. Moreover, the Government has already agreed to propose to Parliament an extensive new Grant in Aid of all Health services, as well as increased Education Grants; and these ought to be sufficient at least to prevent any increase in the rates.

Can Such A Reform Be Got Through Whilst The War Lasts?

It *must* be got through promptly, even whilst we are at war, because it is supremely important to put our social machinery in order before Peace is declared. The very day after Peace is assured the great industrial dislocation and 'general post' of workers will begin. The munition workers will be suddenly and promptly dismissed. The millions of soldiers will be rapidly discharged to a labour market which will, at least, be disorganised, and may (owing to shortage of raw materials) be calamitously over-stocked. More than eight millions of men and women will lose their employment within a year or so. There will presently be hundreds of thousands of men and women seeking situations. And disease will increase. The close of a war has always been a time of increased sickness. Many thousands of 'carriers' of disease from foreign countries will be scattered among the whole population. However optimistic we may be as to 'Trade after the War,' the nation cannot fail to have to face Unemployment, Disease, and Want in thousands of homes. We need to set our house in order before the time comes. 'Do it now' rather than 'Wait and See.'

The Ministry of Health Bill is waiting. The Maternity and Infancy ('Baby-saving') Bill is overdue. Would it not be the right course – one overcoming many objections – to insert the necessary clauses abolishing the Poor Law in the same Bill as the other two reforms, and thus put through the whole reorganisation at once.

You are requested –
1. To get resolutions passed by every organisation with which you are connected asking the Government promptly to carry the Abolition of the Poor Law.
2. To get such resolutions sent to the Prime Minister and also to the member of Parliament for the constituency.
3. To get deputations sent to your member of Parliament asking for his help in the matter.
4. To make it a test question at any Parliamentary Election.
5. To get it brought forward for discussion in your Town or County Council.
6. To write a letter to the local newspaper urging the necessity for the Abolition of the Poor Law.

Appendix

For further information see the following, any of which would be sent on receipt of remittance by the Fabian Bookshop, 25, Tothill Street, London, S.W.1:–

Report of Local Government Committee of the Ministry of Reconstruction on the Transfer of the Functions of the Boards of Guardians (cd. 8917). Price 3½d., post free.

Poor Law Commission, 1905–9. Majority Report, 2 vols.; Minority Report, 1 vol. (The Minority Report, which was that of the Labour representatives on the Commission, contains a complete account of the Poor Law and the provision for the Unemployed, and remains still the best description of the whole system.)

English Poor Law Policy. By Sidney and Beatrice Webb. 6s. net (postage 5d.). A detailed analysis of the changes between 1834 and 1907.

The Prevention of Destitution. By Sidney and Beatrice Webb. Price 7s. 6d. net (postage 6d.). A policy and programme for actually preventing extreme poverty.

Notes

1 See the significant note by the Minister of Reconstruction prefixed to the Report of the Local Government Committee of the Ministry of Reconstruction on the Transfer of the Functions of the Boards of Guardians (Cd. 8917) which will be sent on application to the Fabian Bookshop, 25, Tothill Street, Westminster, SW1.
2 The complications presented by London and the other Administrative Counties are explained on a later page.
3 See Report of the Parliamentary Committee of the Trades Union Congress, Bristol, 1916.

FABIAN TRACT No. 198
(May 1922)

SOME PROBLEMS OF
EDUCATION

Barbara Drake

INTRODUCTION

The object of this pamphlet is to present a short survey of public
education for the use of members of local education committees
and practical educationists. Under cover of national economy, the
parties of reaction, inside and outside of Parliament, are preparing
an attack on the people's education, which threatens, not merely
to destroy the promise of the Education Act of 1918, but to undo
to a great extent the achievement of the Act of 1902. Hence, lovers
of education have to arm themselves for the children's defence on
one side with a knowledge of facts, on the other side with a
practical policy. There has been no attempt to cover all the ground,
but rather to fix attention on certain central problems. The various
matters connected with medical inspection and care of physical
health have been purposely omitted from the reference, as these
subjects are discussed in other Fabian publications. Nor does the
writer pretend to originality of views, but the pamphlet is mainly
composed of abstracts from official and Labour Party publications,
or from various documents, a list of which is given in the bibliography. If, however, the pamphlet should succeed in strengthening the hands of educationists against forces of reaction in ever
so small a measure, it would not have wholly failed in its purpose.

The thanks of the writer are due to officials, directors of
education, school teachers and others, who, while taking no
responsibility for the opinions expressed, have given generous
assistance in correcting and revising the draft.

The Building of Schools

PUBLIC ELEMENTARY SCHOOLS – According to the Annual Report of
the Board of Education for the year 1919–1920 there are 20,971

public elementary schools in England and Wales, of which 8,705 are provided by local authorities and 12,266 by voluntary agencies. There is a total accommodation for about 7,000,000 pupils. There are in addition 478 'special schools' for physically infirm and mentally defective children, with places for about 35,000 scholars, and 53 'certified efficient schools.' It is incumbent on a local education authority to provide school accommodation for every child of school age within its area, but a rising standard of efficiency, together with fluctuations of population, do not make this duty an altogether simple one. While in some districts there is an accommodation considerably in excess of present needs, elsewhere nearly every school has too many children. Similarly, in some large areas with a total excess of accommodation, there is a deficiency in certain parts of the area. Moreover, owing to the awkward arrangement and unwieldy size of class-rooms in the older schools, the nominal accommodation is often no real guide to the effective accommodation.

A general survey of school premises has not been published by the Board since the year 1908–1909. The Annual Report for that year states that information furnished to the Board indicated that in the case of about 2,000 schools, or 3,000 departments, in England and Wales, the school premises were more or less seriously unsatisfactory, and 660 schools were condemned unconditionally. These figures did not include cases in which the only objection to the premises was the fact that three or more classes were taught in a single undivided room; nor cases in which the only ground for objection was the absence or insufficiency of playground accommodation; nor cases of schools where the accommodation was merely insufficient for the number of scholars taught, and enlargement was the only improvement required. Moreover, the standard embodied in the Board's Building Regulations, which is applicable to new schools, was not employed in judging existing buildings. Such a procedure would have resulted, according to the Board, 'in the condemnation of a large number of school buildings erected within the last twenty or thirty years, and could not in the present state of public opinion be carried to a successful issue.'

Since the year 1908–1909 about 1,200 new schools in England and Wales have been opened, or have taken the place of old ones, making a net increase of 238 schools. The whole advance took place before 1915, for the building of new schools was almost entirely held up by the circumstances of the war. Between 1915 and 1919 there was actually a net decrease of 120 in the total number of schools. In the year 1919–1920 the Board of Education

had 'under consideration how best to meet not only arrears of
building caused by the war, but also the new requirements of the
Education Act, 1918, especially as regards the instruction of older
children.' The year saw the opening of 51 new schools, but the
figure represents barely more than a quarter of the average output
of schools in the five years before the war. Less than nothing has
been done to make good the war-time arrears. The Board has
embarked on a policy of so-called economy, and the prospects of
building are about as bad as they can be.

It is common knowledge that, in areas where the population
is increasing, there is serious congestion in the matter of school
accommodation, accompanied by the usual tendency to deterioration. Under the Board's Building Regulations a new school
should have 'no undesirable surroundings'; a good playing-ground,
with a portion covered for shelter in wet weather; a central hall
for general assembly; a number of class-rooms such that there is
never more than one teacher working in each; as a rule there should
be not less than two class-rooms for every hundred scholars and
not less than 10 square feet of floor space for each scholar in the
class-room; class-rooms should be well lighted from the left of the
pupils, well ventilated and warmed; there should be wide corridors
and safe staircases and exits, adequate cloak-rooms where clothes
can be dried, well-provided lavatories for necessary washing, and
a good supply of drinking water. Schools erected, however, before
1900 fall far short of modern requirements. Even before the war
the standard adopted by the Board in condemning schools was a
very low one indeed compared with the modern ideas of school
planning, and condemned premises have been allowed to continue
in use for years because a new building has not been available. It
is not unusual in old-fashioned schools to find cramped surroundings and no proper playground, no separate hall which is not used
as a class-room, class-rooms made to accommodate 60 to 100
children, and sometimes one large room in which four or more
classes are taught together. Even passages and exits are known to
be used as class-rooms. The Education Act of 1918 requires that
suitable provision should be made by local authorities for 'practical
instruction,' but the lack of accommodation in backward areas
makes this out of the question. Some local authorities, such as the
London County Council, had arranged before the war to rebuild
or remodel systematically a certain number of schools each year,
but these schemes are now held up indefinitely. Local authorities
are not merely permitted by the Board, but deliberately advised
to make do with premises which do not comply in the least with
the Board's building requirements. Even in the case of a new

school, the Board has actually forbidden the provision of a practical room, although the provision of such a room is a statutory obligation. There is practically no new building except in cases where the conditions are actually injurious to health, or the congestion is so great that children are walking the streets. The Board has recently arranged for the purchase by local authorities of disused army huts, and a large number of these are being used as temporary accommodation; but makeshift premises of this kind are necessarily unsatisfactory to run, and tend to cost more in the end than the building of efficient schools. It is true that owing to the decline of the birth-rate during the war, the number of children proceeding to school in the next few years will fall below the normal. There will be for a time a decrease rather than an increase in the demand for elementary school accommodation, but this is no reason why children should be taught in unsuitable premises. The Board of Education ought to carry out the survey of existing school buildings which was begun before the war, and should put pressure on local education authorities to make good deficiencies by giving notice that after a reasonable interval it will decline to pay grant on account of schools held on premises which are obviously unsuitable. At the same time, labour members of local education authorities should call for regular reports on the school accommodation of their area, and should press for the erection of new schools in place of those which are condemned. Educationists may reasonably claim that the rebuilding or remodelling of the schools in the coming year should be at least equivalent to the average achievement in the five years before the war.

NURSERY SCHOOLS – The advent of nursery schools, provided for under the Education Act of 1918, seems as far off as ever. Under the new Act, local education authorities are expressly empowered to make arrangements for 'supplying or assisting the supply of nursery schools (which expression shall include nursery classes) for children over two and under five years, or such later age as may be approved by the Board of Education, whose attendance at such schools is necessary or desirable for their healthy physical and mental development.' The Board issued its regulations in respect of nursery schools in January, 1919, twenty-nine such schools being recognised up to March, 1920, but of these only three have been provided by local authorities. During the last twelve months the Education Committee of more than one town has been offered as gifts suitable and substantial buildings for use as nursery schools. Owing to the fact that the Board of Education would be required to contribute annually their proportion of the cost for carrying on the school, the Board has refused to approve the acceptance of buildings for nursery school purposes.

'GRANT-AIDED' SECONDARY SCHOOLS – 'The primary need of the moment,' the President of the Board of Education has declared, 'is the multiplication of secondary schools.' The total number of grant-aided secondary schools in England and Wales is 1,140, with places for about 308,000 pupils, and 206 other schools are recognised by the Board 'as efficient.' The comparative prosperity among certain classes of workers during the war resulted immediately in an increasing demand for secondary education, a fact which refutes the middle-class contention that working-class parents do not appreciate the value of education. Secondary schools became rapidly filled to overflowing, with the result that thousands of would-be scholars, among them intending teachers, have to be refused admission because there are no places for them. In 1910 the London County Council arranged to establish a number of 'central' schools with the object of providing advanced instruction for children over 11. At the end of 1921, there were fifty-one such schools in being, with accommodation for 17,000 children, and the Council proposed to extend the scheme so as to bring up the total number to 100 schools, with 40,000 places, but the scheme is held up with every other reform. The Board has found it necessary to suspend its rule limiting the size of classes to thirty-five pupils, and it is admitted that 'the enforced stoppage of building' has caused serious overcrowding in the great majority of secondary schools. The clamant need for a large increase in secondary school accommodation is discussed in a later chapter.

The standard of accommodation and equipment required by the Board's Building Regulations in 'grant-aided' secondary schools is higher than in elementary schools, as regards both class-rooms and playing-fields, but 'higher elementary schools' and schools of the type of the L.C.C. 'central schools' are required to 'be planned in accordance with the principle applicable to an ordinary public elementary school.'

The Law as to School Attendance

WHOLE-TIME SCHOOL ATTENDANCE – It is estimated that in 1919 the total number of scholars on the books of public elementary schools in England and Wales was 5,419,137, with an average attendance of 5,123,526 per day. The age-limits of compulsory whole-time school attendances are fixed by law, but these may be varied by local authorities to some extent. Section 8 (1) of the Education Act (1918), which has not yet, however, been brought into operation, requires that 'no exemption from attendance shall be granted to any child between the ages of 5 and 14 years.' Under the same section labour certificates must not be granted to children under 14, but the local authority may, if it pleases, raise the higher age limit of school attendance to 15. Further, the Board of Education may, on the application of the local authority, 'authorise the instruction of children in public elementary schools till the end of the school term in which they reach the age of 16, or (in special circumstances) such later age as appears to the Board desirable.' Thus there is nothing in the terms of the Act to prevent school authorities from providing education for children up to 16. Children over 15, it is true, cannot be legally compelled to attend school, but parents may be persuaded to let them remain. Not merely does whole-time school attendance up to 16 exempt young people between 16 and 18 from part-time attendance at continuation classes, but local authorities are empowered to provide allowances for maintenance in the case of children over 12, so that there need be no hardship to poor families from the loss of children's earnings. The payment of fees in public elementary schools, which was the practice until recently in some voluntary or 'non-provided' schools, was finally abolished by the Education Act of 1918.

Unfortunately, however, the Education Act of 1918 is in a state of suspended animation. The Act comes into operation on a day appointed by the Board, different days being appointed for different purposes. For the purpose of raising school age it was laid down that 'the appointed day shall not be earlier than the termination of the present war.' Month after month the Board refused to take action, pleading in excuse the long delay over the Turkish settlement. Now, however, that the termination of the war has been officially proclaimed, the Board can no longer hide the fact of its ignominious surrender to the pressure of reactionary forces. The baby has been thrown to the wolves, and there seems no immediate prospect of a change of policy. Meanwhile, the earlier law remains in operation. Under previous Education Acts, local authorities are obliged to make bye-laws regulating school attendance for children between 5 and 14. In London, there is compulsory attendance up to 14, but local authorities can and do grant 'labour certificates' to children over 12 who have reached a certain standard in school, or children over 11 in agricultural areas, exempting them from whole-time or part-time attendance. The consequence is that a number of promising young scholars who would benefit greatly from another year of schooling leave school at 13. It is significant of this tendency that the number of children between 13 and 14 on the books of public elementary schools is only about two-thirds of the number in the age-group from 12 to

13. Nor is the Board relieved from responsibility by the passing of the Employment of Women, Young Persons, and Children Act, 1920, which prohibits a child under 14 from employment in 'an industrial undertaking.' The term covers mines and quarries, factories and workshops, works of construction and transport, excepting transport by hand, but children over 12 may be employed in shops, domestic service, agriculture and in casual occupations, and the effect of the new industrial legislation may be merely to prohibit their employment in a regular trade. Pending action by the Board, local authorities would be well advised to make bye-laws enforcing whole-time school attendance on children between 5 and 14. This measure would be preparatory to raising the higher age-limit to 15, when the Education Act of 1918 comes eventually into operation.

SPECIAL REGULATIONS FOR INFANTS – Children under 5 cannot be obliged to attend school, but under the Education Act of 1918 local authorities may provide education for children over 2 and under 5 in nursery schools or nursery classes. The number of children under 5, however, attending elementary schools in England and Wales does not amount in all to over 200,000, and all progress is effectually checked for the time being by the lack of school accommodation. In the case of children under six, the local authority may make a bye-law relieving parents from their obligation to cause the child to attend school, but regard must be had to 'the adequacy of the provision of nursery schools for the area,' and any ten parents of children attending public schools in the area may require the local authority to hold a public enquiry 'for the purpose of determining whether the bye-law should be approved.' It is usual for the infant class to break up in the afternoon half an hour or a hour before other departments, and there is some feeling among parents in comfortable home circumstances that children under seven should not be obliged to attend school in the afternoon. On the other hand, mothers with several young children and perhaps an infant in arms, would find it extremely inconvenient to have children under seven half the day on their hands, and would be thankful in most cases to send infants over two to a nursery school. Experience shows that children coming from poor and crowded homes may greatly benefit, not merely in training, but in health, from early attendance at school. In the case of children under seven, while local authorities should make proper provision, it seems desirable that a certain option should be allowed to parents in the matter of school attendance. The setting up of parents' committees – an experiment which has been made with success in Scarborough – deserves the attention of progressive school authorities.

PART-TIME ATTENDANCE AT CONTINUATION CLASSES – Under the Education Act of 1918, it is obligatory on local authorities to organise a system of part-time education for young people between 14 and 16 (and after the lapse of seven years from the 'appointed day' between 14 and 18) in their respective areas. The Act provides that young people of these ages shall attend continuation schools, at such times and on such days as the local authority may require, for 320 hours in the year, distributed as regards time and seasons as may best suit the circumstances of each locality. Within a period of seven years of the 'appointed day' the number of hours can be reduced to 280, but only by a special resolution of the local authority. Further, attendance must take place between 8 a.m. and 7 p.m., and not on Sundays or on any customary holiday or half-holiday. In short, attendance must take place in working hours. A local authority may, if it pleases, recognise 'works schools' as giving 'suitable and efficient part-time instruction,' but a young person cannot be compelled to attend a 'works school' against his will. Nor is it a sound proposition that a school connected with a private commercial or industrial undertaking, and run for business purposes, should be recognised by the local authority as a suitable place of education.

The Board intended originally to invite local authorities to draw up schemes of continued education, and to fix the 'appointed day' for each area as the local authority was ready to carry out its duties. A few local authorities, including Manchester, began the organisation of a voluntary system of day continuation classes, while London set to work with a compulsory scheme, and the 'appointed day' for the area was fixed as from January, 1921. At the end of a month 90 per cent. of the young people notified had enrolled under the scheme, but the experiment had hardly been tried when the Board decided to change its policy, and local authorities were advised to draw in their horns. In London, a one year's course has been substituted for a two years' course, the size of classes has been swollen beyond the limits, not merely of good teaching, but of ordinary discipline, and the scheme is not given a fair chance. Local authorities ought to act in advance of the Board, and invite young people between 14 and 16 to attend at continuation classes for at least 320 hours per annum, or else offer them the equivalent in some other and better form of secondary education.

The Scope of Elementary Education

CHILDREN UNDER 7 – It is now generally recognised that in elementary education there are three distinct phases, the first covering the period of a child's life from admission to school to 7, the second the period between 7 and 11, and the third the period from 11 to 14, or so long as the child remains at school. The broad lines of the school curriculum are laid down in the Board of Education Code of Regulations, but these admit of considerable variety of interpretation, depending largely on the qualifications of the teaching staff and the nature of the school equipment. The tendency of recent years has been to abolish the system of examinations, and to give teachers as much freedom as possible in framing their curricula.

The period of school life up to 7 is spent in the infant school. According to the Code, the aim is to provide for the free development of mind and body, and for the formation of habits of obedience and attention. Physical exercises should take the form of games, or singing and breathing exercises rather than of set drill. Younger infants should be encouraged 'to employ their eyes, hands, and fingers in suitable free occupations,' to talk and to ask questions. The teacher should tell stories, leading the children to form ideas and to express them in simple language of their own. Older infants should be trained to listen carefully, to speak clearly, to cultivate their powers of observation, and to do simple things with their hands; they should begin to read and write, to count and to sing simple songs. In up-to-date schools an improvement has taken place in methods of teaching infants which amounts almost to a revolution in the last twenty years.

CHILDREN BETWEEN 7 AND 11 – At 7 the child usually passes into the main school. There are in towns separate departments for boys and girls, but departments are 'mixed' in rural districts, and in some schools where all children are under 11. At 11 the normal child is supposed to be able to read and write fluently, and to be familiar with the simple rules of arithmetic. It is a matter of regret to some teachers that in this country, unlike in America, handwork, except in the form of drawing, receives too little attention during the four or five years between the infant classes and the upper standards, when the child is preparing to leave school for industry. There is, however, no question that the education provided in the junior departments of efficient elementary schools does reach a high level of excellence and produce admirable results. The quality of the instruction may be judged, not merely from the number of elementary school children who at the age of 11 win scholarships in first-rate secondary schools, and hold their own in competition with children who have far greater home advantages, but in the high standard of average intelligence. It is suggested in the Report of the Departmental Committee on Scholarships and Free Places that some 75 per cent. of elementary school children in junior departments are intellectually capable of profiting by further whole-time instruction up to 16 or beyond.

CHILDREN OVER 11 – The instruction of children over 11 gives rise to more difficult problems. The child is now qualified to study a growing variety of the subjects which equip him for 'the work of life.' The Code requires that the curriculum should be developed in the direction of history, geography, literature, elementary science and nature study, and further it is incumbent on local authorities to make adequate provision in their areas, as part of the ordinary provision of elementary education, for practical instruction appropriate to the needs of the pupils and the circumstances of the schools. Teaching in the past has been often dull and perfunctory, but teachers are now keenly alive to the fact that the main value of instruction lies in the interest evoked as much as in the actual knowledge acquired. 'There has,' the London Education Committee reports, 'within recent years been a distinct movement towards strengthening the appeal of literature, art, music and drama by an imparting of the spirit rather than an insistence on the letter. Instead of parsing Shakespeare plays, as was the practice a quarter of a century ago, the children now go to see them acted. Instead of listening to a recital of dry facts about Dickens and his writings they read 'David Copperfield' and 'A Tale of Two Cities.' In many London schools, teachers in the upper standards are specialists in their own subjects, and scholars in their final year, more especially pupil teachers, are encouraged to concentrate on studies for which they have particular aptitude, and to work individually or in small groups at intensive courses. The L.C.C. has opened ten 'home workrooms' as an experiment, so that children from poor homes may have the opportunity for private study, and so successful is the venture that it has been decided to open ten more in the immediate future.

The practical side of education is largely inspired with the same spirit. Practical subjects may include handicraft, cooking, laundry work, housewifery, dairy work, gardening, and 'all such subjects as the Board may declare to be subjects of practical instruction.' In London over 92 per cent. of the accommodation necessary for practical instruction of boys over 11 has already been provided. The majority of the centres are for woodwork lessons, but about 20 are for metal work, some of these being furnished with power machines. In other parts of the country there have been successful experiments in using such crafts as printing and bookbinding. Gardening is mostly practised in rural areas. 'The work of a rural school,' the Board advises, 'should centre round such practical subjects as are suited to the occupations of the locality, mainly gardening, handicraft and domestic economy, and associated with these should be subjects teaching the principles underlying the practical instruction, such as arithmetic, drawing, and rural science.' *Practical instruction* which aims at developing intelligence by the use of hand or eye should not be confused with *vocational training*, the primary object of which is to fit the child for his adult occupation.

Nevertheless, it has long been felt by teachers and inspectors that all is not well in the upper part of the elementary school. Teachers are faced with the impossible task of crowding into three short school years instruction in a range of subjects which should properly occupy at least a five years' course. Even such extension of school hours as may be afforded by part-time continuation classes would relieve the congestion to some extent. For example, it has been proposed by the London Education Committee to simplify the teaching of history and geography, as these subjects 'must be taught in future as subjects preparatory for higher work in continuation schools,' a consideration which 'applies in a less degree to the whole of the elementary school curriculum.' Moreover, the ordinary elementary teacher, who is required to take a class through all or the greater part of the time-table, does not, as a rule, possess the wide grasp of a subject which would enable him to inspire enthusiasm in his pupils. Nor is there always the proper equipment for specialised work. The lack of equipment for practical work in many areas has been a serious hindrance to undertaking it.

The London Education Committee has proposed to attack the problem in two ways. The first proposal is to develop the system of 'central schools,' namely, schools providing more or less advanced instruction for selected children over 11, a proposal which has been held up for the time being by the practical embargo on building. The second proposal is to simplify the curriculum in the upper standards for children who remain behind in the ordinary elementary schools, and to specialise in practical work to a greater extent than hitherto. Teachers would be encouraged by means of 'refresher courses' to take up practical subjects, and so far as possible a practical workshop would be attached to each school. 'If all the pupils,' the London Education Committee observes, 'capable or profiting by the more advanced courses of instruction associated with secondary and central schools are removed from the ordinary elementary schools, the problem of dealing with the remainder is greatly simplified and an opportunity is presented for breaking with many old traditions.' The weakness of the scheme lies partly in the fact that it does not go far enough. Witnesses before the Departmental Committee on Scholarships and Free Places estimated that 75 per cent. of elementary school children are 'capable of profiting by the more advanced courses of instruction associated with secondary and central schools,' and the scheme does not propose to provide for more than 20 per cent. at most. Thousands of children will be given mainly practical diet, whose intellectual capacities demand stronger meat. Another serious objection to the scheme is that 'central schools' do not offer, as a rule, genuine secondary education, but are provided 'with a view of giving suitable pupils a course of instruction with a bias to some kind of industrial and commercial work.' Educationists are now commonly agreed that education in adolescence should be solely determined by a child's capacity to profit by it, and not by the needs of his adult occupation.

The Scope of Secondary Education

THE RELATIONSHIP BETWEEN ELEMENTARY AND SECONDARY EDUCATION – Public elementary education, we are told by the Education Advisory Committee of the Labour Party, was originally established by the governing classes for the children of 'the independent poor.' It was designed as a special kind of education, suited to 'the conditions of workmen and servants.' It had no connection with secondary education, which was the education of the well-to-do, and there is still organised opposition from employers' bodies, such as the Federation of British Industries, to education 'which would unfit children for employment they will eventually enter.' Old artificial barriers are, however, breaking down before the pressure of social changes and modern conceptions of education. It is not only school authorities who are aware that the later years at the elementary school are largely wasted, but parents complain that between the ages of 12 to 14 a child is mostly marking time, while the child himself is sick of schooling. The Advisory Committee points out the essential futility of an elementary course which is not related to the laws of a child's natural development. It proposes to throw over the old pernicious doctrine that elementary education is 'a special kind of education designed for the children of a particular class,' and to substitute a system under which it would form 'the preparatory stage in a course extending through childhood and adolescence.'

335

This modern view of education is recommended by the Committee for adoption by the Labour Party as an essential part of a progressive programme. 'The Labour Party is convinced that the only policy which is at once educationally sound and suited to a democratic community is the one under which primary education and secondary education are organised in two stages in a single and continuous process; secondary education being the education of the adolescent and primary education being the education preparatory thereto. Its objective, therefore, is the development of public secondary education to such a point that all normal children, irrespective of the income, class or occupation of their parents, may be transferred at the age of 11 from the primary or preparatory to the secondary school and remain in the latter till 16.' The Labour Party holds that all immediate reform should be carried out with that objective in view and in such a way as to contribute to its attainment. In particular it regards all 'central schools,' 'junior technical schools and part-time continuation classes' as at best transitional arrangements, which must on no account be allowed to conflict with 'the creation at the earliest possible date of a system of free and universal secondary education.' The general lines of the Labour Party scheme for giving practical effect to these views may be briefly indicated under the following headings.

THE CONTINUATION SCHOOL – From the educational point of view, part-time attendance at continuation classes forms a miserably inadequate substitute for full-time secondary education. From another standpoint, non-labour members of the L.C.C. have declared that 'the continuation school stops employment and ends discipline without adequate result,' and that it would be more satisfactory to keep the children full-time until a later age. Similarly, parents protest that the loss of children's earnings is not sufficiently compensated by a few hours a week of instruction, or mere physical drill or dancing in an overcrowded class-room. Half a loaf is, however, better than no bread. Local education committees are advised by the Labour Party to extract what good they can from the Education Act of 1918, and to press forward voluntary schemes of continuation classes, but to keep always in mind that the ultimate goal of any scheme is whole-time secondary education. Not merely should there be provision for at least 320 hours per annum, but schools should be staffed and equipped up to the standard of 'grant-aided' secondary schools. The curriculum should be framed on broadly humanistic lines, and narrowly vocational subjects should not be taught to children under 16.

HIGHER ELEMENTARY SCHOOLS – By the mere practical necessities of the situation, local authorities have found themselves committed now for many years past to the organisation of some form of post-primary education, which they have tacked on to the elementary school under such names as 'higher elementary schools,' 'higher grade schools,' 'higher tops,' 'junior technical schools' or 'central schools.' The type of 'central school' which in London is superseding the earlier forms of 'higher elementary school' provides instruction of a comparatively advanced grade, the time-table including at least one foreign language. Nevertheless, in general academic standing, these schools fall definitely below the standard of a 'grant-aided' secondary school, and are modelled on somewhat different principles. The general characteristic of the 'central school' is inferiority to secondary schools in teachers' qualifications and salaries, in the ratio of staff to pupils, in school buildings and equipment, and in surroundings and playing-fields, while the curriculum is framed with a vocational bias and children do not generally remain at school after 15. 'Central schools' are favoured by school authorities, partly because the vicious doctrine persists that a child's education should be determined by the needs of his adult occupation, but principally for the sake of cheapness.

'We have not yet gone so far,' the Director of Education for Darlington has declared, 'as to establish vocational schools for intending doctors, lawyers, and those who intend to take up the higher branches of engineering. A good general education is essential whatever calling a boy or girl proposes to follow.' From a broad statesman-like point of view it is bad economy on the part of a local authority to provide schools of a type which offer merely a cheap substitute for secondary education, and would certainly have to be scrapped when the nation faces seriously the problem of education. As opportunity occurs, higher elementary schools should be remodelled on the lines of a true secondary school, and transferred to the proper authority, where separate local authorities are responsible for elementary and secondary education. The methods of staffing and equipment should be approximated so far as possible to the secondary school model, and the curriculum freed from a vocational bias. Pupils should be encouraged by means of maintenance grants to remain at school until 16.

THE SECONDARY SCHOOL – The Education Act of 1902–1903, by placing responsibility for secondary as well as elementary education in the hands of county and borough councils, made it possible for a child to pass on from the elementary to the secondary school, and in some rare cases from thence on to the university. The L.C.C. awards annually 1,700 junior county scholarships to elementary school children, tenable for three or five years, and there are similar schemes in operation elsewhere. A ladder of this kind is, however, reserved to children of exceptional talent and ability. It is estimated that something under 9 per cent. of elementary school children between 11 and 12 – the normal age of transfer – pass on to secondary schools, and the majority of these children leave school before they reach 15. Fresh powers and new duties were conferred by the Education Act of 1918, and local authorities are under the obligation of using their powers in such a way that 'adequate provision shall be made to secure that children and young persons shall not be debarred from receiving the benefits of any form of education of which they are capable of profiting through inability to pay fees.' For the first time the provision of secondary education has been made a statutory duty, and local authorities have to hold themselves responsible for the failure of suitable candidates to gain admission to secondary schools. The Departmental Committee on Scholarships and Free Places has revealed that in all probability as many as 75 per cent. of elementary school children are intellectually capable of profiting by full-time instruction up to 16 or beyond. It is significant that in 1919–1920 over 8,000 children were refused admission to secondary schools because there were no free places, and over 9,000 children because there were no means of accommodation at all. Nor do these figures represent by any means the full extent of the demand. In hosts of cases a child does not apply for admission to a secondary school, for the simple reason that there is no such school within reasonable access of his home. And these are not the worst difficulties. Apart from the payment of fees, few working-class parents can afford to maintain children over 14 at school without hardship to other members of the family, and the present provision of allowances for maintenance is quite inadequate to the need. The total number of children who receive maintenance grants may be roughly estimated at 30,000, the average grant being about £8 10s. per annum. Further, there is a tendency for a higher standard of intellectual acquirements to be required from children of poor parents than from children of the well-to-do. The London Education Committee has made the amazing proposal that, 'in the interests of the community,' the children of fee-paying parents should be admitted to public secondary schools on easier intellectual terms than children who apply for free places, while a still higher standard should be required from children whose parents are so poor as to claim an allowance for maintenance.

For practical reasons it would be idle to suggest that the present shortage of secondary schools should be made good all at once. The Advisory Committee of the Labour Party has therefore put forward the very moderate proposal that local authorities should provide places for at least twenty children between 11 and 16 for every 1,000 of the general population in their areas. This is the standard laid down by the Departmental Committee on Scholarships and Free Places 'as the basis of a reasonable development,' and one which has been recommended for adoption in the scheme of the York Education Committee. From this basis the number of places could be increased each year until it covered all children capable of profiting by secondary education. The proportion among elementary school children has been variously estimated by educational experts as from 75 to 90 per cent. So as to make the most of existing accommodation, it is proposed that the preparatory departments of 'grant-aided' secondary schools should be abolished. These departments now provide about 10,000 places for fee-paying children under 10, and could be turned to the better use of providing for children over 11. The remodelling of higher elementary schools would be another means of providing further secondary school accommodation. In sparsely populated areas, where secondary schools are few and far between, a motor service could be organised for the conveyance of pupils to and from school. The normal age of transfer from the elementary to the secondary school would be 11, and children would normally remain at school until 16, but provision should be available for late developers up to the age of 14.

Students' fees in grant-aided secondary schools, under the Labour Party proposal, would be abolished straight away. Bradford has already taken this step, while Durham has prepared a scheme under which the number of free places would be systematically increased each year until all places would be free at a given date. There should be a generous system of allowances for maintenance. Children in need of this assistance should receive it as a matter of course, and the grants should be adequate in amount, the scale rising automatically with the child's age and growing expenses. Under the Education Act of 1918, local authorities have power to make grants for maintenance in respect of children over 12. Finally, there should be one uniform test of admission to 'grant-aided' secondary schools, and children of poor parents should not be required to exhibit exceptional intellectual attainments. The central purpose of the Labour Party scheme is that secondary education, from being the privilege of a few specially intelligent or fortunate children, should become the right of every child of normal intelligence.

UNIVERSITY SCHOLARSHIPS – It would be premature to consider a general scheme for the development of public university education. Apart from special arrangements for ex-service students, the Board established in 1920 a scheme offering 200 university scholarships to students in grant-aided secondary schools in England and Wales, but this scheme is now suspended. Present holders of scholarships only are allowed to complete their course. There are other scholarships provided by local authorities for poor students at the universities and various places of higher learning, but the total provision is too small to affect seriously the problem of education for the general mass of young people.

Miscellaneous Provisions

SIZE OF CLASSES – The excellent work of teachers in elementary schools is too often handicapped by the unduly large number of pupils in a class. The following table shows the number of adult teachers of various grades for every thousand scholars in average attendance for the year 1919–1920:–

	Head Teachers	"Certificated" Assistants	"Uncertificated" Assistants	Other Adult Teachers	Total
London	3.7	24.3	.3	.3	28.5
County Boroughs	4.0	19.0	4.6	.5	28.0
Boroughs	5.3	15.5	8.4	1.2	30.4
Urban Districts	3.8	19.4	4.8	.5	28.7
Counties	9.2	9.3	9.9	5.4	33.7
Total	6.0	15.8	6.3	2.3	30.4

These figures indicate that the average size of a class does not greatly exceed 30 pupils, but head teachers are not supposed to take a class in any but very small schools, so that the average size of classes is larger than the figures would suggest. Nor do the figures refer to the number of children on the register, but to the number in average attendance, and the attendance on full days would be considerably above the average. Further, the average is reduced by the inclusion of small rural schools. In urban areas the size of classes is considerably above the average. On the other hand, the proportion of 'uncertificated' or supplementary teachers in village schools is nearly twice as large as for the country as a whole.

The Board's Code of Regulations requires that the number of scholars on the register of any class, or group of classes, under the instruction of one teacher should not exceed 60; while 'in no case will a staff be considered sufficient if, in the aggregate, it is not at least equivalent for the average attendance of the school or department, measured by the following scale':–

340

Head teacher	35 children
Each certificated assistant teacher	60 ,,
Each uncertificated assistant teacher	35 ,,
Each student teacher	20 ,,
Each supplementary teacher	20 ,,

In the old-fashioned type of school, however, where class-rooms are built to seat as many as 80 or 100 pupils, local authorities are hampered in carrying out even the minimum prescriptions of the Code. The L.C.C. adopted a scheme in 1912 under which the size of classes in existing schools would be reduced at the end of fifteen years to the limits prescribed by the Council in new schools, namely, 40 children in senior departments, and 48 children in infant departments, and in the last ten years the number of classes with from 50 to 60 pupils has been reduced by about 200. Nevertheless, there were in London no fewer than 4,800 classes of this size in 1920. Meanwhile, the recent restrictions on building have caused a general suspension of new schemes, and there is already a noticeable tendency to discharge teachers and increase the size of classes. For example, Sheffield has proposed to economise by a general inflation of classes to a 50–60 standard, and also to relax the rule by which the head teacher is relieved from the ordinary duties of teaching. In the spring of 1922 it was stated in the House of Commons that, out of 150,000 classes in elementary schools in England and Wales, 39,000 classes had between 40 and 50 pupils, 31,000 classes between 50 and 60 pupils, and nearly 7,000 classes over 60 pupils.

Classes in 'grant-aided' secondary schools are subject to special rules. The Board prescribes a limit of 30 pupils, but, owing to the present lack of accommodation, it has recently been decided to raise this limit to 35. There are no special rules as regards higher elementary schools, but, broadly speaking, the ratio of pupils to teachers is greater than in secondary schools, but not as great as in an ordinary elementary school. By swelling the size of classes beyond their proper proportions, so that teachers and pupils alike find that their best efforts are discouraged, local authorities do not achieve economy, but merely a waste of public time and money. Moreover, teachers in elementary schools should not be required to teach under conditions which would not be tolerated in other schools. Local education authorities would be well-advised to reduce the size of classes in elementary schools to at least the standard of a 'grant-aided' secondary school.

SPECIAL CLASSES FOR BACKWARD CHILDREN – In a report by Mr Cyril Burt to the London Education Committee, it is estimated that about 10 per cent. of elementary school children, though not mentally defective, may be classed as backward. For children of this type it is necessary to provide either special classes, or special schools. Mr Burt is in favour of special classes, on the ground that there is no hard and fast line in the case of backward children, who ought not to be completely segregated from their normal school-fellows. Backwardness in many cases may be traced to under-feeding, illness or similar physical cause, or merely to perpetual 'migration' from one school to another, so that there is no continuous education. Many backward children develop later so as to reach the full normal standard. Mr Burt advises that classes for backward children should be limited to 30, and that the curriculum should be predominantly manual in character, and for older children adapted to their probable future employment. For children of limited intelligence there seems an actual advantage in early vocational training. It is observed that backward children are by no means deficient in aesthetic appreciation, and may be keenly susceptible to music and drama.

PHYSICAL TRAINING – The Code of Regulations requires that children should be afforded every opportunity for the healthy development of their bodies, not merely by training them in appropriate physical exercises, but by encouraging them in organised games. Instruction and practice in swimming may be included in the time-table. For the proper encouragement of organised games the London Education Committee advises that additional playing-fields inside and outside the county are badly needed, and it is most desirable that more use should be made of the royal parks and the parks belonging to the L.C.C. and the Borough Councils. The Committee has in view proposals for the provision of additional school swimming baths, these classes being most popular among the pupils, but the Board's present policy of economy has thrown back every development in this direction. In some areas organised games have been restricted to one hour instead of four hours a week, so that all the time is taken up in going to and from the playing-fields, and organised games are practically cut off altogether. It is not necessary to believe that 'Waterloo was won on the playing-fields of Eton' in order to realise the importance of physical exercises and games for growing boys and girls.

THE 'PREFECT' SYSTEM – 'It is incumbent on the school,' the London Education Committee states in a memorandum on the 'prefect system,' not only to see that the child has every opportunity for full development as a child, but to see also that the training shall be a real preparation for future duties and responsibilities, social, utilitarian and cultural. Perhaps one of the greatest needs of the time is the development of a social conscience and a keen sense of corporate life in the schools. 'With these ends in view older pupils are invited by enterprising school authorities to take an active part in the good government of the school. Prefects are appointed by the head teacher in some cases, but in schools where the tone and discipline are of a higher order it is preferred that prefects should be selected by the scholars within certain limits on a democratic basis. Each school has to work out its own scheme, but there seems unanimity of opinion as to the educational value. 'One head teacher after another,' the Director of Education for Warwickshire has stated, 'tell of its marvellous results: how it has made manly boys and womanly girls of children who, at the best, had kept their good to themselves, how the whole school has easily responded; how swearing and foul talk and smoking have disappeared, or nearly so; how manners in the street and road have been metamorphosed by the new code of honour which has appeared; how the parents have risen up and blessed it; how corporal punishment has nearly gone; how new activities of school life have appeared spontaneously; how the whole relationship of teachers and children has been changed.'

SCHOOL LIBRARIES AND PICTURES – 'There is,' the London Education Committee reports, 'great need for the establishment of a really good library in each school, for nothing is likely to have a real influence on the older children than to place at their disposal a wide range of stimulating literature.' Something has already been done by the Committee in developing a system of circulating libraries. Sets of carefully chosen books are circulated among the schools, the sets being so arranged that each child in each class has three or four books every term, and there are now about two million volumes in circulation under the scheme. In Sheffield and in some other boroughs and districts there is useful co-operation between the school libraries and public libraries, and teachers act as vouchers and advisers to boy and girl readers. There seems room for further development in this direction.

Teachers interested in stimulating a child's natural love of beautiful things attach a great importance to the educational influence of school decoration. Reproductions of famous pictures and statues may be purchased at a comparatively low cost. In Buckinghamshire the local authority has recognised a voluntary organisation, which will lend pictures to a school in return for a small annual subscription. The pictures are changed each year, so that a child may become familiar with a wide variety of styles during his school life.

SCHOOL JOURNEYS – According to the Code, 'time occupied by visits paid during school hours to places of educational value and interest, or by field work or by rambles' may be reckoned as school attendance, and academic teaching in art and science may be supplemented by this means from living experience. The London Education Committee puts aside habitually a certain sum each year for expenses of this sort. Children have been taken in school term for journeys in the country, extending in some cases for a fortnight, so that they may have experience of camp life. They have visited museums and picture galleries and been taken to the theatre. Elementary school children have formed some of the most enthusiastic audiences of the classic performances at the 'Old Vic,' and the Committee assisted recently in organising in various parts of London special performances of Shakespeare plays. The latter expense, however, was subsequently disallowed by the District auditor. The matter was referred to the Courts, which upheld the auditors' decision, and the judge further questioned how far a child's attendance at the performance of a play in a theatre could be brought within fair interpretation of the term 'visits to places of educational value and interest.' Children may derive from good drama, not merely exquisite delight, but keen stimulus to imagination and intellectual activity; and this unfortunate judgment, together with the policy of stringent economy preached by the Board, has resulted in a real deprivation to London children. The L.C.C. has decided to cease its expenditure on school journeys for the coming year, thereby saving a round sum of £13,500. It is left to the enthusiasm of the teachers to raise a voluntary fund and to keep the system going.

The Supply of Teachers

THE SHORTAGE OF TEACHERS – On the supply of teachers depends the future of education. There are in England and Wales something over 166,000 adult teachers of all sorts in elementary schools. The supply of qualified teachers is already insufficient for present needs, and the general shortage would be immediately apparent under conditions of normal development. In the event of the Education Act of 1918 being brought fully into operation, it is estimated that there would be a deficiency of at least 20,000 teachers. Even before the war teaching was, in fact, a 'decaying trade,' the number of entrants each year being too few to replace the normal wastage caused by death and retirement. It is significant of the present tendency that the number of persons recognised by the Board of Education for the first time as intending teachers was 9,614 in 1908, but had declined to 6,088 in 1918. The falling-off in numbers since 1914 can no doubt be partly attributed to war circumstances. At all events, there was a certain recovery after the Armistice, so that the figure was raised to 6,604 in 1919, but this reversal of the general tendency may have merely a passing significance. Meanwhile, the shortage of teachers has had disastrous effects, not merely in hindering natural development, but in giving countenance to the employment of unqualified persons, and dragging down the standard of the service. At the present moment nearly one-third of the total adult staff in elementary schools are 'uncertificated' or supplementary teachers. In London the proportion is only about 2 per cent., but the figure rises to nearly one-half in rural areas. Under healthy conditions, it should be as impossible to employ an 'uncertificated' teacher as an unqualified medical practitioner.

In secondary schools there is not quite the same acute problem. The superior conditions of service attract, not merely a good proportion of university graduates, but the cream of students from State-aided training colleges – further depleting the supply of elementary teachers. It is, however, obvious that a multiplication of secondary schools would depend on the multiplication of secondary school teachers, and the present supply would have to be largely increased so as to meet the needs of a reasonable rate of progress. The causes of the present decline in the supply of elementary teachers may be grouped under two heads according to whether they relate to difficulties experienced by candidates during the stage of preparation, or to the ultimate prospects of the profession.

TRAINING OF ELEMENTARY SCHOOL TEACHERS – The system of training elementary school teachers, as it stands to-day, cannot be said to exhibit any definite unity of plan. Rather less than one-half of the teachers in elementary schools have undergone a course of instruction in a training college beginning at the age of 18 or over, while about one-third have received the Board's certificate without going through a training college. The remainder are composed of persons who have only passed an examination of inferior grade, and are known as 'uncertificated' teachers, or they belong to the anomalous unqualified class which goes by the name of 'supplementary' teachers.

There are, broadly speaking, three types of training college, namely, residential colleges provided by private initiative and having mostly a religious and denominational character; day colleges attached to a university; and residential or day colleges provided by local authorities, either as independent institutions or in connection with a university or other place of higher learning.

345

The students' fees amount to about £30 per head per annum, impecunious students being usually assisted by their local authority in this respect. These fees are supplemented by grants from the Treasury, and colleges have to conform to certain requirements laid down by the Board. For example, half the places in a denominational college must be open to students not belonging to the denomination of the college. At the head of each college there must be a responsible principal of university standing, and at least two-thirds of the teaching staff must consist of persons holding academic qualifications approved by the Board. The principal of a woman's college should be a woman, and a woman vice-principal should be appointed where there is a woman's department. Students are still partly recruited from pupil teachers who have had considerable practice in teaching, but whose general education has been, as a rule, incomplete and unsatisfactory. The majority, however, have now received a substantial period of secondary education. Thus, the training college has to perform a double function. It has to continue the general education of students as well as to train them in the principles and practice of teaching. There is normally a two years' course, but a limited number of students reading for university degrees remain for a third or fourth year; or an extra year may be allowed for a special course at a school of art or science, or for foreign travel. Further, a small number of 'certificated' teachers or university graduates take a one year's course of professional training. The Board's final examination is normally taken at the end of a two years' course, and students who pass are recognised as 'certificated' teachers, but university degrees and various university examinations not necessarily leading up to degrees are accepted by the Board as equivalent to the 'certificate' examination. Men students receiving grants from the Board are required to pledge themselves to serve for seven years as teachers in a 'grant-aided' school within a period of ten years following training, and women for a term of five years within a period of eight years.

The system of training for elementary teachers has undergone important changes in recent years, and facilities have been largely increased since the Education Act of 1902. There are, however, wide gaps which still remain to be filled. Most serious of all is the lack of secondary school accommodation. Though the majority of free places in 'grant-aided' schools are occupied by prospective teachers, there are not nearly enough places to go round. The Board has made certain proposals for the attendance of rejected candidates at pupil teacher centres or at higher elementary schools, but cheap makeshifts of this sort do not take the place of true secondary education. It is clearly undesirable that intending teachers should be confined through childhood and adolescence within the close atmosphere of the elementary school, where they expect to remain as adults, and the whole system of boy and girl pupil teachers should be completely abolished. A generous provision of secondary school accommodation is the preliminary step in a sound system of training, and incidentally would act so as largely to increase the supply of potential teachers.

Other defects of the present system are due to the limitations of the training college, which has to perform the double function of providing both higher education and professional training within the limited space of two years. The curriculum has been lately remodelled, so as to give opportunity for a more liberal course of study to two-year students than had previously been allowed, but the mere fact of so short a course practically prohibits the average student from undertaking advanced studies in special subjects. The number who do so falls admittedly below the needs of the schools. So far back as 1846 it was the intention of the Education Department to provide a normal course of three years, but this ideal has never been realised for any but a small minority of students. The time seems already overdue for establishing a minimum three-years' course, and encouraging the rank and file of students to read for university degrees. Students who are intellectually not up to the university standard should not, as a rule, be admitted to the teaching profession. Further, there are defects of training due to the isolated circumstances of intending teachers. It has been recognised by the Board for many years past, in principle if not in practice, that a system which segregates students for two years in a residential training college tends to develop an unduly narrow and professional outlook. It was, in fact, realisation of this defect which led to the movement for establishing day training colleges attached to a university. For the first time students were privileged to take part in the general social and academic life of a university, where they were brought into touch with teachers who were men of eminence in their subjects, and capable of kindling intellectual enthusiasm, as well as able to secure passes at examinations. Day training colleges have, however, been found wanting in other respects. Apart from the difficulties of students who live at a distance from the college, young people living at home, or in cheap lodgings, do not enjoy the privacy and facilities for uninterrupted study which are afforded in a residential college. Another serious danger which threatens municipal training schemes is the danger of excessive provincialism. It is not good that teachers should have been brought up, educated and trained within a single county or borough, and for this reason some local authorities arrange to draw part of their school staff from outside areas. There is, indeed, no royal road to training so long as higher education is closed to students capable of profiting by it, and the immediate need is for a generous provision of university scholarships. Under an efficient system young people would not be called upon to decide on a profession, but would pass on as a matter of course from the preparatory school to the secondary school, and from thence on to the university, intending teachers mixing freely at every stage with students of all types. The training college would be reserved to graduates who required a period of professional training at the end of the academic course. It is the survival of the old pernicious doctrine that elementary education is a special kind of education designed for the children of a particular class which is the root of all trouble. The training of elementary school teachers should, in fact, not differ substantially from that of secondary school teachers, who are already largely drawn from the universities. It is a condition of progress that the student of to-day shall be trained so as to teach in the school of to-morrow.

TEACHERS SALARIES – In comparing the various hindrances to a proper supply of teachers, the Board has expressed its opinion that by far the most important and fundamental of these have arisen from insufficient ultimate prospects. The slight increase in the number of candidates since 1919 is principally attributed to the fact that 'substantial progress has been made in the direction of improving these prospects by the provision of more adequate salaries, and better pensions and disablement allowances.' A Standing Joint Committee, composed of representatives of the various associations of local education committees on one side and of the National Union of Teachers on the other side, was appointed in 1919 under the chairmanship of Lord Burnham. A national agreement was drawn up, prescribing scales of salaries for elementary school teachers, which was unanimously adopted by the Committee and approved by the Board. These scales are as follows:–

Scales for Certificated Assistant Teachers (Two Years College Trained) in Elementary Schools:–

Scales.	MEN.			WOMEN.		
	Minimum.	Annual Increment.	Maximum.	Minimum.	Annual Increment.	Maximum.
	£ s.	£ s.	£ s.	£ s.	£ s.	£ s.
Standard Scale I	172 10	12 10	325 0	160 0	12 10	260 0
Standard Scale II	172 10	12 10	340 0	160 0	12 10	272 0
Standard Scale III	182 10	12 10	380 0	170 0	12 10	304 0
Standard Scale IV	200 0	12 10	425 0	187 10	12 10	340 0

Scales for Uncertificated Assistant Teachers in Elementary Schools:–

Scales.	MEN.				WOMEN.			
	Minimum.	Annual Increment.	Maximum.		Minimum.	Annual Increment.	Maximum.	
			Appointed on or after 1st April, 1914.	Appointed before 1st April, 1914.			Appointed on or after 1st April, 1914.	Appointed before 1st April, 1914.
	£ s.	£ s.	£	£	£	£ s.	£	£
Standard Scales I & II	103 10	7 10	160	204	96	7 10	150	164
Standard Scale III	109 10	7 10	180	228	102	7 10	160	182
Standard Scale IV	120 0	7 10	200	255	112	7 10	170	204

The scales vary according to the district, Scale I. relating to rural areas, and Scale IV. to London and the extra metropolitan areas. Certificated teachers who have completed a three-years' course of training, or are university graduates, receive one increment in addition, or two increments in the case of four-years students. An assistant teacher who is appointed as head teacher, or a head teacher who is promoted to a higher grade school, retains his or her existing salary, and receives in addition a 'promotion increment' of £20–£25 for men and £15–£20 for women. The maxima for head teachers vary again with the size of the school, Grade I. including schools with not over 100 pupils, and Grade V. schools with over 500 pupils.

Maxima for Head Teachers in Elementary Schools:–

Scales.	GRADE I.		GRADE II.		GRADE III.		GRADE IV.		GRADE V.	
	Men.	Women.	Men.	Women.	Men.	Women.	Men.	Women.	Men.	Women.
	£	£	£	£	£	£	£	£	£	£
Standard Scale II	374	300	408	328	442	356	476	384	510	412
Standard Scale III	418	335	456	366	494	397	532	428	570	459
Standard Scale IV	467½	374	510	408	552½	442	595	476	637½	510

Corresponding scales were drawn up by a second Standing Joint Committee for teachers in 'grant-aided' secondary schools, viz:–

Scales for Assistant Teachers in Secondary Schools:–

	Men.	Women.
Graduate assistant teachers	£240–£500	£225–£400
Non-graduate assistant teachers	£190–£400	£177 10s.–£320

In the case of secondary school teachers, there is an addition of £50 for men, and about £40 for women, who are employed in and about the London area, and certain other additions for teachers with special qualifications. Owing to the variety in the type of school and differing local conditions, there is no fixed scale of salaries for head teachers in secondary schools, but it was agreed by the Committee that the minimum commencing salary should be £600 for a head master and £500 for a head mistress.

Teachers were notoriously underpaid before the war, and the new scales when agreed did little more than compensate the rise in the cost of living. The scales were, in fact, only accepted by the teachers' side of the Standing Joint Committee in the expectation of an immediate fall in prices, and it was agreed by the Committee, with the approval of the Board, that salaries should not be revised until September, 1925. It would be in the highest degree unfortunate should the new economies to be effected by the Board now hinder in any way local authorities from observing their part of the agreement. Not merely a grave injustice would be done to the present generation of teachers, but so gross a breach of faith would have disastrous and far-reaching effects on recruiting.

The Departmental Committee on Teachers' Salaries which considered the question of 'equal pay' for men and women teachers rejected the proposal as impracticable. The Committee took the view that a salary which would attract a woman would not necessarily attract a man with similar qualifications, owing largely to the fact that, under existing social and fiscal conditions, financial liabilities fall on a man in connection with his family which do not fall on a woman to the same extent, and that a difference between the scales of men's and women's salaries is inevitable. The War Cabinet Committee on Women in Industry, after considering this report, advised that, 'in order to maintain the principle of "equal pay for equal work" where it is essential to employ men and women of the same grade and capacity, but where equal pay will not attract the same grade, it may be necessary for the State to counteract the difference of attractiveness by a payment for the services rendered to the State in connection with the continuance of the race, or, in other words, by the payment of children's allowances to married men.' It seems worth while to give the proposal a trial, provided that women's salaries are levelled up to the men's standard, and not men's salaries levelled down to the women's standard. It is, however, important that local authorities should be under no temptation to prefer unmarried teachers. For this reason the whole of the additional cost of the children's allowances should be borne by the Treasury. The practice of discharging women teachers on marriage, though admittedly fit for their work, has been universally condemned by women teachers and all women's organisations as socially unjust and economically unsound. It cannot be urged too strongly that this practice should be discontinued, and women teachers receive the same allowances as men for dependent children.

The Regulation of Children's Employment

RESTRICTIONS ON EMPLOYMENT – Children's employment is regulated under the Factory Acts, and by various special legislation. Under the Women, Young Persons and Children's Act (1920), a child under 14 may not be employed in 'an industrial undertaking.' The latter term covers mines and quarries, factories and workshops, works of construction and transport, excepting transport by hand. Further, children's employment is restricted by the law of school attendance, and local education authorities have wide powers of regulating conditions for children of school age not coming under special industrial legislation. Under the Employment of Children Act (1903), the local authority may prescribe for children employed in any occupation the age below which employment is illegal, the hours between which employment is illegal, the maximum number of hours to be worked per day or per week, or may prohibit employment in a specified occupation. There are certain statutory requirements. A child under 12 may not be employed for longer than two hours on Sunday, or for longer than one hour before and one hour after school on any day when he is required to attend school. Also, a child under 14 must not be employed between the hours of 8 a.m. and 6 p.m., or in street trading, or in public performances without a licence from the local authority. It is these statutory requirements which form the basis of local bye-laws, but local authorities may exercise a wide discretion over and above the statutory minimum. In London and in most large towns, local authorities have used their powers to prohibit children's employment in the sale or delivery of intoxicants, in lathering or similar processes in barbers' shops, and have taken advantage of their option to prohibit street trading for girls up to 16. Children's employment is prohibited in different localities, in such various occupations as billiards or bagatelle marking, the sale of programmes or shifting of machinery in theatres and cinemas, working in hotel and restaurant kitchens, acting as messenger, tout, or agent to bookmakers, soliciting for the letting of apartments, sorting rags or refuse, and cleaning doorsteps.

The weakness of the Employment of Children's Act lies in its mainly permissive character. Backward local authorities, not only neglect to make suitable bye-laws, but seem unable to enforce such legal restrictions as exist. Moreover, the reports of school medical officers reveal that any employment out of school hours, beyond the lightest errand work, tends to impair the child's physical development. The obvious remedy would be that a child under 14 should be unconditionally prohibited by law from employment for wages. The simplicity of such an enactment would give it the further advantage of being comparatively easy to enforce. During a recent revision of local bye-laws by the L.C.C., some members interested in education brought forward a proposal to the effect that 'a child shall not be employed on any day when the school is open,' but the motion was defeated by the reactionary parties. It has not been clearly established in the courts that local authorities have power to make a general order prohibiting children's employment, but they may achieve practically the same result by prescribing the strictest limits to employment, and by a rigid enforcement of bye-laws.

The need for raising the age of school attendance, and for abolishing labour certificates in the case of children under 14, have been discussed in a previous chapter.

CHOICE OF EMPLOYMENT – Under the Choice of Employment Act, 1910, local education authorities have power 'to make arragements, subject to the approval of the Board of Education, for giving boys and girls under 18 years of age assistance with respect to the choice of suitable employment, by means of the collecting and communicating of information and the furnishing of advice.' About 600,000 boys and girls leave the public elementary schools each year, and of these a large and increasing number seek help, either from local employment committees acting as sub-committees of the local education authority, or from juvenile advisory committees appointed by the Ministry of Labour. Unfortunately, however, the existence of this dual authority has led to conflicts between the Ministry of Labour and local authorities, which have seriously jeopardised the success of the service. Young people between 14 and 18 are in a period midway between the educational life of the child and the industrial life of the adult. It is necessary to consider their interests from both points of view, and the alternative is, either a system of local administration by local education committees, reinforced by assistance from the Ministry of Labour, or a centralised system where the Ministry of Labour is the supreme authority, acting in co-operation with local education committees. Following the Chelmsford Report, the most recent proposal is that local education authorities should within a specified period declare, whether or not, they will undertake in their areas the duties under the Choice of Employment Act. If a local authority decides not to act, then the Minister of Labour can, and presumably will, take action instead. The policy is that there should be an organisation of some kind in each area, but it has always been recognised by the authorities on both sides that 'the employment of juveniles should be primarily considered from the point of view of their educational interests and permanent careers rather than from that of their immediate earning capacities.' Local education authorities neglect a great opportunity who do not make efficient use of their powers under the Choice of Employment Act.

UNEMPLOYMENT – 'When there is unemployment among adults,' the Labour Party has laid it down as a general principle, 'the entry of juvenile workers into industry should, as far as possible be arrested, provision being made by means of adequate system of maintenance allowances to prevent the family suffering from loss of earnings.' The opposite effect has, however, been achieved by the policy of the present Government in holding up the Education Act of 1918 regardless of the growing volume of unemployment. It is a common practice among employers in some industries deliberately to discharge adult men or women in preference to young people who are content with low wages. The Labour Party proposes that powers of emergency should be conferred on local authorities to raise whole-time school age from 14 to 15 (this being the highest age-limit under the Education Act of 1918), at times of acute unemployment in their areas. Further, local authorities should open special training centres, and provide suitable instruction and maintenance for unemployed young people.

The Cost of Education

Precise figures as to the actual expenditure on education from central and local funds are not available for any recent year. The following summary figures are computed from the published estimates of the Board of Education and the local education authorities as to their expenditure in the year ending March, 1922. They are, of course, approximate only.

ESTIMATED PUBLIC EXPENDITURE ON EDUCATION IN ENGLAND AND WALES IN THE FINANCIAL YEAR ENDING MARCH 31ST, 1922.
A.–*Elementary Education.*

1. Net Expenditure of Local Education Authorities
   (a) Salaries of teachers   £43,795,000
   (b) Other expenditure   £19,853,000
                          Total   £63,648,000

2. Grants from the Board to Local Education
   Authorities   £36,900,000
3. Grants from the Board to other Bodies   £98,000

B.–*Higher Education.*
(*Including Secondary Schools, Technical Schools, Training Colleges, etc., but not Universities*).

1. Net Expenditure of Local Education
   Authorities   £13,469,000
2. Grants from the Board to Local Education
   Authorities   £6,647,000
3. Grants from the Board to other Bodies   £2,130,500

C.–*Total of* A *and* B.

1. Total Net Expenditure of Local Education
   Authorities   £77,117,000
2. Grants from the Board to Local Education
   Authorities   £43,547,000
3. Other Grants to Local Education Authorities
   (Local Taxation Grants, etc.)   £950,000
4. Difference to be met by Local Education Auth-
   orities from rates   £32,620,000

D.–*Other National Expenditure on Education.*

1. Pensions to Teachers   £1,575,000
2. Grants to Students – ex-Service Students   £2,248,000
   Other Students   £192,000
3. Expenditure on Universities   £1,500,000
4. Other Expenditure by the Board (Museums,
   Administration, etc.)   £722,000

E.–*Total Public Expenditure on Education.*

	1913–14.	1921–22.
1. Grants from the National Exchequer	£15,320,000	£53,400,000
2. Local Rates	£16,190,000	£32,600,000
Total Local and National Expenditure	£31,510,000*	£86,000,000

*Actual expenditure.

Between the years 1913–14 and 1921–22 there was an increase of 168 per cent. in the total sum of public expenditure on education.

The rise is most acutely marked in the amount of national grants, the national exchequer bearing at present a substantially greater proportion of the total expenditure than before the war, but the figures taken as a whole do not represent an excessive rate of advance. They err rather on the side of moderation. Apart from special items of expenditure in the estimates for 1921–1922, such as provision for ex-service students, and a fall of at least 100 per cent. in the value of money, there has to be taken into account the necessities of growth in an undeveloped but vital public service. Broadly speaking, it is true to say that the progress of a nation in civilisation may be measured by the sum of its expenditure on education.

The primary need of the moment, Mr. Fisher has told us, is the multiplication of secondary schools. The Labour Party scheme, put forward as 'a basis of reasonable development,' would involve a net additional expenditure of about £15,000,000 per annum. This estimate, which takes into account the corresponding saving on elementary schools, would cover the abolition of fees in grant-aided secondary schools, places for at least 20 children between 11 and 16 for every thousand of the general population, and maintenance grants for children over 14. The immediate cost would be a comparatively small one, and there is no better time than to-day to undertake this and other schemes entailing the building or rebuilding of schools. There are at the time of writing as many as 150,000 building operatives out of work, and at least a part of the outlay on building would be compensated by a corresponding saving of public money on unemployment benefit and poor law relief. For this reason building schemes undertaken immediately should be generously financed by the Treasury. Nor is it desirable on other grounds that fresh burdens should be thrown on local rates, which are so high in some poor localities that local authorities find their best activities paralysed. Not merely 'the poor pay for the poor' in working class areas, but rents have been forced up to a point which practically prohibits the provision of decent working-class dwellings. Under the present rating system, local rates amount virtually to a single tax on housing, which presses necessarily more heavily on the poor man than on the rich man, and with the utmost severity on large families. A further rise in local rates would be the cause of grave injustice and hardship to hundreds of thousands of poor tenants. There is an overwhelming case that further expenditure on education should be met by increased grants from the national exchequer. The London Labour Party has proposed that at least 75 per cent. of the cost of education should be borne by the Treasury, and the proportion seems a fair one. In respect of measures directly undertaken for the relief of unemployment, the proportion of national expenditure should not be less than 90 per cent.

For the time being, however, forces of reaction are paramount in Parliament. 'Education,' Lord Inchcape has told us, 'is an excellent thing in its way, but there is a limit to its economic usefulness.' Hence, the Geddes Economy Committee, of which Lord Inchcape is a member, advises the Government to cut down the education estimates for the coming year by no less a sum than £16,000,000, or nearly one-third of the total national expenditure on education. The Committee makes no attempt to discriminate between one public service and another, and would cut down the education estimates by about the same proportionate amount as the swollen army estimates. Its members view apparently with complacency the total exclusion from school of children under 6 regardless of home convenience, enlarging the average size of classes in elementary schools to 50 or 60 pupils, a drastic curtailment of the school health services, a breakdown of the scholarship system, so that the number of children who now pass from the elementary school to the secondary school or to the university would be still further diminished, together with the wholesale discharge of teachers and a general reduction of salaries contrary to the 'Burnham' agreements. And this saving of money on public education the Committee proposes to devote to the purpose of relieving taxation on private incomes. In short, the business man's idea of national economy is to shift the burden of paying for the war from off his own broad back on to the shoulders of the poor man's child!

The signs of unexpected public indignation at the ruthless attack on the people's education, together with the prospect of a general election, seem to have had their influence on the Government, which has rejected the more sensational of the Geddes proposals. The reductions foreshadowed in the education estimates for 1922–1923 do not exceed £6,000,000. The outlook is nevertheless a sufficiently grave one. Working-class opinion has so far been conciliated that children between 5 and 6 are not to be excluded from school without their parents' consent, but there are to be economies where staffing is on a lavish scale, and a number of teachers are to be discharged. This method of economy is preferred by the Government to a reduction of teachers' salaries. Pensions are to be placed on a new contributory basis, but the Burnham scales are to be maintained intact. In spite of unemployment, school feeding must be kept within normal limits, and necessitous children referred to the Poor Law. Similarly, the quality of entrants into secondary schools is to be narrowly watched, and there is practically an end to progress. The general policy of the Board is, however, not to make specific proposals for cutting down of this or that branch of the educational services, but to ration local authorities up to a fixed maximum grant in aid of local expenditure. The policy of percentage grants which was condemned by the Geddes Committee as a 'money-spending' device, has been referred by the Government to a separate committee for further consideration, but seems in effect to have been already abandoned. Local authorities will be obliged either to cut down their expenditure or else to raise local rates, and so spare the taxpayer at the expense of the ratepayer.

There is, of course, a limit to 'economic usefulness,' in education as in everything else. It is a question of degree, and the first step towards a sound system of economy is a proper sense of economic values. The product of education is 'brains,' which from the most commercial point of view are the nation's most valuable asset. To save on education, while vast sums are spent on less 'excellent' things, such as tobacco, drink, or armaments, which are not conspicuous for 'economic usefulness,' or money is lavished on mere wanton luxury, this is not economy but waste.

The business man has, however, his own axe to grind, and he is not such a fool as he seems. The manner of his attack on the workers' education and his desperate anxiety to thrust it back within the old limitations 'suited to the conditions of workmen and servants,' suggests, indeed, that he appreciates its significance for himself, not too little, but too well. Education is a double-edged tool. It makes good servants but bad slaves, and capital is afraid of losing its hold over labour. It is possible that a reactionary Government may succeed in cutting down the people's education so that the effects would be felt for a generation or longer, but this is not the political broom which will sweep back the rising tide of democracy. For men do not wait to seize power merely because they may not be 'fit to govern.' The danger which threatens democracy is that radical social and economic changes may take place unaccompanied by a forward movement in the schools.

Summary of Proposals

I. School Premises. – Local authorities should proceed at once with their schemes for the building or rebuilding of schools in accordance with the Board's Building Regulations and the requirements of the Education Act of 1918. These schemes should make provision for a proper number of nursery schools and for increasing the number of secondary schools. The provision for building in the coming year should be at least equivalent to the average achievement in the five years before the war.

II. School Attendance. – Pending the operation of the Education Act of 1918, local education committees should enforce whole-time school attendance for children between 5 and 14, and the higher age-limit should be raised to 15 as soon as the new Act comes into force. Nursery schools, or nursery classes, should be available for children between 2 and 5, but a certain option should be allowed to parents as regards the attendance of children under 7. Local authorities should forestall action on the part of the Board of Education and invite young people between 14 and 16 to attend continuation classes for at least 320 hours per year, or offer them an equivalent in some other and better form of secondary education.

III. The Scope of Elementary Education. – As regards children under 11 the curriculum should be framed in accordance with the Board's Code of Regulations. For children over 11, there should be provided advanced courses of instruction of the type generally associated with secondary education. It should be the ultimate goal of local education committees that all children of normal intelligence should pass as a matter of course from the elementary school to one type or other of secondary school about the age of 11. Provision should, however, be available for late developers up to the age of 14.

IV. The Scope of Secondary Education. – Local authorities should immediately provide secondary school accommodation for at least 20 children between 11 and 16 for every thousand of the general population in their areas, the number of places being increased each year until all children of normal intelligence are provided for. Meanwhile, continuation classes and higher elementary schools should be developed so far as possible on the lines of true secondary education, and vocational subjects should not be taught to children under 16. Students' fees in grant-aided secondary schools should be abolished, and adequate maintenance grants provided for children over 14.

V. Miscellaneous Provisions. – (1) The size of classes in elementary schools should approximate so far as possible to the standard of secondary schools and be limited to 30 pupils. (2) Special classes should be arranged for backward children, and instruction in their case given a practical bias. (3) Playing-fields should be enlarged and public parks opened so as to encourage children in physical exercises and organised games. (4) Increased attention should be paid to school libraries and pictures. (5) The prefect system should be encouraged in senior departments.

(6) Increased facilities should be given for school journeys and visits to places of educational value and interest.

VI. The Supply of Teachers. – The supply of teachers may be encouraged (*a*) by increasing the facilities for training, and (*b*) by improving the ultimate prospects of the profession. Training schemes should provide for full-time secondary education up to 18 and a three years' course in a training college, or preferably at a university, to be followed by a period of professional training. Teachers should be assured against any breach of the agreements of the Standing Joint Committee in respect of salaries, and the present scales should be gradually raised so as to compare not unfavourably with earnings in other learned professions. The Standing Joint Committee should consider a proposal for 'equal pay' to men and women teachers, to be supplemented by children's allowances.

VII. The Regulation of Children's Employment. – Pending an amendment of the law so as to prohibit children under 14 from employment for wages, local education authorities should make bye-laws restricting children's employment within the narrowest limits, and in every area should make efficient use of their powers under the Choice of Employment Act. At times of acute unemployment local authorities should be given power to raise school age from 14 to 15, while suitable training with maintenance should be provided for unemployed young people.

VIII. The Cost of Education. – The burden of fresh expenditure in order to meet the growing needs of education should not be thrown on local rates, but met by additional grants from the national exchequer. At least 75 per cent. of the total public expenditure on education should be borne by the Treasury, the proportion being raised to 90 per cent. in respect of measures undertaken for the relief of unemployment.

FABIAN TRACT No. 205
(March 1923)

CO-OPERATIVE EDUCATION

Lilian A. Dawson

ALTHOUGH the Co-operative Movement started with the object of providing commodities for the workers at reasonable prices and freeing them from the adulteration and credit system of the little shopkeeper and the truck shop of the employer, the ultimate purpose which lay behind the mind of the twenty-eight flannel weavers of Rochdale was their emancipation from wage slavery by such a reorganization of industry as would enable them to provide themselves with employment and – to use their own words – 'so to arrange the powers of production, distribution, education, and government as to create a self-supporting home colony.'

How far this ideal has been reached may be realized by the study of the Movement as it is to-day, with its individual membership of over four millions, and an organization which provides, in addition to wholesale production and retail distribution of material goods, educational services which include Scholarships and College facilities, Holiday Homes and Rest Houses, Camps and Travel Bureaux, Convalescent Homes and Sick Room Appliances, Summer Schools and Social Institutes, Men's and Women's Guilds, a Political Party, a Publishing Society, and two Churches. It is true that it has not been wholly successful in providing employment for its members, and it has not yet achieved that self-supporting Home Colony which it set out to create, but it has gone a long way towards laying its foundation; it is for the next generation to carry it forward.

The old pioneers recognized that to make people wealthier without making them wiser would merely perpetuate the evils of the society which they were out to destroy, and in all their schemes education played a large part. If the educational development of the Movement has not kept pace with its material side, still a great deal has been done; and to-day there are Co-operators who realize that it is along the educational line that ultimate success lies. A Movement which, except for a small minority, has never gone outside the working classes, and yet has built up such an organization as we see to-day, cannot be said to have failed in its higher ideals, whatever the obstacles may be to their full realization.

Whilst appreciating all the work which has been done by the Movement for the education and social welfare of co-operators, a criticism may be advanced, not belittling those efforts, but accentuating future possibilities of development.

It is a common error for people who only think of the Co-operative Movement as a trading concern to accuse it of being a capitalistic enterprise run on commercial lines, but they forget the difficulties with which it has to contend. As a group of idealists it must produce goods of the best quality and provide good conditions for its workers. As an ordinary competitor in the markets of the world it must keep its prices on a level with other competitors who do not pretend to be idealists, but merely businessmen. Its difficulties are further complicated by the psychology of its members, many of whom are not co-operators in the true sense of the word, but join societies for the material advantages they can obtain. They care nothing for education, conditions of the workers, or other social questions. The view of such members is obscured by dividends – if dividends are good, they think it is progress; if dividends are low or non-existent, they visualize the collapse of co-operation. In the larger questions of health, culture, and education they are not interested. If it is not quite as true to-day as it was in 1897, when, at the Jubilee Conference, the proposal for a halfpenny a month for knowledge was put forward, and a delegate stated, 'We want no eddication, give us a bonus,' there are still members who have not got beyond that stage of mentality; but if co-operators cannot see farther than this, then the Movement will lose its value as an educational influence, which influence should be one of its greatest assets.

It might be useful to revise the present method of returning dividends on purchases, and to consider the possibility of using a definite proportion of surplus or profit for educational purposes for the whole Movement; such a proceeding might eliminate a certain number of members who only understand co-operation through the dividend, but it would establish a solid band of real co-operators and enable them to organize an educational policy of great value.

There seems to be some difference of opinion among co-operators as to the type of education which should be provided. Should it be co-operation pure and simple, or co-operation supplemented by culture? The Co-operative Movement possesses a large and expensive machinery for the purpose of educating its members; is it being used to the best advantage and what is its aim?'

Like the growth of national and international trade, provision for education has developed with the growth of the Movement, and in this way it has been uneven; in those societies which have had an educational conscience, it has progressed; in others it has remained stationary or non-existent. It is inevitable that there should be a lack of uniformity in a system which is the result of haphazard growth rather than preconceived policy. The result is that, while it is true that, nominally, education is accepted as part of the work of all societies, actually it is only fully adopted by a comparatively small number.

The educational work is carried on through two main channels – the education committees of the local societies and the Central Education Committee of the Co-operative Union. In addition a certain amount of educational work is done voluntarily by the unofficial or auxiliary bodies, such as the Men's and Women's Guilds and the Co-operative Educational Fellowship. Outside the Co-operative Movement, yet in some cases closely allied to it, are such organizations as the Workers' Educational Association, the Working Men's College, the Adult Schools and the various classes carried on by Trade Unions and Socialist and Labour Parties.

Bound up with the educational work, and in fact one of its principal objects, is publicity and propaganda, working through the education committees, the auxiliary bodies, and the co-operative press.

The Education Committee of Local Societies. – A co-operative society acknowledges the advantages of education by setting up an education committee, elected by the members on the same principle as the Management Committee, but without any relationship to it.

In the early days of the Movement these committees, by providing classes, reading rooms and libraries, anticipated the work eventually undertaken by the Local Authorities under the Education and Free Libraries Acts.

It is a tradition that societies should allocate 2½ per cent. of their annual surplus or 'profits' to carry on this particular work.

'The aim of the education committee has been to provide:–

(a) Such general provision for the further education of the members of the society, as the maintenance of a library and reading room for their free use;

362

(b) The organisation of evening classes in literature, science and art;

(c) Popular lectures and entertainments for the members and their wives and children;

(d) Instruction in the 'principles of Co-operation' both for members and employees;

(e) The technical training of the employees in accountancy and book-keeping, salesmanship, &c.;

(f) Propagandist lectures and public meetings for spreading Co-operation and increasing the society's membership.

'In most societies, and particularly in the larger ones, revolving round the educational committee are "social institutes" and all sorts and kinds of associations and clubs: debating societies, literary societies, choral societies, drill and dancing classes; chess societies, photographic societies, football and cricket clubs, field clubs, rambling clubs, cycle clubs, "summer schools" and "holiday fellowships" for home and foreign travel.'[1]

In order to co-ordinate the work of the local societies, the education committees have their Educational Associations, in each Section of the country – Northern, North-Western, Southern, & c.

The principal object of these Associations is to stimulate educational activities in the societies within the Sections, and to interest persons engaged in educational work outside the co-operative movement. They are composed of representatives from the Central Board of the Co-operative Union, from groups of societies, and, in some sections, from outside bodies such as the Working Men's College and the Co-operative Brotherhood Trust.

The Central Education Committee of the Co-operative Union. – The Central Committee is intended to direct and guide the educational activities of the societies. It is a committee of the Union, composed of representatives appointed by the Sectional Boards, the Sectional Educational Associations, and the English and Scottish Women's Guilds. In 1915, the Union appointed a Director of Studies, who draws up the syllabuses for the use of local committees.

Through its Adviser of Studies it promotes classes for teaching the history and principles of co-operation, book-keeping, management, and other allied subjects. It issues an annual programme and lecture list, provides lecturers and teachers for classes; it also awards scholarships, certificates, &c. Of late years, one of its most successful undertakings has been the organization of summer and week-end schools. As an outcome of these schools, small associations have been formed, such as the secretaries' association and the managers' association, for the purpose of a mutual exchange of views.

There is no compulsion on societies to accept the programme issued by the Central Education Committee, but many of them find it useful and base their studies upon it.

The Central Education Committee works in co-operation with other bodies, such as the Publications Committee, the Co-operative Party, the Workers' Educational Association, Ruskin College, the Young Men's Christian Association, Joint Universities Committee, the various University Joint Tutorial Classes Committees and the Society for the Advancement of Education in Industry and Commerce.

Through the Publications Committee, it issues an annual programme with sets of syllabuses for local education committees and publishes a bi-monthly journal, 'The Co-operative Educator,' the organ of the Co-operators' Educational Fellowship, an organization formed by the amalgamation of two former bodies – the Students' Fellowship and the College Herald Circle. The Fellowship seeks to gather to its membership all those co-operators who are interested in education; it thus forms the nucleus from which to invite members to summer schools or educational conferences.

Part of the work of the Central Education Committee has been to interest societies and individual members in the establishment of a Co-operative College. This is no new vision, but has been in the minds of co-operative educationalists for many years. It is now coming within the realms of possibility, and the Central Board of the Co-operative Union has issued an appeal for £50,000, of which about £16,000 has been collected. In the meantime college work is being carried on at Holyoake House, Manchester, under the direction of Professor Hall, the Adviser of Studies.

Auxiliary Bodies. – A great deal of Educational work has been done by what may be called the unofficial bodies of the Movement, which have come into being as the outcome of certain necessities which arose as the Movement grew. Of these, the most important are the Women's Guilds – Scottish, Irish and English. It is sufficient to speak only of the English Women's Guild, since it is the model on which the others were formed, and has taken a very much greater part in local and national affairs than the others.

Its educational work among working women has been of enormous value both inside and outside the Movement. Formed in 1883, from a few co-operative women meeting together to do their needlework and discuss co-operative questions, it now has a membership of 46,000, and declares itself to be a 'self-governing organization of women who work through co-operation for the welfare of the people seeking freedom for their own progress, and the equal fellowship of men and women in the Home, the Store, the Workshop and the State.'

It depends for its income on contributions from its branches and two subsidies of a few hundreds a year from the Co-operative Wholesale Society and the Co-operative Union respectively. But it has never allowed this monetary assistance to interfere with its right to express an independent opinion on any subject for the advancement of women. By taking part in local politics it has influenced the educational policy of local authorities, but its activities have extended beyond this, its members have sat on Departmental Committees, and it may be said that of late years very little legislation dealing with women and children has been framed without consultation with the Women's Co-operative Guild. Its educational work includes lectures to the Branches on various subjects, such as the History of the Guild, the Place of Co-operation in the New Social Order, International Co-operative Trade, Co-operative Politics, the Workers' Press, and the National Care of Maternity.

It is now helping to build up an International Women's Co-operative Guild Movement, thus bringing it into line with other International bodies of the Co-operative Movement.

The National Co-operative Men's Guild. – The Men's Guild has never had the same influence as the Women's Guild, perhaps because men have had other opportunities for expressing themselves. Its numbers are smaller, only 5,320, and under present conditions its educational work is almost negligible It depends for its finances upon the Central Education Committee, whose secretary performs its secretarial work. It has been responsible for a few week-end schools and has arranged conferences on educational subjects.

Press and Publications

The line of demarcation between education and publicity and propaganda is so thin, that, before dealing with criticisms and suggestions, it may be well to glance at the actual work which is being done in the Movement on this side. The machinery of the Press is essentially a part of education, and the Co-operative Movement, through its publications, has sought to educate its members in co-operative principles, and to attract the outside public to the advantages which co-operation offers.

It seeks to effect this by means of weekly newspapers, of which it maintains two – *The Co-operative News* and the *Scottish Co-operator*, formerly issued separately but now jointly – six monthlies:

the *Millgate Monthly, Woman's Outlook, Our Circle* for young persons, the *Co-operative Official* for secretaries and managers, the *Co-operative Monthly,* the *Wheatsheaf* and the *Producer* – and a quarterly, *The Co-operative Educator.* Of these papers, three are published by the Co-operative Union, two by the English Co-operative Wholesale Society, and four by the National Co-operative Newspaper and Publishing Society.

In addition to the periodicals, there is a considerable output of other publications, including books for children, and technical works on co-operative administration. The English and Scottish Wholesale Societies have each published Histories and the English Co-operative Wholesale Society issues a People's Year Book.

Some local societies, in self-defence against the boycott of co-operative activities by the capitalistic Press, publish local papers of their own. Of these, the best known are the *Keighley Co-operative Bee,* the *Kettering Co-operative Magazine,* the *Cairncross and Ebley Co-operative Economist* and the *Paisley Provident Magazine.*

Ireland produces the *Irish Homestead,* a weekly paper brilliantly edited by G. Russell (AE.) and the Irish Agricultural Wholesale Society *Bulletin,* issued by the Irish Agricultural Wholesale Society; also a quarterly magazine, *Better Business,* now called *The Irish Economist,* issued from the Co-operative Library, Plunket House, Dublin.

Other publications are the monthly *International Co-operative Bulletin* of the International Co-operative Alliance, and the *New Dawn* (formerly the *Co-operative Employee*), the monthly publication of the National Union of Distributive and Allied Workers, also the Scottish Co-operative Wholesale Society *Magazine,* published by the employees of the Scottish Co-operative Wholesale Society.

The Problem of Education And Its Solution

The question which confronts us is, are all these means of education being put to the best advantage; if not, what are the alternative proposals?

The great problem before co-operative educationalists to-day is the lack of interest which so many of the members have in education. In many societies, the tradition of the 2½ per cent. of the annual surplus or 'profits' allocated for educational work, has been entirely fictitious. In some cases, notably in the mining villages of the North, no grant is made at all; in others, it has been very much less than 2½ per cent.; in only a few cases has it been realized that the claim of education is as important as the trading interest.

There are various reasons for this diversity; in some societies of late years there has been little or no surplus, in others the majority of the members have not been sufficiently interested in education. The method by which the Movement has grown has prevented any clear policy of education from being developed. Each society, as it has been formed, has tended to be individual in its outlook, and to be jealous of its privileges. In this way societies have overlapped in their trading and educational activities, with the result that competition instead of stimulating interest has had the effect of producing a number of small societies, too feeble to do any real constructive work, and too selfish to federate under one Central Body which could direct the education for the district.

The aims of Education Committees have been as divergent as the ideas of the members who form the Management Committees and allot the grant. If one considers the membership of the Movement as a whole, only a very small number take education seriously, and, although a few societies have elaborate schemes for classes and scholarships, the majority limit their strictly tutorial work to book-keeping classes for their younger employees, while others do not go as far as this, but use their funds to provide entertainments, such as teas and whist drives, or in pushing the sale of the *Co-operative News* and paying delegates' fees to Conferences. There is a feeling among the more enlightened members of the Movement that a great portion of the education grant is wasted on frivolous amusement, which, useful as it may be as a means to promote social intercourse among members, would be of greater value if it were employed in providing education, not only in co-operative ideals, but in general culture.

This brings us to the very important question – *What should the Co-operative Movement teach?*

In the days before the passing of the Education Act, there was little or no education for the working classes, and by providing reading rooms, libraries, and classes, the Co-operative Movement gave some educational facilities to those working men and women who cared to avail themselves of them. But with the State provision for free education and free libraries, there was no longer any necessity for the Co-operative Movement to undertake this work, and it turned its attention to the education of its members in co-operative principles.

No one, whether a co-operator or not, would to-day urge any other course. The State, and not the Movement, should supply a general education, and co-operative education, if it is to exist, must take as its subjects those which do not fall within the curriculum of a general education and which have some definite connection with the objects or principles of Co-operation. At the root of the ineffectiveness of the educational side of the Movement lies the fact that there is no general agreement, indeed very little appreciation of, the existence of this problem. In societies which vote money to an education committee, there is probably a vague idea that the society should do something to 'educate' its members and that that education should be 'co-operative'; but only too often, when the committee gets to work, it is helpless and the grant is frittered away, because neither the members of the society, nor of the Management Committee, nor of the Education Committee have any clear idea of what subjects or objects are included in 'co-operative education.'

It may be suggested that the first thing which the Movement requires to do is to educate its Education Committees. No Committee will ever do good work unless it has this clear idea of the subjects or knowledge which it is to offer to the rank and file of the society. There are two alternatives before a committee. Arguments can be found for confining co-operative education to subjects strictly connected with the work and organization of the Movement. Co-operation is a vast industrial system based upon certain economic and social principles or ideals. It is clear even from a cursory examination of the Movement that an immense amount of work might be done in (1) improving the technical organization and working of the Movement, and (2) in teaching the members what Co-operation, its principles and aims are. Such education, properly so called (as distinguished from entertainments and social amenities) which the Movement offers to its members through the local committees and the educational organization of the Co-operative Union, is mainly confined to this strictly co-operative type. It consists of lectures or classes for the technical training of employees, instruction in the history and principles of Co-operation, and lectures and discussions of current co-operative problems. It would be absurd to underestimate the amount and value of this kind of educational work which has been and is being done in the Movement. On the other hand it is capable of immense extension. Development is required along several different lines. As was said above, the first necessity is to educate the Education Committees. Every society ought to have an Education Committee and every committee ought clearly to understand that it is its duty to give at least an opportunity to every member of the society of acquiring a knowledge of the history and principles of Co-operation and to every employee of acquiring technical knowledge. This is certainly not the case at the present time. In the vast majority of societies no organized or consistent effort is made to provide this kind of instruction or, if it is provided, to induce members to take advantage of it. The result is that nine out of ten co-operators remain in ignorance of the meaning of co-operation and of the possibilities in the Movement. The remedy must come both from the central organization of the Union and from the local committees. The central educational department of the Union should be in much closer touch than it is with the local committees, perpetually stimulating them to carry out this work and advising them with regard to difficulties. It should be said that the quality and quantity of the educational work of the Union has in recent years, owing to the appointment of an Adviser of Studies and other reasons, been greatly improved, but an immense amount of work remains to be done in the particular point under discussion.

Hitherto we have been discussing educational work in so far as it consists in the education of co-operators themselves in the history, theory, and technique of co-operation or co-operative industry. But education committees have always undertaken other functions which some people would call propaganda rather than education; they have attempted to put before persons who are not members the aims and advantages of co-operation. This is a work which obviously ought to be performed somewhere in the Movement and the societies, and it ought to be performed much more vigorously and effectively than it actually is. The question is whether it should be part of the province of the educational side of the Movement or should be entrusted to special propaganda organizations or departments. In a Movement like the Co-operative the partition between education and propaganda must in places be very thin. The object of a society is not, like that of an ordinary shop, merely to get an extra customer; its object is or should be to make a man or woman who is not a co-operator into an active believer in co-operation and an active member of the society. To do this effectively would require an organized, persistent, and strenuous effort to explain to non-members what co-operation means and stands for and what it has effected. Much of this effort would have to consist of strictly educational work performed among non-members, and it seems almost inevitable that it should be performed by the educational organization of the Movement. At the present moment it can scarcely be said to have begun in this country.

It may be suggested, with regard to these two functions, that the relations between the Union and local committees should be more closely and more consciously organized. No one who knows the Movement would suggest that the Central Education

Committee should control the local committees; what is wanted is that stimulus should be given to the backward committees and societies and advice and materials for educational work to the non-backward. To do this kind of work adequately the central organization would require a large and efficient staff of inspectors and organizers constantly in touch with Management and Education Committees of local societies.

So much for education in the narrowly co-operative sense. But there is a wider sense in which co-operative education has been understood and practised in the Movement. The Movement is an industrial system of a revolutionary kind when compared with the ordinary capitalist system. The Co-operative Commonwealth, which is its ultimate end, would imply a very drastic alteration in the whole constitution of society. The beliefs of the convinced co-operator, and his problems and the problems which in fact beset the Movement, wander very far afield and become entangled in the questions which cannot possibly be included in a strict interpretation of 'the history and principles of co-operation.' If the Movement is to consist of members having the knowledge necessary for the understanding of these wider issues and problems – and if it does not, co-operation will become stagnant – it must give to its members the opportunity of acquiring such knowledge. Such education would touch not only political science, economics, sociology, but the whole science and art of citizenship, and must necessarily become involved in the dangerous ground of current controversial politics.

A certain amount of this wider education can be, and actually has been, given by the official organs of the Movement, the local education committees and the Co-operative Union. But there are real obstacles in the way of the official educational activities being made too wide. The Movement would have quite enough on its hands, if it undertook the task of making co-operative education in the narrower sense really efficient. Moreover, where education touches upon highly controversial questions of a political or social nature, or where it is a question of exploring new methods or new ground within or without the Movement, an official organization with an open membership like the Co-operative Movement is necessarily chary of doing anything which may seem to identify itself with any particular side or party in the heated controversies. It is here that the unofficial organizations, like the Women's Co-operative Guild, have in the past performed, and should in the future perform, a very great work. The official Movement, if it were wise, would encourage such organizations to preserve their independence or autonomy and to undertake this education in the widest sense, and that task of exploration and innovation without which the Movement cannot remain living and progressive.

Finally, there is the relation between Co-operative education and the educational activities of other parts of the Labour Movement. At present, there is a tendency for each section of the Labour Movement to confine its educational work strictly within the limits of its own views, and this produces a limited outlook, some waste, and serious overlapping. There should be a much closer contact between all sections of the Labour Movement. Co-operation, Trade Unionism and the Political Labour Party are all bound together by their aims and ideals, and there should be some system of education which would embrace them all. By this means, much of the dissipation of energy which exists might be avoided.

A general educational Council with representatives from each section of the Labour Movement might evolve an educational policy which could be adopted by all and yet which would contain the essential elements of each. Such a policy would pave the way to the Labour University which every educationalist in the Labour Movement has in view as an ultimate achievement. There exist at present some nine Labour Colleges,[2] in addition to which the Workers' Educational Association, the Adult School Movement, and the Co-operative Movement give shorter or longer residential courses, and perform some of the functions of colleges. Each is inclined to be too narrow in its outlook, and there is not sufficient interchange of views between them.

It is, perhaps, natural that at this early stage there is an indisposition on the part of the co-operators, if not indeed on that of other sections of the Labour Movement, completely to merge themselves in one common Labour College. But that is no reason why a series of colleges should not exist, each financed and supported by the various sections and yet with a definite bond of association between them. This association might at first take the form of interchange of students and lecturers and, where possible and desirable, joint courses. Eventually the colleges might be federated or affiliated in what would, in effect, be a Labour University.

Co-operative Press and Publishing

There can be no doubt that one of the most potent influences on education is wielded through the Press, and it is a weakness of the Labour and Co-operative Movements that, although a great deal of money has been spent on publications, it has never had an efficient newspaper. Considering the amount of printing and publishing that is done by the Co-operative Movement it is remarkable how little is known of its publications outside. The circulation of its newspapers among the general public is negligible, and the sale of its publications rarely extends further than to a minority of its own members. Perhaps the best known of its books is 'Maternity,' the work of the Women's Co-operative Guild, which has a widespread appreciation, and 'Industrial Co-operation,' by Catherine Webb, which is used as a text book by students of Industrial History.

There can be no complaint made of the number of publications issued. In 1920, 14 new books were published, in addition to an output of 74 leaflets, pamphlets, and posters. If one may make a criticism, which is accepted by Co-operators themselves, it is, that on the whole, the publications lack scientific and literary quality, and their make-up is not attractive. But it is in their distribution that the greatest need for criticism lies. The volumes remain almost unknown, alike to the public libraries and to the bookselling world, and they obtain scarcely any notice, not merely in the ordinary Press, but even in the economic reviews and the Trade Union and Labour journals. At Congress in 1920 the Central Board acknowledged that 'the chief difficulty still to be overcome by the Publications Committee is that of distribution . . . Little has yet been done to organize the demand for Co-operative Union publications.' The total receipts from literature sales (including pamphlets and leaflets as well as books) were, in 1919, only £4,014, and in 1920, £6,237, in a Movement counting four million members.

Books and pamphlets, useful as they are, pre-suppose a certain amount of education on the part of the consumer for whom they are written. But for the education of the mass of the general public, the daily newspaper affords the most successful medium. At the present time very few of the general public have ever heard of the *Co-operative News*, and yet it is safe to say that there is scarcely a hamlet in the most remote part of the British Isles to which the *Daily Mail* has not penetrated. If we look at the circulation of the various periodicals we can see that, even within the Movement, they reach only a fraction of the membership.

In 1921 the circulation of the *Co-operative News* was 120,000, the *Scottish Co-operator* 25,000, the *Millgate Monthly* 14,000, the *Woman's Outlook* 55,000, *Our Circle* 24,000, the *Co-operative Official* 3,000, the *Co-operative Monthly* 10,000, the *Wheatsheaf* 650,000, the *Producer* 25,000, the *Co-operative Educator* 6,000, making a total of 932,000, little more than 24 per cent. of the whole membership. But even this does not represent the exact proportion, since one member possibly subscribes to or receives more than one paper.

The question of a daily newspaper has been in the minds of Co-operators for some years. The *Co-operative News* and the *Scottish Co-operator*, both issued weekly and dealing with the same matter, have satisfied neither the outside public nor the inside Movement. The recent amalgamation of these two papers will lessen the over-lapping and will be a saving in expenditure, but it does not fill the place of a daily paper, distributed in the ordinary way to the general public, and the question which divided co-operators at Congress was not whether there should be a co-operative daily paper, but whether it should be published by the Movement alone or in conjunction with the National Labour Party and Trade Union Congress.

A great deal of money is spent annually by the Labour Move-ment on sectional journals, many of which are never read. A combined pooling of funds would result in the amassing of sufficient capital necessary for running such a paper. The difficulty lies in the sectional interests, which prevent the Labour and Co-operative Movements from taking a wide view of the situation as a whole. There is, in theory, no reason why one daily Labour paper should not be the mouthpiece of the three wings of the Movement, and at the same time provide the general public with news.

In practice, however, there are some very real obstacles and difficulties and they have already had their effect. The question of the Co-operative Movement joining with the other sections of the Labour Movement, namely, the Trade Unions and Labour Party, in the financing and controlling of a common daily paper has actually arisen on the proposals with regard to the *Daily Herald*. The last Co-operative Congress decided against participation, and the present policy of the Movement is to aim at a strictly co-operative daily paper. The reasons for this decision are obvious. There is first the same difficulty which confronts the Movement when it is compelled or proposes to take political action. The fundamental principle of the Movement is open membership, and though its membership is overwhelmingly 'Labour' in origin and sympathy, it necessarily and rightly includes minorities of every political and social complexion. It cannot, if it is to maintain this principle, take action which would bar its doors to particular classes or persons. Such is the argument used against the proposal that the Movement shall officially join with the trade unions and Labour Party in financing a paper. But there is a further difficulty. In the Labour Movement itself there is a considerable cleavage of opinion between the Right and Left wings. It is not unnatural that there should be objection on the part of persons holding one set of opinions to the financing of a paper which really only represents the other. There is, however, one way in which, with a certain amount of toleration, this difficulty could be got over. No single daily paper can of course really cater for the whole country. A separate London and Northern edition is at least necessary, and a Labour press would not really begin to exist until there were separate Labour dailies or at least separate editions in the north, south, east, and west of the country. This, as has been suggested, would allow the various grades and shades of opinion to be represented in a common Labour press.

Appendix

List of Colleges for Working People

WORKING MEN'S COLLEGE	Crowndale Road, N.W.1.
WORKING WOMEN'S COLLEGE	The Holt, Rectory Road, Beckenham.
LONDON COLLEGE FOR WORKNG WOMEN	Fitzroy Street, W.1.
MORLEY COLLEGE	Waterloo Road, S.E.1.
THE LABOUR COLLEGE	11a, Penywern Road, Earls Court.
RUSKIN COLLEGE	Oxford.
VAUGHAN MEMORIAL COLLEGE	Leicester.
FIRCROFT COLLEGE	Bournville, Birmingham.
WOODBROOKE	Selby Oak, Birmingham.
W.E.A. HOUSES – HOLYBROOK HOUSE	Castle Street, Reading.
THE EDWARD MCKNIGHT COLLEGE	Chorley, Lancashire.
THE ADULT SCHOOL MOVEMENT (16 Houses as Colleges)	30, Bloomsbury Street, W.C.1.
THE CO-OPERATIVE COLLEGE	Holyoake House, Manchester.

Notes

1 <i>The Consumers' Co-operative Movement.</i> p. 36. Sidney and Beatrice Webb.
2 See Appendix.

FABIAN TRACT No. 227
(March 1929)

LABOUR'S FOREIGN POLICY:
What has been and what might be

Helena M. Swanwick

There is no department of politics in which the policy of Labour is more markedly opposed to that of the two older parties than the department of foreign affairs. From its very constitution, we might infer this difference; for the British Labour Party is the only one of the three parties in Parliament which is a member of an International organisation: the Labour and Socialist International.

Sir Austen Chamberlain has explained on more than one occasion that the true Briton abhors a general principle. Even if this be true, it may yet be possible for an eccentric who does happen to be interested in general principles to infer them by observing the long-continued actions and utterances of politicians – even of the most 'unprincipled.' They may not themselves be aware of it, but all past Liberal and Conservative Governments have based their foreign policy on the ancient and outworn conception of a world composed of independent, competing, a-moral Sovereign States, which were compelled by the very law of their being to adopt in relation to each other methods essentially those of war. In direct opposition to this ancient conception is the new one, accepted whole-heartedly only by the Labour Party: that of States whose sovereignty is voluntarily limited by the obligations of law, the acceptance of arbitration and the development of co-operation. This conception leads to the adoption of methods of peace.

The development of this co-operative and international view of the relation of States was extended over many decades, and it would be absurd to claim that it has been the discovery of the Socialist Party alone, here, or in any other country. What Socialists may justly claim is that theirs is the political party which has most whole-heartedly adopted and made propaganda not only for this ideal in the abstract, but for the practical measures necessary for its realisation. While in this country Conservatives and Liberals alike do lip-service to the new principles of law, arbitration and co-operation, as laid down in the Covenant of the League of Nations, yet many of their past actions have belied these principles. While all parties in this country declare that they stand for peace, only one, the Labour Party, is willing to pay the price of peace.

It cannot be too clearly understood that the two above-mentioned conceptions of the relations of States to each other are mutually destructive and that, by his timid clinging to indefensible portions of the old conception, Sir Austen Chamberlain has been hindering the development of the new, not only here but – because of the importance of the British Empire – all the world over. The old conception always looked towards war, concerned itself with methods appropriate to war and converted statesmanship into strategy; peace was merely an interval between wars. The new conception looks towards peace, concerns itself with methods appropriate to peace, and puts statesmanship at the service of co-operation.

Effete diplomacy, based on the doctrine of the absolute sovereignty of States, gets round the obligations of the League Covenant (which cuts deeply into that doctrine) by every available subterfuge and ingenuity. The letter of the law had not been broken by this Government, but the spirit is being broken most of the time.

It is proposed here to examine very briefly the record of Mr. Baldwin's third Administration in regard to foreign affairs, and to contrast it with the policy which Labour would have pursued and has declared its intention of pursuing, if returned to power at the General Election.

The Labour Programme

I. – STRENGTHENING THE LEAGUE OF NATIONS

Taking in their order the main points of the foreign policy of the Labour Party, as officially set forth by the Annual Conference, at Birmingham, in October, 1928, we find the first place given to the strengthening of the League of Nations. Obviously, if international co-operation is to take the place of international anarchy based on nationalist exclusiveness, the great organ of international co-operation – the League of Nations – must rely on the passionate loyalty of members and the respect of non-members. It will be possible for the League to resist any formidable outburst of belligerent feeling only when it has attained a secure place in the hearts of the peoples, so that in a clash of loyalties, the greater will overcome the less.

What has been this Government's record in regard to creating this loyalty to the League? Under Mr. Baldwin's third administration, Great Britain has (1) not broken the Covenant, (2) paid the assessed contribution to League expenses, (3) sent its Foreign Secretary regularly to attend sessions of the Council and the Assembly. Beyond this, it would be hard to find any direction in which Great Britain has strengthened the League in the course of the last four and a half years. On the other hand, there have been many occasions when our Government has definitely obstructed the development of the League, and it has on no occasion been the initiator of forward movements, such as the Economic Conference, the Disarmament Conference, or the renunciation of all war.

Among many examples which might be given, the following will illustrate this judgment:-

Alliances. The League Council having the duty of judging impartially between States which are in dispute, it is obvious that no State-member should – in Mr. Wilson's phrase – 'play favourites' with any other State. We should have no alliances, understandings, commitments, or bargains, which might prevent our giving as impartial a judgment in any quarrel as is consistent with human frailty. Yet frequently the language and still more frequently the conduct of our Foreign Secretary have indicated relations, now with France (in regard to Germany and the occupation), now with Spain (in regard to Mosul and a permanent seat on the Council), now with Fascist Italy (in regard to Abyssinia), which suggest, not friendship alone – a wholly admirable state – but a common front against some other Power or Powers.

League Finance. It is obvious that the finances of the League must be subjected to the most rigorous scrutiny and conducted with intelligent economy. They are, as a matter of fact, far more carefully scrutinised by International Committees than are most national budgets, and rightly. But 'economy' does not mean 'not spending,' and it should have been anticipated that, as the League grew and developed, the amount of its expenditure would necessarily increase. At the 1928 Assembly, the British delegation, which had been for years past objecting to increased expenditure, proposed to refer back the proposal of the Budget Committee for an increase of 1,500,000 Swiss francs over the previous year's expenditure of 25,371,244 Swiss francs; this increase was chiefly due to expansion in the work of the International Labour Office (I.L.O.), and to new work recommended by the Economic Conference of 1927. It would have brought the League budget up

377

to £1,070,000, this sum including the work of the Secretariat and its many Committees, the Council and Assembly, the Permanent Court of International Justice, the I.L.O. and its Committees. No one in his senses could deny the world's crying need for economic co-operation; yet Mr. Godfrey Locker-Lampson was put up to propose a reduction of the estimates by one million francs. It is satisfactory (though humiliating to our national feeling) to record that, in the event, the Assembly actually increased the sum, not by 1,500,000 francs, as originally proposed, but by 1,800,000 francs.

It is well to ask ourselves what proportion of our total expenditure goes to the maintenance of the League, and what we get in return for it. Great Britain is at present assessed at (roughly) 10 per cent. of the League's expenditure. Upon the League budget for 1929, therefore, we shall pay only £108,000, and even some of this may be returned. Our total national expenditure in 1927 was £838,585,000, and out of this the League receives about one-eighth of a farthing in the pound. If Great Britain derived no direct cash advantage out of this expenditure – ludicrously small as peace insurance, when compared with our expenditure on armaments (£118,600,000 in 1927) – it would still be immensely profitable in indirect ways. But it happens that we have also derived remarkable financial profit, directly. The British loan to Austria of 2¼ millions, which was, in 1922 threatened with complete loss through the bankruptcy of that country, has, as a consequence of the League reconstruction scheme, been paying a steady interest of £187,134 yearly; or nearly £80,000 more than our annual contribution for League expenses.[1]

Such results should not, of course, be anticipated as a necessary consequence of our membership of the League, but they do expose the meanness of the Government's attitude. Although a Labour Government would certainly not encourage any slackness in League expenditure, we may feel sure it would not starve or cripple work so essential to civilisation.

The Eight Hours' Convention. The conduct of the Government in regard to this Convention is a crying scandal. It was signed in 1919 at Washington by the British representative. The British Government has postponed ratification from year to year till, in 1926, a Conference of Ministers of Labour from the more important industrial countries in Europe met in London in order to define the terms. Ratification was to follow, but did not. On March 11th, 1929, Sir Arthur Steel-Maitland gave to the Governing Body of the I.L.O. a more detailed criticism than his Government had yet published, but he made no constructive proposals. Labour, as usual, stood firm and the representatives of the French and German Governments also opposed the united forces of the Employers, declaring that revision would embarrass them.

Mandates. The conception of the Mandated areas as a 'sacred trust of civilisation' is magnificent if honestly held, but repulsive if made a hypocritical cover for annexation or exploitation. The honest conception possesses one guardian in the Mandates Commission of the League, which exists to enquire into the way in which the 'sacred trust' is exercised. In September, 1926, the Commission, which has always acted tactfully and discreetly, presented to the Council two requests – one was that certain questions (covering no new ground, but methodising enquiry) should be permitted, and the other that, under exceptional circumstances, the Commission should be entitled to receive, in person, petitioners from Mandated territories. The whole body of Mandatory Powers on the Council – France, Belgium and the British Empire – rallied to the attack on the Mandates Commission, and Sir Austen Chamberlain's rebukes lacked none of the asperity for which he has an unpleasant reputation. He makes no secret of the fact that he dislikes even the very small interference with national sovereignty contained in the Minorities Treaties and the Mandates system.

II. – THE RENUNCIATION OF WAR

The Pact of Paris, commonly known as the Kellogg Pact, was, after sixteen months of negotiations, signed in Paris by the United States, France, Belgium, Czechoslovakia, the British Empire, Germany, Italy, Japan and Poland, and was then open to all the nations of the world to sign. By it the signatories (1) renounce war 'as an instrument of *national* policy' (an undertaking which excludes acts of war committed under *international* authority), and (2) agree that the settlement of disputes 'shall never be sought except by pacific means.'

This epoch-making declaration was ratified first by the Union of Socialist Soviet Republics, and then by the United States, after a prolonged debate in the Senate. The British Government, whose loud and interminable trumpeting of the Locarno Treaty has become a subject for derision, has ratified the Pact of Paris without any reference to the House of Commons, on the plea that everybody is agreed about it. Is it not lamentable that the Government, so lavish with pageantry and pomp for militarist or imperialist occasions, should have no public honour to offer this occasion? Is

379

it indeed because we are all agreed? Or is it because the British Government fears some reference to the 'understandings' under which we agreed to sign the Pact? These include (1) the maintenance of the 'inherent right' of every sovereign State to self-defence and (2) the condition that 'there were certain regions, the welfare and integrity of which constituted a special and vital interest for the Empire's peace and safety' and that 'the Government accepted the proposed Pact on the distinct understanding that it did not prejudice their freedom of action in that respect.'

The Government has not named these regions; they certainly include Egypt (which would prefer the protection of the League lead); possibly a region round the Persian Gulf; conceivably Afghanistan. There is nothing to prevent this 'understanding' from being extended to any region we please. On the same grounds, France might have excluded Belgium, or Poland, or Czechoslovakia; Italy might have excluded Albania, and for the matter of that, so might Yugoslavia; Germany might have excluded Austria. But they did not. And the Covenant of the League provides us with all the safeguards to which we are entitled, for Article XI, declares that –

> 'Any war or threat of war, whether immediately affecting any of the Members of the League or not, is hereby declared a matter of concern to the whole League, and the League shall take any action that may be deemed wise and effectual to safeguard the peace of nations.'

It is an indirect but very effectual method of discrediting the League to insist upon a sort of 're-insurance' instead of boldly relying on protecting our legitimate interests in and through the League.

The two 'understandings' mentioned by the British Government are not properly called 'reservations,' and they are not incorporated in the Pact. The Labour Party has therefore formally announced that it repudiates them and proposes to be bound by the strict terms of the Pact itself.

III. – DISARMAMENT

The third Baldwin Administration has played solemnly farcical variations on the theme of Disarmament. It sent representatives to five sessions of the League Preparatory Commission for a Disarmament Conference, and in 1927, at Geneva, took part in a Naval Disarmament Conference (commonly called the Coolidge Conference) with the United States and Japan; it is difficult to see that it did anything on any of these occasions, or subsequently, except entangle the question further and rouse considerable suspicion of our policy in America, Germany, and even France. In the Preparatory Commission, the British, Japanese and American representatives wished that naval armaments should be limited by categories, but the British and Americans could not agree as to the types of ships and guns to be excluded from limitation and this difference of opinion appeared irreconcilable at the Coolidge Conference. The Americans wished to limit all classes of combatant vessels, including light submarines (peculiarly desired by the French), and 10,000-ton cruisers, armed with 6 to 8 inch guns (peculiarly desired by the British); the British wished to limit ships over 10,000 tons, whether aircraft carriers or cruisers (peculiarly desired by the Americans). The French had presented a scheme for reduction by total tonnage which would have enabled them to have a larger number of the small vessels, submarine and otherwise, which they desire.

When at the Fifth Session of the Preparatory Commission, in March, 1928, the deadlock appeared to be complete all round, Mr. Hugh Gibson (U.S.A.) suggested that various Governments and groups of Governments might try by direct negotiation to eliminate their difficulties. Accordingly, Sir Austen Chamberlain negotiated privately with M. Briand, and between them the two Governments agreed to accept the Anglo-American plan of reduction by categories, but to propose the reduction of the big ships which America wanted and retain the smaller ships which France and Great Britain wanted. As a *quid pro quo*, Great Britain offered to withdraw her opposition to the French claim regarding trained military reserves.

Naturally, when this proposal leaked out through the French Press, Germany, whose trained reserves have been so drastically limited by the Treaty of Versailles, took alarm at the last point. Sir Austen's telegram in reply to our Minister in Berlin was in the very best style of old diplomacy, for he considered he had reassured Herr Stresemann by explaining that 'the *text* of the compromise' proposed by France and Great Britain referred exclusively to naval limitations, while there was only an '*understanding*' with France about the withdrawal of our opposition to her mass of trained reserves. Later on, Lord Cushendun, left as caretaker when Sir Austen's health broke down, actually asserted in a telegram to Washington that it would be a 'misapprehension' to represent the arrangement with France as a bargain; it was nothing of the sort; the British Government had quite independently come to the conclusion that 'it would be impossible to move the French and the other European Governments' from their position in this matter. In reply to this it is enough to quote the actual text of a note by Sir Austen Chamberlain to Lord Crewe, dated June 26th, 1928, in which, after detailing the naval part of the suggested compromise, he concluded:–

> 'You should add that the adoption of this suggestion, which His Majesty's Government recognise would be a concession to their views on naval classification, *would enable them to meet the French Government* by withdrawing their opposition to the French standpoint in regard to army-trained reserves.'

The words italicized (by me) plainly show that the proposal was intended to be a bargain: 'You roll my naval log and I'll roll your military log!' We cannot be surprised that Germany was alarmed. Neither can we be surprised that the United States was indignant at the Anglo-French Agreement, which, in the words of the American Ambassador in London, 'appears to fulfil none of the conditions which to the American Government seem vital.'

Small wonder if it began to be thought that there was some strategical basis for this British complaisance to French submarines and that the frequent revival of the phrase 'Anglo-French Entente,' even on ministerial lips, alarmed not only America, but all those Europeans who regard strategical alliances as dangerous to the League. More particularly must Germany ask herself how Great Britain is to carry out impartially her guarantee under the Treaty of Locarno, if she has tied herself up in this way to one of the possible disputants. If French and British fleets are to be considered as making one, this Entente is explicable; not otherwise.

Moreover, we induced Germany to sign the disarmament clauses of the Treaty of Versailles by the statement that it was 'to render possible the initiation of a general limitation of the armaments of all nations,' and it is simply putting our heads in the sand to refuse to see that by their unjustifiable delay in carrying out their side of the undertaking, the victors in the late war are tempting Germany to seize upon every device by which she can protect herself against the militarism to which we refuse to put an end and which is encamped on her very soil.

The fact is that, on this question of disarmament, none of the victor powers have had any policy but that of a scramble to keep as much as they each could. They have consulted their military, naval, air and chemical experts and have attempted to pursue the old policy of 'trying to make every tree in the garden taller than every other tree' precisely as if the League of Nations did not exist.

It may be said that we are not worse or more foolish than many other Powers, and this would be true if we were not greater than most and therefore more deeply responsible for holding up disarmament. For in a matter like this, it is for the strongest to lead the way.

In contrast with this confused grasping at contradictories the Labour policy is plain. Meaning what it says by 'the Renunciation of War,' intending to accept All-In-Arbitration, it declares its aim to 'abolish the element of force from international relations' and not to rest content 'until all nations have mutually agreed to reduce their armaments to the minimum required for maintaining national and international order.' It is the only party which could give confidence to the world that it meant what it said in the matter, and its return to power would probably result in the decay of many militarisms in other countries.

IV. – ARBITRATION.

The 'gap' in the Covenant. The Covenant makes it much less easy to wage aggressive war, but such wars are still possible and it was the intention of the Labour Government in 1924 to render them impossible by continued action with other powers through the celebrated Geneva Protocol. This instrument, unanimously recommended to all the Powers by the Fifth Assembly, would have introduced All-In-Arbitration and have coupled with it a Disarmament Conference to take place in 1925. One of the first acts of the Conservative Government was to reject the Protocol, and it has ever since then firmly rejected pleas for All-In-Arbitration and even the offer of Treaties on the part of such peaceful and non-provocative states as Switzerland, Sweden and Holland.

The General Act. The Ninth Assembly (1928) recommended for signature a treaty called 'The General Act for the Peaceful Settlement of International Disputes.' In it there is full provision for all varieties of national settlement, but the British Government has received it with marked coldness and obviously intends to do nothing about it. This Act is the positive side of the negative in the Pact of Paris, by which we bind ourselves never to seek the solution of a dispute 'except by pacific means.' If we mean this, we must develop the 'pacific means' and our refusal to do so bears a, perhaps undeservedly, sinister interpretation; just as many men, who had not cared one way or another about the enfranchisement of women were forced, at last, to ask themselves why, after all, it was being so obstinately opposed. If Great Britain will not sign the General Act, if she will not herself accept the very undertakings which she pressed upon France and Germany and backed by her guarantee in the Treaty of Locarno, will not all her asseverations fail to reassure people who ask why she still keeps ajar the little door of lawlessness leading back to the old European anarchy which was the ultimate cause of the war?

The principles of the General Act have been accepted by the Labour Party and we may feel confident that its signature by Great Britain would be followed by many other signatures and would, as it was intended to do, greatly facilitate the process of Disarmament.

The Optional Clause. When Great Britain became a member of the League, she recognised the League's Permanent Court of International Justice as suitable for the adjudication of certain (legal or justiciable) disputes; but she did not sign the 'Optional Clause' of the Statute establishing the Court, by which she would have bound herself (with or without qualifications) to carry such disputes to the Court. As time has gone on, over 26 States-Members have in one form or another accepted the obligations of the 'Optional Clause,' including Germany, who signed as soon as she became a Member in 1926. There is little doubt that, if we signed, the rest of the Members would fall in with us, and the Labour Party has declared its intention of signing, with, possibly, one or two qualifications which would in no way affect the binding nature of the undertaking never to seek the settlement of international disputes except by pacific means.

V. – ECONOMIC CO-OPERATION

It is obvious that so long as States feel there is a danger of war, there will be a tendency to try to be self-sufficient. In the case of Great Britain it is so mainfestly impossible that these islands should be self-sufficient that the tendency has been to try to attain self-sufficiency within the Empire, and the struggle for this has been responsible for many of our wars and annexations and for our attitude in regard to sea-power. Once the danger of war were reduced to a minimum by the methods already suggested, we could not only throw down barriers of trade, but we could develop, by means of the League and of all-inclusive organisations of trade and industry outside the League, a degree of economic co-operation which would in time set every man, woman and child beyond the reach of want and out of the power of exploitation. The consumer, as well as the worker, could be protected by international action, if only confidence could be established.

VI. – PUBLICITY

Open Diplomacy. It will be remembered that when the Labour Government was in office it made a declaration that it would enter into no treaties or agreements without the consent of Parliament, and in 1925 the Labour Party went so far as to pass a resolution that –

> 'No Treaty or Convention of any kind shall be binding upon this country or will be recognised as such by any future Labour Government until it has been confirmed by Parliament.'

On July 11th, 1927, Sir Austen Chamberlain declared that the Government will undertake no future engagements on behalf of our country without submitting those engagements to Parliament and having the approval of Parliament for them.'

Nevertheless, Sir Austen's preference for pre-League methods of diplomacy does not diminish. He has used Geneva far more as a meeting-place for private confabulations than for action in and through the League, and he contributed largely to the disastrous failure of the Extraordinary Assembly in March, 1926, when his secret undertakings to France and Spain and Poland served to encourage the aspirations which prevented the admission of Germany at that time. Again, it was not till the Abyssinian Government appealed to the League that the British people became aware of the mapping out in that country of 'Spheres of Influence' between the British and Italian Governments. It is methods such as these that bring us to the edge of an 'inevitable war' without our knowing our danger.

It is significant that Sir Austen should have proposed that the League Council should meet only three instead of four times a year on the ground that it has not enough to do. But it is a popular gibe that 'the Council touches nothing which it does not adjourn,' and this is mainly because anachronistic diplomacy, like that of Sir Austen, cannot bring itself to treat frankly the problems that come before the Council, but prefers the old secret methods, by which all sorts of unavowed pressure can be used.

Espionage. Diplomatic spying and all the shady methods of the Secret Service are not only ineffectual for good, but a positive bar to frankness and understanding. Unavowable shady characters who frequently sell the same valueless 'secrets' to a number of mutually hostile gulls and who become expert in manufacturing those which they cannot find, lead by the nose men who should be responsible statesmen; the Foreign Office becomes an appendage of Scotland Yard.

VII. – POLITICAL CO-OPERATION

The kind of co-operation which the Labour Party contemplates is with *all* Powers *all the time*, and not with one Power or set of Powers in opposition to another Power or set of Powers; a co-operation which shifts about and has no significance or stability. When Spain failed to get a permanent seat on the League Council, her representative complained openly that she had been ill rewarded for the support she had given to Great Britain over Mosul! We have joined with Fascist Italy in some very queer dealings over Abyssinia (kept secret from Abyssinia as well as from the British people), and, in spite of the admirable reciprocity (on paper) of the Treaty of Locarno, our foreign policy, whether from fear or friendship, leans always to the side of France.

We not only pocketed a share of the French receipts from the invasion of the Ruhr (which we had declared illegal), but to oblige the French Government we continued our occupation of the Cologne area for many months after evacuation was due, according to the Treaty. We do not, or dare not, speak clearly about the total evacuation of the Rhineland, which should have taken place as a consequence of the Locarno Treaty and the entry of Germany into the League of Nations.

In regard to Russia, Conservative policy has led us further and further away from an understanding, has certainly not prevented Bolshevik propaganda, and has lost us many millions of pounds' worth of trade at a time when it was of vital importance to us to extend our commerce. The Arcos raid in 1927 was an outrage which, while it certainly damaged Russia, damaged us at least as much. Undoubtedly one of the first acts of a second Labour Administration would be to resume diplomatic and commercial relations with Russia and settle outstanding differences by Treaty or by arrangement.

The folly of our alienation of America in order to oblige France scarcely needs to be enlarged upon. The United States, by its negotiation of the Pact of Paris, by its signature and ratification, has made the greatest step towards the rest of the world since its repudiation of the Versailles Treaty and its refusal to join the League. It has, in fact made a treaty of eternal peace with all the world, including Russia. It is as difficult for a great Power to be truly international as for a camel to enter the needle's eye, and yet the greatness of the United States, as of the British Empire, depends precisely on whether they can achieve this miracle. For this it is absolutely essential that we should discuss the whole question of the Freedom of the Seas with the United States and come to the only – which is the international – solution: that they shall never be closed by any Power *as a matter of national policy*. If we do not come to terms with the United States on these lines, nothing is more certain than that it will increase its navy until it is in a position to turn the tables upon us and claim against us the belligerent rights which we claimed in the last war.

CONTINUITY?

Lord Grey of Fallodon last November renewed the plea for continuity of Foreign Policy. But the Labour Party cannot travel the same road as the other two parties. They look back; the Labour Party looks forward.

Lord Grey hoped that Foreign Affairs might not be made an election issue; the Labour Party regards it as one of the most important of all issues and one on which this Government (as well as previous Liberal and Coalition Governments) has gone disastrously wrong.

Lord Grey suggested that the Anglo-French naval agreement had perhaps been an 'isolated blunder.' Such blunders are too costly and this one was not isolated.

Sir Austen Chamberlain is, in one respect at least, too modest; he has some principles; and he acts on them.

They are not the principles of the Labour Party, and the Labour Party intends to oppose them.

Note

1 The figures in this paragraph relating to the Austrian Loan are derived from *Headway*, November, 1928.

FABIAN TRACT No. 236
(April 1931)

A NEW REFORM BILL

Beatrice Webb

To-day there is a deepening conviction that our machinery of
government is no longer equal to its task. Indeed, there are many
who think, and not a few who say, that unless we can rationalise
the constitution and activities of British Parliamentary institutions,
so as to render them an efficient organ for continuous social
readjustment and progress, there will ensue a slow decay of our
standards of civilisation; accompanied, it may be, by a dictatorship,
either a Fascist dictatorship, in the exclusive interest of men of
property and men of rank, or a Communist dictatorship in the
assumed interest of manual workers eager for the equalitarian State.
To those who believe in political democracy and desire equitable
social reconstruction, such a prospect spells disaster – a disaster all
the more tragic because it is unnecessary. Hence it is imperative
on all students of the world of politics to discover the evil and
seek the remedy.

The Evil to be Remedied

First let us realise the nature of the evil complained of. It is the
paralysis of public business in the House of Commons that leaps
to the eye. 'The House of Commons,' Mr. Lloyd George told a
representative of *The Manchester Guardian* the other day, 'is like an
old windjammer – which was equal to the traffic of 100 years ago,
but cannot cope with one-hundredth part of the enormous trade
of to-day.' 'Each session of Parliament,' he added, 'is over-loaded
and the Plimsoll line is completely submerged.'

1. – AN OVER-TAXED CABINET

I am disposed to put the emphasis higher up. The primary evil is
an over-taxed Cabinet; over-taxed beyond human capacity for
thinking and taking decisive action.

Year by year the public affairs transacted by this little group of some twenty persons have become ever more multitudinous and diversified. Think of the growth of the social services – each branch with a technique of its own. There is the old-established postal, telegraph and telephone services and the startling emergence of broadcasting with all its implied political and educational uses. There is public education from the infant school to the university, from technical institutes to public libraries. There is public health, including not only the prevention and cure of all sorts of diseases, but also house sanitation and main drainage, slum clearance and plans for re-housing the inhabitants. There is the control of the lunatic and the care of the feeble-minded, together with the maintenance of prisons and reformatories. There is town planning, rural amenities and the country's water supply; there are old age and widows' pensions (not to mention war pensions), and there are the recently established social services of Labour Exchanges and of State insurance in all its branches. There is the supervision of local government, including local finance and Local Acts, the rectification of areas and the granting of new powers; there are the semi-centralised services of roads and transport, of electricity, docks and harbours and the newcomer – hydraulic power. Beyond and above all these centrally controlled and sometimes centrally managed social services, there is the ever-extending regulation of private enterprise in the interests of the producer and the consumer alike, from Factory and Mines Regulation Acts and Trade Boards to the Development Commissioners; from the adulteration of food to the Consumers' Council. During the last decade, successive Cabinets have had to grapple with unemployment, not merely the maintenance and training of the unemployed, but the actual prevention of the occurrence of unemployment from whatever cause it may be due. A bare thirty years ago, Mr. Gladstone rebuked Keir Hardie for daring to mention unemployment in the House of Commons – a subject which the Great Man thought totally unfit for the consideration of the Cabinet or Parliament. To-day a Conservative Opposition proposes to turn out a Labour Government expressly on account of its failure to prevent the mass unemployment brought about by the world's slump in prices. Nor is this enlarged and complicated task merely a question of administration or the supervision of administration: it entails a perpetual stream of new legislation involving several scores of bills each session, each one initiated and drafted in the department of a Cabinet Minister to be passed by him through all the stages of Parliamentary procedure. Finally, there is the annual raising, through a wide range of taxes, the right incidence of which is of vital importance to all sections of the community, of eight hundred million pounds annual revenue; together with the allocation of this enormous sum, according to priority of need, between such diversified and often conflicting claims as growing establishment charges, the repayment of the war debt, national defence, the organisation of nationalised services, the grants in aid to local authorities, and the subsidising, directly or indirectly, of certain spheres of profit-making enterprise.

When we pass from home affairs to the external relations of Great Britain we see a like increase in magnitude and complexity. In pre-war days foreign affairs consisted, in the main, of alliances, avowed or unavowed, with or against particular Governments; alliances secretly contrived by the Ambassadors and the Foreign Ministers of the various Powers. To-day we are building up a new public authority, a super-state, with its international assembly, its international executive, its international law and its international courts to interpret that law. That is why our leading Ministers, the Prime Minister, the Foreign Secretary, the Chancellor of the Exchequer, even the President of the Board of Trade, spend so much of their time at the Hague, at Geneva or Washington, or in London itself, immersed in discussion with the representatives of other Powers. And if we turn to the other department of external affairs, Great Britain's relation to its sister Dominions and dependent Colonies, the three Secretaries of State for India, for the Dominions, and for the Colonies respectively, not only survey an area and population ever so much larger than that of the British Empire of fifty years ago, but they are met in every direction by problems and questions immeasurably more intricate and dangerous than those of the Victorian era.

Is it surprising that, with such an impossible task, the Cabinet has ceased to be an effective Council of State?

Each Minister has necessarily to manage his own department with the minimum of consultation with his colleagues. This avoids delay; but it sacrifices co-ordination and Cabinet solidarity. The activities of the isolated Ministers do not form a policy; and their claims on the present all-too-scanty Parliamentary time, or on the revenue, are settled by a scramble instead of by a carefully concerted allocation. In Parliamentary circles, it is an open secret that the Cabinet Council never considers the forthcoming estimates of national expenditure as a whole. The Chancellor of the Exchequer, advised by Treasury officials, is left to settle the estimates of each department with the Minister concerned, the matter not being brought up for Cabinet decision unless agreement cannot be reached. There is like concentration of responsibility in the Chancellor of the Exchequer and his department in respect of the

nature and amount of the proposed levies; a decision revealed to
the Cabinet usually only just before it is published in the Budget
speech.

Once we have adequately realised the unmanageable bulk and
complexity of the home and foreign affairs assumed to be transacted by the twenty Cabinet Ministers, either individually or
collectively, it is easy to understand, though not to excuse, the
two more notorious and sensational evils arising out of the present
machinery of government, first, the growth of what is decried as
'bureaucracy' and, secondly, the congestion of business in the
House of Commons so vehemently criticised by Mr. Lloyd
George.

2. – AN HYPERTROPHIED BUREAUCRACY

I will take for granted, to quote the words of John Stuart Mill,
that it is 'inexpedient to concentrate, in a dominant bureaucracy,
all the powers of organised action in the community.' But how
can this evil be avoided if each Cabinet Minister, however
assiduous and able he may be, has neither the time nor the energy
for the business he is assumed to control? For, in order to avoid a
too unwieldy Cabinet, some of the ministries have come to include
so many different services, that it is impracticable for one Cabinet
Minister to survey and control the day-by-day administration of
his department. How is it possible, for instance, for a newly-
appointed Minister of Health to master the technique of a score of
branches, with separate and distinctive activities, ranging from the
prevention and cure of all diseases to the supervision of local
government, from slum clearance, housing and water supply to
the intricacies of health insurance? And is it likely that the President
of the Board of Trade can tackle even the more important of the
issues raised in the seven or eight thousand letters which arrive
addressed to him each morning? Moreover, owing to social pres-
tige and apparent autocratic power, the Cabinet Minister is
expected to interview innumerable personages representing organisations or interests closely connected with his official work; whilst
his evenings are taken up with public dinners and social functions
more or less concerned with the office he holds. Over and above
these departmental duties are the frequent Cabinet Council and
Cabinet Committee meetings and attendance in Parliament. Hence
the undue reliance on the judgment of the permanent officials; not
only in matters of routine and technical detail, but in questions
involving crucial principles, with which the official concerned may
be honestly out of sympathy with the party in power. 'The nearest
thing to a puppet in our political system is a Cabinet Minister at

the head of a great public office' scoffs Mr. Bernard Shaw in his Preface to *The Apple Cart*. I may add that, after forty years' experience of trying to get this or that legislative proposal or administrative reform adopted, if I have easy access to his permanent officials, I hesitate to trouble the Cabinet Minister, for the sufficient reason that I assume that he will be ignorant of the ins and outs of the subject, and that he cannot have his hand on all the parts of the working machine.

3. – An Emasculated House of Commons

Now it is evident that this over-loading of the Cabinet, while it inevitably magnifies the responsibilities and the activities of the civil service, must disable and demoralise the House of Commons.

The six hundred members, many of whom enter the House full of enthusiasm, brimming over with determination to cure the social evils they have witnessed – evils that they and their families may have actually experienced – over-crowding, sweated wages, constant terror of unemployment – find themselves, not with too much to do, but with nothing whatever to do that seems to be worth doing. For the first six months of a member's life he may be amused, even enlightened, by looking on at carefully staged performances by Ministers and ex-Ministers: if he is a caricaturist or a journalist, he may pick up remunerative copy. But this passive listening to one debate after another, with the sole relaxation of walking through the division lobbies according to the instructions of the Party Whips, is deadening to the strong and demoralising to the weaker brethren. Their rebellion against it only makes matters worse. The tumultuous exuberance of the rank and file of the Members of Parliament of the present century is such that a large proportion of them, unlike their predecessors of the nineteenth century, refuse to listen silently to the few score of regular debaters – largely drawn from the front benches – who expound and criticise the Government Bills. These Bills have themselves increased in number, owing to the ever-widening range of legislation and administration. But the number of members who insist on taking part in debate has increased tenfold. Against this incessant determination of hundreds of members to talk on every subject, every improvement in procedure of the past half-century, from the excision of merely formal resolutions to the encroachments on 'Private Members' time,' and even the closure itself, has proved ineffective. The cumulative result is that not one-tenth of the subjects can be dealt with that the 615 members are burning to bring forward; not one-fifth of the legislation called for in the public interest can be put into any King's Speech; and only a small proportion of the

Government measures actually proposed in any one session can be, even by every permissible use of the closure, either made law or definitely rejected by Parliament; whilst all concerned – advocates of reforms and sufferers from grievances, local administrators and departmental heads, Ministers and rank and file members – endure an abiding sense of wanton frustration due solely to the imperfection or inadequacy of the Parliamentary machine.

There are some who say that this alternating enervation and exasperation of the M.P.'s would be remedied by so altering the constitution and procedure of the House of Commons, that each Cabinet Minister would be required to submit, to an appropriate Standing Committee, not only his legislative proposals in all their technical detail, but also his day by day administration, exactly as is habitually done by the chairmen of the various committees of municipal bodies, such as the London County Council. As will presently appear, I see great advantage in the committee form of government for home affairs. But quite apart from the constitutional question whether government by *responsible bi-party committees* can be grafted on to government by *a responsible one-party Cabinet* – any such procedure would be an unendurable addition to the toil of the already over-taxed Minister. The plain truth is that the greater the congestion of business – the more multitudinous and diversified the affairs transacted – the less Cabinet Ministers can take the Members of Parliament into their confidence; and the more they are driven to rely on the closure. British Parliamentary Government, whether surveyed from the Cabinet or from the House of Commons, is to-day like the stomach of a man who habitually over-eats. The only remedy is to reduce the amount of food he has to digest. That is why, among the wiser heads of all parties, you have the cry of devolution.

'I am not sure,' sums up that experienced and level-headed parliamentarian, Sir Herbert Samuel, 'whether the best way to relieve the present congestion in Parliament is not to invite our Scottish friends to manage their own business in their own Parliament in Edinburgh.'

Granted: but why endow the Scot with a first-class liner running thirty knots an hour and leave the Englishman and Welshman with what the Liberal leader has politely termed a windjammer. Why not ask our friends in England and Wales to manage their own internal affairs in their own assembly or assemblies?

Here I may observe that neither Sir Herbert Samuel nor the present writer can claim originality for the proposal to devolve a large portion of the business of the Cabinet and the House of Commons on a directly elected but subordinate national assembly and its executive. Indeed, it is one of the oddities of British politics, that so long as Irish Home Rule was an unsettled question, the leaders of both political parties played about with the notion of national assemblies, designed to legislate on and administer the internal affairs of the three or four separate nationalities constituting the United Kingdom. Even as late as June, 1919 – owing to the devoted propaganda of Mr. Murray Macdonald, M.P. – the House of Commons passed a resolution setting up a conference of both Houses, to work out a scheme of federal devolution for England, Scotland, Wales and Ireland respectively. Presided over by the Speaker (Lowther, now Lord Ullswater), this conference actually presented a unanimous report (Cmd. 692 of 1920) in favour of a devolution of extensive powers to separate legislatures for England, Scotland and Wales, Ireland having been meanwhile otherwise dealt with. But the 32 representatives of the Lords and Commons differed widely, and as it seems to me, irrevocably, as to the constitutions and powers of such subordinate legislatures. Rather than criticise this somewhat muddle-headed and inconclusive report and its dissenting memoranda, I prefer to set out the following scheme of reform.

The Plan of Reform

I do not propose any radical alteration in the British Constitution. Under my plan of reform, the supreme authority for Great Britain remains, as at present, formally with King, Lords and Commons in Parliament assembled; substantially, under the Parliament Act of 1911, with the Cabinet and the House of Commons. It may be desirable to 'mend or end' the House of Lords. It may be expedient to alter the method of election or the procedure of the House of Commons. It may be wise to reduce the number of M.P.'s to about 300. But these changes are irrelevant, and can take place or not take place, without affecting the present scheme.

1. – DEVOLUTION

The essence of this scheme is summed up in the word devolution – the devolution of business from the Cabinet and the House of Commons to another authority. Hence the pivot of this scheme is the creation, by a Parliamentary statute, of a new National Assembly, and what is most important, with its own national executive, for Great Britain, or alternatively for England and Scotland separately; it may be, if Welshmen insist on it, also for Wales. Personally, I think it would be a mistake to separate Wales from England; partly because of the relative poverty of Wales, but also because North Wales and South Wales seem to have less in common with each other than each has with the neighbouring English counties. Indeed, so far as the distinctive purpose of devolution is concerned, I should be glad if the Scot would insist on his immemorial right to govern England and refuse to be restricted to an assembly sitting in Edinburgh. I should prefer one assembly and one executive for the whole of Great Britain. For the larger the area comprised within the jurisdiction of the new authority, the more complete can be the devolution of work, from the Cabinet and the House of Commons, to this new authority. For instance, it would be inexpedient, if not impracticable, to break up into separate units of administration, for England, Scotland and Wales respectively, the Factory, Workshop and Mines Regulation Acts, the Trade Boards, the Labour Exchanges, and the network of unemployment insurance, the control of transport and the activities of the Consumers' Council. Moreover, owing to the motorcar and the telephone, mass production and mass distribution, *the smaller area, as a unit of administration, is always tending to become obsolete.* But I recognise that efficient administration is not the only test of good government; there is also the consciousness of consent, and this may take the form of racial self-consciousness and a consequent demand for separate authorities for what are deemed to be distinct species of human beings, with different faculties and different needs, inhabiting England, Scotland and Wales respectively. Moreover, in Scotland, at any rate, there is already a peculiar body of law, a characteristic structure of local government and separate executive departments, located in Edinburgh, for education and health, for agriculture and fisheries, for lunacy and prisons. Hence I suggest one or two compromises. Three separate assemblies might be set up for England, Scotland and Wales; and the services necessarily common to the United Kingdom might be administered by a series of joint committees, on the model of the existing Joint Committees for Health Insurance, the decisions of these indirectly elected bodies being ratified by each assembly. Or, as I should prefer, as more likely to combine economy with efficiency, one National Assembly might be created for Great Britain. In this case the Scottish, Welsh and English members might meet separately in London, Edinburgh and Cardiff, for purely sectional business; whilst the whole of the members might assemble in London for the formal ratification of the sectional decisions and for the administration and legislative development of such services as are necessarily co-extensive with Great Britain.

In order to facilitate the exposition of the scheme, I will assume that this latter compromise is adopted, and that there will be one National Assembly and one executive; and I will leave it to any

reader who prefers the plural to the singular, to substitute, in the
following pages, the numerals 'two' or 'three' for the 'one' I prefer.

2. – THE NATIONAL ASSEMBLY

I propose that the members of this National Assembly should be
directly elected on the same franchise as the House of Commons
– I suggest about 300 members for England and Wales and perhaps
50 members for Scotland. I think that they should be elected for a
fixed period, preferably three years, without liability to premature
dissolution, and should thus be quite disconnected from the polling
day of the House of Commons. Whether the single-member
constituency, with or without the alternative vote, or the multiple-
member constituency with proportional representation, be adopted
as the electoral basis of the new authority, will probably depend
on the balance of opinion in the particular House of Commons
translating the scheme into law.

3. – SPECIFIC STATUTES TO BE DEVOLVED

At this point let us consider the intriguing question of the type of
devolution to be embodied in the statute. The usual procedure
in establishing federal constitutions appears to be devolution by
subjects; some subjects being reserved for the larger, or more
sovereign authority, whilst others are devolved on the smaller or
subordinate authorities. Sometimes this subject definition is of the
vaguest character; for instance, in the British North America Act,
1867, establishing the Dominion of Canada, Section 92 allots a
number of specified subjects to the provincial governments, ending
up with the general power to 'make laws in relation to all matters
of a merely local or private nature in the province.' I venture to
suggest that it would be wiser to adopt a more limited and explicit
type of devolution: a devolution not of subjects at all, but of
specific statutes or groups of statutes. It might be inferred that this
leaves the proposed National Assembly without any legislative
powers; in fact, in exactly the same position as the London County
Council or the Manchester Municipal Corporation. But that need
not be so. In a fit of absent-mindedness – another phrase for the
subconscious wisdom of the British race – the House of Commons,
plagued with acute congestion, emitted what is now termed
'administrative law' – a type of devolution arousing the wrath of
eminent jurists. 'It is one thing,' indignantly declares Lord Hewart,
in describing this 'New Despotism,' 'to confer power, subject to
proper restrictions to make regulations. It is another thing to give
those regulations the force of a statute. It is one thing to make
regulations which are to have no effect unless and until they are

approved by Parliament. It is another thing to make regulations, behind the back of Parliament, which come into force without the assent or even the knowledge of Parliament. Again, it is a strong thing to place the decision of a Minister, in a matter affecting the rights of individuals, beyond the possibility of review by the Courts of Law. And it is a strong thing to empower a Minister to modify, by his personal or departmental order, the provisions of a statute which has been enacted.' (*The New Despotism*, by Lord Hewart, p. 19).

It would be easy to cite endless examples in the statutes of the last two decades of this devolution of wide legislative powers to Government departments, under such plausible headings as 'power to remove difficulties,' or 'in order to meet unknown future conditions'; coupled with the clause, 'that the Rules and Orders shall be of the same effect as if they were contained in this Act.'

Now it is clear that, whilst there may be grave objections to this new type of 'administrative law' if it be devolved on Government departments, which may mean, in practice, on a permanent official, not even the Lord Chief Justice can object, on constitutional grounds, to the devolution of these powers of amendment and extension of existing statutes to a National Assembly, having exactly the same moral authority, from the standpoint of political democracy, as the House of Commons itself. Incidentally, I may observe, that this new device of administrative law, more especially the clause 'shall be of the same effect as if they were included in the Act,' would, according to recent judgments, exempt the National Assembly from having its administrative and legislative activities open to *ultra vires* proceedings in the Courts. And if it were thought necessary to curb this unlimited power 'to remove difficulties' and 'to meet unknown future conditions,' in order to invade spheres quite unconnected with the original Act, it might be left to the Speaker of the House of Commons, on the complaint of a member of the National Assembly, to certify or refuse to certify as within the meaning of the clause, the proposed amendment or extension of the statutes. Should the Speaker refuse certification, it would be always open to the National Assembly to promote a Bill in the House of Commons to alter the statutes in any way that was necessary for the new departure.

I may remark in passing, that under this plan of reform, amendment or rejection by the House of Lords, in all the devolved services, automatically disappears.

4. – THE SERVICES TO BE DEVOLVED

Upon this new National Assembly and its Executive, would be devolved a long row of public services. Thus, the plan contemplates the transfer to the new authorities, from the Cabinet and Parliament, of the business of half-a-dozen or more of the present Ministries – the Ministry of Health, the Board of Education, the Ministry of Labour, the Ministry of Agriculture and Fisheries, the Ministry of Transport, the Ministry of Mines and the Office of Works, together with certain branches of the Home Office and the Board of Trade, *e.g.*, the Factory and Workshop department, the Patent Office and the Consumers' Council.

Thus the National Assembly and its Executive will supervise, not only the local authorities exactly as they are at present supervised by the Cabinet and the House of Commons, but also the new specialised Commissions, such as the Electricity Commission, the London Traffic Board and the B.B.C. Private Bill legislation, whether affecting the constitution and powers of railways and other companies, or of local authorities and public utility corporations, will plainly fall, not to the House of Commons, but to the National Assembly. Besides this first instalment of statute law there is no reason why there should not be a progressive devolution from the House of Commons to the National Assembly, of statutes creating public services yet undreamt of, exactly as there has been a progressive enlargement of the spheres of existing local authorities.

It will be noted that all these departments of administration have been invented since 1832, mostly in the last thirty years. They constitute, in fact, a new kind of government – national housekeeping – quite separate and distinct from the exercise of sovereignty, national defence and the maintenance of Courts of Justice. The services involved partake ever less and less of the nature of the exercise of sovereign power, determining the relation between individuals or groups of individuals in the manner of a monarch dealing with his subjects. They become more and more of the nature of a mass of rules and conventions adopted, as occasion arises, for the organisation of social utilities so as to secure their regular and uninterrupted function. This modern State, indeed, is now increasingly seen as a congeries of public corporations – central and local – analogous to the consumers' co-operative movement, except that membership is necessarily universal in order that, by careful and continuous planning, the whole body of citizens may attain higher standards of civilisation.

5. – FINANCE

But what about finance – the biggest puzzle in any scheme of devolution? In the space at my disposal I could do no more, even if I had the requisite knowledge of detail, than set out the fundamental considerations. It is, I think, essential to the completeness of the devolution, that the National Assembly should have its own revenue, independent alike of the House of Commons and the Chancellor of the Exchequer. It is indispensable to genuine efficiency, no less than to economy, that the National Assembly should be made to feel effectively its responsibility to the electorate whose money it is expending. But, on the division of services proposed, the National Assembly will be much more of a supervising and legislative than a spending authority.

The total expenditure of the British Government is approximately eight hundred millions, of which I reckon the Chancellor of the Exchequer and the House of Commons will, under this scheme, continue to be responsible for about six hundred millions, a sum which includes the service of the national debt, national defence, war pensions, post office, Courts of Justice, and prisons, together with foreign, dominion and colonial affairs. The National Assembly, on the other hand, would require for devolved services, something less than two hundred millions (education, health, labour, agriculture, transport, etc.). But this includes the one hundred and ten millions for grants in aid of the local authorities, now paid by the Chancellor of the Exchequer. If these were stabilised (say decade by decade) and paid in a lump sum to the National Assembly for distribution among the local authorities, there would remain only some eighty millions to be provided annually for all the other expenditure on the devolved services. Whether this need could best be met (as was proposed by the Ullswater Committee of 1920) by the devolution of suitable existing taxes; or by allowing the National Assembly to issue precepts to the local authorities; or by permitting it to devise new forms of taxation, such as the taxation of site values, not conflicting with those required by the Chancellor of the Exchequer – or by any combination of these – must be left to be settled by more experienced financiers than myself. I will only suggest that, whilst there are undoubtedly advantages in putting the National Assembly under an obligation to bring home to the consciousness of every elector the fact that the national expenditure is rising, this is not necessarily secured by the simple device of causing the aggregate of expenditure to result in an increase in the rates and taxes. It is not merely that the financial revolution involved under the Local Government Act of

1929 in 'de-rating,' together with the sudden exaggeration of the system of Grants in Aid, will, for a number of years, prevent any precise or accurate comparison of the successive yearly burdens in particular localities. Apart from this transient difficulty, the device of making taxation vary with expenditure has, to a great extent, lost its efficacy in producing economy. Merely to increase the fees for local licenses or the entertainment tax, the taxes on motor vehicles or wireless sets, the precepts to the local rating authorities, or even a directly levied separate rate on every householder, would not, in fact, bring home to the consciousness of the average elector that the National Assembly has become extravagant in its staffing, excessive in its requirements from the local authorities, or unduly ambitious in its legislative schemes. On the other hand, it would clearly be desirable to require the Finance Committee of the National Assembly to consult the Chancellor of the Exchequer privately, and in due time (and perhaps to obtain his sanction) before even proposing to raise a loan, or to recommend to the National Assembly any expenditure on capital account involving a loan.

7. – MEASUREMENT AND PUBLICITY

If, however, we are to bring home to the consciousness of the electorate any recklessness or profligacy in the financial policy of the National Assembly – and the same is true of the House of Commons – we must adopt some more effective device than making its extravagance result in an increase of taxation. The first requisite is a comprehensive independent audit in its most modern developments, including stores as well as cash, not merely verifying initial outlay, but also comparing maintenance charges, and above all not stopping at surcharging illegal expenditure, but going on, year after year, to report fully in the frankest terms on the financial position and policy of the National Assembly, as disclosed by the continuous investigations of the audit. This duty might well be imposed by statute on the Comptroller and Auditor General, who would need for the purpose a separate highly qualified staff, and who should make his reports, not to the House of Commons, but direct to the National Assembly, which might be required to deal with them, as is the practice of the House of Commons, in its own Public Accounts Committee, independent of its Finance and other committees. But in the stress and complication of modern life, in an electorate numbering 28 millions, a mere auditor's report is not enough. Why should it not be published at a nominal charge (say, one penny); or even officially posted to every elector? Why should not the purport of the report be broadcasted to every licensed wireless receiving set, and the members of the National Assembly be invited to explain, at meetings of their constituents, their reasons for the expenditure that they have incurred, and their justification of the financial policy that they have adopted?

8. – GOVERNMENT BY ADMINISTRATIVE COMMITTEES

How would the National Assembly be organised? In what way would it administer all the social services for which it was responsible? We have two models before us. There is the ancient constitution and procedure of the House of Commons – what is called the Cabinet system of government. In this case the score of members of the Cabinet, nominally appointed by the King, are actually selected by the incoming Prime Minister – the statesman 'sent for' by the King because he is the recognised leader of the party in power in the House of Commons. Once in the seat of office, the Government, through its several members, controls Whitehall, and is responsible for all the legislative activities of the House of Commons. The 600 private members, as I have already described, are practically powerless, except for purposes of obstruction, in deciding what shall be the legislation enacted by Parliament.

On the other hand, we have the modern system of administration by committees as worked out by the British municipalities and county councils. To my mind the second of these two models is the one that ought to be adopted for the new National Assembly. Let me explain exactly what would happen. At its first meeting the Assembly would elect its chairman and other officials and pass its standing orders. At the second meeting a whole series of committees would be elected, to direct the work of the Whitehall departments, including a General Purposes Committee and a Finance Committee. The heterogeneous departments now making up the Ministry of Health might, for instance, be presided over by a series of separate committees, for such subjects as housing and town planning, hospitals and medical treatment, open spaces and rural amenities, lunacy and mental deficiency, pensions, insurance and public assistance, and Private Bill legislation. All the members of the Assembly would find themselves on one or other of these committees, political parties being represented according to their strength on the National Assembly. Each committee would elect its own chairman, who, besides presiding over its deliberations, would become the head of the executive department concerned. Every new departure in administration, every proposal for legislation, would be brought by the chairman before the committee, and it would be the committee's proposal which would be submitted by him to the National Assembly.

Note how far greater under this system of government would be the control exercised by the elected representatives than it is in the House of Commons. Every item of the proposed expenditure of any committee of the National Assembly (exceeding some stated amount) would be reported to the Finance Committee for its prior sanction, either as part of the routine disbursements under previously sanctioned Annual Estimates, or as new expenditure urgently required which has to be subsequently authorised by Supplementary Estimates. The annual budget of the National Assembly, with its proposed reductions and additions in expenditure and taxation – instead of being sprung on the House of Commons overnight, would also have to pass through the Finance Committee, prior to its submission to the National Assembly.

Further, any need for 'administrative law' in its bureaucratic form of 'departmental legislation' would automatically cease to exist; all amendments and extensions of existing statutes, together with the appropriate statutory rules and bye-laws, would be discussed and decided by the committee concerned with the particular service and afterwards submitted by the chairman to the National Assembly for enactment.

But this is not the only advantage of the committee system. Under the Cabinet system, one team goes out as the other team comes in, and any experience and keenness which may have been developed in a Minister, is lost to the administration. Under the committee system, zealous and experienced members of the Minority Party will continue to share, sometimes as vice-chairmen, or at any rate as members, in the work of the particular committees in which they are interested. To my mind, this continuous use of the abler members of all parties, in the day by day administrative and legislative activities of the National Assembly, is of immense value in any machinery of government. So far as party interests are concerned the group of chairmen chosen by the numerically superior party to preside over the politically crucial committees would doubtless confer regularly together on questions of party policy. In this way there would be evolved (as in the London County Council) as much of concerted party influence as is desirable and no more. The pivotal feature of our party system, the sudden dissolution and change of Government following the rejection of any Government measure, would, from this sphere, vanish completely.

A *new reform bill*

9. – What Would be Left to the House of Commons

What, then, it may be asked, would be left to the Cabinet and the House of Commons? Quite as much, I reply, as any one group of Ministers and any one Assembly can adequately attend to. First, of course, constitutional legislation and reform. Then all the issues of foreign affairs; all the problems connected with the Dominions; our relations with India; our direct administration of territory exceeding in area the whole of India, namely, the fifty odd separate colonies, protectorates, mandated territories and other dependencies. With all this goes necessarily the steadily growing work connected with the League of Nations, the Hague Court, the Permanent Mandates Commission, and the International Labour Office. Allied to these are control of foreign trade, of currency, of weights and measures, and of migration. Nor can we forget the complicated issues and essential services of disarmament on the one hand, and national defence on the other – the Army, Navy and Air Force. Moreover, there is the huge burden of the national debt, with its obverse in the swollen income tax, surtax and death duties, and along with these also the customs and excise duties. There is, further, the greatest of all national services, the Post Office, which is becoming every day more bound up with the postal, telephone and wireless services of the dominions and colonies, and also with those of foreign countries. We may imagine Parliament also keeping its hand on the main body of law and the administration of justice.

Finally, Parliament would keep all its sovereignty. It could at any moment end or mend the National Assembly; it could by new legislation amplify or contract – above all, it could interpret or clarify – the powers which it had devolved, whenever practical experience or some unforeseen judicial decision called for their amendment. In fact, under the foregoing scheme, the Cabinet and the House of Commons would retain all the functions of government known to Pitt and Canning, to Peel and Palmerston, and even to Gladstone and Disraeli prior to the seventies.

The Basic Principle of the Scheme

My final word brings me to the philosophy of the subject. The scheme here advocated involves the advance of the British Constitution to a new kind of federalism. In the United States, in Canada, in Australia, and now in several of the new European States, we see federations based on unions of geographical areas, where every citizen votes at two elections, one for the smaller area – State or Provincial Parliament and Executive and another for the Federal

Government and Executive. For the relatively small and densely populated Great Britain, where urban and rural districts are inextricably entangled, the splitting up of authority by geographical areas is out of date. What we require, if we are to sweep away the threefold evil of an over-taxed Cabinet, an hypertrophied bureaucracy and a paralysed House of Commons, is the differentiation of one authority from another according to the services rendered. Governmental functions in Great Britain of the twentieth century fall easily into two main groups, one concerning sovereignty, overseas relations, national defence, the main body of law, and the administration of justice between man and man, all functions based on the exercise of power; the other relating to social services, such as public health and education, pure air and pure water, insurance and industrial regulation, town planning and open spaces – all essentially subjects for organised co-operation amongst citizens to supply their common needs and fulfil their aspiration for a better and nobler life.

To mix together the issues arising out of these two strongly contrasted groups is illogical and confusing. How can electors vote intelligently on such lumpings of widely disparate issues about which they may want to give contradictory verdicts? They may approve of the Government policy in one group of questions and condemn it in another. An elector may be an internationalist and a pacifist, whilst upholding competitive profit-making enterprise as the best form of social organisation; he may be a fervent believer in free medical treatment and the endowment of motherhood, and yet be a militant imperialist intent on holding and extending a distinctively *British* Empire. It is only by making 'cross-voting' practicable in regard to the two fundamentally contrasted groups of issues that the true verdict of the electorate can be given. And the same is true about representatives in Parliament and colleagues in the Government. So far as international affairs are concerned or the relations of the white to the coloured races, Lord Cecil and Lord Irwin may find their spiritual comrades in Mr. MacDonald, Mr. Henderson and Mr. Wedgwood Benn; but they may altogether object to government control of industrial enterprise, extension of the school age, or maintenance with training for the unemployed. It is this heaping up of multitudinous and disparate issues and of problems irrelevant to each other in the Cabinet, in the single representative assembly and at the polling booth, that is jamming the existing machinery of government and bringing political democracy, with its implication of the consciousness of consent on the part of the people, into a discredit as dangerous as it is unwarranted.

A new reform bill

Notes

HOUSE OF COMMONS COMMITTEES

1. The proposal to convert each Cabinet Minister into the chairman of a committee drawn from the membership of the several parties in the House of Commons – a proposal with which the Rt. Hon. F. W. Jowett, M.P., has specially associated himself – is best described in a report embodied in *The Reform of Parliament*, a pamphlet published by the Independent Labour Party. The same pamphlet contains also a rival report, which sets forth the disadvantages and difficulties of applying such a system to the present work of Cabinet Ministers and Parliaments; and examines an alternative suggestion, namely that of establishing, in connection with each Ministry, a purely advisory committee of Members of Parliament, whom the Minister may consult without necessarily accepting their decisions. I may observe that either of these schemes for the reform of the House of Commons would be all the more practicable if that body were relieved of half its present work by devolution to a new National Assembly.

The arguments against the substitution of administrative committees for Ministers, as set out in the second report, appear to me, in respect of the greater part of the present work of the Cabinet and Parliament, unanswerable. At any rate, in connection with Foreign Relations, Dominion Affairs, Colonial Administration and Fiscal Policy, the attempt to base a one-party Cabinet system upon a series of bi-party committees seems hopelessly unpracticable.

Moreover, whatever improvement in House of Commons procedure might result from either form of committee, it is clear that their establishment would do nothing to relieve Ministers from their insupportable burden. It would, on the contrary, greatly increase their work, and make their position quite impossible. Even the mild alternative of giving each Minister an advisory committee of Members of Parliament of all parties, whilst it might occupy and even educate the members, would be a new tax on the time of the Foreign Secretary, and a new opportunity for premature 'leakage'; calculated to lessen efficiency without in any way increasing the control of the House of Commons as a whole and without diminishing the influence of the bureaucracy. There seems, in fact, no half-way house between the device of government by a single supreme one-party committee (the Cabinet), responsible to the elected assembly for every department, and that of government by a series of bi-party committees, each separately responsible for its own department to the elected assembly. The

405

former device, with its concentration of authority, its avoidance of premature publicity, and its presentation to the electorate of a definite choice between alternative administrations, appears the more advantageous, if not unavoidable, for foreign and overseas relations, for issues of supreme importance, and for momentous new departures in policy. The latter device (the so-called Committee system) offers advantages in securing greater concentration of thought on each department, enlisting the willing co-operation of all sections of opinion, and in ensuring greater continuity of administration. For these reasons I have adopted it as best suited to the proposed National Assembly, which would, in the main, be concerned not with supreme issues but with developing policies already determined in principle in respect of public health, education, unemployment and the maintenance of the standard of life.

But the House of Commons is not likely to multiply, in either form, little committees of members as screens between Ministers and itself. More probable, and as I think, more dangerous, is the growth of a demand (as in Australia) for the control of Ministers, not by Committees of the Legislature at all, but by Committees of the Party Caucus. In Australia, the Party Caucus openly decides who shall form the Cabinet, and now seeks to dictate the measures which the Cabinet shall initiate, and which the Party Majority in the Legislature shall enact. This, in my view, is the very negation of Political Democracy.

ADMINISTRATIVE LAW

2. This term is loosely used (as by Lord Hewart in *The New Despotism*, 1929) to include four different objects of dislike, between which it is important to distinguish. Originally the term meant only the *droit administratif* of France, where a special code of law is applied by special tribunals in suits against the State or its officials (see *Précis de Droit Administratif*, by Hanrion; *History of French Public Law*, by Brissaud; *Law in the Modern State*, by Duguit, translated by H. J. Laski). This has no relation to English practice. But apart from legislation by Parliament, we have much Delegated Legislation, specifically entrusted under Statute to particular legislative organs (e.g. the Bye-Laws of Local Authorities and of Railway Companies; the Orders of the Privy Council under the Emergency Powers Act; even the quasi-legislative 'warning notices' of the General Medical Council). This may be distinguished from Departmental Legislation, now denounced as law-making by bureaucracy, where Parliament has empowered particular Ministers, either to make Rules or Orders amplifying

general statutes in elaborate detail (the voluminous Statutory Rules and Orders which far exceed in length the Statutes themselves); or to do what is necessary to bring Statutes into operation, or 'remove difficulties' in their application, even to the extent of altering the provisions of the Statutes themselves. The furthest extension of the term is to the procedure by which, under Statutory Authority, not only Parliament, but even the Courts of Justice are left on one side. This development, better termed Departmental Awards, is seen where Parliament gives power to particular Ministers to act as the final, and, indeed, as the only tribunal of appeal against orders by Local Authorities (e.g. the Arlidge case). For all these varieties of British practice, see *The New Despotism*, by Lord Hewart, 1929; *Administrative Law*, by F. J. Port, LL.D., 1929; *Justice and Administrative Law*, by W. A. Robson, B.Sc.(Econ.), LL.M., Ph.D., 1928; *Comparative and Administative Law*, by F. J. Goodnow, LL.D., 1903; *Delegated Legislation*, by Cecil J. Carr, LL.D., 1921.

COMMITTEE PROCEDURE

3. This committee procedure has, in England and Wales, been elaborated in a century of practice substantially on identical lines, but with local differences, first by the Borough Councils under the Municipal Corporations Act, and since 1888 by the County and District Councils under the Local Government Act. It may be added that it forms a part of the new Constitution of the Colony of Ceylon, coming into force in 1931. Based essentially on the necessity of each committee submitting successive reports of its provisional decisions for ratification by the full council, this procedure has reached in the London County Council a high degree of efficiency, at the relatively small cost of extensive printing. It now achieves, in combination (a) the private consideration by each committee of reports by officials; (b) the communication to the whole council of all the decisions or proposals of the committee; (c) the accompaniment of each of these by adequate printed explanations, prepared by the Chairman of the Committee, of the facts and reasons on which the committee's recommendations are based, thus dispensing largely with Ministerial oral expositions; (d) the printing in special type of the actual recommendations, to which alone the council will be committed; and (e) the accompaniment of them, on the same page, by any necessary report by the Finance Committee on the subject. The printed agenda of the London County Council – in marked contrast, it must be said, with that of many important Municipal Corporations, which often contain little more than an 'epitome' of the committee's minutes – is thus

a lengthy document, not only constituting an intelligible record but also placing every Councillor, if he will but read, in possession of everything needed for his understanding of every issue coming before the Council. No adequate comprehension can be gained of the working of the London County Council without careful study of the form of its agenda, a little known but invaluable contribution to Political Science. At each Council Meeting the Chairman of the Council calls upon the Chairman of the Committee to move the reception of his Committee's report, which is almost invariably done without any speech. The Chairman of the Council then puts each numbered paragraph separately to the Council, whereupon discussion may ensue. As each paragraph affords its own explanation, and most of them are non-controversial, the majority are rapidly agreed to without discussion. But any recommendation, large or small, may be challenged, debated, amended to any extent, or rejected; and every controversial issue is thus fought. It should be said, however, that the London County Council imposes a time limit for speeches of fifteen minutes, at the expiration of which the Chairman asks whether it is the pleasure of the Council that the speaker continue. Permission to continue is habitually accorded, nem. con., but, except in cases of important explanations or arguments, this is hardly ever taken advantage of for more than a few minutes beyond the quarter of an hour.

The National Assembly would, like the London County Council, frame its own Standing Orders, subject to any statutory prescription. One of the matters to be thus prescribed would doubtless be the limits of the latitude to be allowed to the Committees for immediate action without prior ratification by the full Council. Another might deal with Payment of Members. It may be suggested that proper provision for the necessary expenses of members should be made by Statute, whether (as a minimum) travelling and hotel expenses, together with payment for loss of remunerative time, as now given to Scottish County Councillors; or (as I think preferable) a common minimum of £400 a year and railway fares (as in the House of Commons) for what would be, during the sessions, practically full time service. In lieu of the present Ministerial salaries, the National Assembly might be left free to settle what additional payment should be made to the Chairman and Vice-Chairman of the Council and the several Chairmen of Committees, which might vary with the amount of executive work thrown upon each of them.

A new reform bill

FEDERATION BY SUBJECTS

4. The historical student will not think the analogy too far-fetched. The federal states of modern times, created when the territorial basis had become dominant in law and administration, have naturally been based on the geographical distribution of their populations. Yet it is easy to trace in every federal constitution, the influence of 'subject' equally with that of 'place.' The functions of the State or Province are always largely those relating to a common 'house-keeping' by the citizens, whereas those reserved to the superior federal authority deal principally with subjects of another kind, such as external relations, means of transport and communication, the common indebtedness, etc. It may be suggested that the present tendency towards a transfer of functions from states or provinces to the federal authority is largely because its smaller area is no longer suited to the administration of some social services. In the United Kingdom, the relations between the National Government and the Local Authorities exhibit a like tendency, the supply of electricity and the regulation of road traffic being better administered in larger units and less narrowly circumscribed areas. In Governmental organisation it is the influence of neighbourhood, not that of subject, that is passing away. In the new services of state insurance and pensions, for instance, the areas over which the central or subordinate authorities have jurisdiction are, geographically, indeterminate; the obligations and benefits involved following the insured or pensionable persons, wherever they may be resident; in some cases to places outside Great Britain.

Moreover, both unitary and federal governments to-day, leave an increasing share of authority to vocational organisation, which often ignores geographical boundaries. Thus, in the United Kingdom, the General Medical Council which has, in fact, both legislative and judicial authority, exercises these functions over all its registered practitioners, whatever their race, nationality or residence. The current tendency is for other professions to become 'self-governing' on a vocational, not territorial basis. A 'union of professional associations' would be, so far as its quasi-governmental functions extended, a federation by subjects. But this tendency to subordinate the area to the subject matter of the service, wherever it may occur, has its limitations. There are still many services, where the primary consideration is that of the common neighbourhood of the persons concerned, and it is these services which are still best managed by the inhabitants of particular localities within the sovereign state: for instance, cleansing and paving, small parks and playgrounds, baths and wash-houses, public libraries and local museums and art collections, and, I think, the all-important service of elementary and secondary education. Hence the persisting need for maintaining and perfecting our system of local government, even if we make it responsible to the National Assembly instead of to the House of Commons.

FABIAN TRACT No. 240
(December 1933)

STARVATION IN THE MIDST OF PLENTY: A New Plan for the State Feeding of School Children

Barbara Drake

Introductory

'Nutrition,' the Chief Medical Officer tells us, 'is everything in childhood. Childhood is the particular and only occasion when it is true to place nutrition in the first rank. Indeed, it stands unique, for it is the only foundation of growth.'[1] Lack of food is not the only cause of malnutrition; the debilitated child may lack fresh air, exercise, rest, but a principal cause is insufficient, improper, irregular, unsuitable, or unappetizing food.

A child in a civilized community has then a first claim on the food resources of his country. This is commonly recognised in war-time, and adults, if necessary, must go without. In peace time, when there is plenty for everyone, we are apt to forget it. Never before in our history have we been better supplied with so rich a variety, or such abundance, of foodstuffs. Yet, in spite of this, thousands of our children are known to be living on diets which do not even provide the minimum conditions of health and growth. Not only socialists are discovering the folly of an economic system which makes 'profit,' in the narrow sense of mere 'financial results,' the test of social utility. 'We have to remain poor,'[2] says Professor J. M. Keynes in deploring our failure to use the vast technical and material resources at our disposal to build a wonder-city, 'because it does not "pay" to be rich.' Worse, our children must starve in an age of abundance, because it does not 'pay' to feed them.

The Facts About Malnutrition

THE TEST OF A SATISFACTORY DIET

A satisfactory diet, as defined by the Chief Medical Officer, is one that provides for full natural growth – 'for the full unfolding in growth of the best potential qualities, physical and mental, inherent in the child at birth.'[3]

For practical purposes, we are told,[4] one has to judge a diet in four different respects, namely, the supply of calories (units of energy), the quantity of first-class or 'animal' protein, and the supply of mineral matter and vitamin content. The minimum needs of the adult man may be taken as 3,000 calories, that of the adult woman as 2,500 calories, while that of children varies from 40 per cent. of the 'man' value at the ages 2–3 to the full adult value at the age of 14. The experts are, in fact, not sure that a boy or girl of 14 does not need even a larger share than a full-grown man or woman.

The next criterion of a sufficient diet is the supply of first-class protein, which is only to be found in animal products, such as meat, fish, eggs, cheese, milk, etc. In a satisfactory diet, first-class protein should form at least 5 per cent. of the total calories. The estimate is admittedly a modest one. In ordinary middleclass diets, 'animal' protein is said to form about 7.5 per cent. of the calories.

The remaining criteria may be considered together. There are no means of measuring the amounts of the different kinds of vitamins and salts which are necessary to prevent 'deficiency' diseases, e.g., rickets, scurvy, undue susceptibility to certain infections; but milk and milk products, green vegetables, fresh fruit, salads, 'fat' fish, such as herrings, are known to be rich in them. If, therefore, the diet contains a fair share of these so-called 'protective' foods, there is little danger that it will be lacking in vitamins and salts. It is important to remember that a satisfactory diet must be complete *in all respects*. No amount of calories, for example, will make up for a deficiency in 'first-class' protein, or in vitamins and salts.

COMMON FAULTS OF DIET AND THEIR CAUSES

With the enormous range of foodstuffs procurable, it is plain that no one with money to spend need have a defective diet, but where economy has to be considered it is a different matter. That serious defects are due to ignorance, to established customs and tastes, no one is likely to dispute. 'I am perfectly satisfied,' the School Medical Officer for East Suffolk writes,[5] 'that ignorance on the part of the mothers exerts the greatest influence on the causation of malnutrition. They fail, not because they lack interest, not because they are careless and slovenly, but simply because they know no better. The distribution to the best advantage of a very slender weekly wage is far from being a simple matter and, in the absence of guidance, it is little wonder that failure so often results.'

Cereals (flour, oatmeal, rice) are relatively cheap and easy to get, and consequently bulk largely in working-class diets. 'It is unusual,' Dr. M'Gonigle (M.O.H., Stockton) states,[6] 'to discover children suffering from the effects of actual shortage of food-stuffs, but the ill-effects of deficient quality of nutrition are widespread.' Where large appetites must be satisfied at a very small cost, it is inevitable that the more expensive 'animal' foods, meat, fish, butter, eggs, should be cut down. An analysis of the dietaries of 22 unemployed families by Dr. M'Gonigle showed that, while the calory value equalled on an average 80 per cent. of the normal, and the carbohydrates 94 per cent., the value in first-class proteins was only 55 per cent. of the normal, and the value in fats 59 per cent.[7] 'There is abundant evidence,' reports the Chief Medical Officer[8] 'that a direct result of poverty is to reduce the amount of protein and fat in the diet, and relatively to increase the carbohydrates.'

It is, however, in the protective foods, milk, green vegetables, fresh fruit, that a deficiency is most likely to be met. 'All the defects,' the Chief Medical Officer has stated,[9] 'which may exist in diets in common use can be readily corrected by the addition of milk and green vegetables.' If a diet is supplemented by milk and green vegetables, the other materials of which it is composed can, it is said, quite safely consist of articles which are easily obtained and relatively cheap, such as bread, flour, potatoes, roots, pulses, sugar, fats.

Milk is the perfect food for the young. It is now generally recognised that one pint of milk per child per day is a minimum allowance, not merely for very young children, but for children up to 16. Unfortunately, we are not a milk-drinking country. There are countless homes where milk is said to be only used for tea, or is bought for the cat! The total daily average consumption of milk in this country is about one-third of a pint (against one pint in the U.S.A.); in some populous areas, it is only 0.08 or even 0.06 of a pint. When this is realized, and also that one pint of milk is said to contain about two-thirds of the total daily first-class protein requirements of the average child, more than one-third of his total fat requirements, and to be rich besides in vitamins and salts, some conception can be formed of the inadequacy of the amount of this most valuable food which children are receiving,

413

and the improvement in their growth and vigour that might be expected to follow a more adequate use of it.

The Minimum Cost of a Satisfactory Diet

The cheapest possible diet upon which healthy subsistence is possible is said to consist of oatmeal, herrings and cabbage,[10] but no one could swallow the necessary quantity of oatmeal, nor tolerate the monotony of such a diet, even if he had the physiological knowledge to buy it, and the practical skill to cook it and serve it so that it would not be revolting. That appetite, apart from hunger, has much to do with proper digestion is a well-known physiological fact. Starting then from the assumption that a satisfactory diet must be reasonably varied and palatable, the minimum cost per man per week has been variously estimated (February, 1933, prices) between 4s. 10d. (M'Gonigle) and 6s. 8d. (Crowden).[11] The average sum works out at 5s. 8d., but Dr. V. H. Mottram suggests that the sanest figure to adopt for practical purposes would be 6s. per week per adult male. These estimates presuppose 'the most economical purchasing and household management, and demand a knowledge of dietetics and a skill in the laying out of money and in the preparation of food which few housewives are likely to possess.' On the basis of 6s. per 'man,' the minimum cost of a child's diet may roughly be estimated at:

Age.	Cost per week.
14 and over	6/–
12–14	5/5
10–12	4/10
8–10	4/3
6–8	3/7
3–6	3/–

About the same figure is reached as a result of an enquiry into diets in poor law homes. The Advisory Committee on Nutrition state:[12] 'In a home containing about 200 children we estimate that the weekly cost, allowing for one pint of milk per child daily, would be about 4s. 6½d. per head, if all provisions were bought at contract prices.' The Chief Medical Officer,[13] however, thinks that, unless the numbers are large and there are facilities for obtaining foods at contract rates, a more reasonable sum would be 5s. 6d. a week. It is plain that, on the lowest estimate, a man, wife and, say, three children, should spend on an average on food alone not less than about 25s. a week.

DIET AND WORKING CLASS BUDGETS

'More than any other factor,' the Chief Medical Officer has declared,[14] 'the amount and quality of food are likely to vary with changes in the economic status of individuals, and the danger to the health of children resulting from reduction of income is to be sought for mainly in this sphere.' Food is not the only necessary of life. Rent, for example, is a fixed charge which must be paid whether or not a margin is left for food. The Ministry of Labour base their present calculation of the cost of living on the assumption that 17 per cent. of the total weekly budget goes in rent, but circumstances may decide otherwise. Big families especially must often pay large sums in rent because owners and agents refuse to let rooms to people with children.

From an examination of the budgets of poor families living in London, Dr. G. P. Crowden calculates[15] that, on an average, 35 per cent. of the total income goes in rent, or about twice the official estimate. The Medical Officer of Health for Hammersmith has found[16] that, after rents have been paid, a number of working-class families, both employed and unemployed, have only a very small margin left for food, clothing and other necessaries. Among employed families, this margin per head per week may be as little as 3s. 8d. and 2s. 9d.; among unemployed families, 1s. 11d. and even 1s. 7d.

A recent enquiry carried out by a Committee of the Hull Community Council[17] into the budgets of poor families, some of them unemployed, showed that in Hull rent usually takes about one-quarter of the income, food two-fifths, clothes rather less than one-tenth, leaving one-quarter for fuel, light, cleaning materials, and sundries. Some families of four persons, i.e., man, wife, and two children, have thus only 11s. or 12s. a week for food. The diet in many cases, say the Committee, 'shows a serious omission of nutritious food, especially for children, and cannot but result in serious ill-health.'

The Sheffield Social Survey Committee[18] have worked out a 'minimum needs standard,' covering food, clothing, cleansing materials, light and fuel, below which a family in Sheffield may be said to be living below the 'poverty' line. According to this standard, the minimum working income per 'man' should be 6s. 11d., or 24s. 11½d. for a husband, wife, two school children and an infant. The estimate takes no account of rent, insurances, fares, holidays or conventional luxuries, and assumes that the family income is spent to the greatest advantage. The Committee report that even on this low basis: 'Nearly one-fifth of the working-class families of Sheffield were either living below, or bordering on, the "poverty" line during the winter of 1931–32, and that, even if all those available for work had been on full-time employment at current rates of wages, one in seventeen of the families would still have been in or on the margin of poverty.' The proportion of children under 14 living below the 'poverty' line was much greater than that of families, 'nearly one-third of them being on or below the "poverty" line.'

When we remember that, even in organized trades, the full-time wages of semi-skilled and unskilled workers have fallen in some industries to between 35s. and 40s. a week, the rates for agricultural labourers being as low as 30s. and even 28s. a week; that hundreds of thousands of workers are employed on short time; that nearly two million adult men are wholly unemployed; that the rates of unemployment benefit have been cut down to 23s. 3d. a week for a man and wife, *plus* 2s. for each dependent child; that few public assistance committees are willing to grant assistance to able-bodied families beyond this point; we are forced then to the conclusion that hundreds of thousands of children, unless they are receiving school meals, are living on diets which do not provide for 'full natural growth,' and may result in serious ill-health.

EVIDENCE OF MALNUTRITION

The risk to health of underfeeding is all the more insidious in that deficiencies in the quality of diet may produce no immediately obvious results. 'A diet,' the Chief Medical Officer explains,[19] 'may be very defective and yet, if sufficient in amount, may satisfy children's appetites leaving no craving behind, and may maintain apparently normal vigour for a considerable time. The inevitable results of such a diet are, however, ultimately to be seen in its failure to promote a full measure of growth, in lessened immunity to disease and possibly in the presence of some form of "deficiency" disease.'

It is then not surprising that, in spite of the depressed state of industry, the official figures do not show as yet any marked physical effect on the child population. Of children submitted to routine medical inspection in 1932, not more than 1.07 per cent. were notified as suffering from malnutrition, though the percentage has risen slightly from .95 in 1929. These figures, however, do not tell the whole story. The School Medical Officer for London reports that, while the proportion of definitely ill-nourished children is only about one in 6,000, the proportion of children with subnormal nutrition was as high as 4.8 in 1931 and 4.9 in 1932. Considerably higher figures are revealed in the depressed areas. Evidence collected by a Committee of the Save the Children Fund[20] shows that the proportion of children with subnormal nutrition is 9.2 per cent. in Leeds, 13.0 per cent. in Merthyr Tydfil, 17.2 per cent. in Newcastle, 21.0 per cent. in Pontypridd. The School Medical Officer for Wolverhampton reports:[21] 'Under this particular heading [malnutrition], there is a distinct increase in the figures, and it is doubtful whether the figures represent the whole of the picture.' Of the children notified in Wolverhampton as subnormal in nutrition, no less than 95 per cent. were found to be necessitous. 'There appears,' the report continues, 'to be established here a definite link between unemployment and malnutrition of children.' The Chief Medical Officer's report for 1932 concludes:[22] 'Though the medical reports recently received contain no signs of widespread physical degeneration, there is an undercurrent of forewarning as to the possibility of mental instability in the adult man, and prolonged undernourishment of women and children.'

Nor is it certain that all the children suffering, in one degree or another, from malnutrition are discovered by the school doctor. From a recent medical examination carried out by Dr. Someville Hastings in West London, it appeared that, of 53 children belonging to 21 unemployed families, no less than 33 children showed some sign of malnutrition. Yet, of this number, four children only were receiving extra nourishment at school. The truth is, as Dr. Someville Hastings points out,[23] that the effects of under-nourishment are by no means easy to detect by physical examination. The signs may be readily missed unless they are specially looked for – which is rather a long business. Nor do they become evident at once. It is easy, moreover, to confuse the *average* with the *normal*, so that the doctor's standard varies with a rise or fall in the proportion of ill-nourished children. Even where light weight is associated with chronic sepsis of the tonsils, teeth, ears, etc., the septic conditions may be secondary to food deficiency, which may be the more direct cause of the low weight.[24] The situation has been admirably summed up in a leading article in the 'Medical Officer':[25] 'Unfortunately, we cannot make a sensational story out of malnutrition as it occurs to-day – it produces a slow silent rot of virility, vitality and fibre from which recovery soon becomes impossible. It takes a lot of ill-feeding to kill a child. It takes very little to sap his value seriously.'

The Provision of School Meals

THE 1906 ACT

The power to supply meals to children in ordinary elementary schools was first given to local education authorities under the Education (Provision of Meals) Act, 1906. Before, however, any expense connected with the purchase of food can be incurred out of local rates, the authority must resolve that there are children attending school within the area who are unable, by reason of lack of food, to take full advantage of the education provided, and that voluntary funds are not available or are insufficient for the purpose. Out of 317 authorities, more than half have never at any time taken steps to exercise their powers. The total number of meals supplied in 1931 was about 48,000,000, of which 27,000,000 were milk meals, 16,000,000 were dinners, and the rest breakfasts, teas, cod-liver oil, etc. The number of children fed was 320,000, or less than 6 per cent. of the total elementary school population. About one-fifth of the cost of the food was recovered from the parents. In addition to meals supplied by authorities under the 1906 Act, some 800,000 children are receiving milk meals under a scheme established by the National Milk Publicity Council. Use in this case is made of the school organisation, but the milk is paid for by the parents.

The great weakness of the 1906 Act is its permissive character. Authorities are not obliged to operate it. The report of the Save the Children Fund Committee[26] makes it clear that, where a decline in the nutrition and health of school children is recorded it may be attributed to the fact that the provision of school meals has not kept pace with the need. The inadequacy, where it exists, is said to be due in general to one of two causes: either there is lack of initiative, or of a sense of responsibility, on the part of the authority, or the authority is so much impoverished that it is not possible to incur the expense of providing meals.

THE SELECTION OF CHILDREN TO BE FED

The practice of authorities in selecting children to be fed varies in a marked degree. Some authorities give meals to all children for whom extra nourishment is advised by the school doctor. Others appear to be under the impression that they should only feed children actually classed as 'malnourished.' Other authorities again regard the service as a measure of public assistance, or an emergency expedient for meeting an industrial crisis. They make, therefore, their selection primarily on an 'income' basis. It is usual in this case for an application to come from the parents, while the selection is made by the head-teacher or the care committee. As a rule 'each case is decided on its merits,' but a few authorities have adopted definite income scales below which a child is classed as 'necessitous.'

Thus, under the Sheffield scheme, where the weekly family income (after deducting rent and rates) does not exceed 6s. per head, dinners and breakfasts are given on six days a week, and during the holidays as well; and, where the family income is less than 4s. 6d. per head, teas are given in addition. Wolverhampton[27] allows free meals where the family income, after deducting rent and clubs is less than 6s. per head, and reduced charges are made where the family income is below 7s. per head. In Cardiff, dinners and milk are given free of charge where the family income, after payment of rent, is less than 7s. per head with two in family, (one child), 6s. per head with three or four in family, and 5s. with five in a family. Bradford gives free dinners where the family income, less rent and rates, falls below 23s. with three in family, rising to 66s. with twelve in family, and there is a graduated scale of reduced charges. Free breakfasts are given in addition in the case of very poor families.

The claim made by some authorities that only on an income basis can the needs of the situation be properly met has been disputed by the Board's medical officers, who think that this claim is unjustified.[28] In areas, it is said, which have adopted the method, considerable numbers of children who are either actually suffering from malnutrition, or are on the borderline, do not for various reasons get it. It is certain that many parents, through ignorance, a sense of false shame or – a very potent factor – because they fear that the cost of the food will be deducted against their public assistance allowance, do not apply for school meals. Where it is left to the care committee 'to decide each case on its merits,' not merely may individual committees hold widely different opinions as to what constitutes a sufficient family income, but they may have their own ideas as to parental responsibility and their own ways of enforcing it.

The Chief Medical Officer recommends[29] that the selection of children to be fed should be made by the school doctor on physical criteria, borderline cases being fed as well as cases of actual malnutrition. Apart, however, from the fact that, as we have seen, the early signs of malnutrition are by no means easy to detect, the underfed child does not always come at once to the notice of the school doctor. Routine medical inspection takes place normally only three times in the course of the nine years of elementary school life. The doctor has to rely in the intervals very largely on the judgment of the teacher or care committee, who may be little qualified to observe any but obvious and urgent cases. The truth is that on any basis the selection of the under-nourished child is an extremely difficult business. The best results seem to be obtained where the selection takes place on either basis, and one method is used to supplement the other.

RESULTS OF SCHOOL FEEDING

Serious as are the defects of the 1906 Act, where school meals have been provided, the benefit to the children can hardly be exaggerated. More than anything else, according to the Report of the Save the Children Fund Committee, school meals have prevented ill-health in children during the present crisis. Evidence collected by them from nineteen typical areas show a very close connection between school feeding and malnutrition. 'It will be noted,' the Report states,[30] 'that in the majority of cases 1932 is worse than 1931. Only in four places – Oldham, Bradford, Leeds and Glasgow – are the malnutrition figures less in 1932 than in 1931, and only in Bradford and Oldham, where the increase in school meals has been greatest, is there a substantial improvement recorded in 1932 compared with 1931. In the case of Coventry, Manchester and Walsall, there is no change. In the other twelve places shown on the table there is deterioration.'

Even more striking than the figures showing the connection between school feeding and malnutrition are the results of enquiries carried out by the Board's medical officers into the relation between diet and growth. School feeding is supplementary feeding. The addition to the dietary of foods commonly lacking in poor homes may indeed give in some cases as good results as a more complete meal. An experiment made by Dr. Corry Mann[31] under which supplementary rations were added to the ordinary dietary of a large institution showed that:-

(1) Sixty-one boys receiving the ordinary diet only gained an average of 3.85lbs. per boy and grew an average of 1.84 inches in twelve months.

(2) Thirty boys receiving, in addition to the ordinary diet, a ration of protein daily which about doubled their consumption of 'animal' protein, gained an average of 4.01lbs. in weight and grew an average of 1.76 inches in twelve months.

(3) Forty-one boys receiving, in addition to the ordinary diet, one pint of milk daily gained an average of 6.98lbs. in weight, and grew an average of 2.63 inches.

Dr. Corry Mann experimented at the same time with supplementary rations of New Zealand butter, castor sugar, vegetables, margarine, and fresh watercress. Such additions all resulted in increase of weight, but, except in the case of the butter ration, there was little or no increase in height.

The value of milk as a supplementary diet has been abundantly proved. In an experiment conducted by Dr. J. B. Orr[32] four groups of children were selected, one group receiving whole milk, a second separated milk, a third a biscuit ration of the calorie value of the milk, while a fourth group acted as controls. Taking all the children (1,157) together and dividing them into milk-fed and non-milk-fed groups, it appeared that there was an average increase in height of 23.5 per cent., and in weight of 45.37 per cent., in favour of the milk-fed groups over the non-milk-fed groups. The evidence of school medical officers further shows that, where supplementary milk meals are given, not merely is there a general improvement in weight and height, but school attendance is more regular, the children are more alert and energetic, and the improved physical condition makes them more attentive and receptive of school teaching. This is specially noticeable in the latter periods of the afternoon. Teachers also testify to a greater propensity to mischief.[33]

Where, however, as a result of underfeeding, growth has already been impaired, there is a limit to what can afterwards be done in order to repair the damage. 'At the start,' states the School Medical Officer for Rotherham in describing the results of careful observation of 815 children receiving milk meals, 'the malnourished children were on the average, one inch below the normal child in height and three pounds lighter in weight. The immediate effect of the milk was to cause these children to increase in both height and weight faster than the normal child; after eleven months of milk feeding the deficiency had been reduced by some 40 per cent. as regards height and weight. A further eleven months of feeding, however, produced no further closing of the gap; the children increased in height and weight, but showed no tendency to make good the remainder of the gap.'

Some indication of what may be done by systematic good feeding appears in a comparative study of the physical development of boys at the age of fifteen in four well-known public schools and in a South London riverside district.[34] This showed that the calorie value of the public school diets varied between 3,325 and 3,819, compared with a calorie value of 1,935 to 2,421 for the industrial district diets, the public school diets being superior especially in the proportion of fat and 'animal' protein. There was a difference of 15 to 20lbs. in the weight of the typical public school boy and the boy of the same age coming from an elementary school.

All the evidence points to the same conclusion. It is not enough to feed the 'necessitous' or debilitated child. To achieve 'full natural growth,' it is imperative that the essentials of a satisfactory diet should be assured throughout the period of childhood and adolescence.

The Economics of 'Community' Feeding

'AFTER BREAD, EDUCATION'

Nearly thirty years ago, a Committee of the Fabian Society urged[35] that all children, destitute or not, should be fed, and fed without charge, at the expense of the State or municipality. The first need, they argued, of a people is food; without proper feeding instruction is useless, and worse than useless – it is indefensible cruelty. Feeding is of infinitely greater importance than education for, in the last resort, you can do something with a race that, however ignorant, is healthy and physically well developed; with anaemic degenerates you can do nothing though you offer them all the schools in the world.

It is not enough, they declared, to feed the destitute only. For it is by no means certain – and since then the contention has been abundantly proved that this way the children who most need food will get it. It may be very unfortunate that parents should feel their own sense of dignity before the well-being of their off-spring, but it is an indubitable fact that a great many of them do. Few out of the many parents whose children do not get sufficient nourishment are willing to write themselves down as 'necessitous' and those who do may not be those who most need and most deserve assistance. The method further leads to a very undesirable distinction between those children who are fed out of public funds and those who are not. The provision of universal free meals does not destroy parental responsibility, but only *communalises* it. If you feed destitute children only, there may be something in the argument that you are relieving the parent of part of his responsibility, but, if all citizens pay for the provision of meals through rates and taxes, direct and indirect, and all parents can send their children freely to eat the meals, then they are simply providing for their children by co-operative methods, and there is no more interference with parental responsibility than if all the parents in a particular block of tenements agree to start a common kitchen. The 'communal' meal, provided under proper discipline in humane surroundings has, indeed, a civilising effect upon the children, who learn what a dinner ought to be and, when they grow up, make all the better fathers and mothers in consequence. To suggest that school meals 'break up the home' is absurd. The Eton or Harrow boy is kept at school, not merely for meals, but for the whole of the term. Yet no one fears for the home life of the plutocracy!

These and other arguments used by the Fabian Committee of 1905 are as sound to-day as they were a generation ago.

PREVENTION IS CHEAPER THAN CURE

The great opposition, however, to the Fabian scheme came, as it comes to-day, from those who maintain that its cost would be ruinous. Undoubtedly, the expense would be considerable, but sooner or later, in one way or another, it is the State which must pay for underfeeding its children. If a child grows up underfed, the chances are heavy that it grows up a weakling and inefficient worker, or falls the victim of disease. What we save to-day on food, we are likely to spend many times over tomorrow on medical treatment and special schools, on sickness benefit and hospitals, on poor relief and charities, to say nothing of the lowered efficiency of the workers and the loss of working days.

Sir John Bray, in his presidential address to the Institute of Municipal Treasurers and Accountants (1931), estimated that we spend nearly £200,000,000 per annum on the prevention and treatment of disease and combating their results. In addition to the cost of the prevention and cure of disease, there is the loss of productive power that ill-health causes. A very conservative estimate by Sir Francis Fremantle, M.P., puts the total annual cost to the nation of ill-health at £300,000,000. Less than one-twelfth of this sum would go a very long way in school feeding.

THE ECONOMY OF THE 'COMMUNITY' FEEDING

It is wiser to spend on food than on sickness, but this is no reason to spend on food extravagantly. From the standpoint of good housekeeping, it is plain that 'community' feeding has over the family meal many advantages. The objection raised by some people, who would prefer to cater for themselves, or at least to choose their own caterer, does not apply to children. A child does not in any case determine his own diet. Not merely have public authorities access to expert knowledge and advice which is not generally open to the private housewife, but they have opportunities of buying in the wholesale market good food cheaply which are obviously closed to her. Her facilities for buying may, indeed, be extremely limited, and confined in practice to those of the small local shop. Nor has she always the necessary facilities for cooking. Cooking is a highly-skilled craft. Every mother does not take to it naturally. There can be no question that, where food is prepared on a large scale in up-to-date kitchens, with the aid of a trained staff and modern equipment, it is possible to provide a variety and excellence of cooking which is quite beyond the reach of the small household, and yet to make substantial economies in materials and fuel. The growing use in working-class homes of tinned and semi-cooked foods, which are seldom the ideal diet for children, must at least partly be connected with the lack of proper cooking conveniences in small flats and tenements, and the excessive cost of fuel, which is bought and used in small quantities.

Reference has been made in a previous section to the urgent need of children to drink more milk. We are told, on the other hand, that too much milk is produced in this country. Yet the retail price of milk is more than half again as high to-day as it was before the war. About one-half of this price goes to the dairy who distributes the milk between arrival at its place of destination and its delivery to the housewife; the other half goes to the farmer. It is plain that the farmer fares less well than the dairy, but he does not in this case fare so badly. His trouble is that he sells to the dairy something less than two-thirds of his total product. His surplus he must sell to the manufacturer, who is only prepared to pay him one-half, or even one-third, of the price that he gets from the dairy. If a new market could be found for liquid milk, and the milk delivered wholesale direct from the farm or dairy, to the school, there is clearly here a margin for a substantial reduction of price, which would yet leave a fair profit to the farmer.

Nor is it a matter of price only. Milk is a highly perishable food and one which is quickly contaminated; it may be the carrier of tubercle or other infectious disease. As the great consumer of milk in the district, the authority would be in a favourable position to secure, not merely a cheap, but a clean and pure supply.

There are other excellent foods, of which this country has abundant supplies, but too little use of them is made in children's dietaries. Many common kinds of fish come within this category. The herring is a 'fat' fish of exceptional dietetic value, but its place in working-class dietaries is now being very largely taken by the less nourishing and more expensive 'fish and chips.' Fresh fish very quickly deteriorates, while supplies may fluctuate wildly from one day to another. A glut of fish at the port is a common occurrence. Costs of distribution are high in consequence. Between the port price and the price charged to the housewife, there may be a difference of several hundred per cent. An enterprising authority should be able, not merely to buy fish at wholesale prices, but to come to some arrangement with the fishing industry to take at short notice exceptional catches of suitable kinds of fish on terms satisfactory to both sides.

Green vegetables and salads contain properties essential to healthy growth. There is no shortage of these foods in the country, but for one reason and another our children do not eat them in anything like sufficient quantities. They are bulky and, therefore, costly to handle. Except from street barrows, they are not cheap to buy at retail prices. In the smaller and less expensive shops, they are not always too fresh, and in the winter months sometimes hard to get. Yet the grower may get practically nothing for them, or find a difficulty in selling them at all. Here is another opportunity for wholesale deliveries from the growers or dealers to the school, which should enable the authorities to obtain ample and cheap supplies. Some schools in country districts, which have established school canteens, have adopted the practice of growing their own vegetables. Costs per meal in this case have been greatly reduced, and the practice could be followed in suitable circumstances.

It was reported the other day in the Press that a valuable cargo of oranges had been dumped into the sea because, since tariffs were imposed, it did not 'pay' the dealers to handle them. Where dealers fear to tread, the authority should be able to step in. The tax, which is prohibitive to the private trader, could be recovered by the authority from the Exchequer, into which it is paid, in the form of grant. What the Exchequer lost on the swings, it would gain on the roundabouts, and no harm would have been done to anyone.

A New Market for Agriculture

Apart from economies to be made in the buying and preparation of food, school feeding could be used to play a new important part in developing the food resources of the country. 'It is to the market,' the Minister of Agriculture has declared,[36] 'that both the consumer and producer must for the present bend their attention . . . It would be black treachery to place men on the land without markets for their product.' Our children lack food, our farmers lack markets. Cannot the two be brought together?

Milk is a food which this country is eminently fitted to produce. We produce already on the lowest estimate about 1,200 million gallons of milk a year, but we do not consume in liquid form more than about 700 million gallons. The pressing need of the industry is thus an outlet for fresh milk. The importance of the school as a prospective market has even gained recognition in the House of Commons. So good a Conservative M.P. as Sir Edward Grigg has placed milk meals for school children in the forefront of measures which would restore prosperity to this country. A new market for 80,000,000 gallons of milk a year, he has declared, would 'transform the problem of the milk industry.'[37]

The problem of the fishing industry again is one of marketing. In spite of a shifting of demand from the herring, a decline in the consumption of white fish has been evident since 1931. The amount of fish that our trawling industry can market is known to be substantially below its productive capacity. The home consumption of herrings has declined since before the war by about one-third, while a marked contraction has taken place in exports. When the fishing fleet assembled for the East Anglian autumn fishing last year, it numbered 150 fewer vessels than in the previous year. On many occasions in 1932, the price of sprats fell so low that fishing was abandoned. It may be estimated that the addition of fish meals as a weekly item in children's dietaries, extended to the present school population, would create a new demand for at least another million cwts. of fish a year. In the absence of an expanding home market, the present 'Eat More Fish' campaign is for the most part mere waste of money. No country could be better suited than our own to grown green vegetables. There are thousands of unemployed workers ready to grow them. A new market for green vegetables, extending to every town and village, would give to the Minister of Agriculture the opportunity for which he is waiting to place men on the land. The children, meanwhile, would have acquired a taste, which they would not afterwards lose, for fresh wholesome home-grown food.

The home farmer has a monopoly of the fresh milk market. It is otherwise with meat, cheese, butter, etc., which are important items in children's dietaries, but these are also foods that this country is admirably adapted to produce. According to high medical authority,[38] no matter how carefully food is chilled or preserved, the resulting product is inferior to the fresh material. For this reason alone, it is urged that encouragement should be given to the consumption of home-grown produce. This is not the place to discuss how far it is wise, or practicable, to give protection to the home farmer against foreign competition. It may, however, be pointed out that, so long as the Exchequer continues to make grants in aid of local expenditure on school meals, it is open to the Government to bring pressure to bear on authorities to buy, so far as possible, only home-grown produce and to make good, if necessary a difference of price. Such a subsidy to agriculture would anyway be a much more sensible plan than the present subsidies amounting to some £8,000,000 per annum granted by the Government to the growing of wheat and of sugar-beet!

The Government's present agricultural policy, which is more concerned to make farming 'pay' than to develop the food resources of the country, has done nothing to expand markets. It is aimed instead at restricting supplies in order to raise prices. While tariffs and quotas have been imposed on foreign foods, new machinery has been set up designed to assist the home farmer to limit production at home. The effects are now beginning to be felt. We pay more for our food, but we buy less of it. The children are worse off, and the farmers no better off than before.

The Outline of a Scheme

AMENDMENT OF THE 1906 ACT

The Provision of Meals Act, 1906, has never at any time been accepted by socialists, except as a half-way measure. When the Act was passed, school feeding was at the stage of experiment, but after nearly thirty years of experience its value has been proved beyond all dispute. While there may be practical difficulties in the way of establishing all at once a universal scheme of school feeding, the time is clearly overdue when further steps should be taken to meet the more urgent needs of the position. The first step to this end would be a revision of the 1906 Act.

The weakness, as we have seen, of the existing law is its permissive character. Authorities are not obliged to operate it. In order, moreover, to do so, they must first of all declare that there are 'necessitous' children in the area and voluntary funds are not forthcoming to feed them. Where the parents are able to pay, they are under a legal obligation to recover a part, or the whole, of the cost. The time has now come when these conditions should be removed. Authorities should be granted full and unconditional powers in respect of provision of meals, and the duty further imposed on them to secure that no child attending a state-aided school should lack the essentials of a satisfactory diet.

MILK MEALS FOR ALL

The case for supplementary milk meals, and the urgent need to extend the present provision, has been fully discussed in previous sections. Under the scheme instituted by the National Milk Publicity Council, a daily ration of one-third of a pint of milk is supplied to any child whose parents have agreed to pay for it. The milk allowance, admittedly, is inadequate, but the Council are not at the moment in a position to increase it. Experience shows that few parents are willing or able to pay more than 1d. per day, and the dairies do not see their way to supplying more milk at the price. The choice of a dairy rests with the teachers, who are responsible for serving out the milk, and also for collecting the pennies from the parents. The milk is delivered by the dairy in bottles, one bottle for each child, out of which he drinks his portion. A minimum of trouble is thus caused to the teacher, and practically no outlay is needed on the part of the authority. The great obstacle in the way of extending the scheme is the difficulty of collecting pennies from poor families.

The proposal is that this scheme should now be extended to all state-aided schools, and authorities required to supply, free of charge, not less than half-a-pint of milk per day to every child under the age of sixteen. In the case of debilitated children, an additional half-pint could be given on the advice of the school doctor. Milk meals would thus be made a part of ordinary school routine. Apart from the objections already discussed to dividing the children into 'necessitous' and 'non-necessitous' groups, the collecting of pennies in a *compulsory* scheme would be almost impossible to carry out.

If milk meals are to be provided on a large scale, some inconvenience may be caused to farmers and dairies, who have to adjust their supplies to the days when the schools are closed, and this in turn would be reflected in the price. For this reason, as well as from the standpoint of health, it would be desirable that milk meals should be continued so far as possible on Saturdays and during the holidays. It is not a case for compulsion; but, where parents gave notice that they wished their child to receive milk meals on other than school days, the authority should be required to make the necessary arrangements at the school or some other convenient centre. It is the poorer families who may be expected to take the greater advantage of an opportunity of this kind. In the case of better-off families, any falling off during the holidays in the school demand would tend to be compensated to some extent by increased consumption at such times in the homes.

NOTE. – Children under five not attending school are outside the reference of the present discussion, but it is plain that all the arguments in favour of the provision of milk meals are equally strong in their case. The necessary arrangements could be made by the local public health authority, and the milk distributed through the infant welfare centres.

CHILDREN OVER ELEVEN AND THE SCHOOL CANTEEN

Half-a-pint of milk is estimated to supply about one-third of the total first-class protein requirements of an *average* child. The value of such a meal as a supplementary diet would obviously be greater in relation to total requirements in the case of younger than of older children, whose dietetic needs approximate to, or may even exceed, those of adults. It is also at the stage of adolescence, when growth is accelerated and the onset of puberty imposes an exceptional drain on vitality, that the results of underfeeding are likely to be most serious. The cost to the parents of maintaining the dependent family bears at the same time each year more heavily as the children grow older, and relief to the family income is at this point most needed. The high incidence of defect discovered in working boys aged 14–16 – in London, a recent enquiry into boys' clubs showed a figure of 75 per cent. – cannot be wholly unconnected with deficiencies of diet in earlier years, and the consequent absence of physical reserves to fall back upon. Malnutrition is by no means unknown in secondary schools. In London, 7.2 per cent. of secondary school boys and 12.2 per cent. of girls are reported as subnormal in nutrition.[39] The figures are actually higher than those for London children in elementary schools. From the physiological standpoint, there is thus a special case as regards adolescents for the provision of something more than milk meals.

The concentration of children over eleven in separate senior of 'central' schools, which may be situated at some distance from the children's homes, has at the same time created in many areas a new problem. Where the distance between the school and the home compels large numbers of children to remain at school for the midday meal, authorities have for practical reasons been obliged to establish school canteens, which provide some form of hot dinner. The school canteen is already a well-known feature of the secondary school, and many authorities to-day, in building new senior or 'central' schools, include a kitchen and dining-hall as part of the normal equipment. These canteens are run for the most part on a voluntary and self-supporting basis. The cost of the food is charged to the parents and, in secondary schools, costs of cooking and service as well. For this reason, full use of the school canteen is only made by children of a relatively well-to-do class. The poorer children either struggle to get home for dinner, or else they bring their sandwiches to school and buy at most a cup of hot coffee or cocoa. It is customary for the teachers to take turns in supervising the school meal, while the children wait for the most part on themselves. The need for supervision and attendance, which are important factors in the cost of school dinners, and may involve a heavy burden on the teachers, is obviously much less in the case of older children than it is in that of little ones, many of whom require constant personal attention. Experience shows that meals provided directly through the school organisation are in general much more satisfactory in character than those contracted for through an outside agency.

It is, therefore, proposed that authorities should be required to establish school canteens in all schools or departments for children over eleven, and to supply dinners, free of charge, on each school day, as part of the ordinary school routine. The scheme should be extended to grant-aided secondary schools as well as to schools coming under the elementary heading. Where fees are charged, the cost of the food supplied could, if desired, be added to the fee. The dinner should be required to contain, as advised by the Chief Medical Officer,[40] not less than two-thirds of the child's total requirements of 'animal' protein. A child over eleven receiving school dinners as well as milk meals would thus be assured his full supply of 'first-class' protein.

PROVISION FOR NECESSITOUS AND DEBILITATED CHILDREN

The universal provision of milk meals, together with dinners for children over eleven, would go at least a long way to make good the present deficiencies in children's dietaries. The younger children coming from normal working-class homes would not be entitled under the scheme to school dinners, but, in large families especially, they would gain to some extent indirectly from the fewer mouths to be fed at home. The great merit of the scheme is that it would place school feeding for the first time on a proper basis as part of the ordinary school routine, and remove it definitely from the sphere of mere public assistance or medical relief.[41] Special provision would, however, still have to be made for the poorest families. The remedy for unemployment, or for low wages, is not the 'soup kitchen,' but so long as these evils persist it is obvious that such children must be properly fed, and also the child referred by the school doctor as subnormal in nutrition.

The best plan here seems to be that the Board of Education should prescribe an income scale, to be based on the minimum cost of a satisfactory diet (say 6s. per 'man' value at current prices), below which authorities would be required, on application from the parents, to provide, in addition to milk meals or other meals supplied as part of the ordinary school routine, school dinners and, if necessary, school breakfasts and teas, free of charge, to all children, irrespective of age, in need of them. Such an income scale may be expected, under present conditions, to cover the great majority of unemployed families, who have no means of subsistence other than unemployment benefit or transitional payment, and also a proportion of employed families living below the 'poverty' line. It would be a definite advantage of the scheme that the school meal, unlike any form of money allowance, could not be diverted to the payment of rent, or to any other purpose. The full value received would go in extra nourishment for the child. Children should not be debarred from enjoying school meals because their parents are receiving poor law relief. The Government's present policy, which discourages the provision of meals to such families, except in special circumstances, should be reversed. In the case of very poor families, it would be necessary that dinners should be given on Saturdays and during the holidays as well as on school days.

The perodical physical examination of the children should at the same time be made as thorough as possible, and authorities required to feed borderline cases as well as cases of actual malnutrition. Extra nourishment ordered by the school doctor should be given without reference to the family income, and in such form as he may prescribe. The cost in this case, if desired, could be recovered from well-to-do parents.

THE COST OF THE SCHEME

The cost of carrying out the scheme would depend on many variable factors, and can only, therefore, be very roughly estimated. It would be determined, on the one hand, by the number of children to be fed each day; on the other hand, by the price of food and the ability of authorities to buy cheaply in the wholesale market.

The total number of children in state-aided schools, who would be entitled under the scheme to receive milk meals, is approximately 6,000,000, of whom about 2,000,000 are children over eleven who would receive dinners in addition. The latter figure includes, however, some 400,000 children over eleven in secondary schools, trade schools, etc., of whom about one-half are fee-payers. Assuming that the parents in this case would continue to pay the cost of the dinner, either directly or in the form of increased fees, the number of children over eleven who would receive dinners, free of charge, may be estimated at 1,800,000.

The number of 'necessitous' children, for whom additional provision would be required, is not so easy to determine. It would obviously diminish with a return to prosperity. There are to-day (September 1933) some 2,000,000 adult men on the unemployment registers, equivalent to about 22.5 of the insured population. On the assumption that the proportion of school children, whose fathers are unemployed, to the total school population is about the same as the percentage of unemployment among insured male persons, the number of children belonging to unemployed families

431

would be roughly 1,200,000. These children, however, would anyway be entitled under the scheme to milk meals, and children over eleven to dinners besides. This would leave 800,000 children under eleven, of whom at least one-half, or 400,000, may be expected to apply for dinners. To this number must again be added some thousands of employed families living below the 'poverty' line, or where the breadwinner is working half-time, say, another 100,000 children under eleven, for whom it would be necessary to provide dinners. The needs of the 'debilitated' child would, in great measure, be met by the general provision of milk meals, together with dinners for adolescents. The number of 'debilitated' children under eleven (other than those belonging to 'necessitous' families) may thus be expected to be relatively small. The cost of the meal could, moreover, be recovered in this case from well-to-do parents.

No exact calculation can be formed of the number of children who would require meals on Saturdays and during the holidays. For the purpose of a rough estimate, it may be assumed that about one-third of all children, or some 2,000,000, would apply for milk meals, and about one-half of 'necessitous' children, or some 250,000, would apply for dinners on other than school days.

Costs per meal would vary mainly with fluctuations in food prices. Under the present arrangement between the National Milk Publicity Council and the dairies, the price of milk supplied to the schools has been fixed at 6d. a gallon. The price is about the same as the average charge made to the private householder, and 1d. more than the charge made to hotels and restaurants which buy milk at contract prices, but the price does not here provide for costs of bottling, etc., such as are included in the school price. In view, however, of the wide margin which exists between the dairy price and the price received by the farmer (between 1¼d. and 2¼d. a quart in the case of surplus milk), the authority should certainly be able to contract for large supplies of milk at the hotel price of 5d. a quart, or 1¼d. per half-pint, including all costs of bottling, etc. There is no reason to suppose that costs of bottling would be greater in the case of half-pint than of third-pint bottles.

Costs per meal in the case of school dinners vary widely from one area to another. Thus, London reckons the cost of food alone at 4d. per meal. In some places, where each school caters for itself, the cost is 5d.; while other schools, those especially which grow their own vegetables, have brought down the cost to 2d., and even to 1½d. In order, however, to secure that the meal should contain a full share of 'animal' protein, it would be wise to take an average figure of 4d. Some further adjustment would be needed to meet differences in the food requirements of older and younger children. Assuming an average food cost of 4d. per dinner, the adjusted figure could be stated at 4½d. for older children and 3¾d. for younger children. These figures take no account of possible reductions in food prices, where the authority may be able to deal directly with the producer.

To the cost of food something more must be added for costs of cooking, fuel, etc., and service. In London, where wages are relatively high, these costs are estimated at about 2d. per dinner, making an average total cost of 6d. per dinner. Costs of service, however, could be substantially reduced in the case of school canteens for children over eleven, who may be expected for the most part to wait on themselves. Costs of cooking, fuel, etc. vary again to some extent with the number of children to be fed, and the regularity with which the dinners are supplied. An all-round total cost of 6d. per dinner would be a not unreasonable estimate. Of this sum, expenses other than food would represent about one-quarter as regards older children supplied regularly with dinners, and rather more than two-thirds in the case of younger children receiving dinners only from time to time.

On the above basis, the cost of the scheme may be stated as follows:-

	£
Milk meals supplied to 6,000,000 children at 1¼d. per meal on five days a week for 44 weeks	6,875,000
Extra milk meals supplied to 2,000,000 at 1¼d. per meal on Saturdays and during the holidays	958,000
Dinners supplied to 1,800,000 children over eleven at 6d. per meal on five days a week for 44 weeks	9,900,000
Dinners supplied to 500,000 necessitous children under eleven at 6d. per meal on five days a week for 44 weeks	2,750,000
Extra dinners supplied to 250,000 necessitous children at 6d. per meal on Saturdays and during the holidays	575,000
Total	£21,091,000

HOW THE MONEY SHOULD BE RAISED

Under the present grant formula, education authorities are able to recover from the Board of Education one-half of their total net expenditure on school meals. The cost is thus borne equally between local rates and the Exchequer.

The larger the volume of public expenditure the more important

it is that the burden should be equitably spread. Local rates to-day
bear very unevenly over the country. They press lightly on rich
areas, but heavily on poor areas. Thus, in well-to-do residential
resorts, such as Bournemouth, Eastbourne, or Hove, rates in the
£ are 7s., 7s. 6d., 7s. 11d. respectively, while in poverty-stricken
industrial areas such as Rhondda, Caerphilly, or Merthyr Tydfil,
they are as high as 23s., 23s. 6d., even 27s. 7d. The result is that,
where the need for school meals is greatest, the authority can least
afford to provide them. Rates bear again unfairly on households
within the same area. They are, in effect, a tax on house-room.
Large families pay more than small families. There is no necessary
relation between rates and family income. Unlike income-tax, rates
are a direct charge on industry and commerce. They have to be
paid before a profit can be made, or if no profit is made at all.
This unfairness has, in fact, been recognised by Parliament, and
substantial relief given in recent years to manufacturers and
farmers, but at the expense of the householder and the shopkeeper.
High rates are at least a contributory factor in the high level of
retail prices, which bear again more heavily on small incomes than
on large ones. In any but the richest areas, a rise in rates would
be a much more serious affair than an increase in national taxation.

It is, therefore, proposed that grants from the Exchequer in
respect of school meals should be raised from 50 per cent. to 80 per
cent. of the total net expenditure. In order to avoid extravagance on
the part of local authorities, as well as to secure the greatest measure
of efficiency, it would be advisable that the Board should fix a
maximum cost per meal (subject to price fluctuations) and a
minimum content. It would be a definite advantage that school
dietaries should be brought under the more direct supervision of
the Board's medical staff. The marked improvement in recent years
in the dietaries in children's residential homes may be very largely
attributed to the guidance coming from the Central Department.

CONCLUSION

Great as would be the gain to the children from the scheme and,
ultimately, to the nation as a whole, it may yet appear to the
taxpayer, who has to pay the bill, that a sum of £21,000,000 a year
is a lot of money to be spent on the feeding of school children.
We are, most of us, creatures of habit. We are accustomed, as
taxpayers, to spend largely on some things, say, wars and war
debts, and we do so as a matter of course. We are not accustomed,
as taxpayers, to spend largely on other things, say, education and
the school medical services, and to do so seems to us shocking. It
is then primarily a matter of a change of fashion.

Starvation in the midst of plenty

A sum of £21,000,000 is no doubt a lot of money to be spent on anything. Yet it is only a fraction – hardly more than 0.5 per cent. – of the total national income. It is roughly equivalent to, say, another 4½d. on the income-tax, or an all-round rise of 6d. a week on the earnings of all occupied persons. We are, after all, a rich, even an extravagant, people. In our more frivolous moods, we do not hestitate to spend in hundreds of millions of pounds on, say, tobacco and drink, joy-rides and cinemas, sports, gambling, cosmetics, and such-like adult indulgencies. Nor does it appear that there is a particular virtue in *not* spending. The economists teach, on the contrary, that the purpose of money is to spend it. That is, they say, what money is for. We may, of course, spend wisely or foolishly, productively or wastefully, for public or private purposes. We may be the richer, or the poorer, in consequence, though hardly so poor as we should be from not spending at all. It is up to those who are opposed to school feeding on the ground of expense to explain how money could be better or more productively spent than on 'the slow unfolding in growth of the best potential qualities, physical and mental, inherent in the child at birth.'

Summary of Proposals

The main proposals of the scheme may be summed up as follows:–

(1) The Provision of Meals Act, 1906, should be amended so that authorities would be granted full and unconditional powers in respect of school meals, and the duty further imposed on them of securing that no child in a state-aided school should lack the essentials of a satisfactory diet.

(2) Authorities should be required to establish a system of milk meals in all state-aided schools, and to supply, free of charge, not less than half-a-pint of milk, on each school day, as part of the ordinary school routine. Milk meals should be supplied on Saturdays and during the holidays on notice being given by the parents that they wished the child to receive them.

(3) Authorities should be required to establish school canteens in all schools or departments for children over eleven, and to supply dinners, free of charge, on each school day as part of the ordinary school routine. The provision should be extended to grant-aided secondary schools as well as to senior schools and departments coming under the elementary heading. In the case of fee-paying parents, the cost of the meals could, if desired, be added to the fee.

(4) The Board of Education should prescribe an income-limit, based on the minimum cost of a satisfactory diet, below which authorities should be required, on application from the parents, to provide, in addition to

milk meals and other meals given as part of the ordinary routine, school dinners, and if necessary, breakfasts and teas, free of charge, to all children, irrespective of age, in need of them. In the case of very poor families meals should be given to 'necessitous' children on Saturdays and during the holidays as well as on school days.

(5) Authorities should be required to provide extra nourishment in all cases, including borderline cases, where the child is referred by the school doctor as subnormal in nutrition, without reference to the family income, and in such way as he may prescribe. The cost in this case could be recovered from well-to-do families.

(6) The Board's grant in respect of school meals should be raised from 50 per cent. to 80 per cent. of the total net expenditure. The Board should fix a maximum cost per meal and a minimum content.

Notes

1 'Health of the School Child,' 1928, p. 67. Board of Education.
2 'The New Statesman and Nation,' July 15, 1933.
3 'Health of the School Child,' 1931, p. 92.
4 'Criticism and Improvement of Diets.' Ministry of Health, 1933.
5 'Health of the School Child,' 1931, p. 108.
6 'Health of the School Child,' 1931, p. 88.
7 'The Lancet,' March 18, 1933.
8 'Health of the School Child,' 1931, p. 96.
9 'State of the Public Health,' Ministry of Health, 1926, p. 185. – The statement refers to a relatively prosperous year, and may to-day need some modification.
10 'Food and Health; The Physiological Minimum.' *The Lancet*, March 18, 1933.
11 Ibid.
12 'Diets in Children's Poor Law Homes,' November, 1932.
13 'Health of the School Child,' 1931.
14 'Health of the School Child,' 1931, p. 88.
15 'Week-end Review,' March 4, 1933.
16 Annual Report for 1931.
17 'Unemployment in Hull,' 1933.
18 'Survey of the Standard of Living,' 1933.
19 'Health of the School Child,' Board of Education, 1931, p. 88.
20 'Unemployment and the Child,' 1933, p. 57.
21 'The State of the Public Health,' 1932, p. 31.
22 'The State of the Public Health,' 1932, p. 41.
23 'The Lancet,' March 25th, 1933.
24 'The Medical Officer,' April 29th, Dr. Dunstan, M.O.H., Lewes.
25 April 29th, 1933.
26 'Unemployment and the Child,' 1933, p. 126.
27 'Unemployment and the Child,' pp. 53–55.
28 'Health of the School Child,' 1928, p. 69–71.
29 Ibid., p. 69.

30 'Unemployment and the Child,' pp. 61–62.
31 'Health of the School Child,' 1925, p. 117.
32 Annual Report of the Chief Medical Officer, Board of Education, 1928, p. 71.
33 Ibid., 1931, p. 110.
34 'Health of the School Child,' 1927.
35 'After Bread, Education,' Fabian Tract, 1905.
36 Statement in the House of Commons. *Times*, July 11th, 1933.
37 'The New Statesman and Nation,' July 15th, 1933.
38 Dr Alexander Lander. Address to Agricultural Section of British Association, September 6th, 1933.
39 Annual Report on Public Health, 1932, p. 14.
40 Annual Report, Board of Education 1931, p 96.
41 It is interesting to note that in 1922 the Standing Joint Committee of Industrial Women's Organisation put forward proposals for school dinners, and other allowances in kind, as part of a general scheme of family endowment. This scheme was subsequently adopted by the Labour Women's Conference.

Index

For Product Safety Concerns and Information please contact our EU
representative GPSR@taylorandfrancis.com
Taylor & Francis Verlag GmbH, Kaufingerstraße 24, 80331 München, Germany

www.ingramcontent.com/pod-product-compliance
Lightning Source LLC
Chambersburg PA
CBHW060128280326
41932CB00012B/1455